In Pursuit of the *Essex*

In Pursuit of the
Essex

A Tale of Heroism and Hubris in the War of 1812

Ben Hughes

Pen & Sword
MARITIME

First published in Great Britain in 2016 by
Pen & Sword Maritime
an imprint of
Pen & Sword Books Ltd
47 Church Street
Barnsley
South Yorkshire
S70 2AS

ISBN 978-1-47382-364-8

Typeset in 11/13 Ehrhardt by Replika Press Pvt Ltd, India
Printed in the UK by CPI UK

Pen & Sword Books Ltd incorporates the imprints of Pen & Sword Archaeology,
Atlas, Aviation, Battleground, Discovery, Family History, History, Maritime,
Military, Naval, Politics, Railways, Select, Social History, Transport, True Crime
and Claymore Press, Frontline Books, Leo Cooper, Praetorian Press, Remember
When, Seaforth Publishing and Wharncliffe.

For a complete list of Pen & Sword titles please contact
PEN & SWORD BOOKS LIMITED
47 Church Street, Barnsley, South Yorkshire, S70 2AS, England
E-mail: enquiries@pen-and-sword.co.uk
Website: www.pen-and-sword.co.uk

Contents

List of Illustrations

Preface: Behind the Hyperbole

In the United States the story of USS *Essex*'s commerce-raiding Pacific cruise, perhaps the most daring exploit of the War of 1812, is relatively well-known. The truth, however, has been blurred by the prevailing fabrications of President Madison's incumbent Republican government and Captain David Porter's self-serving memoir released soon after his return. As the Bostonian would have it, his mission, despite ending in the capture of one of the United States' few remaining men-of-war and the death or mutilation of over one-third of his 300-strong crew, was a spectacular success. His claims of crippling the British whaling industry, making a fortune from captured prizes and diverting the Royal Navy's over-stretched resources on a year-long game of cat and mouse, do not stand up to close scrutiny, yet still form the basis of the generally-accepted narrative told to this day in the United States.

In Britain, Porter's story and that of the men of HMS *Phoebe* who defeated him is virtually unknown. Embroiled in a 23-year-long fight to the death with Revolutionary and Napoleonic France, the war with America was considered a sideshow. It received little attention from contemporaries and was soon all but forgotten. In modern times Patrick O'Brian revived the tale with his Jack Aubury novel, *The Far Side of the World*. Although a thin veil is cast over the story (USS *Essex* becomes USS *Norfolk* and the final showdown takes place off the Galapagos Islands rather than in Valparaiso Bay), O'Brian's tale largely sticks to the facts, but his efforts have since been overshadowed by a recent Hollywood adaptation. *Master and Commander: the Far Side of the World* is an imaginative and entertaining amalgamation of naval lore, fact and fiction in which Russell Crowe stalks the Pacific seeking a French frigate rather than an American one.

In Pursuit of the Essex: A Tale of Heroism and Hubris in the War of 1812 aims to tell the true story. Dedicating equal coverage to the hunter and the hunted without regard for reputation, it immerses the reader in the world of the British and American seamen who struggled for supremacy in the sunset years of the Age of Sail. In compiling the narrative, I have exploited a variety of British sources hitherto untapped by the historians who have covered the subject. The National Archives in Kew and the National Maritime Museum in Greenwich hold a host of primary accounts. The masters' and captains' logs of the British ships; secret coded journals intended for the High Lords Commissioners of the Admiralty;

surgeons' notebooks; ships' musters and pay lists; courts martial records; and official correspondence, wills and personal letters penned by the chief protagonists all cast new light on the story as do several contemporary newspaper reports and the recently-published journal of Midshipman Allen Gardiner, an eyewitness to events from the moment HMS *Phoebe* left Portsmouth until the story's bloody denouement in Valparaiso Bay.

Acknowledgements

I would like to thank my editor, Rupert Harding, for his professionalism, kindness and encouragement; my parents, Dave and Jane Hughes and Stephen W. H. Duffy, author of *Captain Blakeley and the Wasp: the Cruise of 1814*, for their help in proof-reading and correcting the draft; and my wife and daughter, Vanessa and Emily Hughes, for their love and support.

Maps

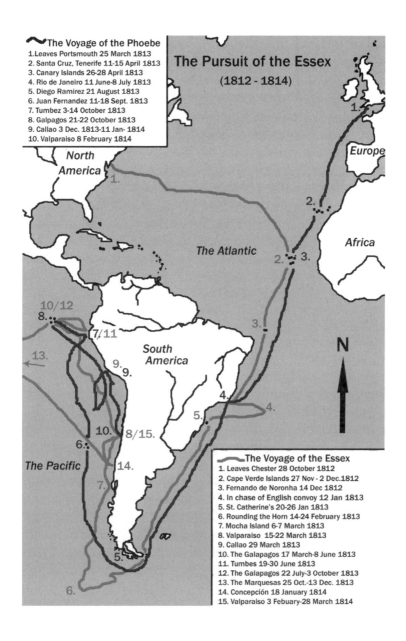

The Voyage of the Phoebe
1. Leaves Portsmouth 25 March 1813
2. Santa Cruz, Tenerife 11-15 April 1813
3. Canary Islands 26-28 April 1813
4. Rio de Janeiro 11 June-8 July 1813
5. Diego Ramirez 21 August 1813
6. Juan Fernandez 11-18 Sept. 1813
7. Tumbez 3-14 October 1813
8. Galpagos 21-22 October 1813
9. Callao 3 Dec. 1813-11 Jan- 1814
10. Valparaiso 8 February 1814

The Pursuit of the Essex
(1812 - 1814)

North
America

Europe

The Atlantic

Africa

South
America

N

The Pacific

The Voyage of the Essex
1. Leaves Chester 28 October 1812
2. Cape Verde Islands 27 Nov - 2 Dec.1812
3. Fernando de Noronha 14 Dec 1812
4. In chase of English convoy 12 Jan 1813
5. St. Catherine's 20-26 Jan 1813
6. Rounding the Horn 14-24 February 1813
7. Mocha Island 6-7 March 1813
8. Valparaiso 15-22 March 1813
9. Callao 29 March 1813
10. The Galapagos 17 March-8 June 1813
11. Tumbes 19-30 June 1813
12. The Galapagos 22 July-3 October 1813
13. The Marquesas 25 Oct.-13 Dec. 1813
14. Concepción 18 January 1814
15. Valparaiso 3 Febuary-28 March 1814

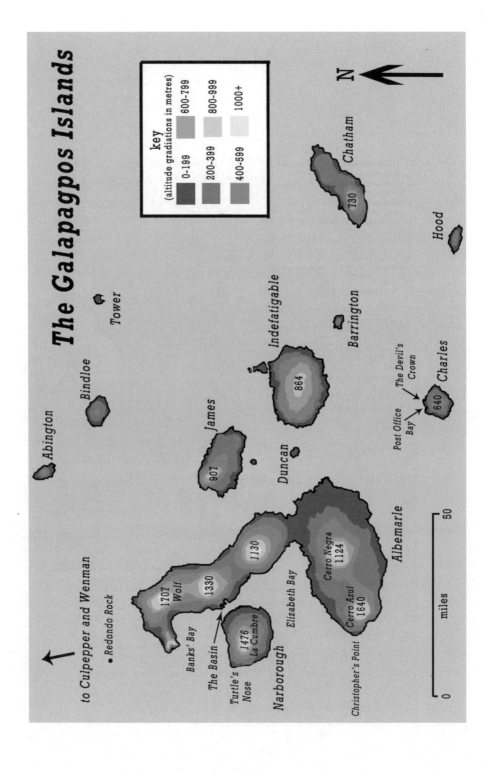

The Galapagos Islands

to Culpepper and Wenman

• Redondo Rock

Abington

Bindloe

Tower

Banks' Bay

The Basin

1707 Wolf

1330

1130

Turtle's Nose

1476 La Cumbre

Narborough

Elizabeth Bay

Cerro Negra 1124

Cerro Azul 1640

Christopher's Point

Albemarle

James

907

Duncan

Indefatigable

864

Barrington

Post Office Bay

The Devil's Crown

640 Charles

Chatham

730

Hood

key
(altitude gradiations in metres)

0-199	600-799
200-399	800-999
400-599	1000+

N

miles

0   50

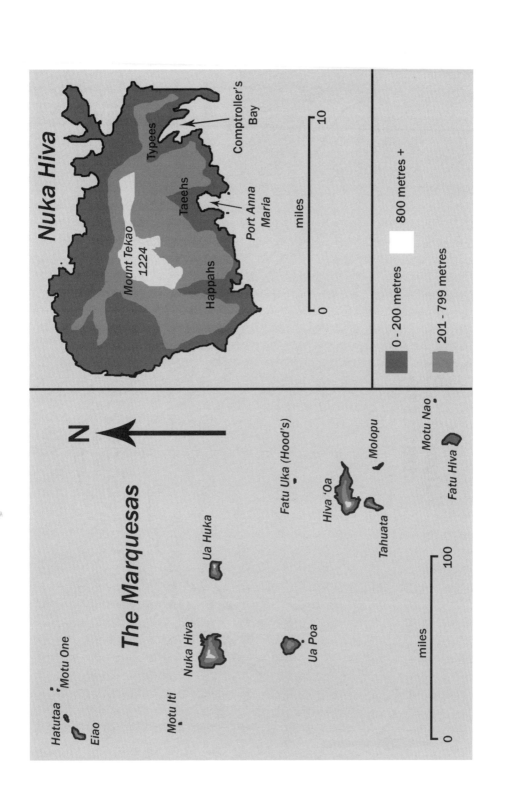

The Marquesas

Hatutaa
Motu One
Eiao

Motu Iti

Nuka Hiva

Ua Huka

Ua Poa

Fatu Uka (Hood's)

Hiva 'Oa

Tahuata

Molopu

Motu Nao

Fatu Hiva

N

miles

0   100

Nuka Hiva

Typees

Comptroller's
Bay

Taeehs

Mount Tekao
1224

Port Anna
Maria

Happahs

miles

0   10

0 - 200 metres

201 - 799 metres

800 metres +

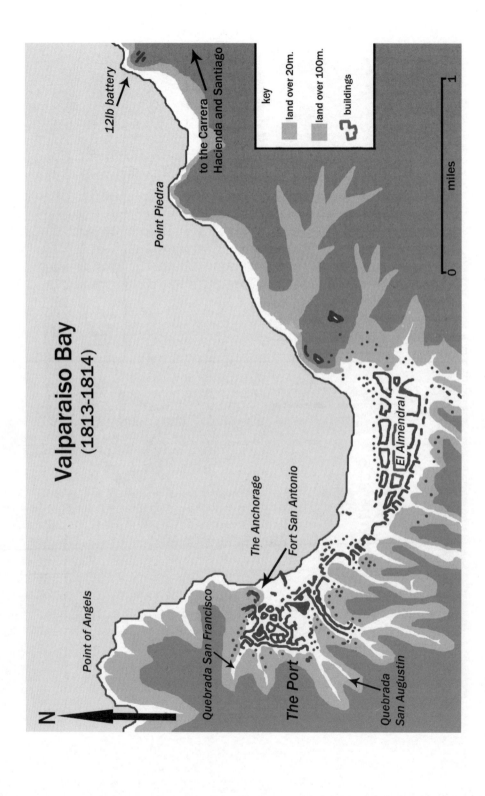

Valparaiso Bay
(1813-1814)

N

12lb battery

Point Piedra

to the Carrera
Hacienda and Santiago

Point of Angels

Quebrada San Francisco

The Anchorage

Fort San Antonio

El Almendral

The Port

Quebrada
San Augustin

key

land over 20m.

land over 100m.

buildings

0   miles   1

sailplan of a Napoleonic-era frigate

1. flying jib
2. outer jib
3. inner jib
4. fore royal
5. fore topgallant
6. fore topsail
7. fore mainsail
8. main topgallant stays
9. main topmast stays
10. main stays
11. main royal
12. main topgallant

13. main topsail
14. main course
15. mizzen topmast stays
16. mizzen stays
17. mizzem royal
18. mizzen topgallant
19. spanker or driver

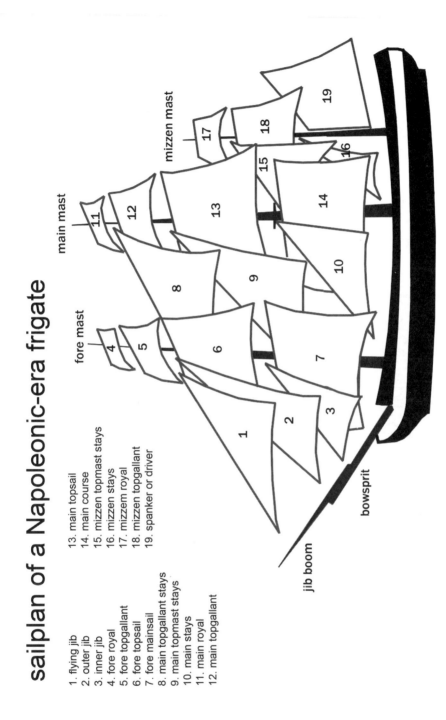

main mast

fore mast

mizzen mast

jib boom

bowsprit

deck plan of a typical Napoleonic-era frigate

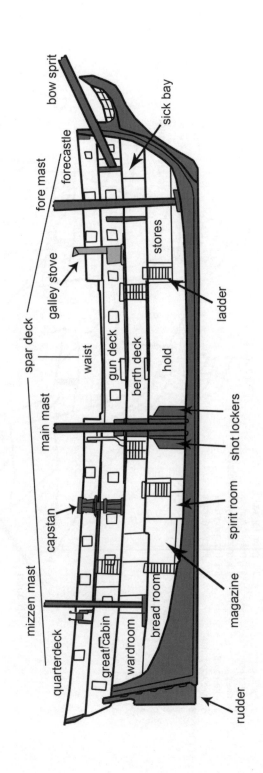

bow sprit

sick bay

fore mast

forecastle

galley stove

stores

spar deck

waist

gun deck

berth deck

hold

ladder

main mast

capstan

shot lockers

mizzen mast

quarterdeck

great cabin

wardroom

bread room

spirit room

magazine

rudder

Prologue: 'A Prodigious Slaughter': USS *Essex*, Valparaiso Bay, 6.30 p.m., 28 March 1814

His ears ringing from the concussion of two hours of cannon fire, Captain David Porter surveyed the scene. Dozens of dead were strewn amongst his frigate's shattered spars. On the quarterdeck the bodies lay in heaps around three dismounted 12-pounders. Cut down as they had attempted to return the British fire, some of the men had been decapitated. Others were disembowelled. Many resembled pincushions, their flesh pierced by clouds of jagged wooden splinters punched through USS *Essex*'s oak sides. Limbs had been torn from sockets, fingers severed, flesh ripped open to the bone. Brains spattered the holed and blackened sails. The stench of seared flesh and gunpowder lay heavy in the air. Shredded rigging lay limp amongst blocks shot from the tops and rivulets of blood ran off the spar deck, down the hatches and into the hold from whence the sound of exploding cartridges emanated.

As tears began to roll down Porter's sunburnt cheeks, a handful of British deserters staggered out of the hatchways. Lowering two boats, they abandoned the ship to escape their compatriots' imminent revenge. Others dived overboard. Dodging wreckage, they braved the currents on the mile-long swim ashore. Below decks two teenage midshipmen threw small arms through the open gun ports. Another sheepishly emerged from his hiding place, while Ruff, a negro boy, searched for his master. Some of the wounded bravely mouthed defiance. Others wept or called for their mothers or rolled overboard, seeking oblivion in the swirling brine.

Introduction: A Tale of Two Navies

At the turn of the nineteenth century the Royal Navy dominated the seas. Since the Seven Years War (1756–63), Britain's European rivals had been struggling to compete and repeated crushing victories over the French, Spanish, Dutch and Danish during the French Revolutionary War and early Napoleonic period saw all claims to equality quashed. After Trafalgar, the service's reach was all-encompassing: solitary cruisers patrolled the world's oceans and tried and tested battle fleets could be mustered with relative ease in the Mediterranean and on both sides of the Atlantic. Such was the respect that the service commanded, that the surviving French ships-of-the-line would spend the rest of the war blockaded in their home ports. From 1805 to 1812, aside from a few frigate squadron encounters in the Indian Ocean, the most serious threat the British faced at sea was from the French privateers which infested the English Channel and the cays and inlets of the Caribbean.[1]

Equally ubiquitous in the early nineteenth century was the US merchant marine. Lacking the blessing (or curse) of internationally-desirable resources, such as sugar, slaves, silver or gold, but gifted with excellent deep-water harbours and an enterprising population, between the sixteenth and eighteenth centuries the ports of New England grew rich through 'the carrying trade'. Loading up with pork, beef, flour, rum and salted fish, the merchants of Boston, New York, Philadelphia, Baltimore and Providence, Rhode Island, sailed for the British colonies in the Caribbean. There the sugar monoculture employed on the plantations ensured American products fetched a good price.[2] At Kingston, Port Royal, Bridgetown, Charlestown and Saint John's the Americans loaded sugar destined for Britain where manufactured luxury goods were purchased for the North America market or guns, destined for the west coast of Africa, were stowed. In the Gulf of Guinea, off Cape Lopez or at the islands of São Tomé and Principe slaves were loaded to fuel the plantations of the Caribbean where molasses, a by-product of sugar manufacture, was purchased to be transformed into New England rum, thus completing this cyclical and highly-lucrative trade. The shipbuilding industry of New England, boosted by access to the virgin timber of the vast American interior, prospered hand-in-hand with the colonies' merchant class, while contacts with the British Caribbean saw the plantation system trans-located to Virginia and Carolina. In place of sugar, cotton and tobacco were grown.[3]

The European wars of the late seventeenth and early to mid-eighteenth centuries saw discontent arise between Britain and her transatlantic colonies. The North Americans saw no reason to stop trading with the French and Spanish just because London had declared them the enemy, especially when the molasses sold at Martinique, Guadaloupe and Hispaniola could be had for a third of the price demanded at Barbados, Jamaica, Nevis and St Kitts. The Navigation Acts of 1651 and 1660, the Molasses Act of 1733 and the Sugar Act of 1764, implemented to put a stop to such treasonous activities, merely led to a rise in smuggling and the seeking-out of legal loopholes, which in its turn, brought about the Royal Navy's increasingly heavy-handed policing of North American trade. With their mercantile interests blatantly subordinated to the economic priorities of the mother-country, in 1775 the North American colonies rebelled.

At sea the War of Independence went badly for the Americans. Despite their shipbuilding expertise, the colonists had little experience of naval warfare and their fleet was hopelessly outnumbered. Of thirteen American frigates built during the conflict, seven were captured and incorporated into the Royal Navy and four were destroyed to prevent them falling into enemy hands. Unwilling to run the risk of trading on the open seas, the American merchants turned their hand to privateering. With fast ships and experienced seamen, they enjoyed some success. On land the Americans grew in confidence as the war progressed. Despite convincing victories at Long Island and White Plains, the British had since struggled to get to grips with an elusive enemy and between 1778 and 1780, with the entry of the French, Spanish and Dutch into the war, Westminster began to view the conflict as a lost cause and started channelling resources into the protection of her Caribbean colonies instead. In 1783 the United States gained its independence, while, with the defeat of the French Navy at the Battle of the Saintes the previous year, Britain's all-important sugar plantations were retained.[4]

The post-war period saw a dramatic slump in the New England economy. Barred from trading with the British West Indies, whole seafaring communities went bankrupt. The shipbuilding industry suffered and a number of American sailors emigrated to Nova Scotia. Lured by financial incentives established by Westminster, some Nantucket whalers even crossed the Atlantic to set up business in London and Wales. To compensate, New England's merchants sought fresh markets overseas. In 1784 the *Empress of China* was the first US vessel to trade at Canton. Others exploited the opportunities offered by a still-independent Bengal or braved the pirate-infested waters of the Mediterranean; trade consuls were dispatched to nineteen foreign ports and commercial relations were established with Sweden, Prussia, Russia and the Dutch. The response of the French, however, was disappointing. Despite being Revolutionary Washington's principal ally, the trade policies of the tottering *Ancien Régime* mirrored those of Westminster. Instead of welcoming American vessels, Versailles established a restrictive system to protect the interests of her own merchant class.

Everything changed with the French Revolution. At first the resulting European conflict played into American hands. With the French mercantile fleet devastated by the Royal Navy, Paris relaxed its trading laws and invited the Americans to take up the slack. Exploiting a legal loophole known as the re-export trade, New England's merchants were able to carry cargoes between France and her Caribbean colonies by stopping *en route* at American ports to briefly unload then re-stow the goods. In this way their cargoes could be reclassified as US products and therefore avoid confiscation by the Royal Navy. The US merchant fleet rapidly expanded, forcing its captains to take on an ever-increasing number of foreign, principally British, hands to whom they could offer wages in excess of what they would receive at home. A knock-on effect was that the Royal Navy believed itself increasingly justified in stopping and searching American vessels and pressing men whose nationality was suspect onto her men of war.[5]

In 1794 the situation changed once more. Worried that their policies were pushing the Americans ever further into the French orbit, the British agreed to trading concessions with the Jay Treaty. The terms saw US bottoms return to Britain's Caribbean colonies, in exchange for Washington's acquiescence in Westminster's anti-French naval policies. Anglophile at heart, appalled by the barbarities of the Reign of Terror and firmly believing that America's future would be fuelled by ocean-going trade with Britain and her colonies, the New England merchants were only too happy to oblige. The issue of impressment, however, remained unaddressed and as a result of the treaty an undeclared conflict known as the Quasi-War broke out in 1798 between the US and Revolutionary France. Fought entirely at sea, the conflict saw the rebirth of the US Navy. Supported by a number of armed brigs and sloops, the force was built around a dozen solidly-constructed and superbly-crewed frigates. The largest, which could outgun any ship of their class including those of the Royal Navy, mounted 44 guns, were built of exceptionally resilient live oak and boasted broadsides of heavy 24-pounders. Although small in number, the US Navy was highly efficient, her officers scored several morale-boosting victories in the Caribbean against French privateers and men of war and in 1800 the Quasi-War was brought to a negotiated close as the result of the more conciliatory stance adopted by the new French government led by Napoleon Bonaparte as First Consul.

In February 1801 Thomas Jefferson became the third President of the United States. As a Republican, his sympathies lay with the Southern landowners. He favoured inland expansion, opposed overseas trade, distrusted the Anglophile New England merchant class and discouraged the growth of the navy. Many promising young officers went on furlough into the merchant trade as a result, but within months of Jefferson's appointment, the US found herself at war once again. This time her opponents were the Barbary States of North Africa: petty princedoms financed by piracy which had been a thorn in the side of Mediterranean trade for 500 years. While North American merchants had previously enjoyed the protection of the British flag, since independence US ships had been targeted and the late 1790s and early 1800s saw several highly-publicised cases come to light.

The First Barbary War saw the US Navy grow in experience and prestige. As the enemy's pirate galleys and feluccas were no match for the Americans' men of war, blockading, bombardment and cutting-out operations were the order of the day. The US performed well: a number of ships were captured; a young lieutenant named Stephen Decatur McKnight emerged with particular credit, receiving rapid promotion as a result; and the Bashaw of Tripoli was eventually forced into a negotiated settlement which saw the lucrative Mediterranean trade reopened to US shipping. Things were not entirely one-sided, however: the squadron's most powerful frigate, the 44-gun USS *Philadelphia* commanded by Captain William Bainbridge, ran aground while chasing two enemy ships into Tripoli harbour. Although Decatur McKnight later destroyed the *Philadelphia* in a daring night-time raid, her crew, which included a young lieutenant named David Porter, were only released at the conclusion of the conflict in June 1805 on the payment of a $60,000 ransom.[6]

Four months later, the Battle of Trafalgar dramatically altered the balance of global naval power for a century. With French impotence at sea matched by the British army's inability to challenge Napoleon on land, both sides implemented policies to cripple their opponents economically. In May 1806 the British government placed the European coast between Brest and the Elbe under blockade, thus prohibiting neutral nations from shipping produce from France's colonies to her home ports. Napoleon responded with the Berlin Decree in November, excluding British trade from mainland Europe. One side-effect was a major disruption to the neutral carrying trade. By 1807 the US in particular was beginning to suffer. Combined with the Royal Navy's aggressive stance towards neutrals suspected of trading with France and the continuation of impressment, the governments of Britain and America became increasingly polarised. President Jefferson hit back by banning British imports, but this policy backfired: Britain was not about to let herself be influenced by the protestations of a 'minor nation' when engaged in total war. The end-result was an increase in smuggling and a rebellion which broke out along the US Canadian border where Jefferson's countrymen relied on international trade.[7]

In June 1807 the pressure intensified. Ordered to the Mediterranean to protect the US's mercantile interests, Captain James Barron of USS *Chesapeake* was intercepted by a British frigate a few miles east of his home port of Hampton,

Virginia. The commander of HMS *Leopard*, Captain Salisbury Price Humphreys, had received intelligence that several Royal Navy deserters were amongst the *Cheaspeake*'s crew. When Barron refused to allow the British to search his ship, Humphreys fired a warning shot across his bows. When this failed to have the desired effect, the British fired three broadsides in quick succession. Never suspecting that he would face combat so close to home, Barron was hopelessly unprepared and only managed to loose off a single cannon shot in return before striking his colours. Three Chesapeakes were killed and fifteen wounded. Going on board, the British identified four deserters. One was hanged, the others imprisoned.[8]

The *Chesapeake–Leopard* affair caused outrage. In Norfolk, Virginia, a mob prowled the streets looking for Royal Navy officers to lynch; the press called for war; the militia and inshore gunboat fleets were mobilised; President Jefferson demanded all British ships leave the US seaboard or face an embargo; and the American men-of-war cruising the Mediterranean were recalled for national defence. Barron was court-martialled in October. Found guilty of negligence and want of judgement, he was suspended for five years without pay. The British press was equally bullish. 'Three weeks blockade of the Delaware, the Chesapeake and Boston Harbour would make our presumptuous rivals repent of their puerile conduct', *The Morning Post* opined. The leading officers of the Royal Navy stood to make a fortune from US prizes, while the country's merchant class was keen to see their transatlantic rivals humbled. Admiral Sir George Cranfield Berkley, the commander-in-chief of the Royal Navy's North American Station at Halifax, also pressed for action to cow the 'upstart Johnathons', but eventually calmer heads prevailed. Westminster remained focussed on the threat of Napoleonic France, while the US was split between hawkish southern Republicans and the powerful merchant class of the Federalist states of New England who loathed the idea of entirely losing British trade.[9]

In 1809 James Madison was elected President. Putting an end to Jefferson's embargo, Madison presided over a partial economic recovery, but the relationship with Britain remained strained. In 1811, with the US once again moving into the French orbit, two British ambassadors were obliged to retire from Washington in quick succession. The American representative at the court of Saint James' followed suit and Madison enlarged the US Navy from 1,440 to 2,000 personnel and ordered four frigates to sea. Meanwhile, the third British ambassador to serve in Washington in a single year made it clear that his country had no inclination to concede ground on neutral trade restrictions and in May 1811 a second violent encounter occurred on the high seas. On the night of 16 May USS *President*, one of the country's 'super' frigates, spoke HMS *Little Belt*, a 20-gun sloop, off the Virginia Capes. With neither captain willing to identify himself without first knowing the name of his interrogator, a stalemate ensued. Accounts of who fired the first shot vary. The result was never in doubt. At 10.30 p.m., having had nine killed and twenty-three wounded and most of her guns disabled, Lieutenant John Creighton of the *Little Belt* struck his colours. A diplomatic spat ensued, but as both Commodore John Rodgers of the *President* and Lieutenant Creighton refused to accept responsibility, the question was left unresolved.[10]

In November 1811, the Republican War Hawks gained the ascendency in Congress. Henry Clay, a charismatic Kentuckian who, at thirty-five, was too young to remember the horrors of the War of Independence, called for an increase in naval spending and an attack on British Canada which he blamed for inciting Indian attacks in the Northwest Territories. Former president Jefferson opined that the Canadians would be happy to join the US and claimed that the conquest would be 'a mere matter of marching'. Madison backed the Hawks and in April 1812 announced a ninety-day embargo against British products to enable US merchantmen to return to their home ports prior to war. The British government, for its part, remained opposed to the conflict. Defeating the French remained the priority; rioting Luddites required 10,000 troops to be deployed at home; the recent assassination of the anti-American prime minster, Spencer Percival, had robbed the country's hawks of their leadership, while Percival's successor, Lord Liverpool, favoured peace. Neutral trade restrictions were relaxed and a move made towards conciliation. The news reached the US too late, however. Congress had already voted to go to war and on 18 June the bill passed through the Senate.[11]

Few in Britain took the threat seriously. Many thought that Madison's declaration of war was mere bluster and that a truce would be called once news of Liverpool's policy changes reached Washington. In the Royal Navy's North American Station, Vice-Admiral Herbert Sawyer, Berkley's successor as commander-in-chief, was wary of antagonising the enemy and ordered all captured US merchantmen released pending instructions from London. Anticipating a windfall from prize money, Sawyer's junior officers were more bellicose, but their overblown sense of confidence and lack of respect for their new rivals would prove their undoing in the opening two years of the war. Interestingly, the officers of the US Navy would labour under their own psychological shortcomings. Desperate to prove themselves the equal of their highly-rated opponents, the Americans would throw themselves into the fray without due consideration of the impact on their country's wider strategic goals which, due to their numerical disadvantage, required a more patient, measured approach.[12]

The Royal Navy's overconfidence was mirrored in the British press. In a piece of rhetoric as provocative as it was ill-informed, *The Evening Star* dismissed the US Navy as nothing more than 'a few fir-built frigates ... manned by a handful of bastards and outlaws [with] ... striped bunting flying at the mastheads'.

Nevertheless, such an attitude seemed justified when word of the initial land exchanges across the Canadian border reached London. Rather than the matter of 'mere marching' envisioned by Jefferson, the opening moves saw the senior US general, William Hull, a Revolutionary War hero who was well past his prime, surrender with 2,500 men to a British force of redcoats backed by militia of just a little over half his strength, while Fort Michilimackinac on Lake Huron was captured by the Governor-General of Canada, Sir Isaac Brock, without a single British casualty. Brock's success not only brought an important fur-trapping concern under British control but also assured the allegiance of the region's powerful Indian chieftain, Tecumesh and his numerous followers.[13]

By sea the initial exchanges followed a different course. Having convinced Madison that the US Navy's best chance was to take the war to the enemy, Commodore John Rodgers set sail from New York on 21 June. Amongst his five-strong squadron were two of the service's 44-gun 'super' frigates: USS *President* and *United States*. Rodgers' mission, to intercept the 110-strong British West Indian convoy as it made its way east across the Atlantic, would ultimately prove frustrating, but before he returned home USS *Essex* and *Constitution*, captained by David Porter and Isaac Hull respectively, would score the first of several stunning successes won by the US Navy in the first two years of the war. Porter's cruise of the Caribbean saw him take several British merchantmen between Bermuda and the Grand Banks and capture the sloop HMS *Alert* on 13 August. The *Essex* then sailed for the Delaware River where she arrived in early September having narrowly avoided a British blockading squadron led by Captain Philip Broke of HMS *Shannon*. Isaac Hull, meanwhile, had set sail from Boston on his second cruise of the war on 2 August intending to meet up with Rodgers' squadron in the mid-Atlantic. On 17 August, about 750 miles east of Boston, he sighted HMS *Guerriere* under Captain John Dacres, lately detached from Broke's squadron to return to Halifax for resupply. The two frigates closed rapidly. Displaying the over-confidence which typified British officers, Dacres assured his men that the contest would be won within thirty minutes. He was proved correct, but it was *Constitution* which emerged victorious. In a bloody encounter, *Guerriere* was shattered by 24-pound American shot while her own 18-pounders had comparatively little effect on *Constitution*'s solid live-oak sides. By the time Dacres struck, twenty-three of his men had been killed and fifty-six wounded. *Guerriere* was so badly damaged that Hull had little option other than to set her on fire after taking Dacres and the rest of the survivors on board.[14]

September saw a new commander-in-chief arrive at the Royal Navy's North American Station. Although Vice-Admiral Sir John Borlase Warren had been issued with orders to 'attack, sink, burn or otherwise destroy' enemy shipping, he had also been told to seek peace: his first official act was to write to President

Madison offering an armistice. The move was indicative of the lack of direction behind British policy. With Warren's hands tied, it would be some time before the full weight of British naval superiority would be brought to bear on the enemy. Meanwhile, the US Navy, unhindered by such considerations, was preparing for the second phase of the war. The fleet would be divided into three squadrons for commerce raiding. Commodore Rodgers would take the 44-gun *President* and the 38-gun *Congress* to cruise the Caribbean; Commodore Decatur would sail off the Cape Verde Islands and Azores with the USS *United States* and the brig *Argus*; while Commodore William Bainbridge would take the *Constitution*, supported by Captain Porter in the *Essex*, to the South Atlantic. It would prove the beginning of one of the greatest naval cruises of all time.[15]

Chapter 1

'Yankee Warriors True': Captain David Porter and the *Essex*, 1 September 1812 – 25 January 1813

Throughout the autumn of 1812, the Pennsylvanian village of Chester was alive with activity. At anchor in the Delaware, the black bulk of USS *Essex*, an 850-ton Fifth Rate frigate, was preparing for her latest cruise. By the quayside, Lieutenant John Gamble's marines kept guard as boats rowed back and forth with provisions. Flocks of geese splashed down near Chester Island in mid-river and some of the *Essex*'s 319 crew threw fishing lines into the sluggish brown waters to hook the white perch, catfish, shad, herring and giant sturgeon with which the Delaware abounded. Three hundred barrels of salt beef and salt pork, 200 gallons of vinegar, 100 barrels of molasses and quantities of anti-scorbutic lime juice were stacked in the *Essex*'s hold. Nearly 22,000lbs of hard tack filled the bread room and 1,700 gallons of spirits was packed in the liquor store. In the warrant officers' storerooms on the orlop deck were ten boxes of spermaceti oil, seventeen of tallow candles and 50lbs of nails. Hundreds of gallons of paint, turpentine and varnish, sewing twine, fishing lines, fire buckets, barrel hoops and soldering irons had been squeezed on board; coal for the galley stove and forge was loaded and 500lbs of musket balls, a thousand flints, 100lbs of slow match, seventy cartridge bags, hundreds of roundshot, grapeshot and canister and several thousand pounds of powder were stacked in the magazine. Fresh fruit and vegetables were stored in net bags hanging from the rigging and each of the ship's messes had penned chickens and tethered pigs on the spar deck for their private supply.[1]

Built fifteen years earlier by Enos Briggs of Salem, Massachusetts, to the design of Captain William Hackett, the *Essex* was a 'tight little' craft. One hundred and thirty-eight feet in length, with a beam of 37 feet and a draft of 12 feet 3 inches, she dwarfed the cutters, barges, shad boats and two-masted shallops circling around her. Unlike the original six frigates, which had been funded entirely by the government, the *Essex* had been partially built by public subscription. Half of the $150,000 required had been raised in Essex County on the back of a wave of patriotism inspired by the outbreak of the Quasi-War. Elias Hasket Derby and William Grey, the two principal shipping merchants in town, had donated $10,000 each. The government had made up the shortfall. The 53-year-old Briggs was at the height of his powers when he began work in April 1799. After laying down a 128-foot keel cut from four mighty white oaks at Winter Island, Briggs placed an advert in *The Essex Gazette* calling on all 'true lovers of liberty' to supply the rest of the materials. The response was swift. Spruce and pine were cut for the spars, masts and decking. White oak was felled for the knees and structural supports in the wood lots of Danvers, Peabody and Beverly and dragged to the yard on ox-drawn sleds through the winter snows. Local hemp was used for the cables and rigging and the sails were cut from duck at Daniel Rust's factory in Broadstreet. Malleable copper spikes were obtained from Colonel Paul Revere while copper plating to protect the frigate's hull from barnacles, shellfish and the dreaded *teredo*, a wood-eating ship worm of tropical climes, was imported from England. At midday on 30 September 'the Stars and Stripes were unfurled on board' and, to the sound of a salute fired by the frigate's cannon arrayed on a nearby hill and the applause of a crowd of 12,000, the *Essex* was launched into Salem Sound.[2]

Thirteen years later, Captain David Porter, a darkly intense 32-year-old, was in command. Born in Boston into a seafaring family, Porter had grown up on his father's tales of sea-faring derring-do and had made several voyages to the West Indies as a merchant sailor in his teens. After twice escaping impressment by British men-of-war, he joined the US Navy in 1798, securing a midshipman's commission during the build-up to the Quasi-War. 'My son . . . is just entered his nineteenth year', his father wrote, 'he is active and promising . . . [,] understands navigation well [and is] a tolerable good scholar otherways.' Porter's first posting – midshipman on the 44-gun frigate USS *Constellation* – was under the fiery Captain Thomas Truxtun, a former merchant captain who had rounded the Cape of Good Hope three times and made a name for himself as a privateer in the Revolutionary War. 'Swear at you?' Truxtun had bellowed after Porter had complained about the harsh discipline on board. 'Damn it, sir, every time I do that you go up a round on the ladder of promotion . . . Go forward and let us have no more whining.' Porter took Truxtun's advice to heart.[3]

On 9 February 1799, eight days after his nineteenth birthday, Porter had his baptism of fire. Cruising the Caribbean during the Quasi-War, the *Constellation* took on *L'Insurgente*, a frigate of 36 guns, six leagues northeast of the Island of Nevis. In the chase *L'Insurgente*'s main topmast was brought down by a squall. Principally armed with carronades and therefore reliant on forcing a close-range encounter, Captain Michel-Pierre Barreaut found himself at the mercy of Truxtun's long 24-pounders. In an hour and a quarter the American had hammered *L'Insurgente* into submission. With his ship wallowing and his decks littered with twenty-nine dead and forty-one wounded, Barreaut struck his colours, giving the US Navy its first significant prize of the war. Porter was amongst those charged with bringing *L'Insurgente* and her 173 surviving crewmembers into the neutral harbour of St. Kitts, an achievement that helped bring about his promotion to lieutenant. Eleven months later Porter once more demonstrated the bullheadedness that would characterise his career. As second officer of the 20-gun schooner USS *Experiment*, the twenty-year-old was escorting four merchantmen when they were attacked by Haitian pirates. As his superior, Lieutenant Maley, countenanced surrendering, Porter assumed command and saved the *Experiment* and two of her charges. Maley, a long-term malingerer, was dismissed from the service. Porter was praised for his aggression and initiative, attributes which he possessed in spades.[4]

Twelve years on, on the eve of taking the *Essex* on one of the most remarkable cruises in US history, Porter remained as impulsive as ever. On 18 September 1812, whilst the crew awaited a set of replacement sails and rigging and a new bowsprit from the navy shipyard in Philadelphia, a traveller arrived at Chester bearing a challenge from Sir James Yeo, the commander of the 36-gun HMS *Southampton*, part of the British fleet blockading the coast. Yeo requested a '*tete-a-tete* anywhere between the capes of the Delaware and the Havanna', a neatly-couched opening which was followed by the sort of tirade that Englishmen reserved for berating upstart Americans. After capturing the *Essex*, Yeo boasted, he 'would have the pleasure to break [Porter's] own sword over his damned head and put him down forward in irons'. Yeo's ire was no doubt provoked by his opponent's most recent success. While on a commerce-raiding cruise of the Caribbean on 13 August 1812, the *Essex* had captured HMS *Alert*, a 20-gun sloop-of-war, after an eight-minute exchange of fire – the first time the Royal Navy had lost a warship to the Americans.

His pride piqued, Porter promptly penned a reply. '[I] accept ... with pleasure [Sir James'] *polite* invitation', he began, '[and,] if agreeable ... would prefer meeting near the Delaware, where, captain P. pledges his honor ... [,] no other American vessel shall interrupt their *tete-a-tete*. The *Essex* may be known by a flag bearing the motto – FREE TRADE AND SAILORS' RIGHTS; and when that is struck to the *Southampton*, captain Porter will deserve the treatment promised.' As well as providing Porter with an opportunity to prove his own worth, accepting Yeo's challenge would allow him to perform a reconnaissance. It would not be long before Porter received orders to set sail and his first task would be to avoid the British fleet blockading the eastern seaboard. If he was to get amongst the rich prizes of the Atlantic, Porter would first have to get past the Royal Navy.

On 27 September Porter hoisted the cornet to call all officers back on board. The hemp mooring ropes were thrown off and the *Essex* set sail. Working a large ship down a tidal river was no easy task. With a local pilot pointing out the Delaware's hidden banks and shoals, the sounding lead was kept in constant use and the anchor carried cock-billed, hanging from the cathead, ready to drop into the muddy waters at a moment's notice. Slipping by the port and naval hospital at New Castle, the frigate rounded Pea Patch Island, where local militia were constructing fortifications to repel any would-be British invaders, and swept on into the thirty-mile-wide Delaware Bay. Bracketed by extensive salt flats, it narrowed at the Capes before spilling out into the grey-blue depths of the Atlantic.

On 28 September the *Essex* spoke an American schooner. Her captain informed Porter 'he had been captured a few days since off the South shoal of Nantucket by a squadron of seven British frigates & a Brig'. With a breathtaking disregard for secrecy which smacked of the arrogance bred by a decade of the Royal Navy's unchallenged dominance of the seas, the British officers had explained that they were on the lookout for 'Comm[odo]re [John] Rodgers ... and stated their intention to run into Boston Bay'. After thirty-six hours they had liberated the schooner only for her to go on to meet another British frigate, the 36-gun *Orpheus*. After transferring some prisoners on board the American, the *Orpheus*' captain explained that 'he had spoke ... [Captain Yeo's HMS] *Southampton* a few days since bound to the West Indies with three prizes in company'. The *Orpheus*, which the American noted was badly in need of repair and with a crew both 'weak and ... sickly', was bound for Halifax and the American later learnt that another frigate, HMS *Belvidera*, had been seen off Barnegat Bay to the north. Despite being denied his showdown with Yeo, Porter was delighted. With the entire British blockading squadron either sailing south for the Caribbean or north to Nova Scotia, it appeared his passage into the Atlantic would be without incident. His reconnaissance complete, Porter gave the order to tack. With a cry of 'the Helm's a lee', the sailors hauled on the buff-coloured ropes on the windward side while casting loose those on the lee. The *Essex* swung through the water, the main and mizzen sails were braced to the opposite side, caught the wind and billowed taut, the foreyards were brought round to the same tack and the frigate picked up pace as she headed back upriver. Before his next cruise, Porter had some final preparations to make.[5]

On 6 October, back at Chester, Porter received the orders he had been waiting for. Commodore William Bainbridge, the Bostonian's friend and the newly-appointed commander of USS *Constitution*, directed Porter to join a cruise to the South Atlantic. 'I shall sail from ... [Boston in convoy with the sloop-of-war USS *Hornet*, under Master Commandant James Lawrence,] by the 25th [October]', Bainbridge's letter began, 'and shall shape my course in the most direct way for the Cape De Verd[e] Islands ... to fill up my water ... I shall leave there at furthest by the 27th November and hope I shall meet you there.' After detailing several possible points of rendezvous, Bainbridge explained that he intended to follow the Brazilian coast before cruising the shipping lanes of the South Atlantic in search of British East Indiamen.[6]

News of the *Essex*'s imminent departure prompted a final flurry of activity. The new sails and bowsprit ordered from Philadelphia were brought on board along with miles of hemp cordage which the crew used to reset the rigging, splicing, worming, hitching and bending the ropes into place, while Carpenter Waters and his assistants drilled holes into the hull above the gun-deck to take the cleets from which the men's hammocks would swing. Typically, a frigate's crew slept on the berth deck, but Porter reasoned that 'permitting the men to sleep on the gun deck with the ports open ... [would] contribute ... to the preservation of their health'.[7] Whilst keeping his precise destination a secret, Porter 'gave the officers and men intimation of the probable length of [the] ... cruise, in order that they might supply themselves with such comforts as their means would admit of'. The men made modest purchases: an extra stock of fresh fruit or vegetables or some new clothing, while the officers, having been advanced three months' pay, could afford somewhat more. Midshipman William Feltus, the fifteen-year-old son of a New York rector who had joined the *Essex* on July 1, bought a journal to keep a daily record of his adventures, while acting Fifth Lieutenant Stephen Decatur McKnight, a short-sighted native of Philadelphia and the spitting image of his famous uncle, had his writing desk stowed in his six-foot square cabin on the berth deck.[8] Several of the crew also smuggled some New England rum on board. Chief amongst them, no doubt, were the regular offenders: Third Lieutenant James Wilson, the ship's senior drunk, Quarter-Master James Rynard, a troublemaker with mutinous leanings, and Lawrence Miller, the ship's gunner whose inveterate thirst would eventually result in his arrest.[9]

Porter spent his last nights in Chester with his family. Following his wedding to the seventeen-year-old Evalina in 1808, his father-in-law, William Anderson, a Republican Congressman, had presented him with a comfortable, three-storey stone mansion near Welsh Street as a wedding gift. Porter had renamed the house 'Green Banks' for its proximity to the tree-lined Delaware and it was now home to the couple's three year-old son, William David and their daughter, Elizabeth, a sickly toddler of twenty-one months affectionately nicknamed 'Little Rib'. Porter's other ward was James Glasgow Farragut. Following the death of the boy's mother from Yellow Fever, Porter had taken him under his wing while commanding the naval station at New Orleans. A tough yet charismatic eleven-year-old, Farragut had been serving on the *Essex* as a midshipman since the age of nine. He was said to be made up of 'three pounds of uniform and seventy pounds of fight'.[10]

While the *Essex* had performed admirably in her first cruise of the war, Porter still harboured doubts about her sailing abilities. With a top speed of 11.4 knots or 8.4 knots when sailing close-hauled to the wind, she could outrun the majority of ships she was likely to encounter, but would lag behind the fastest frigates. The Royal Navy's HMS *Endymion* had recorded an exceptional 14.4 knots, while USS *Constitution* was capable of 13 knots. On the positive side, despite her relatively small size, the frigate was strongly-built. She was a capacious ship, with an ample hold and proved an easy sea-boat. She was weatherly, making little leeway when close hauled and handled well, despite being a rather heavy pitcher in high seas. Of more concern was the *Essex*'s armament. Besides three long 12-pounders mounted on the quarterdeck and forecastle and another three on the gun deck, her main armament was forty stubby-barrelled, 32-pounder carronades. Known as 'smashers' due to the punch they packed at close range, carronades were hopelessly inaccurate at distance. As such, although the ship's nominal weight of broadside was an immense 676lbs, only 36lbs of those could be deployed at long range. If the *Essex* was disabled in the early part of an action or encountered a highly-manoeuvrable opponent armed with long-barrelled guns, she was sure to come off second best. Accordingly, on 14 October Porter wrote to the Secretary of the Navy, Paul Hamilton, requesting a transfer to USS *Adams*. Citing his 'insuperable dislike to Carronades and the bad sailing of the *Essex*', he claimed she was 'the worst frigate in the service'. It was an exaggeration that Hamilton rightly ignored.[11]

The *Essex*'s sailing master, John G. Cowell, was also feeling underappreciated. A father of two of military stock from Marblehead, Essex County, Massachusetts, Cowell was suffering from the perennial sailing master's gripe. At twenty-six, he was older than most junior lieutenants and had more seafaring experience. Although he might not have been so refined in manners and, with his gold hoop earring and old-fashioned braided queue, resembled those before the mast as much as those behind it, Cowell considered himself a superior seaman and of more value to the service. Nevertheless, lieutenants received better annual compensation: $624 when the value of their rations was factored into the equation, as compared to the $552 Cowell received, a portion of which he no doubt sent home to Abigail Lindsey, his wife of three years. Even more vexing from a sailing master's point of view, was the fact that the position was a dead-end job. Only a minority rose to the rank of master commandant, whereas lieutenants, often blessed with having been born into a 'superior' family and possessed of more influence, enjoyed the fast track. During wartime when the rates of attrition rose, many could expect to achieve their captaincies. Such perceived injustice worried sailing masters' pride and formed the basis of Cowell's complaint to Paul Hamilton, written in the gloom of his cabin on the berth deck on 24 September 1812. 'The many mortifications incident to the situation of master loudly demand that I should aspire to [a] more dignified situation' he began, before requesting promotion. Though it appears that

Hamilton chose not to reply, Cowell would amply demonstrate his professionalism during the forthcoming cruise and eventually achieve his ambition.[12]

During their last few days in Chester, the Essexes were in buoyant spirits: having recently been paid a proportion of what they were owed for their Caribbean prizes, they had money in their pockets; they enjoyed their captain's energy and drive and trusted in his abilities to enrich them further at the cost of the hated Royal Navy. Volunteers from the seafaring communities of New York and New England, the Essexes had long resented Britain's heavy-handed treatment of American merchantmen. Many would have had their ships seized by the Royal Navy and some, like Porter himself, had fallen foul of British press gangs. Others may have spent time on board the infamous 'hell-ships', hulks moored in New York's East River which had housed American prisoners during the Revolutionary War. Such deep-rooted animosity no doubt led to the crew's almost whole-hearted embrace of the declaration of war in mid-June 1812. 'Captain Porter [had] called his crew together', a local journalist had recorded, 'and ... received ... three hearty cheers.' The feeling was not quite unanimous. When called upon to make an oath of allegiance, John Irvine, the ship's sailmaker, had refused. A native of Newcastle upon Tyne, Irvine was unwilling to fight his countrymen. Disgusted, the crew persuaded Porter to let them tar and feather the 'traitor' after which he was bundled ashore. The incident blew into a full-scale riot and the police were forced to lock Irvine in the local jail for his protection. Although Porter was chastised by Naval Secretary Paul Hamilton, he confirmed the Bostonian's acting promotion to captain two days later. Irvine's disgrace also served to bond the frigate's crew.[13]

The men of the *Essex* were a heterogeneous mix. Volunteers to a man, unlike their peers in the Royal Navy, who were obliged to serve until dismissed, each had signed a twelve-month contract, on the expiration of which they were free to leave. Fifteen boys were on the ship's muster. Employed as officers' servants ('shoe boys') or to brave the slender high yards of the tops, some were no more than twelve, while the eldest man on board, Ordinary Seaman Edward Sweeny, was a veteran of 'upwards of sixty-four' years of age. Several of the crew were related: there were two Tuckermans, Ordinary Seamen Matthew and Bartholomew; four Millers; three Whites; three Browns; two Gardeners; and no less than seven Smiths. Although the vast majority were American, with a hard-core of original hands hailing from Essex County, Massachusetts, John Witter, a marine private in whom Lieutenant Gamble placed considerable faith, was from Germany and a significant proportion was British. Some had deserted the Royal Navy. Others had joined from the merchant marine seeking the higher wages available on the US seaboard. As capture would mean a traitor's death, most were careful not to leave an official record of their roots, but at least one, Able Seaman Robert

White, a man whose rating revealed that he had over seven years' experience, identified himself as an Englishman, while seven others, including Boatswain's Mate Thomas Belcher, whom Porter thought 'a consummate villain' and a young Scot named John Glasseau, were British. Several others were of African-American origin. Pete Almy was employed as a 'powder monkey' on the gun-deck and Henry Ruff was the 'negro boy' of Second Lieutenant James P. Wilmer. There was also variety of experience. While the majority had served with Porter for under a year, several had fought in the Barbary War at the turn of the century, a handful had seen action in the Quasi-War against France and one old seaman, Levy Holmes, whose bow-legged gait and tar-stained hands betrayed the number of years he had spent at sea, had served aboard USS *Trumbull* in the Revolutionary War.[14]

On 21 October, on the advice of Surgeon Robert Miller, who himself had advanced liver disease, Porter decided to leave nine of his crew at the naval hospital in New Castle. They were suffering from a variety of complaints: William Stanwood, one of eight quarter-gunners, John Francis, a carpenter's yeoman and John Anderson, a seaman, had sexually-transmitted diseases; William Hubbell, one of nine supernumeraries, and James Wallace and Charles Frederic, both seamen, were suffering from tuberculosis; another seaman, Peter Johnson, complained of a 'rupture' caused when he had been working at the New York Naval Yard in the summer; Charles Smith, seaman, had chronic constipation caused by a perineal fistula; and John Smith complained of a 'diseased testicle'. The final chronic case, William Klaer, a seaman with liver disease, 'through mistake' remained on board.[15]

On 23 October the *Essex* set sail. Slipping downriver in incessant rain, the frigate came to at Morris Liston's, an early settler's house at the mouth of Cedar Creek on the edge of Delaware Bay. On the 24th and 25th, as Midshipman Feltus noted in his new journal, 'nothing remarkable happened', but the following morning Porter, who had stolen a few extra days at home with his family, came on board in a ceremony known as 'Tending the Side', part of the ritual that helped establish the captain's semi-regal position on board ship. Flanked by saluting men who doffed their caps reverently, Porter climbed the gangway – rigged with decorative side ropes – before being welcomed by the frigate's lieutenants and midshipmen and taking up his customary position on the quarterdeck, the entire windward side of which was reserved for his solitary promenade. In later years, Porter would compare his role to that of a 'little tyrant'. A navy captain 'dare not unbend', he opined, 'lest he should lose that appearance of respect from his inferiors that their fears inspire. He has, therefore, no society, no smiles, no courtesies for or from anyone.' It was a lonely role and one that heaped considerable pressure and responsibility upon its holder.[16]

Porter's first task was to establish standing orders for the cruise. Not knowing when he would next resupply, he cut salt provisions by one-third and the bread ration by half. The latter was replaced by 'half a pound of potatoes or the same quantity of apples … in regards to the health of the crew'. The candle ration was reduced by 50 per cent and an 'economy established respecting the consumption of wood and the expenditure of the ship's stores'. Porter instructed John R. Shaw, the *Essex*'s Annapolis-born purser whose job was to supervise the men's provisions and balance the ship's accounts, to keep a full record and assured the men all losses would be reimbursed when they next arrived in port. This, a general pardon issued for all previous misdemeanours and the fact that the rum ration remained untouched, meant that 'not a murmur [of discontent] was heard from any person on board'. Orders were also issued regarding the consumption of fresh water and the crew were reminded 'to lose no opportunity of catching rain-water for the stock'. Guidelines were laid down for personal hygiene and cleanliness of quarters and daily fumigation was ordered to take place 'in every part every morning, by pouring vinegar on a red-hot shot'. Acting Fourth Lieutenant William B. Finch was tasked with maintaining the berth-deck 'in a cleanly and wholesome state' and all officers were reminded to pay 'the strictest attention' to matters of discipline. The men were warned that the first to be punished would receive three dozen lashes, but Porter also expressed a hope 'that punishment during the cruise would be altogether unnecessary'. He promised that those who performed exceptionally would be rewarded and that the hours of 4 p.m. to 6 p.m. would be reserved for leisure and amusement 'when the duties of the ship would admit'.[17]

On 27 October, with the marines sweating at the frigate's double capstan, the anchor was raised and the *Essex* got under way. At 3 p.m. the river pilot was discharged. He took a bag full of letters from the officers on board, but Porter confiscated those written by the men in case any happened to reveal sensitive information. On the 28th the *Essex* passed between the Capes and entered the Atlantic Ocean. That afternoon the wind swung round to the west driving the frigate towards the shoals of Chincoteague. The next morning the wind 'increased to a gale', the topmen raced up the standing rigging and reefed the topsails to reduce the strain on the masts. With the *Essex* rolling violently and waves breaking over her gunwales, the berth-deck, level with the waterline, was repeatedly flooded. On 30 October the wind abated, the topsails were unfurled and the day ended clear. Porter ordered all clothes and hammocks brought up for airing and the berth-deck was scrubbed clean and swabbed dry. That afternoon, the gun crews were exercised. 'We found the powder in several guns wet', Porter recalled, 'all of which we reloaded and more carefully secured.' The captain had learned the importance of combat-readiness at an early stage of his career. Drill with the great guns had regularly punctuated Captain Truxtun's Caribbean cruises and

Porter now mirrored his old mentor's insistence on 'every Article, at any Time, Night or Day, be[ing] ready for Action in a Moment's warning'.

On 2 November, after a few days of squally weather and intermittent rain, the sun broke through the clouds. The apples and potatoes which had been damaged during the storm were thrown overboard, leaving a trail in the *Essex*'s wake as she cut southwards, heading for the busy British shipping lanes to the northeast of Bermuda. Porter hoped to snatch up a merchantman or, better yet, to encounter a Royal Navy frigate to test his mettle, before heading east for Bainbridge's first rendezvous – the Cape Verde Islands. The rest of the stores were left to dry, repacked, returned to the berth-deck and stored under oiled tarpaulins, while windsails, cylinders of sailcloth two feet in diameter and several dozen yards long, were looped down through the hatches to funnel fresh breezes to the orlop deck and expel the fetid air which had accumulated whilst the gunports had been closed.[18]

On the morning of the 3rd a lookout spotted a strange sail to the southwest. Porter ordered the British ensign hauled up to the mizzen peak, a ploy commonly adopted to lull the enemy into a false sense of security, and gave chase. The able seamen scrambled up the rigging, all sails were set and by 8 a.m. the stranger was obliged to heave to and identify herself. '[She was] discovered ... to be a Portuguese merchant brig', Porter recalled. Although allies of the British in the Napoleonic Wars, the Portuguese had not taken sides in the conflict with America. As a result, the brig, whose crew remained none the wiser as to the *Essex*'s identity, was allowed to sail on.[19]

November 4th dawned bright and pleasant with 'breezes and flying clouds'. Several days of fine weather followed. With the winter sun warming the spar deck, further adjustments were made to the rigging, tears in the sails were sown up and life on board took on a routine. Every hour, on the hour, the officer of the deck rang the ship's bell, affixed near the fore-hatchway on the main deck. Every eighth hour it signalled the rotation of two of the ship's three watches. The newly-arrived topmen, the most experienced and nimble sailors in the crew, stood ready, waiting for the watch lieutenant to give the frigate's seven quartermasters the command to send them up the rigging and across the yards. Once aloft, dozens of feet above the deck as the ship rolled with the Atlantic swell, they set, furled or unfurled the sails to order, buffeted by the wind, while the waisters took up the ropes below. Midshipman Feltus recorded the rhythm of the days. At 4 p.m. on 4 November the sailors 'took in the light sails put down the royal yards & housed the masts'. The next day they 'unbent the ... mizzen topsails & bent others [and] at 8 p.m. shortened sail'. Meanwhile, those off duty descended to their quarters beyond the main mast. Divided into eight-man messes, each centred round a small table, they snatched a few hours' sleep swinging in their hammocks; ate salt rations by candlelight, flickering in the stale air; speculated on the destination of their current cruise and the amount of prize money it would afford them; complained about their officers; recounted old anecdotes; sang and played flutes or fiddles; or drank their grog and gambled over cards, backgammon, chequers and fox and goose.[20]

On 8 November, the weather turned 'fresh and ... squally' and at 4 p.m. another strange sail appeared off the lee bow. Porter gave the order to clear for action. As Boatswain Edward Linscott, a New Englander three and half years in his post, blew his whistle, the men rushed to their stations. Muskets, pikes, hatchets and blunderbusses were handed out by Mr Field, the ship's armourer. The hammocks on the gun-deck were unlashed, rolled into tight cylinders and stowed in racks around the gunwales to provide protection from splinters, the canvas partitions dividing the lieutenants' and warrant officers' cabins on the berth deck were taken down, marines were ordered up the ratlines to the tops from where they could pick off enemy officers on the quarterdeck and the gun crews rushed to their carronades. By 8 p.m. the chase had 'dodged' the American. The next morning she was nowhere to be seen. Porter speculated that she had been the sloop of war USS *Wasp* commanded by Captain Jacob Jones which had sailed from Philadelphia on 13 October. His deduction was wrong in several particulars. Five days after leaving the Delaware the *Wasp* had run into trouble after attacking HMS *Frolic*, a 22-gun sloop-of-war, escorting six merchantmen. The resulting fire-fight had seen the British lose dozens killed and wounded, while the *Wasp*'s sails and rigging were cut to shreds by the British shot crashing through the tops. After a final, devastating broadside, Jones' men had boarded their adversary, but at the moment of victory HMS *Poictiers*, one of the Royal Navy's lumbering 74-gun ships-of-the-line, had appeared. With both his ship and his prize in no state to fight, Jones had surrendered.[21]

The storm continued on 11 November. Despite being buffeted by a heavy swell, Porter had the men exercised at the great guns. Amidst the acrid smoke and the thunder of the carronades, the officers timed their crews with stopwatches. Friendly competition was encouraged, wagers placed and rewards distributed. Below, in the filling room, Gunner Miller and his assistants made up cartridges behind a lead-weighted leather blast curtain for the powder monkeys to lug up the ladders to the gun deck. The next morning dawned clear, the gun ports were pushed out and the carronades exercised yet again. To barked orders, each ten-strong crew sponged out the barrel, loaded the charge, shot and wadding and rammed them home. The gun captain pricked the powder bag through the touchhole and poured some powder into it. The crew stood clear, the captain adjusted his aim and gave the order to fire. A match was touched to the priming and, with a thunderous crash, the gun lurched up its slide as the roundshot hurtled across the ocean to send up a distant plume of water unseen through the smoke.[22]

As she cut southeast across the Atlantic the *Essex*'s rate of fire steadily improved, as did the health of her crew. Adversely affected by the ease with which rum had been procured on the Delaware, the sea air and exercise restored the men and by 16 November, when the winds dropped and the frigate was bathed in warm sunlight, only eight men remained on Surgeon Miller's sick-list. Six, including the British boatswain's mate Thomas Belcher, were able to continue with light duties. Levy Holmes, the aging Revolutionary War veteran who was suffering from an 'intermitting headache' and William Klaer, the serial skiver with a chronic liver problem, remained in the sick bay, 'a comfortable place . . . fitted up' especially for their accommodation on the berth-deck behind the main mast.[23]

The next morning an old Portuguese brig fifty-two days out from Brazil with a cargo of tobacco for Gibraltar was spotted. 'The only news she could give us', Porter noted, 'was that an embargo had been laid on American vessels in the Brazils on news of the war.' On 20 November, as the *Essex* fell in with the trade winds and was swept swiftly south-southwest, the temperature rose and a heavy rain fell. Spreading the spare sails across the deck, the crew caught sixty gallons to add to the stock. Two days later another stranger was spotted. At first Porter thought her a British East Indiaman, but after an exhilarating one-hour pursuit with the salt-spray whipping across deck, she turned out to be yet another Portuguese schooner, bound for New York from Lisbon with a cargo of salt.[24]

On 23 November the *Essex* crossed the Tropic of Cancer prompting an age-old initiation ceremony. 'When the ship was supposed to be about on the line the man at the mast head was directed to cry Sail Oi', Feltus recorded. 'Being asked by the officer of the deck . . . what she looked like[,] he answered a small boat on the Lee bow . . . [and] that it was Neptune's the god of the seas, & that he wished permission to come on board with his train. As soon as it was granted one of the B[oatswain's] Mates with some others being in the fore chains, came over the Bows.' Playing Neptune was William Kingsbury, 'a trusty' 39-year-old 'seadog' with a 'stentorian voice' from Wiscasset, Maine. Once on board, he was seated beside a seaman impersonating his wife on chairs lashed to a converted gun carriage 'drawn by 4 men[,] some with their shirts off & their Bodies painted[,] & others with their trowsers cut off above the knees'. Behind came several 'Barbers' carrying makeshift 'razors made of an Iron hoop & constables & [a] Band of music'. Neptune dismounted at the quarterdeck and asked Porter's permission to proceed. The Bostonian had little choice. Although the ceremony was a thinly-veiled excuse for the men to momentarily lord it over their officers while getting thoroughly drunk, it had become so imbedded in the mariners' psyche that non-compliance would be tantamount to inciting mutiny. Clambering into one of the ship's boats, which had been placed on the quarter-deck and filled with seawater, Kingsbury and his nereids called for the first of their victims to step forward. While officers who had not crossed the line before were only required to pay a tribute of a bottle of rum, the novices from before the mast were roughly shaved with the iron hoops and dunked repeatedly under the water. 'In the course of the afternoon all . . . were initiated,' Porter recalled. 'Neptune, however and most of his suite, paid their devotions so frequently to Bacchus, that before the ceremony . . . was half gone through, their godships were unable to stand . . . On the whole, however, they got through the business with less disorder and more good humour than I expected; and although some were most unmercifully scraped, the only satisfaction sought was that of shaving others in their turn with new invented tortures.'[25]

On 24 November the captain of a Portuguese trading brig destined for St. Barts informed Porter 'that an English frigate, bound to the Cape of Good Hope, had touched at Madeira and brought intelligence of the war . . . As we were under English colours,' Porter recalled, 'I . . . affected much surprise at the news and questioned him accordingly.' The next day the crew rigged the flying jib boom, allowing the *Essex* to harness extra wind and at 6.30 a.m. on the 26th the lookout in the tops sighted the island of Saint Nicholas, the second largest of the Windward Islands of the Cape Verde archipelago. That night Sailing Master Cowell set a course between Sal and Bonavista. Taking to the starlit quarterdeck, Porter watched the islands slip by. After passing Mayo Island, the *Essex* sailed onto Santiago and into Porto Praya Bay, the site of the principal settlement on the Cape Verde Islands and the first of Commodore Bainbridge's appointed rendezvous. The first leg of Porter's cruise had passed without incident.[26]

Chapter 2

The South Atlantic: USS *Essex*, 27 November 1812 – 25 January 1813

Under topsails the *Essex* rounded the east point of Porto Praya Bay at 2 p.m. on 27 November 1812. It was a beautiful day. A light wind blew from the northeast and small clouds scudded across the azure-blue sky. Taking in the arid hillsides, spotted with clusters of whitewashed single-storey houses, Porter thought 'the island had altogether a most dreary and uncultivated appearance'. Aside from several goats sheltering in the shade of a few stands of palm trees, there was little sign of life. A mile on, Porto Praya hove into view. Nestling between hills at the head of the bay, the town was built on a sheer-sided bluff. To the northeast stood a dilapidated fort flying the Portuguese flag. Another had been built on Tubaron Point and several dozen guns mounted on rotting ships' carriages were housed in redoubts on Quail Island. Rising up beyond was the 1,394-metre high Mount Saint Antonio. Noting Bainbridge's absence, Porter sent First Lieutenant John Downes ashore in the gig with a crewmember who spoke Portuguese.[1]

Born in Canton, Massachusetts, John Downes had joined the US Navy at the age of twelve. Through the influence of his father, a purser's steward, he secured a place as a powder monkey on board USS *Constitution* and distinguished himself in his very first fight, a slugging match with a shore battery at Saint Domingo during the Quasi-War. Set on the path to promotion by Captain Silas Talbot, by 1802 Downes had been made a midshipman. Two years later he caught David Porter's eye during a vicious shore action in the Barbary War. Downes had gone on to command a bomb-vessel in the Mediterranean, before being appointed lieutenant aboard USS *Wasp* in 1807. Transferred to the *Essex* two years later, he had served on embargo duty and taken part in a diplomatic mission to Europe by the time Porter took command. Although his annual salary of $480 meant that he was no better remunerated than Lieutenants Wilmer, Wilson and Finch, as First Lieutenant, Downes was tasked with dealing with the day-to-day running of the ship. His thoughtful professionalism provided a counterbalance to Porter's hot-headedness, he was capable of performing a diplomatic role despite his humble origins, and he would distinguish himself on several occasions before the cruise was out.[2]

Downes returned to the *Essex* at 3 p.m. Although the governor had been taking an afternoon nap, Major Medina, the second-in-command, had proved most accommodating. As well as being permitted to resupply, Porter would be welcome to stay as long as he wished. Downes had also learnt that two American privateers, one from Boston and one from Salem, and an armed British schooner had been the only recent foreign visitors. Porter 'consequently concluded on stopping a few days, to ... take in refreshments' and that afternoon the *Essex* came to in seven fathoms, dropped the starboard anchor and saluted with eleven guns. At sundown the topmen lowered the royal yards and stowed them on deck.[3]

Early the next morning Porter and his officers dressed in formal blue jackets, white breeches and black leather boots. Rowed ashore through surf whipped up by the northeast trades, they climbed up to town, watched by negro fishermen sitting under the shade of withered palms. Porto Praya consisted of three streets, extending along an east-west orientation. To the northwest grouped around the plaza, stood the customs house, barracks and jail. After a two hour wait, they were received by the governor and a company of black soldiers, naked from the waist upwards and armed with ceremonial halberds, rusty muskets and broken swords. 'A man of easy and agreeable manners of about forty-five years of age', Don António Coutinho de Lencastre appeared 'much pleased' with his unexpected guests. 'He expressed ... regret that the war had deprived [him] ... of the advantage arising from the American commerce', Porter recalled, 'and assured me ... he would give me every protection against any British force that should arrive.' Later, over a plate of meat and 'an abundant supply of the best tropical fruits' the Americans had 'ever tasted', the governor complained of the treatment he had received at the hands of Portugal's 'haughty, unconciliating' allies. The British demanded supplies, but never brought the trade which the islands so desperately needed. '[He] spoke of the prince regent [Dom Joao VI, then residing in Rio de Janeiro under the Royal Navy's protection] as the ... tool of the British government', Porter added, 'and [was] highly gratified with the accounts I gave ... of our little success over the ships of that imperious navy.'[4]

Don António's Anglophobia matched Porter's own. Mixed with grudging admiration, the Bostonian's prejudice stretched back to his childhood. Both Porter's uncle and father had been captured by the British during the Revolutionary War when USS *Raleigh*, captained by John Barry, had been forced to beach on Wooden Ball Island in Penobscot Bay. Imprisoned on HMS *Jersey*, the most notorious of the 'hellships' anchored in New York's East River, David Porter Senior had escaped after befriending his guards. His brother died on board. As an adolescent Porter's resentment grew. Twice he had been pressed off merchantmen in the Caribbean while serving under his father and on one occasion one of his shipmates had been shot dead at his side by an over-zealous British press gang.[5]

On the afternoon of 28 November the *Essex*'s boats began watering the ship. Hiking to a heavily shaded valley with a solitary well, the men filled the ship's casks, rolled them back to the beach, rowed them out to the anchorage and hoisted them into the frigate's hold. The process was exhausting, but refreshment was close at hand. 'The [local] negroes ... have such a variety of expedients for getting rum on board that it is almost impossible to detect them,' Porter explained. Some buried bottles in the sand for later retrieval. Others filled empty coconuts with liquor and by nightfall several of Porter's men were hopelessly drunk. Some had even sold their winter clothing to purchase rum, while Martin Gilbert and Thomas Ewing had become so inebriated that they had injured themselves loading the casks.[6]

The next day, over dinner at the governor's house, Porter met a Portuguese merchant 'of considerable wealth', while Midshipman Feltus and Acting Fourth Lieutenant William B. Finch explored the town. Out of a population of 3,000, the former noted that thirty were white and the others slaves, free blacks and mulattoes. The rest of the Essexes spent the day stowing supplies. Alongside some 'very poor' and 'very dear' beef, 100,000 oranges and 'a large quantity of cocoa-nuts, plantains, lemons, limes, [and] casada' were loaded. Livestock was also purchased and soon 'every mess on board [had] ... pigs, sheep, fowls ... goats ... [and] turkeys'. Some men bought dogs, young goats and monkeys as pets, prompting Porter to complain that the frigate 'bore no small resemblance ... to Noah's ark'.[7]

Others passed their time fishing. An 'abundance' of wahoo, albacore, yellowfin tuna, grouper and dorado were caught with hooks and lines and Porter sanctioned the use of the frigate's seine net – standard issue for all ships-of-war in the US Navy. Impressed by the Americans' success, Governor Coutinho requested a demonstration and on the afternoon of 29 November made his way to the beach accompanied by several ladies and a number of officers. 'We were not at that time so fortunate as we were afterwards', Porter recalled, '[but still] caught enough ... to be carried to their houses.' Another method of fishing was effected by 'rowing ... a small boat across the mouth [of the bay] ... towing a line ... baited with small fish, for the purpose of catching baracoutas'.[8]

That evening the governor, his officers and family visited the *Essex*. The governor's wife, Teresa Joaquina da Silva Ruas, was hoisted on board and dinner was served by Porter's servants, Francis Green and George Brown. At twenty square feet, the captain's great cabin was the most commodious accommodation on board. Afterwards, an eleven-gun salute was fired from the *Essex*'s carronades. '[Coutinho] was much pleased with the attentions paid him', Porter recalled, 'and next day ... I sent him ... a barrel of flour and pork ... In return he sent me ... six fine turkeys.'[9]

With three men having succumbed to 'inflammatory bilious fevers', attributed to Porto Praya's debilitating climate and 'noxious miasmas', on 2 December Porter gave the signal to weigh. Until the *Essex* was out of sight, Sailing Master Cowell set a course to the southeast for Africa, before hauling round to the southwest: Porter having no wish to inform the residents of his intended destination. The next day having 'laboured under a paralytic affection' ever since the frigate had been at anchor on the Delaware, Able Seaman Levy Holmes, one of the *Essex*'s Revolutionary War veterans, succumbed to 'Palsy'. Sewn up in his hammock with two cannonballs placed at his feet, his body was cast into the deep after a brief service read by Chaplain David Phineas Adams, a 35-year-old farmer's son from Massachusetts who had graduated from Harvard in 1801 and worked as a teacher and journalist before joining the *Essex*. The next few days passed pleasantly. Under a cloudy sky, the thermometer on the spar deck recorded 85 degrees and the frigate flew before an easterly wind, passing several clumps of a 'gelatinous substance ... known by the name of sun-fish ... The landsmen on board were delighted', Porter recalled, 'and the seamen felicitated themselves that [such good progress] was not always the case at sea'.[10]

Porter now turned his attention to the well-being of his crew. 'The utmost cleanliness was required from every person and directions were given for mustering the crew every morning at their quarters, where they were ... examined by their officers'. The men were to take baths in tubs of seawater 'at least once a day' and their officers were 'requested to show them the example'. The watches were to be kept occupied during their shifts and allowed ample time for recreation when not on duty. In this way Porter ensured the men were not only 'active ... [and] healthy ... [but] contented' too.[11]

On 5 December, as a result of leaving Porto Praya before the ship's barrels had been filled, the water ration was reduced to half a gallon per day and all the pigs and young goats taken on board were killed to reduce consumption. 'Many petitions were sent to me to save ... a favourite kid or a pig that had been destined for a Christmas dinner', Porter recalled, 'yet I found it necessary to be inflexible.' The next day, as the *Essex* reached the latitude of 4° North, the weather changed. Heavy rain and periods of calm were interspersed with strong breezes whipping round from the northeast to the south. Lightening occasionally lit up the horizon. The topmen shortened, braced and set the sails as required and some sharp squalls on the 7th saw the frigate running along under bare poles.[12]

On 8 December the *Essex* entered the southeast trades, the temperature dropped to 82 degrees and a heavy shower fell. Hoping to call in at the Portuguese penal colony of Fernando de Noronha, the second of Bainbridge's rendezvous situated 300 miles off mainland Brazil, the men kept a close eye on the birdlife accompanying the ship to judge their proximity to land. 'We saw several ... sheerwaters', Porter noted, 'but as they are to be met with ... in every part of the Atlantic, I did not consider their appearance as a certain indication.' Later, porpoises were spotted riding the frigate's bow wave. At midday Porter took the daily bearings. The longitude, 'by a very accurate chronometer', was judged to be 26° 41' 39" West. Latitude was taken at 3° 2' 6" North. The following evening, believing himself dangerously close to Fernando de Noronha, Porter hove to for the night for fear of running aground.[13]

Porter's caution was a result of a bitter experience. A little over nine years before, while serving as Captain William Bainbridge's First Lieutenant during the Barbary War, his ship, the 44-gun frigate USS *Philadelphia*, had run aground on a submerged reef while pursuing a vessel through Tripoli Harbour. Moments before, a marine had overheard Porter assuring Bainbridge that he knew the harbour well and they had nothing to fear. The Tripolitans had surrounded the frigate with gunboats and forced her surrender. Although the *Philadelphia* was later destroyed during a raid led by the future darling of the US Navy, Lieutenant Stephen Decatur, Bainbridge, Porter and their crew had been held as prisoners of war for nineteen months. Publically, Bainbridge was afforded sympathy, but in private many had vilified him for not fighting to the end. As second in command, Porter escaped such censure, but the humiliation of surrender had left a deep scar on his psyche. He would do his utmost to avoid being captured again.[14]

At daylight on 10 December, with Fernando de Noronha nowhere to be seen, the *Essex* raced on. The following day she crossed the Equator in squally weather and at 2 p.m. on the 12th, with the winds 'moderate' and the weather 'pleasant', the lookout at the masthead decried a strange sail on the weather bow. '[She] bore the appearance of a British brig of war', Porter noted. The topmen made all sail and the *Essex* sprang forward at 11 knots. At 4 p.m., the chase tacked. The *Essex* tacked with her and Boatswain Edward Linscott beat to quarters. The gun deck partitions were hauled down and the hammocks stowed to make room for the crew to work the carronades. In the gloom of the cockpit, Surgeon Miller and his mate, Alexander Montgomery, laid out their instruments in preparation. At 6 p.m. the chase hoisted a signal flag at her halyard. Porter responded using the code book he had captured from the *Alert* several months before, but to no effect and at sunset the chase hoisted British colours. The weather was becoming increasingly squally. Small clouds scudded across the reddening sky. Nervously chewing a wad of tobacco, Porter was well aware of the risk he was taking. With all sail set the frigate could lose a spar or a mast could be wrenched overboard. He pressed on regardless. With night falling and the frigate getting ever closer, the chase displayed a series of signal lights. By 9 p.m., it became clear that she was heavily outgunned. 'Being desirous of doing her as little injury as possible', Porter 'gave orders that the great guns should not be fired.' Muskets were handed out and Porter hailed the brig through his speaking trumpet directing 'her to lower her topsails, haul up her courses and heave to the windward'. Robert Leonard, the commander of the 10-gun brig, the British packet *Nocton*, was not ready to give up. Tacking, he attempted to run to leeward and come under the *Essex*'s stern to rake her. Porter opened fire. Most of the musket shot cut through the brig's sails and rigging. One whipped across her deck, mortally wounding Able Seaman John Williams. Leonard struck his colours and hove to. Sending a boarding party across, Porter had the Noctons transferred to the *Essex* and made a thorough search of his prize. She was carrying over £12,000 in coin. Collected from British merchants resident in Rio de Janeiro, the money was destined for Wellington's campaigns against the French in Portugal and Spain. It was a godsend for Porter. Far from home and with no allied ports in the vicinity, he could use the cash to buy provisions and pay his men.[15]

At 7 a.m. the next morning the *Essex* and *Nocton* 'ran foul of each other … [The frigate] carried away part of Her Starbd quarter & our sprit Yard & cat head', Feltus recorded in his journal. The rest of the morning was spent repairing the damage and 'set[ting] up the [frigate's] rigging, which had become much stretched in consequence of the warm weather'. Interrogating his prisoners, Porter learnt that HMS *Bonne Citoyenne*, a 20-gun corvette laden with gold and silver coin, had left Rio de Janeiro for London six days before the *Nocton*'s departure along with HMS *Montague*, a 74-gun ship of the line under Rear-Admiral Manley Hall Dixon, the commander-in-chief of the Royal Navy's Brazil station. That afternoon Acting Fourth Lieutenant William B. Finch took command of the *Nocton* with a prize crew of thirteen. Amongst them was the long-suffering William Klaer who had not once been off Surgeon Miller's sick list since leaving the Delaware. Porter also embarked seventeen of 'the youngest and weakest' of his prisoners as well as Captain Robert Leonard, who was placed on parole of honour 'with the privilege of embarking on board any vessel they might meet bound to England or elsewhere'. Two English merchants, James Heyworth and Alexander Watson, were also sent on board with a servant, William Rossendale, while the thirteen remaining prisoners, the best sailors 'and strongest men', were held on the *Essex*. At 2.30 p.m. the ships parted company. The *Nocton* sailed north for the United States. The *Essex* continued her search for Fernando de Noronha.[16]

At 5.30 p.m. on 14 December the lookout sighted land on the lee bow. Fernando de Noronha was a desolate volcanic island of eleven square miles. With a variance in the tide of five feet and with just one safe anchorage directly before the guns of a stout citadel, it made for an almost inescapable penal colony. At 10 p.m. the Essexes wore the ship and headed in 'under easy sail'. Daylight revealed the island twelve miles to the southwest. Porter ordered the guns run in and raised British colours. Disguising the *Essex* as a British East Indiaman, he bore up under shortened sail and sent Lieutenant Downes ashore in civilian clothes. '[I] directed him to inform the governor, that we were the ship *Fanny*, captain Johnson, from London, via Newfoundland, bound to Rio de Janeiro, Porter recalled, 'that we were short of water, had several of the crew sick with scurvy and were very much in want of refreshments; but that we could not anchor, as we had lost all of our anchors but one.'[17]

Three hours passed with the *Essex* standing off and on in the bay, before Downes returned. The lieutenant had learnt that two men of war, one of 44 guns, the other of 22, both purporting to be British cruisers, had called in ten days before. Their commodore had left a letter addressed to Sir James Yeo to be sent to England at the first opportunity. Suspecting the 'British' ships may have been Bainbridge's squadron, Porter sent Downes with a gift of cheese and porter for the governor and instructions that he would be only too happy to deliver the letter himself. The governor's catamaran twice braved the surf to bring water, before Downes returned at 4.30 p.m., his boat having been swamped by the waves on two occasions. At first sight the letter appeared innocuous, but a secret message, written in lime juice revealed itself when it was held before a lighted candle – a technique Bainbridge and Porter had employed whilst held in captivity in Tripoli. 'I am bound to off St. Salvadore', the message revealed, 'thence off Cape Frio [north of Rio de Janeiro], where I intend to cruise until the 1st of January. Go [there] . . . and keep a look out for me. Your Friend.'[18]

Sixty leagues off the coast of Pernambuco, Brazil, the weather grew increasingly sultry and apathy spread through the crew. Porter issued summer clothes and set up awnings to provide shade from the sun. On 18 December a strange sail was spotted which turned out to be a Portuguese brig. Two days later another was sighted. Porter approached under British colours and learnt that HMS *Bonne Citoyenne* had put into Saö Salvador da Bahia for repairs. Porter briefly considered going after her, but, with Bainbridge in the vicinity, soon thought better of it. The idea of running into Rear-Admiral Dixon's 74 was also off-putting, besides, Porter's first responsibility was to make directly for the rendezvous.[19]

At noon on Christmas Day a rocky high headland was sighted. Under a hazy sky with high humidity, Porter hauled to the southward and made Cape Frio at 4 p.m. Shortening sail, the *Essex* lay to in the shipping lanes, to see what the tides and winds would bring. That night the hammocks and partitions were cleared from the gun deck and British colours hoisted and the following morning, as several dolphin playing around the ship were hooked for dinner, Porter exercised the great guns. Two days later the *Essex* chased a stranger to within five leagues of Rio de Janeiro before Porter realised she was merely another Portuguese brig.[20]

The Essexes' luck changed on 29 December. That morning the man at the mast head spotted a sail on the weather bow. The crew made all sail in chase while Porter climbed into the tops with his telescope. 'I perceived ... she was a schooner ... standing in for ... Rio' and set a course to intercept. It wasn't until 9 p.m. that the *Essex* got within cannon shot. Running out the 12-pounder bow chasers, Porter fired a few shots. The chase bore up, ran up under the *Essex*'s lee and surrendered. 'She proved to be the British schooner *Elizabeth*, from Rio bound to England', Porter recalled. Having set out with four British merchant ships and a cutter under escort of the ten-gun schooner HMS *Juniper* on 27 December, the *Elizabeth* had sprung a leak two days later and put back to Rio for repairs. One of her crew, Seaman John Bagnell, signed up on board the *Essex* and informed Porter of the whereabouts of the rest of the convoy: 'the cutter had gone to the south-ward to convoy a ship to St. Sebastians ... and ... the *Juniper* had proceeded to the eastward with the ... others, which were deeply laden and dull-sailing ... I also [learnt] that ... the *Montague* ... was still at Rio Janeiro, with all her sails unbent; that a packet had recently sailed for England on Christmas day; and that there were no British vessels there expected to sail shortly'. Having assembled a prize crew of six Americans and three prisoners under Midshipman Charles T. Clarke, a 25-year-old from Georgetown, Maryland, Porter sent them across to the *Elizabeth* 'with orders to go direct to North America'. The six other crewmembers of the prize, including her captain, John Helt, were confined on the *Essex* along with those from the *Nocton*, while Porter ordered all sail set and cut away to the windward in pursuit of the *Juniper* and her convoy.[21]

That night the *Essex*'s 'main-topmast trussel-trees [*sic*]', an integral part of the upper rigging, were 'carried away' by a squall. Despite expecting that 'at any moment ... [the] topmast, rigging and topgallant-mast, would come tumbling about our heads', Porter instructed the topmen to make temporary repairs and pressed on. On the morning of 1 January the lookout at the fore-topgallant masthead spotted four sail. 'The ship was immediately in an uproar', Porter recalled, but the apparition soon 'proved to be nothing but small clouds rising from the horizon'. On 2 and 3 January, two more sails were spotted, but were soon discovered to be Portuguese merchantmen from Salvador. Both informed Porter that the *Bonne Citoyenne* remained in the harbour while a large frigate and sloop of war were cruising off shore. This was the best proof of Bainbridge's whereabouts that Porter had had since the letter at Fernando de Noronha. Meanwhile, the damage to the tops required urgent repair. On 3 January, under lowering skies and heavy rain, the main and mizzen topmasts were brought down and stripped of their rigging while Carpenter Waters and his mate, John Langley, made new trestle-trees. By 6 a.m. the next morning the repairs were complete and the pursuit continued.[22]

On 5 January 1813 a passing Spanish troop transport bound for Montevideo reported that two American men of war were off Salvador and on the 6th the winds turned against the *Essex*, persistently blowing from the northward until 12 January when Porter admitted defeat, wore round and returned south. 'My intention', Porter explained, 'was to run into St. Sebastian's or St. Catherine's, as the wind should suit ... to procure ... wood and water, which were both getting low and ... refreshments for my crew ... I gave the preference to St. Catherine's ... as [it was] ... more distant from Rio ... and I should have an opportunity of getting to sea again, before the enemy could hear of me'. At 3.30 p.m. that afternoon, while 100 leagues off Cape Frio, a large ship was sighted through the haze on the weather bow. Porter made all sail in chase and at 4.30 p.m. hoisted British colours and cleared for action. The chase, a large sloop of war, responded by hoisting the Portuguese ensign and pennant at her mizzen peak. One hour later, after hoisting American colours and firing a gun to bring the sloop to, Porter demanded that an officer be sent across to the *Essex*. The Portuguese obliged. The ship was the *Calypso* of 22 guns. Porter misinformed the officer that the ship under his command was USS *Constitution* and that he was expecting to meet USS *Essex*. '[He] could not be persuaded that we were Americans;' Porter recalled, 'and left us, as I am convinced, under the belief that we were English.'[23]

The next five days passed uneventfully. 'The weather continued remarkably fine', Porter noted. 'We saw and spoke but [a] few ... Portuguese coasters' carrying jerked beef to northern Brazil from Rio Grande. Having been out from Porto Praya for six weeks, Porter reduced the rum ration by half in a bid to preserve his dwindling supplies. The decision caused widespread discontent. Quartermaster James Rynard, a troublesome sailor noted for his rabble-rousing, revolutionary bent who had been on the *Essex* for four years, formed a committee to blackmail the captain into changing his mind. 'Every man in the ship refused to receive any [grog]', Porter explained, 'unless he could get full allowance; stating that when there should be no more on board, they would willingly go without; but so long as it lasted, they wished their full allowance.' Porter was having none of it. 'I ... directed that the grog-tub should be upset in fifteen minutes after they were called to grog; the consequence was, that every man hastened to the tub for fear of losing his allowance. After this, no further complaint was made.' To sweeten the pill, Porter distributed some of the prize money due for the capture of the *Nocton*. A spate of gambling ensued. Losses led to theft and the mood darkened. 'I ... soon put a stop to it', Porter recalled. The chief culprits were punished and an announcement made 'that all moneys, staked ... should be forfeited to the informer, whose name remained secret'.[24]

It seems that on this occasion Porter may have employed a punishment known as Running the Gauntlet. Although the Bostonian was reluctant to give specifics,

British sources, who were to be eyewitnesses of Porter's methods later in the cruise, recalled that it was 'frequent[ly]' used to discipline those guilty of theft. The punishment began with the Boatswain's Mate giving the offender a dozen lashes. Afterwards, he was placed on a seat mounted on top of a tub and dragged between two rows of men ranged along the forecastle. Each was armed with a knotted rope and was obliged to beat the offender until he bled. Any man felt to be slacking was held to implicated in the theft and liable to the same punishment.[25]

On 18 January the *Essex* spoke a Portuguese faluca from Rio. Her captain revealed that HMS *Montague* had sailed for Salvador twelve days before to engage the American force blockading HMS *Bonne Citoyenne*. 'He could not tell me whether the admiral had gone to sea in her or not', Porter recalled, '[but] was disposed ... to give me all the information in his power ... being fully impressed with the belief we were an English frigate, from the River ... Plate.' The next day a lookout sighted the pine-clad highlands of Saint Catherine's to the south. That night, having 'no person on board who knew anything of the place' and reluctant to brave the island's rocky shores in the darkness, Porter stood off and on and ran in the next morning under thick grey skies and intermittent rain. Porter thought Saint Catherine's 'the most delightful country in the world ... Nothing can exceed the beauty of the great bay to the north', he recalled. 'There is every variety ... Handsome villages and houses [are] built around ... shores which gradually ascend in[to] mountains, covered to their summit[s] with trees ... [are] in constant verdure ... [The] climate [is] always temperate and healthy; [and] small islands [are] scattered here and there.'[26]

The main town, Vila do Desterro, was a bustling settlement of 'neatly built' houses and a population of 10,000 which owed its prosperity to whaling. 'Several brigs and schooners were lying' at anchor as the *Essex* approached. A sailor tied to the side of the ship took soundings every few minutes. Heaving a lead-weighted line into the water, he reeled it in once it had struck bottom and used the scraps of brightly-coloured cloth tied at every fathom to keep track of the depth in the morning's half-light. At 6.30 a.m., two and a half miles out from a small fort mounting twenty old, cracked guns, the forecastlemen let go the anchor. Afterwards, Downes was sent ashore. Braving squally winds, 'he returned in about two hours with offers of civilitie ... and a promise from the commander, that he would send an officer and a pilot ... in the morning, to take the ship nearer in ...' The officials arrived at 9 a.m. Porter was obliged to kedge the *Essex* forward. A boat carrying an anchor tied to the frigate's capstan rowed to the roads. The anchor was dropped and the ship hauled towards its destination. Passing the fort, the *Essex* fired a thirteen-gun salute, which the Portuguese returned, before dropping anchor in 6½ fathoms on a bottom of fine sand mixed with a strange blue gelatinous mud.[27]

On the morning of 21 January the frigate's 30-foot barge, 28-foot longboat and 18-foot yawl, began wooding and watering at a small, sandy beach opposite the fort. At daylight Lieutenant Wilmer went to town in the 22-foot cutter to meet the governor. With him were Lieutenant Gamble, the ship's 22-year-old lieutenant of marines, Doctor Richard K. Hoffman, Midshipman Feltus and Purser Shaw. The latter had orders to procure beef, flour, bread and rum. The others took their fellow officers' clothes ashore to have them washed by local women. Meanwhile, a swarm of bumboats surrounded the *Essex*, from which 'well clad' peasants and their 'handsome' wives sold 'hogs, fowls, plantains, yams and onions' at 'the most extravagant prices'. Porter flogged a man 'for paying a dollar for a dozen ... rotten eggs' before negotiating fixed prices and setting up a guard to ensure that no one paid over the odds. That afternoon several of the men and officers enjoyed swimming alongside the frigate before the weather turned foul, with heavy squalls and rain. At 2 a.m. Lieutenant Wilmer returned, 'naked and shivering with ... wet and cold'. Having paid their respects to the governor, Wilmer and his companions had set out from town in a hired boat only for it to be overturned in a squall. For four hours they had clung to the keel before being blown onto Great Rat Island where they managed to right her, but not before losing their clothes and $700-worth of supplies purchased in town.[28]

The next day the ship's cutter returned 'with five puncheons of rum, fresh beef for two days, a quantity of onions and a few bags of flour', but the meat was found to be spoiled and Porter ordered it thrown overboard. 'Shortly afterwards' a 25-foot shark appeared alongside with a quarter bullock clenched in its jaws. Horrified at the thought that many of them had been swimming in the same spot twenty-four hours before, the Americans watched in awe as the 'voracious animal' devoured its putrid prize. 'A man would barely have been a mouthful for him' Porter opined. On 24 January Captain John Helt and the other four prisoners taken from the *Elizabeth* were sent on shore. After signing 'an obligation not to serve against the United States during the existing war, unless regularly exchanged', they were allowed to take passage to Rio in a Portuguese schooner. The next morning, Porter heard a rumour of the capture of an 11-gun American corvette off Rio by the *Montague*. 'She had been in company with a large frigate', the Bostonian was informed, 'and was [taken] off the Abrolhos shoal: the *Montague* had [since] left in pursuit of the frigate.' The source, a Portuguese captain, also informed Porter, 'that the day before he sailed, a British frigate and two brigs of war had arrived from England; that two American schooners had been captured and sent in there; [and] that a Portuguese brig of war had arrived from the Cape of Good Hope and brought intelligence that a British sixty gun ship was to sail the day after her for Rio'. Porter was appalled. It seemed that USS *Hornet* had been taken and USS *Constitution* was on the run. Even worse, if his Portuguese informant was correct,

Rio, just a few days' sail to the north with a fair wind, was teeming with British men-of-war. 'Having strong apprehensions of being blockaded, if not attacked by a superior force, in this port . . . I determined on getting to sea . . . with all possible expedition.'[29]

At 3 p.m. Porter fired a signal gun and raised the cornet indicating his intention to leave. That evening, as the frigate moved to the outer anchorage, Boatswain's Mate Joseph Hawley and Seaman Allen Jones deserted and Porter dashed off an encrypted note to Bainbridge in which he hinted at his future intentions to pursue his 'own course'. That night a double tragedy struck. At 8 p.m. Edward Sweeny, a 64-year-old veteran charged with taking care of the ship's livestock who had 'long been affected by a pulmonary complaint', passed away and at 9.30 p.m., as the *Essex* stood out of the harbour, Able Seaman Samuel Groce fell 50 feet to the deck while loosening the mainsail. His skull split by the impact, Groce lingered on for several hours as the frigate sailed out of the harbour, before dying at 2 a.m. 'His loss was much regretted by us all', Porter noted, 'as he was one of the best men we had in the ship and highly esteemed by everyone on board.'[30]

At 4 a.m., as the lights of Saint Catherine's dropped over the horizon, Porter steered southwards. With all hope of meeting Bainbridge extinguished, he now had the freedom of the seas. Porter's orders clearly stated that in such circumstances he was to act according to his own 'best judgement for the good of the service'. There was only one place he had in mind. For several years, Porter had dreamed of being the first representative of the US Navy to sail into the Pacific. Not yet fully explored, the region held an extraordinary allure: Spanish treasure, deserted islands and the legendary hospitality of the South Seas islanders. As far back as 1809, Porter had put the plan to paper. In a proposal penned to former President Thomas Jefferson capitalising on the recent success of Lewis and Clarke, he highlighted the importance of Pacific trade and colonisation and outlined his wish to lead a voyage of exploration. Jefferson was no seafaring Democrat, however and Porter's pleas were ignored. Nevertheless, a copy of the letter was sent to Charles Goldsborough, the chief clerk of the navy, who forwarded it to the current President. Madison never replied.

Porter wrote a second letter to Madison on 31 October 1810, but it too was ignored. Three months later he made an appeal to be granted command of a Pacific commerce raiding squadron in the event of war with Britain to Paul Hamilton, the Secretary of the Navy. Realising the value of the British South Seas whaling industry as well as the Royal Navy's lack of warships in the region, Hamilton showed interest, but failed to follow up on the idea in the chaos brought about by the build-up to war. In October 1812 Porter made one final attempt. Shortly before sailing from Boston, Captain Bainbridge had solicited his thoughts on the best destination for the cruise they were about to embark upon. Porter proposed the Pacific, but Bainbridge was swayed by the council of another friend, William Jones, a Philadelphia merchant and the future Secretary of the Navy, and decided to cruise the shipping lanes of the Southern Atlantic instead. Even as he prepared to sail from the Delaware, Porter had refused to give up on his dream. Amongst the books and charts in his great cabin were copies of George Anson's *A Voyage Round the World* and maps of the Galapagos Islands made by James Colnett in 1793 – strange choices for someone with orders to cruise off Saint Helena and southern Brazil. The possibility of following up on his ambition grew as the *Essex* had missed Bainbridge at one rendezvous after another. The Bostonian may even have been glad that his old friend had failed to materialise, thus allowing him to fulfil his long-standing dream.[31]

Before committing to the hardships that a trip round the Horn was sure to entail, Porter ordered Purser Shaw to do a stock check. A total of 184 barrels of beef, 114 barrels of pork, 21,763lbs of bread and 1,741 gallons of spirits remained. With the men reduced to two-thirds allowance of meat and spirits and a half-allowance of bread, Porter had enough to last twenty-two weeks. 'I estimated it would not take me more than two months and a half to get round to Conception', he reasoned, 'where I was confident of procuring an abundant supply of jerked beef, fish, flour and wine ... [and] calculated, that the prizes we should make in the Pacific, would supply us with ... articles of naval stores.' These were considerable assumptions. Concepción, a port in southern Chile, along with the entire Pacific coast of South America, was controlled by Spain. Although not officially at war with the United States, as allies of Britain against France, Madrid was unlikely to look kindly on a Yankee captain's requests for supplies. For a man with no knowledge of the Pacific Ocean, no allies in the region and no mandate for travelling there, Porter's plan was a bold one indeed.[32]

Chapter 3

'A finer set of fellows': Captain James Hillyar and the Right Revered HMS *Phoebe*, 27 December 1812 – 11 April 1813

Captain James Hillyar of HMS *Phoebe* was a deeply religious man. Although prone to bouts of temper and a believer in the benefits of the lash, as a committed Evangelical he forbade swearing and a strict observation of the Sabbath was part of the Phoebes' unbending routine. Ever since the 44-year-old had taken command, with the frigate patrolling the icy waters of the Baltic in July 1809, Hillyar had had his men mustered by divisions for divine service twice every Sunday. December 27th 1812 was no exception. At 11 a.m. and again at 4 p.m., as the frigate cut a solitary patrol across the ruffled grey swell of the North Atlantic, Boatswain's Mate George Scargill, a 29-year-old Londoner who had joined the *Phoebe* two years before, ran across the spar deck, pausing at each hatchway to send a blast of his whistle echoing below. Roused from their hammocks, the men pulled on their slops: short, dark jackets with buttoning cuffs, woollen or fur 'monmouth caps' and loose canvas trousers waterproofed with tar. Scargill thrashed any loiterers with a rope's end, roaming the decks until the entire complement of 217 officers, sailors, boys and red-coated marines had emerged. Only then did Hillyar remove his cocked hat, open his well-thumbed Bible and lead his men in prayer.[1]

HMS *Phoebe* was a 926-ton Fifth Rate. One of four 36-gun frigates ordered by the Admiralty in May 1794, she had been designed by Sir John Henslow and built in John Dudman's Thames-side yard. Her elm keel had been laid down sixteen months before her launch at the Deptford Wharf on 24 September 1795. Measuring 142 feet 9 inches from rabbit to rabbit on her lower deck and 38 feet 3 inches across, the *Phoebe* was a sleek, elegant craft, from the bust of the eponymous goddess riding at the bow to the bas-relief carvings surrounding the stern windows on the gun deck. Although not the fastest of the Royal Navy's frigates, she was formidably armed: twenty-six long 18-pounders, measuring 8 feet from breech to muzzle and weighing 37 cwt, were mounted on her gun deck; twelve 32-pounder carronades stood on the quarterdeck alongside two launch carronades, an 18-pounder and a 12-pounder mounted on high-angle carriages which enabled aimed fire into an enemy's tops; the forecastle had four long 9-pounders, to be employed during the chase, as well as two 32-pounder carronades, bringing the frigate's total weight of broadside to 502lbs. In addition, four small guns on swivel pivots were mounted in the tops to rain grape down on an opponent's decks. One, a 3-pounder, was situated in the foretop, two 3-pounders were in the main-top and a 2-pounder was mounted in the mizzentop.[2]

The men gathered at the ship's waist on Sunday 27 December formed one of the most experienced frigate crews afloat. A handful had been on board since 1797 when the *Phoebe* had captured the 36-gun French frigate *Néréide*, after an eleven-hour pursuit off Brest; half a dozen had witnessed the capture of the *Heureux* – a 22-gun man-of-war – in 1800 and the taking of the 40-gun *Africaine*, a particularly bloody encounter fought off Ceuta, north Africa the following year, that saw 200 Frenchmen killed and 143 wounded; at least twenty-nine had helped relay Nelson's signals at the Battle of Trafalgar; a third had been on board when the *Phoebe* had cruised the Baltic, North Sea, Mediterranean and Caribbean between 1806 and 1809; just under half had witnessed Hillyar's subsequent arrival and the refit at Plymouth when the barnacles and weed trailing from the frigate's copper bottom had been burnt free; all but 100 had been present at the capture of the island of Java and the Battle of Tamatave, fought against three French frigates off the coast of Madagascar on 20 May 1811; and over three-quarters had been employed on convoy duty between Portsmouth and Quebec. Most of the Phoebes hailed from the British Isles. Several were from Liverpool. Ordinary Seaman Henry Quintenbarne, a 29-year-old who had been severely wounded at Tamatave, was one of a dozen Londoners. A handful had been born in Newcastle, Ireland or Scotland and a few foreigners stood out amongst the ranks. Landsman John Warren, one of the Trafalgar veterans, hailed from Barbados; Quartermaster John Williams, a 47-year-old tasked with aiding the conning and steering of the ship, had been born in Memmell, Prussia; Able Seaman John Francois was from Madagascar; Kyle Cuester, a 30-year-old member of the carpenter's crew, was from Bremen; Able Seaman Ligorio Philips had been born in Tenerife; Sibidia Land and John Wilson were native New Yorkers; Peter Lewis was a Virginian and Henry Johnson, a 26-year-old able seaman, hailed from Baltimore. Most were in their mid-twenties. At fifty-two, the ship's cook, John Dunn, was the oldest on board, while several boys and first-class volunteers were barely into their teens.[3]

The *Phoebe*'s officers were united by a mutual faith in the benevolent workings of a stern, Protestant god. Hillyar was known throughout the Royal Navy for his faith; judging by his letters to his mother, liberally seasoned with references to 'our blessed saviour' and the 'divine will ... [of] the almighty', First Lieutenant William Ingram, a 26-year-old 'gentleman's son' from Owermoigne, Dorset who had previously served on HMS *Amazon*, was equally pious, while Third Lieutenant Nathaniel Jago, a reverend's son from Devon, had packed several works on theology into his sea chest. Even the frigate's lively young midshipmen and first-class volunteers showed a propensity for religion. Allen Francis Gardiner, a sallow-cheeked 19-year-old midshipman with close-cropped curly black hair, would go on to become a celebrated Protestant missionary, while Samuel Thornton Junior, a 16-year-old MP's son, had faced an uphill struggle to persuade his mother that he wasn't cut out for the church.[4]

The *Phoebe*'s religious streak also ran before the mast. Amongst her complement of forty-eight Royal Marines was William Morgan, a 31-year-old from Martley, Worcestershire. A weaver by trade, Morgan had toured Kidderminster as a Methodist preacher in his free time before industrialisation had driven him to join up in 1806. Initially, his attempts to rebuke the Phoebes for shipboard vice had met with little success, but since Hillyar's appointment in 1809, the fortunes of the 'Methodist Parson', as his shipmates dubbed him, had begun to change. Promoted from a 3rd class to a 2nd class private, Morgan's lower-deck prayer meetings gained official sanction and his breakthrough came with his conversion of James Weir, one of the frigate's three maintop captains. Considered one of the most vicious characters on board, Weir's reformation made a deep impression on his shipmates and he was immortalised following a hero's death at Tamatave, a battle which saw six Phoebes killed and twenty-four wounded. On the voyage home, Morgan's flock grew. He was promoted to corporal, one of four non-commissioned marines on the frigate and by 1813 twenty men were regularly attending his prayer meetings.[5]

On Monday 28 December 1812, as a wan winter sun rose through the clouds, a lookout posted in the *Phoebe*'s maintop spotted a strange sail on the larboard bow. Taking to the quarterdeck, Hillyar levelled his telescope on the fleeing stranger and ordered Acting Sailing Master John Miller, a veteran of nine years who had previously served on HMS *Protector*, *Pluto* and *Ariel*, to make all sail in chase. Miller barked out a series of commands. The Captain of the Top, Stephen Laura, a 29-year-old from Falmouth who had taken part in the capture of the *Néréide* sixteen years before as a third-class boy, responded swiftly. Leading a dozen men up the rigging, he skipped out across the spars, removed the gaskets and shook the reefs out of the topsails. Down below the waisters, led by Matthew Ring, a 28-year-old from Waterford, Ireland, who had fought at Trafalgar, pulled the sails taut. The canvas billowed, catching a fresh, cold breeze blowing from the west, a fine spray flew across the deck and to the sound of ropes creaking as they tightened in the blocks, the frigate cut across the waves.[6]

Several miles to the east, Master Jonathon Upton, the commander of the *Hunter*, a 14-gun Boston privateer, was growing concerned. The chasing frigate, which was flying the British ensign from its mizzen peak, was gaining fast. Having taken a merchant brig and a troop transport bound for Newfoundland since leaving Salem for the West Indies on 9 December, Upton's cruise had been going well, but all would count for nought unless he could evade his pursuer. Over the course of the morning, Upton had his seventy-five strong crew heave twelve of his guns overboard. Riding higher as each splashed into the water, the brig picked up speed, yet still the frigate gained. At 3 p.m. Hillyar ordered a warning shot fired across the American's bows. The gun captain pulled the lanyard, the mechanism snapped shut, the charge caught and, as the gun recoiled across the deck, a 9-pound roundshot hurtled across the ocean to send a plume of foam spiking up a few hundred yards shy of the *Hunter*. Upton had had enough. With over an hour of daylight remaining, he knew he had no hope of escape. Striking his colours, he hove to and waited for the British to board him.[7]

At daylight on New Year's Day the *Phoebe*'s lookouts spotted a schooner. The *Vengence* from New York was bound for Bordeaux with a cargo of coffee, indigo, cotton and sugar. Hillyar changed course to intercept and ordered his topmen to set the larboard studding sails. Extending the pivoting booms from the ship's sides and the yards above, Laura and his crew pulled the sail into place, the frigate picked up speed and at 11 a.m. the forecastle 9-pounder crews opened fire. Officers standing on the quarterdeck spotted the shot fall and sent runners forward to advise the gun captains to adjust their fire. At midday, after several shots had fallen close, the *Vengence*'s Master, G. R. Dowdall, surrendered. Hillyar sent a petty officer and ten men in one of the ship's boats to take possession. Seventeen prisoners were locked below with those taken from the *Hunter*, while Hillyar retired to his cabin under the quarterdeck to peruse the latest New York newspapers courtesy of his prize. The front pages announced yet another US victory. On 25 October the 38-gun HMS *Macedonian* had been defeated by USS *United States* midway between the Azores and Cape Verde Islands. She was the second British frigate to fall into the Americans' hands. Returning to the quarterdeck, Hillyar ordered Acting Sailing Master Miller to set a course for England. The Admiralty would want to know of their latest defeat without delay.[8]

Born at Portsea, Hampshire, on 29 October 1769 into a naval surgeon's family, Captain James Hillyar had always been destined for a life at sea. As a blue-eyed, blonde-haired boy, he had accompanied his widowed father from ship to ship before joining the 50-gun Fourth Rate, HMS *Chatham*, as a ten-year-old first-class volunteer. In the American War of Independence, Hillyar had commanded three of the *Chatham*'s lower deck 24-pounders when the French frigate *Magicienne* had been pounded into submission off Boston and was involved in the capture of no less than forty prizes before the Treaty of Paris brought the conflict to an end. The outbreak of the French Revolutionary War saw Midshipman Hillyar narrowly escaping with his life when his shore battery was stormed by bayonet-wielding Revolutionary French troops at the siege of Toulon. Rapid promotion on board a series of frigates followed and by the age of thirty Hillyar had attained the rank of First Lieutenant. In 1794, while serving on HMS *Aquilon* under Captain Robert Stopford, he took part in his only fleet action, the Glorious First of June, and six years later was made captain of HMS *Niger*, a 12-pounder frigate stationed at Torbay. Hillyar's crowning moment on his first command came on 8 October 1800 when he led a night-time cutting-out operation at Barcelona. With the benefit of surprise, the 31-year-old brought two Spanish corvettes out of the harbour under heavy fire.[9]

Thirteen years of captaining frigates later, with his once-blonde hair steadily turning grey, Hillyar watched as his able First Lieutenant, William Ingram, sailed the *Phoebe* into Plymouth Sound. Three ships-of-the-line, including HMS *Rivoli*, a 74 recently captured from the French, HMS *Salsette* and a number of other frigates, and several armed brigs and sloops lay at anchor. To one side a line of nine dismasted prison hulks were moored. Crammed with French, Danish, Dutch and American soldiers, these once-proud giants served as a reminder of the ongoing European war. Under her previous title, the *Formidable*, HMS *Brave* had served as the flagship of Rear-Admrial Dumanoir at the Battle of Trafalgar. Alongside was a Spanish 74 captured at Cape St Vincent, the *San Isidrio*, two of whose inmates would attempt to escape whilst the *Phoebe* was at Plymouth, only to be caught in the act of cutting a 3-foot-square hole through her tropical hardwood hull.[10]

On the morning of 9 January 1813, having worked his way into the sheltered waters of the Barn Pool to the west of the shore batteries on Drake Island, Hillyar brought the *Phoebe* to anchor. Shore boats selling fresh fruit, fish, meat and vegetables gathered round and the men enjoyed the first fresh bread they had tasted since leaving port. Other boats arrived carrying crewmembers' wives, a number of local prostitutes offered their services for half a crown (a little over double an able seaman's daily pay) and the ship was soon overrun by 'Jew pedlars', small-scale entrepreneurs who set up shop in the hatchway gratings selling everything from handkerchiefs and duck trousers to gold watches and silver rings. The men weren't the only ones to take advantage. Lieutenant Ingram had soon run up a debt of £5.[11]

That afternoon the cutter, yawl and barge were lowered and the ninety American prisoners were put on board HMS *Salvador del Mundo*, a Spanish three-decker captured at Cape St Vincent and since anchored in Cawsand Bay as a receiving ship for pressed men. Four days later, while the rest of the crew was busy taking on supplies, repainting the hull in the distinctive black and yellow pattern known as the 'Nelson Chequer' and repairing the sails and rigging, the

Phoebe's dwindling band of Trafalgar veterans bade farewell to one of their own. Never having fully recovered from a tropical fever contracted at Java in 1811, Able Seaman Robert Hilling, a 42-year-old Irishman who had served on the frigate since 1 November 1803, took one last look at the legendary signal sent by Nelson over seven years before ('England expects every man shall do his duty') embossed in gold lettering on a brass plaque on the *Phoebe*'s quarterdeck, before being discharged into Plymouth Hospital.[12]

On 14 January Hillyar wrote a letter to the Admiralty concerning another long-standing servant: Boatswain John Pomfrey, 'a very worthy man ... [who was growing increasingly prone] to frequent indisposition'. After outlining Pomfrey's good service, Hillyar 'beg[ged]' the Admiralty 'to appoint him to' a role on shore so he could live out his final years in a modicum of comfort. No reply was received. On the 19th the captain took up his pen once more. Patrick Brady, a 27-year-old from County Carlow, Ireland, with a penchant for painting, was to be the *Phoebe*'s new schoolmaster. Tasked with rounding off the young midshipmen's education, Brady was paid a measly £2 6d a month, the exact same remuneration received by his charges. Before he could be entered onto the frigate's books, the Admiralty would have to confirm his appointment. This time Hillyar's plea was answered. Brady lugged his sea chest on board and was assigned a hammock in the cramped confines of the berth deck.[13]

On 2 February orders were received 'to fit for foreign service'. Over the next eight days the Victualling Agent dispatched dozens of barrels of salt pork and beef, dried pease, flour, raisins, butter, vinegar and gallons of beer and spirits from the Weevil yard at Stonehouse. Rowed out on the Hoytaker's boats, they were hoisted on board the *Phoebe* using a line rigged via the yards to the ship's capstan, entered into the books by the Purser's Steward, the 24-year-old Londoner John Higgins, and stacked in the hold. On 7 February orders came to proceed to Spithead. The following day Purser John Surflen, a 26-year-old father of two from Margate who had previously served for five years on HMS *Vulture*, issued an advance on the prize money due for the *Vengence*. Head-money for the capture of her crew totalling £85 was also paid. Divided amongst the crew according to rank, this unexpected windfall allowed the Phoebes to buy some personal supplies.[14]

Over the next two days fifty-seven names were added to the ship's muster, bringing the complement to 274 men. Hillyar had been short of hands ever since the cruise to the Indian Ocean in 1810 and 1811 had seen dozens die of tropical diseases. Twenty more had run at Quebec or deserted while on leave in Plymouth in mid-1812. Sent from the *Salvador del Mundo*, most of the new recruits had been pressed and held just long enough to be examined by a doctor, washed, deloused and issued with new clothing as a precaution against typhus. Others, realising they stood to gain the King's bounty (as much as £5 per head) had volunteered. Once on board the *Phoebe*, the recruits were questioned by First Lieutenant Ingram. Their profession, place of birth and dwelling, name, age and length of time at sea were duly noted in the ship's muster book by Nicholas Nickenson, the 26-year-old captain's clerk. A brief practical examination followed, after which Ingram decided each man's rating. Peter Mortraugh and Peter Carlan, two lads from Drogheda aged seventeen and twenty respectively, were classed ordinary seamen as were William Knowles, a 22-year-old from Reading in Berkshire, and the twenty-year-old John Jackson. Listed as born 'at sea', Jackson opted to send five of the eleven pennies he was paid daily to his mother, Agnes Jackson, in Plymouth.[15]

Thus were the new recruits condemned to a routine of unremitting toil. From sunrise to sundown they would be assigned a series of backbreaking tasks, their only respite coming on the Sabbath, their only amusements the daily issue of grog or small beer, a weak brew typically 2 or 3 per cent proof, and the occasional dance to 'Rule Britannia' which the *Phoebe*'s band were frequently ordered to play. They were deprived of the company of other men as ship to ship visits were discouraged and would only see women in home ports. Psychologically, the most punishing aspect was that they had no idea when their imprisonment would end. Committed to serve until hostilities finished, in early 1813 there seemed little prospect of an early release. The conflict with France had been dragging on for some twenty years. It showed no sign of terminating soon.[16]

On 10 February Hillyar gave the order to raise anchor. With eight merchantmen in convoy, a local pilot guided the *Phoebe* round Drake's Island under leaden skies and out into the Sound where Acting Master Miller set a course for Spithead. Probably the best-known of the Royal Navy's anchorages, Spithead enjoyed several advantages: with the Isle of Wight to the southwest, a number of sandbanks to the east and the mainland to the north, it was well-sheltered; Saint Helen's Roads provided easy access; and it was close to the major dockyards at Portsmouth. Spithead was a major assembly point for fleets bound for both domestic and foreign service and as the scene of frequent naval reviews, it was always crowded with His Majesty's ships. HMS *Mars*, an old 74-gun ship of the line which had fought in the lee column at Trafalgar before being turned into a receiving ship or '*bird of passage*', and HMS *Gladiator*, a 44-gun Fifth Rate which served as Rear-Admiral Sir Peter Halkett's flagship, were present at the *Phoebe*'s arrival on 12 February along with a line of fourteen prison hulks riding at anchor on one side of the bay. Elsewhere, a convoy of merchantmen bound for the West Indies were gathering under the protection of a frigate and several brigs of war. Forty more sail were visible, amongst them eight East Indiamen and the *Isaac Todd*, a lumbering 20-gun storeship commanded by Captain Fraser Smith. Property of the North West Company, the *Todd* was due to sail for the Pacific coast of America and carried a letter of marque, thus giving Smith the right to capture any enemy vessels he might fall in with during the voyage.[17]

On 13 February the *Phoebe* loaded more supplies. Eleven tons of water in twenty-two butts, three tons of beer in twelve hogsheads, a supply of slops and bedding and 300lbs of fresh vegetables were hoisted on board. On 16 February there were fresh gales and intermittent rain. While the men set up the standing and running rigging and fitted a new fore sail, the frigate was blown eastwards. Forced to wear out of trouble, she ran aground on a sandbank, but was soon floated off again. That afternoon the barge took Hillyar ashore leaving First Lieutenant Ingram in charge. At Portsmouth, busy with smartly-dressed officers, gangs of unruly tars and corner-haunting 'Spithead nymphs', Hillyar received a bundle of three packets of orders written by John Wilson Croker, the dour Scottish Secretary of the Admiralty. Marked with the fouled anchor seal and bearing the legend 'secret', each was to be opened at a set latitude and longitude, thus revealing the frigate's mission in stages. The first, which Hillyar unsealed immediately, commanded him to escort the *Isaac Todd* storeship south towards the Bay of Biscay. Once there Hillyar would be permitted to open the second.[18]

As Hillyar may have suspected from the involvement of the *Isaac Todd*, the *Phoebe*'s mission was to take him into the Pacific. Once round Cape Horn, the frigate was to sail north up the coast of the Americas to the mouth of the Columbia River and destroy Fort Astoria, a trading outpost belonging to the Pacific Fur Company, a US enterprise which shipped beaver and sea otter pelts, acquired from the local Tla-o-qui-aht Indians, across the Pacific via the Sandwich Islands (Hawaii) to the Chinese port of Canton, where they were exchanged for porcelain, tea and silk. Previously, the trade had been monopolised by the British-owned North West Company whose two centuries of experience in the Asian market had taught them not to tolerate rivals. Once Fort Astoria had been reduced to ruins by the *Phoebe*'s guns, the passengers on board the *Isaac Todd* were to build a British outpost in its stead. The mission was just one small part of a new policy to bring the Americans to heel. Stung by the news of three embarrassing frigate losses in single-ship actions and enabled to redistribute resources following Napoleon's disastrous retreat from Moscow, the Royal Navy was finally taking her news foes seriously. The coming year would see the strength of the Halifax station increased to eleven 74s and sixteen Fifth Rates, the entire eastern seaboard of the US would be blockaded and several large-scale amphibious raids would be launched.[19]

Captain Hillyar was back on board the *Phoebe* by 18 February. In his absence a new fore gallant sail and spare jib had been completed and 240lbs of fresh beef and 200lbs of vegetables had been taken on board. An outbreak of insubordination among the newly-mustered men had prompted Lieutenant Ingram to order the ship's boats to row guard round the frigate at night to prevent desertion. With the captain back on board, several of the ringleaders were punished. The first was John Jackson, the newly-pressed man who had arranged to send part of his pay to his mother. Stripped to the waist, he was tied to the grating while the ship's company, assembled on the frigate's waist, looked on. Captain Hillyar, flanked by his lieutenants and dressed in white breeches and a navy-blue woollen coat with epaulettes picked out in gold, oversaw the operation from the forecastle, his authority assured by the forty-eight red-coated marines led by Lieutenant William Burrow, who stood to attention around him. After the charges, that Jackson had been guilty of showing contempt to a senior officer, had been read aloud, he was given twenty-four lashes by Boatswain's Mate George Scargill, a 29-year-old Londoner, with a cat-o-nine-tails. James Smith, another newcomer, was given thirty-six for theft and Ordinary Seaman Patrick Burns, a 33-year-old from Kildare who had fought at Tamatave, was given twelve lashes for insolence.[20]

By the middle of February the *Phoebe* was alive with rumours concerning her forthcoming mission. The fact that the North West Company was involved surely meant that she was headed for the frozen furthest reaches of the Pacific Ocean, but the goal of the mission and all other particulars 'were ... matters of conjecture. This is one of the greatest inconveniences of a sailor's life' mused Midshipman Allen Gardiner, who berthed with his five peers in and around the ship's cockpit on the orlop deck, 'but secrecy is a policy in war, without which, even the best concerted plans must fail.'[21]

Born in Basildon, Berkshire, on 28 January 1794, Gardiner was a thoughtful character who kept a journal detailing his experiences. As a child, he had longed to join the navy to see the world and had spent hours producing detailed plans for cutting out the French fleet from La Rochelle and copying the vocabulary of the Mandingo language from an edition of Mungo Park's African travels. At thirteen, having overcome his parents' misgivings, Gardiner entered the Royal Naval College at Portsmouth, at that time still a relatively uncommon route into the service. There, he and seventy other students studied seamanship, navigation, mathematics, physics, astronomy, gunnery and fortification under the college's renowned headmaster, James Inman. Graduating in 1810, Gardiner had volunteered on board HMS *Fortune*, a ship which carried him first to Mauritius and later to Ile de France where he had transferred to the *Phoebe* in March 1811 in time to take part in the Battle of Tamatave. Well-educated and widely-travelled, Gardiner possessed a keen sense of scientific curiosity. Combined with an interest in humanity and a morality coloured by the first signs of the evangelicalism which would dominate his adult life, these qualities would make him an enquiring observer of events.[22]

With the *Isaac Todd* still awaiting the arrival of several key North West Company employees, the Phoebes spent several weeks at Spithead. Captain

Hillyar made numerous forays into town and some of his officers were granted shore leave, although the men were strictly forbidden from leaving the ship, a regulation which must have been particularly trying for Able Seaman John Smith, a 26-year-old who had been born in Plymouth, pressed onto the frigate in 1807 and wounded at the Battle of Tamatave four years later. Being within a few miles of family and friends yet unable to visit them must have stretched Smith's patience to the limits.[23]

For the Phoebes the days passed in a dreary routine. Most mornings, weather permitting, the newly-raised men were exercised at the great guns. Overseen by Captain Hillyar, Lieutenants Ingram, Charles Pearson and Nathaniel Jago and the frigate's six midshipmen, they underwent 'dry-firing' practice to preserve gunpowder and shot. Opening the ports, the crews hauled on the gun tackle to run out the frigate's 18-pounders, the gun captains 'fired' them with their lanyards, the barrels were sponged out, loaded with cartridge and shot which were rammed home and the guns run out once more as the ropes squealed through the tackles and the carriages rumbled across the deck. Small arms practice was also routine, while the Sabbath was a day of rest and meditation. Fresh supplies were brought on board and minor repairs undertaken. On 22 February Boatswain Pomfrey condemned the main mast, braces and luff tackle pulls as 'worn and unfit for proper use'. Later that evening, wine barrel 968 was opened, Purser Surflen noting that it held 67 gallons and on 23 February Pomfrey received 'sundry' supplies, ropes, needles, knives, sailcloth and timber. All was inventoried and locked in his storeroom on the orlop deck. The next morning John Curlin received twenty-four lashes for insolence and Able Seaman Matthew Scott, a 28-year-old from Newcastle who had been wounded at Tamatave, got twelve lashes for drunkenness on duty. Violent squalls that evening necessitated the taking down of the topgallant masts. All the provisions were loaded and by the 28 February the *Phoebe* was supplied with six months' worth of salt meat and hard biscuit and three months' of beer, butter and cheese.[24]

In the interim, the North West Company employees had finally arrived. In charge was Donald McTavish, a 31-year-old fur trader from Strath Errick who had risen to the rank of company partner. His second was John McDonald, a raucous Scot whose withered right arm had seen him nicknamed 'Le Bras Croche' and prevented him from following in the family tradition of joining the army. Having been involved in the planning stages of the mission undertaken at the Admiralty in London, both were fully aware of all details and their ultimate destination. On boarding the *Isaac Todd*, McTavish and McDonald found things far from their liking. The latter thought Captain Smith 'a miserable commander'. He had not even started to stow provisions, the ship was overloaded with guns and ammunition and the crew were 'as mongrel and rascally a mixture . . . as ever was on board a ship'. As well as a Sandwich Islander who was to serve as a pilot when they reached the Columbia River and three different breeds of dog, there were a dozen Canadian *voyageurs* on board. McDonald allowed the latter to take shore leave, but soon came to regret his decision. After a night in which they 'had all made a little free with wine and women', a Royal Navy midshipman pressed two of the Canadians and sent them on board HMS *Mars*. Fortunately, McDonald had excellent contacts and was able to secure their release.[25]

On board HMS *Phoebe* the routine ground on. On 28 February Midshipman Jose S. Rickard, a Cornishman who at twenty-one was the oldest of his rank on board, was made Master's Mate. The promotion saw his pay increase by 12 shillings a month. Three days later 110lbs of sugar and 303lbs of cheese were loaded. The latter was stacked by Purser's Steward Higgins in specially-designed racks in his storeroom on the orlop deck, a cramped space packed with dried provisions which had led to his being nicknamed 'Jack-in-the-dust'. The next morning dawned bright and clear. Five of the ship's marines were exchanged for a new draft from Portsmouth Barracks, while the crew scrubbed and aired their clothes and hammocks. On 3 March the prize money for the *Hunter* was paid, prompting a fresh round of purchases from the bumboats. The following day the newly raised men were trained 'in going aloft and losing the rigging', while Ordinary Seaman Robert Hughes, a 28-year-old from Teddington, Gloucestershire who had volunteered in 1804 and served at Trafalgar, was discharged into HMS *Gladiator* for harbour duty on account of several old injuries.[26]

On 10 March the West India convoy sailed. Three days later Hillyar wrote to Secretary Croker to inform him that his mission had already been delayed. 'The ... [*Isaac Todd*] will not be ready for sea before Monday', he explained, 'having only begun to take in provisions this afternoon [and] the charts [for the South Atlantic and Pacific Ocean] are not yet arrived.' A second letter followed on the 16th with which Hillyar enclosed a missive from Captain Smith blaming his tardiness on the fact that he had to stow extra supplies for his frigate escort 'tween decks'. There was also one final addition to the *Isaac Todd*'s complement. Jane Barnes, a 'lively', 'flaxen-haired, blue-eyed' maid who worked the bar at McDonald's Portsmouth hotel had consented to become his '*compagnon du voyage*'. On 18 March the eight East Indiamen under convoy of HMS *Porcupine* and *Doris* set sail and Michael Lane, a fourteen-year-old Midshipman Ordinary from Sandwich who had graduated from the Royal Naval College, was promoted to Midshipman. That evening he sewed the white shoulder patches to his dark-blue coat with pride.[27]

The newspapers of 20 March brought bad news. 'Another frigate has fallen into the hands of the enemy!' announced the barely credulous *Naval Chronicle*. As Hillyar and his men learnt, on 29 December 1812, while cruising off Salvador de Bahia in the coastal waters of Brazil, Captain William Bainbridge's USS *Constitution* had defeated HMS *Java*, the third British frigate to fall to the Americans so far. *The Times* also carried a report stating that no less than 500 British merchantmen had been captured by US cruisers and privateers. 'Can these statements be true . . . ?' asked the editor.

> Any one who had predicted such a result of an American war, this time last year, would have been treated as a madman or a traitor. He would have been told, if his opponents had condescended to argue with him, that long ere seven months had elapsed, the American flag would be swept from the seas, the contemptible navy of the United States annihilated and their maritime arsenals rendered a heap of ruins. Yet down to this moment, not a single American frigate has struck her flag . . . They leave their ports when they please and return to them when it suits their convenience; they traverse the Atlantic; they beset the West India Islands; they advance to the very chops of the Channel; they parade along the coasts of South America; nothing chases, nothing intercepts, nothing engages them but to yield triumph.

Some publications excused the defeats by stressing that the American ships outgunned their opponents. Others pointed to the fact that the enemy also enjoyed superior gunnery due to regular practice with live ammunition, a lesson Hillyar would take on board. The Royal Navy's pride had been bruised. Humiliated and humbled, the country's senior service longed for revenge.[28]

On 25 March the *Isaac Todd* was finally ready for sea. Hillyar signalled all crewmembers to repair on board and at 10 a.m. the *Phoebe* unmoored. By 4 p.m. all the officers had returned. The forecastlemen, led by John Newbury, raised the small bower while Acting Master Miller ordered the topmen to make sail. Shuffling along the footropes, they spread along the yards. Leaning their weight against the spars to free their hands, they removed the gaskets that held the sails in place and overhauled the buff-coloured clewlines and bluntlines through the blocks. Meanwhile, the afterguard on the deck below pulled on the sheets to stretch the sails taught. With fresh breezes and fine weather, the *Phoebe* sailed serenely out of the bay with the *Isaac Todd* and forty other sail, 'bound for all parts of the world', in company.[29]

Overladen with supplies and top-heavy with cannon, the *Todd* soon proved an extremely dull sailer. By 5 p.m. she was lagging behind. The Phoebes hoisted a yellow and red-striped tricolour above a plain signal flag at the foretopmast head to indicate that she should close up, but at 5.30 p.m. Hillyar was forced to heave to and allow her to catch up. The next four days saw the convoy make slow progress down the Channel, averaging just over thirty miles every twenty-four hours. On 26 March, they passed Portland Bill. The following morning, with seven sail including the *Isaac Todd* in company, Hillyar exercised the great guns. That afternoon, the crew washed their clothes and hammocks and hung them up to dry from the standing rigging, the black ropes that supported the masts and yards, giving the ship the appearance of a floating laundry. The morning and afternoon of Sunday 28 March were marked by divine service and on 29 March, as a thick fog descended obscuring the English shore, the carpenters repaired the ship's boats and the newly-raised landsmen were exercised at the 18-pounders on the gundeck once more.[30]

On 30 March, Gardiner noted in his journal, 'fortune ... smile[d]' on Hillyar and his crew. At noon, while Acting Master Miller was instructing the midshipmen how to take accurate latitude readings with their sextants on the quarterdeck, two strange sails were spotted on the leeward tack. Hillyar bore up to reconnoitre. The lead sail was a French corvette fleeing for the port of Saint Malo on the Brittany coast. Her pursuer was a British frigate, HMS *Unicorn*. Eager to share the spoils, Hillyar gave the order to make all sail in chase. At 1 p.m. HMS *Stag*, another frigate patrolling the Channel, joined the hunt and she and the *Unicorn* opened fire on the chase ten minutes later. The corvette hoisted French colours before striking at 2.30 p.m. A few minutes later, the *Phoebe* hove to and began exchanging signals with the *Stag* and *Unicorn*. The prize proved to be the *Miquelonnaise*, a handsome, copper-bottomed French privateer pierced for twenty guns yet mounting eighteen, with a crew of 130 men. Having left Brest four days previously, she had captured the *Alexander*, a small brig from London, which had been bound for Wellington's troops in Portugal with a cargo of tin and iron. The French had set fire to her and left her to burn into the sea. After making a formal claim for a share in the prize money, Hillyar made sail, but with the *Todd* wallowing behind, at 5 p.m. he was forced to heave to yet again.[31]

The next morning Hillyar opened his second packet of orders. 'We were directed to steer for the Island of Teneriffee', Gardiner recalled, 'there to complete our water and from thence to proceed to Rio de Janiero, where we should open our final orders.' The news sent a buzz of excitement round the ship and that afternoon a strong gale blowing out of the northeast propelled the convoy swiftly across the Bay of Biscay. At 5.30 p.m. a strange sail was sighted and at 6 p.m. Hillyar gave the order to clear for action. At 9 p.m., with the men ready at the guns and the tension building, lantern signals were exchanged revealing the stranger to be HMS *Orestes*, a 16-gun brig-sloop commanded by William Richard Smith. With a mixture of relief and disappointment, the Phoebes stood down.[32]

The next three days were an exercise in frustration. With a steady breeze from the northeast and fine weather, the *Phoebe* could have reached Tenerife within a week. Instead, with the *Isaac Todd* in company, the crew was constantly obliged to heave to, tack and take in sail. Nevertheless, they covered 126 miles on 1 April, 103 miles on the 2nd and 99 miles on the 3rd. The following morning brought strong gales and a high sea. At morning divine service the men struggled to maintain their footing on the rolling deck. All sails were taken in at noon and the frigate ploughed on under bare poles with the *'Isaac Todd* sailing very ill'. At 4 p.m. the *Phoebe* yawed to slow her progress and at sunset, the crew were mustered for divine service once more. The next morning, with the gales continuing and rain falling in torrents, 'a very heavy sea struck the ship on the starboard beam and carried away the gangway stanchions, rails and hammock cloth', but by the morning of 6 April the storm had abated. Warmed by the southern sun, the carpenter and his five-man crew, repaired the hammock rails, while the armourer and his mate took their portable forge up on deck to repair the stanchions and at 6 p.m. the gun crews were exercised at the 18-pounders. All the while the *Phoebe* made a steady 7 to 8 knots cutting ever southwards and by sundown had covered over 180 miles in a single day.[33]

On 8 April Third Lieutenant Nathaniel Jago wrote his will. A reverend's son from Tavistock, Jago was a deeply religious young man, who had reached his current rank on 18 February 1812 after passing his lieutenant's exam. Witnessed by his messmates, First Lieutenant Ingram and Lieutenant Burrow of the Royal Marines, Jago's will bequeathed £100 to each of his elder sisters, Catherine and Anne and £50 to Mary, his youngest. His prize agents, Messrs John and Thomas March, were directed to divide any outstanding money equally between the three sisters. His clothes, watch, globes, sextant, charts, sword and fowling piece were promised to his father, along with a modest collection of books, with the exception of two volumes of David Hume's *Moral and Political Essays*, which were bequeathed to Lieutenant Burrow and a book on theology which was to be given to Captain Hillyar in the event of Jago's death.[34]

On 9 April the *Isaac Todd* raised a signal flag requesting to send a boat on board the *Phoebe*. Moments later, Mr Heatherly, the *Todd*'s first mate, was rowed across with a sullen-looking seaman named William Austen. The Todds had been making mutinous rumblings. Fearing outright rebellion had he punished Austen himself, Smith thought it wiser to request Hillyar to do so instead. The Englishman duly obliged. Tied to the grating at the frigate's waist, Austen was given twelve lashes.[35]

That evening the convoy fell in with the Trade Winds and was swept swiftly along to the southwest. The next day the marines exercised their small arms. Tying marks to the rigging, they loaded and fired their muskets throughout the afternoon. At daylight on the morning of 11 April, after divine service, six strange sail were sighted and that afternoon the cloud-capped, snow-covered peaks of the rugged, volcanic Island of Tenerife rose up ahead. Gazing at the 3,718-metre high Pico de Teide, known to the English as the Peak of Tenerife, Gardiner was inspired to historical musings. 'Had the island been as well known to the ancients as the neighbouring coast', he opined, 'Atlas no doubt would have long since been eased of his ponderous burden.' At 4 p.m., in brilliant sunshine and under azure-blue skies, the *Phoebe* swept round Point Nago and the port of Santa Cruz, infamous with the Royal Navy as the scene of Nelson's 1797 reverse, hove into view. Two forts crowned the headlands and the whitewashed towers of two large churches, San Francisco and Nuestra Señora de la Concepción, dominated the centre of town. Over fifty ships were in the roads. As well as the ten East Indiamen escorted by the frigate HMS *Doris* and the 22-gun HMS *Porcupine* that the Phoebes had sighted at Portsmouth, there were several Spanish merchantmen and a large convoy bound for Brazil. At 4.50 p.m. the topmen shortened sail, the *Phoebe* glided into the outer anchorage, one mile from the shore and came to at sunset with the main bower in fifty fathoms.[36]

Chapter 4

Into the Pacific: USS *Essex*, 26 January 1813 – 11 April 1813

By dawn on 26 January 1813 the *Essex* had left Saint Catherine's Island far behind her. 'The whole of the [day] ... we had fresh gales ... which I took advantage of to get a good offing', Captain Porter recalled. The next morning the wind turned to the east and a 'heavy head sea' pummelled the frigate's bow. The topmen were ordered to take in the sails and it wasn't until that afternoon that the royals could be unfurled and the ship began to make headway. Meanwhile, 'an alarming disease' had broken out and ten to fifteen of the crew were 'suddenly attacked by violent pains in the stomach'. Surgeon Miller, who had considerable first-hand experience, blamed the bad rum procured at Saint Catherine's. His patients' speedy recovery later disproved his diagnosis and Porter attributed the illness to the change from fresh to salt provisions.[1]

On the evening of the 28th, as the *Essex* took a wide-berth of the River Plate estuary, the weather worsened. 'At nine P.M. the wind began to haul around to the southward ... At midnight, after sharp lightening, [it] fixed itself at S. by E ... [and] the cold ... began to be sensibly felt.' Donning woollen coats, the watch speculated about whether their captain was intending to take them round the Horn. The next morning heavy showers burst overhead. Porter ordered the topmen to unbend the light sails and stow them below, while Gunner Miller and his mates, James Spafford and George Martin, lashed the carronades into place on the gun deck and stored the quarterdeck's three long 12-pounders below.[2]

An eclipse of the sun on 1 February set some of the seamen to superstitious mutterings. Two days later the sun broke clear, drenching the deck in sharp sunlight and a fresh breeze sprung up from the northwest. The watch lieutenant ordered all sail set and the *Essex* cut through the waves two hundred miles off the shore of northern Patagonia at 9 knots. 'Flatter[ing] ... [him]self with the expectation of a speedy and pleasant run', Porter took to his cabin in buoyant spirits to pen a note to the crew: 'Sailors and Marines, a large increase of the enemy's forces compels us to abandon a coast that will neither afford us security nor supplies ... We will therefore proceed to annoy them, where we are least expected. What was never performed we will attempt. The Pacific Ocean affords us many friendly ports. The unprotected British commerce, on the coast of Chili, Peru and Mexico, will give you an abundant supply of wealth: and the girls of the Sandwich Islands, shall reward you for your sufferings ... round Cape Horn.' Pinned to the grating at the waist, the note 'diffused a general joy' throughout the ship.[3]

For the next nine days a 'clear and cold' wind blew in from the southwest. 'Occasionally [it was] blowing so hard as to reduce us to our storm staysail', Porter recalled, '[and was] attended generally with a very disagreeable cross sea' which frequently broke over the deck. The topmen alternately set or reefed the top, mizzen and fore sails as the wind dictated while an able seaman sounded, registering from sixty to seventy-five fathoms with a bottom of fine grey sand. At one stage the sea burst in through the rudder coat, flooding the wardroom and the commissioned officers who messed there. Several whales spouted within a mile, sending up faint puffs of white, and huge rafts of kelp floated past, on which a few weary albatrosses had hitched a ride.[4]

At sunrise on 11 February, with the *Essex* somewhere between the Falkland Islands and the southern tip of South America, the wind died away. The air was frigid and the sea smooth. It was a beautiful, crisp Patagonian morning. While the rudder coat was repaired, Porter took to his cabin to determine his route round the Horn. After studying the accounts of Jean-François de La Pérouse, James Cook, George Anson and George Vancouver, he consulted the men on board who had previously made the voyage. Several ratings, including Tameoy, a native of Tahiti whose language skills would later prove invaluable, had served on South Sea whalers, but perhaps the most useful consultant was Sailing Master Cowell. In 1788, as an eleven-year-old volunteer, the father of two from Marblehead had sailed to the Pacific Northwest on a Bostonian merchantman, returning to the US three years later. By midday Porter had made his decision. 'Apprehensive of some difficulties in going through the Streights of Le Marie', he opted to take a longer yet less hazardous route 'to the eastward of Staten Land'. That afternoon the breeze picked up and a thick haze descended. The lieutenant of the watch ordered the men to set the studding-sails and the *Essex* clipped on at 9 knots, foam breaking around her bow.[5]

At dawn on 13 February, with the wind fresh and visibility reduced to a mile, flocks of 'cape pigeons' flew overhead, a clear sign land was nearby. 'I ... caused a good lookout to be kept', Porter recalled, 'took in [the] topgallant sails, double-reefed the topsails, [and] furled the mainsail.' Later that morning breakers were spotted through the fog three-quarters of a mile to the southeast. A dark mass of land reared up and soundings of forty-five fathoms on a rocky bottom were taken. Porter had miscalculated. Rather than being to the east of Staten Land, the

Essex was on a lee shore in the Straights of Marie and threatened with imminent destruction. Banking on riding the wind to safety, Porter ordered the topmen to set all sail and prepared to tack. It was an impetuous move. With such a heavy press of canvas, the forecastle was repeatedly pitched under the waves. All on deck had to hold on or risk being swept overboard. The jib was 'blown to pieces', but the rest of the sails held. Praising God, 'the excellent qualities of the ship' and the strength of New England white oak, the men rejoiced as the *Essex*'s bow swung round to open water. Accompanied by a spouting sperm whale, which the lookouts 'first took for a rock', the frigate was swept through the channel 'with great rapidity' and was soon clear of the straights.[6]

Afterwards Porter 'thought it ... prudent to keep aloof from the land'. On 14 February Cowell set a course for Diego Ramirez, a rocky island southwest of the Horn. At noon, the Cape was in sight. Aside from some storm clouds far to the north, the air was clear and the sun bright. The Horn bore due north and Diego Ramirez stood to the northwest. Thinking themselves over the worst, the men congratulated one another, but it proved premature. 'While we were indulging ourselves', Porter recalled, 'the black clouds, hanging over Cape Horn, burst upon us with a fury ... and reduced us in a few minutes to a reefed foresail and close-reefed main-topsail and in a few hours afterwards to our storm-staysails ... it produced an irregular and dangerous sea, that threatened to jerk away our masts at every roll of the ship.' Steering southwards in an attempt to outrun the weather, Porter only succeeded in burying the frigate in the eye of the storm. That night, the *Essex* pitched and rolled violently. An eclipse of the moon was taken as an omen of imminent doom. The waves swept the decks and forced their way past the battened hatches to drench the men shivering below.[7]

The storm blew for four days. With hard gales, 'heavy rain, cold, disagreeable weather and a dangerous sea', the *Essex* sailed ever further southwest. The sea broke over the deck, filled the fore-topmast sail and carried away the spritsail-yard and the bees of the bowsprit. On the 15th, a fresh, clear day with intermittent squalls, Feltus shot an albatross. It 'proved to be very fat' and measured '10ft across the wings'. Having had the bird roasted in the galley stove, the seventeen-year-old shared the meal with his messmates. With much of the bread, dried peas and beans having been devoured by worms and weevils, the men had taken to hunting the rats infesting the hold. Some even ate the monkeys acquired at Porto Praya.[8]

On 18 February, judging the ship to be sufficiently far to the westward to round the Horn, Porter looked to the heavens for a change in the wind. 'The movement of every passing cloud was anxiously watched ... and our chief employment was comparing the weather ... with the accounts of those who had preceded us.' That afternoon a fierce gale sprung up from the westward. Despite the danger, Porter ordered the men to set a close-reefed main-topsail alongside the fore, main and mizzen storm-staysails he had been using for several days. 'With this . . . we were enabled to force the ship about two knots, through a tremendous head sea', he recalled, but by noon on 19 February, the gale had increased to such a velocity that he was forced to revert to bare poles. At noon, accompanied by sharp falls of hail, the wind hauled round to the southwest. Her storm-staysails set and yards secured with preventer braces, the *Essex* ran northward at 6 knots. It was bitterly cold. There was constant rain and hail. A high wind caused the clouds to scud across the sky and the watch received frequent soakings. To confound their misery, Cook Haden was unable to light the galley stove and no hot meals were served for several days. Some began to suffer the first symptoms of frostbite – losing sensation in their fingers and toes – making even the simplest jobs impossible. The conditions also aggravated old wounds. Porter had been shot once in 1800 during his encounter with the Haitian pirates and twice during the Barbary War. The first had left a deep graze in his right thigh. The second had gone clean through his left.[9]

By 21 February Porter was confident he had rounded the Horn. Although the constant cloud cover meant that no lunar reckonings could be made and the chronometer had been affected by the cold, he anticipated his imminent arrival at a Chilean port by increasing the bread ration to a little over nine ounces a day. With their bellies fuller than they had been since leaving Saint Catherine's, the men began to look forward to the adventures they would have in the Pacific. Some dreamt of the islanders' lack of sexual taboos. Others began to count the prize money they would make. On the night of the 22nd a break in the cloud enabled the officers to make their first lunar reading in several days. The *Essex* was further to the east than Porter had believed, but favourable winds saw her make good headway and by the 24th the meridian longitude reading revealed they had made sufficient westing to turn north for warmer climes. The news, announced from the quarterdeck, had not come a moment too soon. Discipline was beginning to break down. Several thefts had occurred and the culprits been put in irons in the hold.[10]

On 28 February Porter ordered the long guns brought up to the quarterdeck. No sooner had this been achieved, however, than a huge sea rolled in and a gale reduced the frigate to storm staysails and a close-reefed main top. Sightings of birds and kelp led many to fear a lee shore. With the ship rolling violently, the pumps became blocked with ballast and the water in the hold rose. 'The sea . . . increased to such a height, as to threaten to swallow us at every instant', Porter recalled, '[and] the whole ocean was one continued foam of breakers.' Several men were thrown off their feet and down the hatchways. Able Seaman Robert Scatterley suffered a sprained ankle, Quarter Gunner Adam Roach 'contused [his] wrist and arm', Able Seaman John Lingham bruised his hand and Thomas

Charlton suffered a 'contused shoulder and foot'. After falling three times, Porter confined himself to his cabin where he watched his furniture washed from side to side.[11]

On 2 March, Lewis Price, a marine private who had been sick with consumption for several weeks, died. His body was left swinging in its hammock in the sickbay alongside Seaman Benjamin Hamilton, whose amorous exploits at Saint Catherine's had resulted in a dose of venereal disease. At 3 a.m. the gale reached its height. 'We shipped a sea that stove in the [gun] ports from the bow to the quarter', Farragut recalled. '[It] carried the weather quarter boat on to the wheel and took the lee boat off the davits, 'our spare spars [were] washed from the chains . . . [and] our head-rails washed away.' The wave flooded the cramped lower decks knocking several men out of their hammocks 'Many of the marines and . . . sailors [took to] . . . their knees at prayer' and prisoner Richard John, formerly the boatswain of HMP *Nocton*, leapt to his feet and yelled that 'the ship's broadside was stove in and that she was sinking'. The panic spread until Boatswain's Mate William Kingsbury, the 'trusty old' tar who had impersonated Neptune at the line, took control. 'Damn your eyes', he bellowed at John. 'Put your best foot forward, as there is one side left of her yet.'[12]

At 5 a.m. the storm abated. With sunrise, fresh winds set in from the southwest, carrying the *Essex* up the Chilean coast under a serene blue sky. Four hours later Porter mustered the crew. Those who had performed well were promoted to fill the vacancies occasioned by manning the prizes in the Atlantic. That evening rain began to fall, but the wind remained constant and by 5 March the sunshine had returned. The dead-lights were knocked out of the gun ports and fresh breezes expunged the stench that had gathered below decks. Sailmaker Navarro sewed up the tears in the courses; Carpenter Waters and his mate, John Langley, rebuilt the head-rails and repaired the boats; while Porter studied his map of the Pacific, searching for a suitable spot to resupply. Through his telescope, he could make out the waves breaking on the gloomy, black-rock shores of the Chilean coast, twenty miles away. Beyond were green, forested hills, cut by babbling brooks framed by the snow-capped Andes. Ringed by soft cloud, their peaks glimmered in the afternoon haze. Albatrosses, said to be possessed by the restless spirits of bankrupt pursers seeking a ship to make good their debts, wheeled in the air and several sunfish, strange and ungainly giants from the depths, basked alongside the ship amongst slicks of a gelatinous white substance which Porter was at a loss to explain.[13]

On 6 March the island of Mocha was sighted on the starboard bow. A mountainous, verdant height, twenty miles in circumference, Mocha's slopes were blanketed with tall pine. Numerous streams cascaded westward onto black sand beaches. Originally colonised by ocean-going Polynesians, the Spanish had arrived in 1544, but had declined to occupy the island. Over the next 150 years it had hosted a string of Dutch, French and English traders, pirates and privateers, the most famous of whom was Francis Drake. Ambushed by Lafkenche Indians, a coastal tribe of the Mapuche, Drake had been struck by three arrows. Two of his men had been captured and two others had died of their wounds on the *Golden Hind*. In 1685 the Spanish Governor in Santiago, José de Garro, had had the island forcibly depopulated. It remained undisturbed until the latter part of the eighteenth century when British, American and French whalers and sealers began to take advantage of abundant wood, water, fruit, fowl and game. A contemporary visitor was Mocha Dick, an albino male sperm whale. Notorious for his aggression, Dick was said to have survived one hundred skirmishes with whaling boats, many would blame him for the 1820 sinking of the whale-ship *Essex* and it seems likely that he inspired Melville's *Moby Dick*.[14]

Skirting the breakers on the sandy southeast point, Cowell steered round the barren east coast, took a wide berth round the rocks to the north and at 1 p.m. sailed inside a large coral reef that stretched round a bay on the western side of the island. The forecastle-men dropped the larboard anchor in eleven fathoms on a bottom of fine sand. Porter was rowed ashore through a crowd of seals. 'The sea was beating furiously against the beach and rocks', he recalled, 'and it was some time before we could ... [land] in a small cove ... [w]here we found the water perfectly smooth.' Having spotted several hogs and horses running wild, the men hauled the boats up the beach, while the officers set off in pursuit. The day passed pleasantly. The men enjoyed a 'good run on shore' and by dusk the officers 'had killed ... ten hogs, with some young pigs, which the seamen had run down'.[15]

As the Americans were about to embark, another herd of horses was spotted. Positioning his men behind the boats, Porter waited until his quarry approached before firing. 'One horse was crippled', he recalled, 'and ... [three or four] seamen [and Quarter-Gunner James Spafford] ran forward with clubs to knock him down.' Just then a late arrival, the short-sighted acting Fifth Lieutenant, Stephen Decatur McKnight, opened fire. The ball passed through the horse's neck and struck Spafford. 'Sir you have shot me!' he cried. 'I am a dying man!' Coughing blood, Spafford was rowed back to the *Essex* and examined by Surgeon Miller. The ball had entered the right side of his chest and perforated his lungs, exiting below his right shoulder alongside the backbone. Miller's prognosis was not good. 'All were struck with consternation [at the news]', Farragut recalled. 'McKnight was nearly crazed and embraced Spafford, imploring his forgiveness.' Meanwhile, the rest of the crew butchered the animals brought on board. The hogs were tough. The horse was 'much fatter and more tender'.[16]

The next morning the cutter took First Lieutenant Downes ashore. Porter had given him two hours to hunt, but at 7 a.m. the skies 'took on a menacing aspect' and a fresh wind caused the frigate to drag her anchor. Porter ordered the cornet raised and fired three signal guns to attract Downes' attention. In the process of butchering a wild horse, the lieutenant and his men left three-quarters of the carcass on shore in their haste to get back to the ship and at 9.30 a.m. the *Essex* swept northwards out of the bay. That afternoon Feltus admired the view of the Chilean mainland. '[It is] a beautiful prospect', he noted. 'One part of the coast is level to the waters edge & coverd with herbage & another part is perpendicular . . . as if it had been broken off from some other land by an earthquake . . . the rocks and hills are covered . . . with herbage [and] behind all stand the . . . Andes reaching their lofty tops above the clouds.' By 5 p.m. Cowell had brought the ship to within three leagues of the Island of Santa Maria where Porter hoped to stop for supplies, but hazy weather and insufficient knowledge of the shore made the approach dangerous. With a gale picking up, Porter stood off to the north in the failing light.[17]

On 8 March the Essexes found themselves to the north of Concepción. A northerly wind brought a heavy fog which was burnt off by the afternoon sun. Equidistant between Concepción and Valparaiso, Porter believed himself in a good position to cruise for British whalers and rode the currents for the next three days. The fog returned the next day. With visibility at three miles, the Americans' chances of success were reduced, but the lack of wind meant that Porter had little choice but to remain. The crew grew increasingly frustrated. 'We have not had a fair view of the coast since the 8th, Feltus noted '[and] . . . have not seen any thing like a sail since we doubled Cape Horn.' Porter was equally disheartened. 'Nothing could have exceeded our impatience', he recalled.[18]

The Essexes' lack of success was down to bad luck. In the thirty-seven years since its genesis in 1788, when the *Emilia*, a London-based whaler owned by the city's principal whaling firm, Samuel Enderby and Sons, had rounded Cape Horn, the British South Seas whaling trade had grown into an industry that deployed over sixty 300-ton vessels to the Pacific each year. Their principal quarry, the *physeter microcephalus* (sperm whale or cachalot), was hunted for the high-grade liquid wax stored in a 2,000-litre cavity in its head. Prized for its bright, smokeless flame, which made it ideal for interior lighting, spermaceti oil was so lucrative that revenues for the South Seas trade soon overtook those from Britain's traditional whaling grounds off Greenland and by the 1790s the industry was being nurtured by governmental decree. Whalers, along with fishermen, colliers, crews of ships contracted by the Victualing Board and the mates and masters of merchant ships, were given exemption from the press and in 1793 Prime Minister William Pitt ordered Captain James Colnett to find a suitable whaling base among the uninhabited islands of the South Pacific in order to liberate the trade from its reliance on the jealously-guarded Spanish-American ports.

Although Colnett's mission, undertaken in HMS *Rattler*, was of limited value, Pitt's interest remained. Realising that the United States held the advantage due to the unparalleled experience of the whalers of Nantucket, he offered financial incentives to any willing to emigrate to the British Isles. The policy was immediately successful. The islanders considered themselves a breed apart from their mainland compatriots and London, whose streets boasted more oil lamps than any other city in the world, was by far their biggest market. During the American War of Independence the principal players in Nantucket had even sought an independent peace to ensure that their livelihood could continue and the heavy import tax placed on American whale oil by the British government convinced many that Pitt's offer was too good to refuse. Principal amongst those who accepted was a hard-headed Quaker named Benjamin Rotch. Bringing several whaling masters, harpooners, boat steerers and fully-equipped whaling vessels with him, Rotch was instrumental in setting up a colony of 'British' Nantucketers in Milford Haven in Wales.

In 1795, with growing competition from France and Nantucketers operating out of New Bedford, Massachusetts, Pitt pushed an act through the House of Commons establishing a system of cash incentives to boost the British industry. A £600 bonus was offered to the captain who returned with the most oil each year, and £500 was awarded to the seven next most successful. As a result, the industry went from strength to strength. British hands were taken on by Nantucket captains to meet the demand and a consortium set up a base to rival Milford Haven in the British capital. With annual returns of up to 44 per cent, merchants, governors of the Bank of England and even sitting MPs began investing. By 1813 such was the trade's ubiquity that a dozen British whalers were constantly plying the grounds of the Chilean coast. Had the *Essex* arrived off Mocha five days earlier, she would have intercepted at least one of them. The *Comet*, a ship based in Hull, had spent the whole of February off the island catching blackfish and a solitary sperm whale. Her captain, Able Scurr, had spoken three American whalers in the vicinity, the *George*, the *John & James* and the *Gardener* and one British vessel, the *Lima*, before sailing to Concepción on 4 March to resupply. Reaching the port two days later, Scurr found seven more Americans and another English whaler, the 355-ton *Atlantic*.[19]

On 12 March a light wind sprung up from the southwest and the fog lifted. 'Every eye was [immediately] ... searching for a sail', Porter recalled, but nothing was seen but 'a wide expanse of ocean' and the 'barren ... coast of Chile'. With the wind picking up, the topmen set the steering and skysails. That afternoon Porter spotted a fire burning in a cove, lit by Indians or smugglers and at sunset, as the frigate passed a wide river estuary, the crew shortened sail and hauled off from the land. The next morning the *Essex* cruised northwards and that evening hove to off the Point of Quaranilla, a commonly-used landmark marking the route to Valparaiso, the busiest port on the Chilean coast. On the 14th, with a flotilla of local fishing boats scattering on his approach, Porter rounded a rocky headland known as the Point of Angels. Scanning the bay through his telescope, he saw 'a long sandy beach on the opposite side' of the bay. Then 'a large drove of loaded mules coming down the side of the mountain by a zigzag pathway' appeared, 'and in an instant afterwards the whole town [of Valparaiso], shipping with their colours flying and the forts, burst' into view.[20]

Founded in 1536 by the conquistador Juan de Saavedra, Valparaiso was built on land inhabited by the Changos, nomads who fished the bay from precarious seal-hide rafts. Despite several earthquakes and tsunamis and the depredations of Elizabethan seadogs such as Francis Drake and Richard Hawkins, by the early nineteenth century Valparaiso had grown into southern South America's principal Pacific port. Three thousand residents inhabited two neighbourhoods. El Alemendral, a large triangular plain to the east covered with the wooden shacks of the poor, was connected to the port by the principal avenue, a winding road squeezed between the beach and a line of hills rising sharply inland. The San Francisco and San Augustin ravines accommodated two irregular plazas, administrative buildings and the mud-brick houses of the wealthier residents. Down by the beach was the custom house. Beyond were the roads. Protected from the prevailing southerly winds by rocky headlands, the anchorage sheltered ocean-going Spanish merchantmen, coastal traders, foreign whalers and men-of-war.[21]

When the *Essex* arrived, there were seven ships at anchor. Five were Spanish merchantmen. With their topmen spread along the yards, they appeared to be bending their sails in preparation to put to sea. Porter presumed their destination was Callao, the port of the Peruvian capital of Lima, where cargoes of corn, tallow and hides produced in the fertile Chilean interior fetched good prices. Closer in shore was the *Colt*, a deeply-laden, 18-gun American brig. Her captain, Mr Musnon, was fifty miles inland at the capital of Santiago and had no intention of leaving port soon. Alongside was a 'large and clumsy-looking' brig flying British colours. With her bluff-bowed profile, Porter presumed she was a whaler, one of the few ocean-going ships not built for speed. As her sails were unbent and her crew were tarring the rigging, she appeared to have recently doubled the Horn.[22]

Having surveyed the scene, Porter decided to stand out of the bay and sail north. Once out of sight he could await the British whaler while also allowing time for the Spanish ships to put to sea, thus preventing them carrying news of his arrival to the north. Mustering the crew, he announced his decision 'in his usual animated and enthusiastic style'. According to Farragut, the men took the news in good humour and within four hours the *Essex* had left the port behind her. The next morning, however, Porter changed his mind. Concerned that either his rations or his men's patience would not last, at 7 a.m. he ordered the crew to tack. Swinging the *Essex*'s bow to the south, he spent the best part of the day beating up against the prevailing winds.[23]

At daylight, while the *Essex* was being kedged into Valparaiso Bay, Lieutenant Downes was sent ashore to ask permission to purchase supplies. Porter was worried about the reception he would receive: Spain was allied to Britain, recent US encroachments into Florida had created tension between the two nations and Madrid was notorious for jealously guarding her American possessions. Accordingly, Downes had been supplied with a fabricated story about losing a store-ship rounding the Horn. Such 'artifice' was not required. The lieutenant returned within half an hour on the governor's barge bearing 'an offer of every civility, assistance and accommodation that Valparaiso could afford'. To Porter's 'astonishment ... [he] was informed that [the Chileans] had shaken off their allegiance to Spain; ... the ports ... were open to all nations', the new government, the Junta of 1813, 'looked up to the United States ... for example and ... that ... [the *Essex*'s] arrival would be considered the most joyful event, as their commerce had been much harassed by corsairs ... sent out by the [loyalist] viceroy of [Peru]'.[24]

It is somewhat surprising that Porter was so taken aback by the news. South America had been in political turmoil for five years ever since Napoleon's occupation of Spain. On learning of Ferdinand VII's enforced abdication and the subsequent Spanish fight-back led by the Cortes, a temporary Junta of dubious legality set in Cadiz, the continent's creole elite had divided into factions. Some declared their loyalty to the Cortes. Others advocated establishing their own government while remaining loyal to the exiled King. A third group envisioned a break with the Cortes as the first step along the path to true independence. By 1813 Venezuela, New Granada (Colombia) and the River Plate were in a state of civil war. Peru, dominated by its powerful viceroy, José Fernando de Abascal y Sousa, remained loyal to Spain, while Chile was in a state of flux.[25]

Three years before the *Essex*'s arrival, the leading administrative, clerical and military figures in Santiago had established a political council known as the Congress. Initially conservative, this body rejected the authority of the Cortes while professing its loyalty to King Ferdinand. As the French occupation of Spain entered its third year, however, more radical elements began to emerge. In January 1811 the country's ports were thrown open to international trade; in April, following an attempted counter-coup by a conservative colonel, the *Audiencia* – a colonial court representing the establishment – was abolished; and in September, José Miguel Carrera, a 25-year-old creole soldier who had recently returned from fighting in Spain, dissolved Congress and set himself up as a military dictator. With the aid of his brothers Juan José and Luis, Carrera had ruled the country ever since. Although vaguely committed to a revolutionary programme, a stance which brought him into conflict with Viceroy Abascal, Carrera made no formal declaration of independence. Bereft of any particular political ideals beyond a deeply-rooted antipathy towards England and an admiration for the anti-colonial stance of the United States, Carrera's chief concern was holding onto power.[26]

At 10.00 a.m. on 15 March Fort San Antonio, an old stone castle hewn directly from the rock, welcomed the *Essex* with a 21-gun salute. Having returned the compliment, Porter was rowed ashore with Lieutenant Gamble and Purser Shaw. Landing by the town's cavernous custom house, they made their way along the cobbled streets crowded with sailors, fishermen and Indian and *mestizo* peasants dressed in ponchos and straw hats. The governor's palace was a 'shabby-looking' two-storey building. Built on the main square in the grounds of an old fort, it lay deep in the morning shadow of the steep-sided hills behind it. Inside, Porter found the town's principal citizens had gathered to receive him. It was a friendly reception, marked by toasts to republicanism, liberty and revolution. Porter thought the Captain of the Port of Valparaiso, Juan José Tortel Maschet, a Frenchman who had arrived in the New World eleven years before, 'a sterling, honest patriot'. He 'spoke his sentiments boldly', Porter recalled, 'and . . . was resolved to do the utmost to emancipate his [adopted] country'. Francisco de la Lastra de la Sotta, the 34-year-old governor of Valparaiso, was more cautious. Having learnt that a loyalist task force, dispatched from Peru under Brigadier Antonio Pareja, had arrived at the island of Chiloe, he was determined to steer a middle course.[27]

After dispatching a courier to Santiago to alert Joel Roberts Poinsett, the American trade-consul in Santiago, of his arrival, Porter set about securing wood, water and provisions. Beyond the coastal mountain range, Chile's fertile central plain produced an abundance of apples, pears, peaches, melons, strawberries, onions, beans and potatoes. All were available at the daily market in Valparaiso along with coal, jerked beef, flour and live pigs. Poultry was priced at $2½ per dozen and a fine, white bread was flavoured with lard and anise. Fresh pork, beef and chicken were sourced from open-air butchers' stalls set up in a plaza adjacent to the main square. Watering facilities, on the other hand, were inferior. 'The only place whence we could procure it', Porter complained, 'was a small well near the landing-place by the custom house . . . As it afforded a supply of from one thousand to fifteen hundred gallons per day, I concluded to fix the period of our departure on the 22d [March], allowing one week to get all our supplies.'[28]

That afternoon the Americans were informed that Governor Lastra intended to visit the *Essex*. Porter 'went on board to receive him and on his arrival, with a numerous suite of officers, saluted him with eleven guns'. Lastra insisted on a guided tour. 'The visit lasted about two hours', Porter recalled, 'and although [the

Essex] appeared under great disadvantage, from having been so long at sea . . . they were much pleased and astonished that *Anglo-Americans*, as they styled us, could build, equip and manage ships of so large a size.' Among the topics of conversation was the threat posed to Chilean commerce by Peruvian privateers operating out of Callao. Porter learnt that Abascal's letters of marque had been poaching neutral shipping and several American and British ships had been detained. Particularly active were the *Nereyda*, a privateer of fifteen guns which had been lurking off the Chilean coast since July 1812 disguised as a whaler; the *Santa Teresa*, an armed brig captained by Juan Villa; and the *Vulture*, a privateer commanded by Captain Don Domingo Amezaga. The Americans were also informed of the latest international news: the *Essex*'s presence off the coast of the Brazils had been reported and Porter was delighted to learn of the capture of HMS *Java* by Bainbridge's USS *Constitution*. 'It was also stated that the *Wasp*, an American sloop of war, had captured a British sloop of war after a hard-fought action . . . and that the *Constitution* was repairing her damages at St. Salvador, where the British admiral (Dixon) had proceeded with a determination of destroying her.' On leaving, Governor Lastra invited the American officers to a ball at his residence the following evening.[29]

March 16th passed uneventfully. The watering party filled the ship's casks and wooding parties cut timber on the shoreline. The carpenter's and sailmaker's crews made minor repairs and the officers, given an eight o'clock curfew, took it in turns to explore town. Valparaiso was full of grogshops, known as *pulperias*, and whorehouses. No doubt some of the produce of the former and the employees of the latter were snuck on board during the *Essex*'s stay. The men purchased food from the bumboats and dozens of China fowl and over 100 pigs were brought on board. Farragut named one Murphy and adopted it as his pet.[30]

At sundown, Porter and several other officers were rowed ashore to attend the governor's party. The town's richer residents were engaged in an early evening promenade. Tinkers and chandlers hawking bundles of greasy, tallow candles moved amongst them, crossing themselves as the town's six churches called the people to evening prayer. Inside Lastra's apartments over 400 guests had gathered. Despite 'disfigur[ing] . . . themselves' with excessive make-up, Porter thought the local women showed 'considerable taste . . . in their dress'. Many were 'very handsome . . . their complexion[s were] remarkably fine and their manners modest and attractive'. After a blur of introductions in broken English, Spanish and French, a band struck up a minuet. Taking to the dance-floor, the Americans acquitted themselves admirably at first, but struggled with a series of country dances. 'The *ballas de tierra*, as they are called . . . consisted of the most graceless . . . fatiguing movements of the body and limbs', Porter opined, 'accompanied by . . . indelicate and lascivious motions, gradually increasing in energy and violence, until the fair one, apparently overcome with passion ... was compelled to retire to her seat.'[31]

On 17 March Captain Munson of the *Colt* returned from Santiago with a letter for Porter from 'the president and junta ... They considered our arrival as the most happy event', Porter recalled. 'The bells [in Santiago] had been rung the whole day ... and ... it was generally believed that I had brought from my country nothing less than [formal] proposals for a friendly alliance with Chili.' Porter chose to encourage his hosts in their misapprehension. When the local customs officer, whom Porter suspected of being 'of monarchical principles', insisted on charging an export duty on the provisions he had purchased, Porter wrote a letter to Poinsett in Santiago, protesting the imposition and inviting the Carreras to visit the *Essex*. By the morning of 18 March all charges had been waived. That afternoon several sacks of flour, bread and fruit were rowed out to the roads and stowed in the *Essex*'s hold. The following day pork, live hogs, flour and wood were loaded. The 20th saw sacks of beans, coal and bread brought out and by that afternoon the ship was ready for sea. 'As the next day was Sunday', Porter 'determined to devote it to pleasure and invited the ladies and gentlemen of Valparaiso to spend the afternoon on board the ship.' At 3 p.m. Poinsett arrived from Santiago accompanied by Luis Carrera, the president's brother and commander-in-chief of the Chilean artillery. Received with a salute of eleven guns, they joined Porter and Mr Munson of the *Colt* in the *Essex*'s great cabin for dinner.[32]

Porter spent the morning of Sunday 21 March readying the *Essex* for his guests. Bunting and flags were set up, food and drink prepared in the galley, an awning stretched from the rigging to provide shade and the barge, cutter, yawl and longboat were rowed ashore to the landing place. At 4 p.m. just as the first guests climbed on board, a large sail was sighted. Joined by Poinsett and Luis Carrera, both of whom were desperate not to miss out on anything, Porter cleared for action. The partitions were removed, the hammocks brought up to line the bulwarks and the awning and flags cut down. One of the anchor cables was chopped through. The other was allowed to slip to the seabed, its position marked by a buoy and by 5 p.m. the *Essex* was under weigh 'under a cloud of canvas'. From the quarterdeck Porter thought the stranger had the appearance of a frigate pierced for thirty-two guns. Luis Carrera begged to be allowed to board the 'enemy', while 'the hills [around the bay were] crowded with men, women and children, all equally ... anxious ... to see the fight'. With the breeze failing, Porter ordered the boats to tow the frigate and within an hour was alongside the stranger. She proved to be the *Fama*, a large Portuguese merchantman mounting twenty-two guns, sixty-seven days out from Rio. Although her captain, Desidiero Manuel de la Costa, had been chartered to sail to Valparaiso by the British consul, Lord Viscount Strangford, to collect a cargo of flour to feed Wellington's troops in the Peninsula, the *Fama* was neutral under international law. Carrera was crestfallen. With sunset rapidly approaching, Porter decided to stand off and on in the bay for the night.[33]

The next morning the *Essex* worked her way back into the anchorage. The *Fama* came in half an hour later while a thoroughly seasick Carrera was rowed ashore. Later, an invitation arrived to dine at Governor Lastra's and at 1 p.m. a 'great number' of the *Essex*'s officers went on shore to attend. Flags flew around the batteries in the fort and an 'extensive', marquee had been erected in the courtyard. Besides the Americans, several local military commanders, Captain De la Costa and the officers of the *Fama* and a number of English merchants who had taken advantage of Congress' open port ruling to set up business in town, enjoyed a twenty-course banquet served on silver plate. Unused to the local etiquette, Porter committed several *faux pas*. Having stuffed himself with a rather cloying entrée, he struggled with the dishes that followed and was unable to hide his disgust at a peculiarly Chilean habit of sharing bowls and cutlery, a custom which seems to have left all contemporary foreign visitors aghast. After dinner Lastra took Porter on a tour of the fortifications. Dancing followed and several Chilean officers, deep in their cups, proposed toasts to the newfound independence of their motherland. Embarrassed by the slight to Spain, the English merchants retired. That night one wrote to colleagues in Buenos Ayres alerting them of the presence of a US frigate in the Pacific. For the Americans, on the other hand, the evening proceeded with 'much hilarity' and Porter did not retire until 1 a.m.[34]

Discipline had suffered in his absence. Despite the eight o'clock curfew imposed on petty and warrant officers, Carpenter Waters had spent the night on shore. 'As he was a worthless fellow', Porter 'did not permit him to return on board ... again.' Gunner Miller was also in trouble. Caught smuggling rum on board and guilty of 'conducting himself improperly in other regards', he was demoted to ordinary seaman and confined in the hold. On 23 March, the Essexes prepared to put to sea. All the prisoners taken from HMP *Nocton*, with the exception of one who had tried to escape the night before, were released on parole and put ashore along with Mr. Nelson, a Dane taken on board from the *Elizabeth* and permitted to remain as a passenger on the *Essex* thus far. Carpenter's Mate John Langley was promoted to replace his master, Quarter-Gunner James Spafford lingered on in the sick berth and Porter penned a letter updating Commodore Bainbridge on the *Essex*'s adventures so far.[35]

At midday an American whaler, the *George*, dropped anchor in the roads. Porter had her captain, Benjamin Worth, a 44-year-old from Nantucket, rowed on board the *Essex*.

[He] informed me that a few days before he had spoken with two English armed whalers, one off the island of Mocha, the other off the harbour of Conception; that three other American whalers were in company; and that the English ships were the first that gave them intelligence of the war ... They had no orders to capture American vessels, but were in daily expectation of authority to that effect.

Despite flying under the flags of warring nations, the Nantucketers had chosen to help one another. They were islanders first. Whether or not they sailed in US or British bottoms came a distant second. Worth had also heard that several English whalers were cruising the Galapagos Islands and the coast of Peru. The news was all the incentive Porter needed. He gave the order to weigh and at 1 p.m., 'with a fresh breeze from the southward', the *Essex* stood out of the bay. By nightfall, as a thick fog descended, Valparaiso had disappeared from view.[36]

At dawn on 25 March a sail was spotted on the weather bow. The *Essex* gave chase and by 7 a.m. the stranger was boarded. 'She proved to be the American whale-ship *Charles*.' Having left New England thirteen months before, her captain, Grafton Gardner, one of a long line of whalers operating out of Nantucket since the seventeenth century, had rounded Cape Horn only to be captured by a Peruvian privateer and sent into Callao for adjudication. Deemed an unlawful prize by Don Joshua Pasqual de Vivero, the Captain of the Marine Department, the *Charles* had been allowed to continue after paying legal costs and in March 1813, learning of the American declaration of war against Britain, had joined up with two other American whalers – the *Barclay*, a vessel one and half years out of Bedford, Massachusetts with an almost entirely black crew and the *Walker* commanded by captain Stephen West, yet another Nantucketer. The ships had made several kills and were on the point of returning to the United States when they had been chased on 23 March 1813 off Coquimbo. Their assailants were the *Nimrod*, a heavily-armed British whaler captured from the French in 1803 whose captain, William Perry, carried a letter of marque and the *Nereyda*, a 15-gun Peruvian privateer, which had been granted a five-month license by Viceroy Abascal to capture vessels engaged in contraband on the Chilean coast. The *Charles* had escaped by piling on all sail. Gardener's compatriots had not been so fortunate.[37]

Knowing the privateers had a significant head start, Porter acted swiftly. At 8 a.m., after taking the *Charles'* Second Mate on board as a pilot, he ordered Gardner to follow his lead and made all sail in pursuit. Thirty minutes later a stranger was spotted. By noon Porter could make out that the chase was a ship-of-war mounting whaleboats on her quarters by means of disguise. At 1 p.m. he fired a gun to attract her attention and hoisted British colours. The *Charles* followed suit and the stranger hoisted Spanish colours in reply, tacked and fired a gun to leeward. One hour later she fired a gun across the *Essex*'s bows. Angered by the stranger's presumption, Porter toyed with the idea of firing a broadside into his hull, 'but ... contented ... [him]self with firing [six] shot over him to bring him down'. Suitably chastened, the stranger hove to and sent a lieutenant on board the *Essex*. She proved to be the *Nereyda*, which had captured the *Barclay* and *Walker* but had since lost the latter to the *Nimrod*. Maintaining the pretence that the *Essex* was a British ship-of-war, Porter ordered the lieutenant to bring some of the prisoners he had taken from the *Barclay* and *Walker* on board. Captain West and the *Barclay*'s First Mate, Isaac Bly, arrived soon after. Assured they were on board an American frigate, they informed Porter that the Spaniards had stripped their ships of cordage, boats and provisions, robbed the men and even taken the officers' clothes.[38]

With the *Nereyda* close under the *Essex*'s carronades, Porter hoisted American colours and ordered the Spaniards to strike. The Nereydas were confined on board the *Essex* while Acting Fifth Lieutenant McKnight took possession. The next morning Porter brought the other American prisoners on board and had the privateer's cannon, ammunition and small arms thrown into the sea. 'Leaving her only her topsails and courses ... I ... sent back all the Spaniards [on board her] and directed [them] ... to proceed to Lima.' Porter also presumed to address a haughty letter to Viceroy Abascal: 'Your Excellency ... [having been] informed by [the] ... officers [of the *Nereyda*] that they were cruising, as the allies of Great Britain, to capture and send in for adjudication all American vessels they should meet ... I have ... determined to prevent in future such vexatious and piratical conduct ... and have sent her to Lima in order that her commander may meet with such punishment ... as his offence may deserve.'[39]

At noon, as the *Nereyda* limped away to the north, the *Essex* and *Charles* ran up to Coquimbo. At 6 p.m., off a line of rocks called the Chinques, Porter hove to and sent Lieutenant Downes, Captain West and four men to perform a night-time reconnaissance of the bay in one of the *Charles'* whaleboats. Finding no sign of the *Nimrod, Barclay* or *Walker* and with the shore battery alarmed and firing cannon into the night, Downes returned at midnight and the *Essex* and *Charles* stood out to sea. On the morning of March 27 Porter sailed north in search of the *Nimrod*. Before parting company, captains West and Gardner provided a list of twenty-three American and ten British whalers in the South Pacific. 'They both agreed that the Gallipagos was the most likely place to find them' and assured Porter that there were at least ten more British vessels in the area that they couldn't name. 'All [were] fine ships of not less than four hundred tons ... [and] their cargoes would be worth two hundred thousand dollars each.' Porter offered the former American prisoners a choice. They could go with West and Gardner into Coquimbo on the

Charles or join the *Essex*. Nine, including Isaac Bly, took up the challenge. At noon the two ships set sail on opposite tacks and by 2 p.m. had lost sight of each other.[40]

With pleasant weather and fair winds, over the next week the *Essex* travelled over 700 miles. North of Coquimbo, the coastline became more arid as the scrub, scattered trees and thorn bushes of central Chile gave way to the Atacama Desert of southern Peru. Porter filled the time with routine repairs. At 9 a.m. on 28 March the main sail was brought down, the rigging reset and the ship disguised as a Spanish merchantman. A 'broad yellow streak' was painted round the hull 'as far as the fore channels, false waist cloths' while painted ports were rigged round the quarterdeck nettings and a fake poop was constructed. On 1 April the *Essex* crossed the Tropic of Capricorn amidst shoals of flying fish. The next day the guns were scoured and at 6 a.m. on the 3rd the island of San Gallan, a rocky outcrop home to a raucous sea lion colony and numerous Humboldt penguins 150 miles south of the Peruvian capital, was spotted on the starboard bow. Sailing Master Cowell set a course to the northwest 'with a view of crossing the track of vessels bound to Callao' and later that morning Feltus observed that the water had a strange red tint to it. The colouration was caused by thousands of tiny crayfish, 'from one inch in length to one tenth that size'. Porter ordered a bucket pitched over the side and put 'two of them ... in a bottle of sea–water ... On some crumbs of bread being thrown in, they seized and devoured them very ravenously', he recalled.[41]

At 9 a.m. on 4 April, as the *Essex* stood in towards a series of high bluffs, the lookouts spotted a strange sail to leeward. Porter gave chase and over the next two hours two more ships were sighted to windward. Concentrating on the vessel closest to Callao, by midday Porter was convinced he was pursuing the *Barclay*. With the light sails wet to increase the wind they could hold and the boats' crews readied to make a dash, the *Essex* inched closer. At 1 p.m., as the chase came under the lee of barren dunes of the Island of San Lorenzo, which marked the outer limits of the bay of Callao, she was becalmed. Two and half miles to the south, with all sail crammed on, the *Essex* swept into the bay, coming to a halt as the breeze died just 100 yards shy of her quarry. Porter lowered the boats and within minutes they had overpowered the Spanish prize crew and were towing the *Barclay* back out of the bay. Porter noted there were 'a great number of' Spaniards and a single armed British vessel which did not match the *Nimrod*'s description under the guns of an imposing stone fort and two half-moon redoubts which covered the inner roads. Beyond, the church towers of Lima, some three leagues distant, could be made out. At 3 p.m. the second strange sail which the Essexes had spotted ran into Callao. Feltus recognised her as one of the Spanish merchant brigs they had seen at Valparaiso. Within an hour, working hard against the in-draught, the boats had towed the *Barclay* under the *Essex*'s carronades and her captain, Gideon Randall, was ushered on board.[42]

A 'violent tempered' 51-year-old father of five from Hanover, Massachusetts, Randall had been captain of the *Barclay* since 1801. As his former crewmembers, now with the *Essex*, refused to return and the only Americans left on board were sick with scurvy, Randall had little choice but to remain under Porter's protection. 'He ... offered his services ... in any way he could prove useful', the Bostonian recalled, 'giving me assurances that he could take me where the British whale-vessels most frequented, advising me ... to proceed to the islands of Gallipagos ... and on my way looking into Payta', a Peruvian port 500 miles to the north. At 7 p.m., as the mortally-wounded Quarter-Gunner Spafford finally expired, John S. Cowan, a 21-year-old from Baltimore who had been made midshipman in December 1810, took command of the *Barclay* with the aid of Captain Randall and six men and the *Essex* set sail west-northwest. A blue light burning at the frigate's mizzen peak guided the*Barclay* out of the bay.[43]

On 5 April, after an inquiry had cleared Lieutenant McKnight of blame for his death, Spafford's body was committed to the deep. 'He had distinguished himself by his moral and correct conduct', Porter noted by way of an epitaph, 'and I had intended promoting him ... so soon as circumstances would admit.' At 2 p.m. the man at the masthead decried a sail. The *Essex* stood towards it, but it was discovered to be the Rock of Pelado, a barren islet 100 miles to the north of Callao stained white with the guano of the cormorants, blue-footed boobies and pelicans that nested there. Two hours later another sail was spotted. The *Essex* gave chase and at sundown brought the stranger too by firing across her bows. She proved to be a Spanish brig from Callao carrying salt.

> Supposing the *Essex* to be ... [British, the captain] informed me that an English frigate had been for some time expected at Callao from Cadiz, for the purpose of taking in money ... that an English armed ship had put in there a few days since ... [and] that two English whale-ships had sailed from thence ... [in the last few days] ... they [also] informed me that ... [British] vessels [were] treated with great civility, in consequence of being the allies of Spain; but that ... [those of the United States] were held in very little estimation ... that the Americans were notorious ... *contrabandistas* ... and neither received nor expected much civility.[44]

With the *Essex* and *Barclay* coming together at nightfall and parting to signalling distance at daylight to maximise their sweep, over the next few days Porter worked his way up the coast. Two sperm whales were spotted on the morning of

9 April and that afternoon one of the Essexes harpooned a four-foot fur seal as they passed the islands of Lobos de Afuera and Lobos de Tierra off the Peruvian coast. The next day, off Punta Aguja, shoals of fish were forced to the surface by the meeting of the cold waters of the Humboldt Current from the south and the tropical Equatorial Current from the north. The boiling bait-ball was attacked by tuna, seal, dolphin and whales from below while seabirds dived in from above.[45]

On the 11th the *Essex* and *Barclay* stood into Payta Bay. As the men admired the Saddle of Payta, 'a remarkably irregular mountain' which rose out of the otherwise featureless desert, two sails emerged out of the morning haze. Both were six-man catamarans constructed from eight 30-foot logs lashed together with a single mast and a large cotton lug sail. Shocked that they would venture so far from shore, Porter hove to. 'I learnt, to my astonishment, that they were from Guayaquil [a port 300 miles to the north], with cargoes of cocoa, bound ... to leeward of Lima and had already been out thirty days. They were destitute of water and had no other provisions ... than a few rotten plantains ... and [a number of] pieces of fish.' Learning that there were no ships at anchor in Payta, Porter decided to waste no more time on the coast of South America. Steering west-northwest, the *Essex* headed for the Galapagos Islands instead.[46]

Chapter 5

From Tenerife to Rio: HMS *Phoebe*, 12 April 1813 – 9 July 1813

On 12 April 1813 HMS *Phoebe* fired a nineteen-gun salute in honour of the three forts at Santa Cruz, Tenerife. The Spanish guns, which sixteen years earlier had repulsed Nelson's landing with a storm of roundshot and grape, returned the courtesy while the bulk of Hillyar's crew rotated the provisions in the hold to make room for resupply. That afternoon the men were issued half a pint of rum, a boat crew rowed across the bay to assist the ever-struggling *Isaac Todd* and Midshipman Gardiner strolled the main deck, taking in the view under an awning rigged to provide shade from the sun. Over fifty sail were riding on the swell whipped up by a wind blowing from the south. Pounded by the breakers was a large, stone pier known as the mole. Beyond stood the castle of San Cristobal. In its shadow was a large marble column intricately carved with human figures and a number of 'low, ill-built and irregular' one- and two-storey houses dominated by three whitewashed churches. The whole was dwarfed by the lower slopes of the Anaga Mountains whose rocky foothills were planted with corn, grapes and figs in narrow rows.[1]

On the 13th Purser Surflen went ashore to purchase provisions. The water casks were refilled and 6,030 gallons of wine, 400lbs of fresh vegetables, 200 lemons and a single ox were hoisted on board with a rig strung from the spars. The crew stowed the hold under the watchful eye of Acting-Master Miller, while Gardiner visited the Church of Nuestra Señora de la Concepción where he saw two 'English Jacks ... preserved as trophy's of war'. With the roads accommodating the East Indian fleet as well as a number of British merchantmen bound for Brazil and their accompanying escorts, Santa Cruz had the atmosphere of a prosperous, British seaside town. The *Phoebe*'s officers' stay was 'very pleasant [indeed]'. For the *Isaac Todd*'s French Canadian *voyageurs*, on the other hand, it proved a painful visit. When soldiers from the local Spanish garrison mistook them for escaped French prisoners 'a scuffle ensued'. Half 'were wounded and locked up, but were soon after released'. Another member of Hillyar's command, Able Seaman Ligorio Philips, was also having a difficult time. A native of Santa Cruz, Philips had served nineteen years with the Royal Navy without visiting his home town. 'Immediately on our arrival ... he asked permission to go on shore', Gardiner recalled, '[but] returned on board the same evening ... His parents who were both living when he left ... had long since paid the debt of nature, all his friends had left ... nor could he hear any account of the remainder of his unfortunate family.'[2]

At 9.30 a.m. on 15 April the *Phoebe* and *Isaac Todd* got under way with a light breeze from the northeast. Hillyar took two East Indiamen, the 532-ton *Ocean*, commanded by Captain Thomas MacTaggart and the larger *Devaynes*, under Captain John Short, under convoy. Left behind when their sister vessels had sailed that morning, both were carrying supplies, passengers and soldiers to Madras and Bengal. That evening the *Phoebe*'s officers gathered on deck to see the Peak of Tenerife, but 'the darkness of the night concealed it from ... view'. On Good Friday a barrel of cocoa was opened, Hillyar held extra divine service and the convoy covered 125 miles. The next morning brought fine weather and moderate breezes. The Phoebes washed their clothes and scrubbed their hammocks, hanging them from the rigging to dry. Steering south-southwest, Hillyar made for the Cape Verde Islands to catch up with the East India convoy and rid himself of the *Ocean* and *Devaynes*.[3]

April 19th brought a dead calm. For the next forty-eight hours the convoy idled under a burning sun and covered no more than six miles. At 11 a.m. Ordinary Seaman William Dougherty, a 23-year-old Tamatave veteran from Derry, was punished with eighteen lashes for swearing and disobedience of orders. That afternoon the sailroom was cleared and the spare courses aired on deck. On the 21st a breeze sprang up from the northeast and at daylight the *Phoebe*'s lookouts spotted a stranger on the weather beam. She proved to be a Spanish schooner from Majorca bound for Puerto Rico. On the 25th, as the *Phoebe* covered over 100 miles, Acting Sailing Master Miller steered south for the Cape Verde Islands. Gardiner sighted San Antonio the next morning: 'As the weather was very hazy, the ... barren summit ... was all that we could ... distinguish, rising ... majestically above ... mists which entirely concealed its base.' Hoping the India fleet was astern, Hillyar 'lay too till morning in expectation ... that ... [he] might resign [his] ... charge' and at noon lookouts spotted a strange sail approaching. She proved to be the *John*, a British merchant brig originally part of the convoy bound for Brazil that the Phoebes had seen at Tenerife. Having separated from his escorts, her captain was obliged to join Hillyar's command.[4]

The next day the flotilla passed the tiny island of Brava, and then on the moonlit night of the 28th the night watch enjoyed spectacular views of the 2,829-metre high volcano rising from the island of Fogo. The 30th brought moderate breezes and cloudy weather. Scudding along at 7 knots, the convoy covered 145 miles. That afternoon Hillyar had Ordinary Seaman Thomas Staines promoted to Trumpeter.

The post brought the 38-year-old from Donegal who had served on the frigate since February 1802 an extra ten shillings per month. The next morning the landsmen were exercised at the great guns and at 2 p.m. Hillyar backed the mizzen sail to allow the *Devaynes* to catch up. As the convoy neared the Equator, the humidity rose. Dark clouds gathered and on the evening of 4 May a thunderstorm broke out. The next morning Gardiner noticed a solitary swallow trailing the ship. 'After flying [round] several times ... as though unwilling to approach ... it at length alighted', he recalled, 'and hopping about from one rope to the other, seemed to share in the general amusement [which its sudden appearance had caused] ... under ... mistaken notions of kindness ... [the sailors] determined to catch this little wanderer following it from one place to another till at last weary of such inhospitable treatment ... it left us as quickly as Noah's dove when she found no rest for her foot.' The incident left Gardiner in melancholy mood. 'Such a ... visit, so common in England, could not fail to present to a sea–green imagination, many of those rural and social scenes, kind friends and affectionate relations whose influence on the mind only increases as distance separates', the young midshipman mused.[5]

Nine days of frustrating calms followed. On 6 May Mary Fanning, the wife of an East India Company private on the *Devaynes*, gave birth to a daughter. Eight days later, 'the long wished for breeze at length sprung up from the Southward and brought [the convoy] into the S.E. trades'. The captain of the *John* attempted to take advantage by sailing ahead, prompting Hillyar to fire several guns across his bows and the next morning, in the longitude of 22 degrees, the convoy crossed the line. Neptune was invited on board and the 140 men and boys on the *Phoebe* who had never sailed the southern seas were ducked and shaved. On 17 May the *John* parted company. Ignoring the *Phoebe*'s blue, white and black-striped signal flag, she disappeared over the horizon near the Racers, a hazardous, rocky shoal off the easternmost point of Brazil. The next three weeks saw the *Phoebe* and her remaining charges beating south down the coast towards Rio. Hillyar exercised his men at the great guns and small arms, a precaution also taken by captains MacTaggart and Short who knew they would soon have to fend for themselves. The next day Hillyar took the *Isaac Todd* in tow. Three days later squalls split the *Phoebe*'s maintopgallant sail 'from the foot to the head'. Those on board the *Isaac Todd* passed the days harpoon fishing for 'fierce sharks' and green turtles, the latter of which proved 'very superior ... eating'. On the 26th the *Koddington*, another member of the wayward Brazil convoy, joined Hillyar's flock and two days later the *Devaynes* and *Ocean* hoisted their colours in farewell and sailed for the Cape of Good Hope.[6]

The last day of May saw the Phoebes gathered at the waist for a punishment parade. Ordinary Seaman John Evans, a 22-year-old Tamatave veteran from

Branton, Northumberland was given twelve lashes for drunkenness. On 3 June, after a boat had been sent aboard the *Delfina*, a Portuguese ship from Rio bound for Oporto, soundings recorded a depth of 107 fathoms. Over the next week, as the convoy neared Rio, dozens of sails were seen and on the 9th, as the *Phoebe* rounded the lofty promontory of Cape Frio, seventy miles to the east of the Brazilian capital, Hillyar gathered his men at the waist once more. 'I told them [that they would not be] allowed to go on shore at any of the ports we visited ... [and] to make up their minds on the subject and to forgo the comforts of liberty until their return to England', while 'promis[ing] them that if we should be spared to see our native country ... [I would] request their Lordships to indulge them with long leave.' As an added incentive, Hillyar made several promotions. John Lunn, a fourteen-year-old First Class Volunteer, was made midshipman and William James, a 23-year-old who had been with the frigate for a little over a year, was promoted to able seaman. The new rating, which would see James' wages increase by eight shillings a month, meant that he had served at sea for a minimum of three years. Able seamen were required to know every inch of the frigate's miles of standing and running rigging; tie, worm, parcel, serve and splice ropes; run up the ratlines, furl or reef a wind filled sail; rig tackle from the yards; steer at the helm; heave the lead; load and fire the guns; stow the hold to retain the ship's trim; and use a sailmaker's needle to repair tears in the shrouds.[7]

On the morning of 11 June the *Phoebe*, *Isaac Todd* and *Koddington* entered Rio's Guanabra Bay. The views were stunning. Beyond the Sugar Loaf, which jutted 'almost perpendicularly' skywards at the southern entrance, several 'high and singular peaks ... softened with ... luxurious foliage' surrounded a vast anchorage dotted with fortified islands. Amongst the vessels at anchor were the *John* merchant brig, whose captain Hillyar promptly rebuked for breaking convoy and two British sloops-of-war, the 18-gun HMS *Cherub*, commanded by Captain Thomas Tudor Tucker, and the 24-gun HMS *Raccoon* under Captain William Black, both of which had recently returned from an uneventful cruise off Salvador de Bahia in search of American privateers. To the south stood the city. Built in a verdant valley leading gently upwards from the beach, Rio de Janeiro boasted several 'pretty' churches and public buildings and was dominated by an aqueduct whose double arches brought water six miles from a mountain named the Parrot's Head.[8]

The *Phoebe*'s arrival was a godsend for Rear-Admiral Manley Dixon, the 53-year-old commander of the Royal Navy's Brazil Station. With no more than a handful of frigates and sloops and a single 74, Dixon was tasked with monitoring the volatile political situation in the Spanish colonies of Chile and the River Plate, protecting British trade across the South Atlantic and South Pacific, and providing convoy for quantities of gold and silver bullion generated by the growing number of British merchants resident in Rio de Janeiro, Salvador, Buenos Ayres, Santiago and Valparaiso. The opening of these new markets was a direct result of Napoleon's 1805 closure of European ports refocusing British mercantile attention on emerging New World markets and the French invasions of Spain and Portugal which had forced Spanish America to allow foreign trade. By 1813 revenues amounted to over £1,000,000 per year. Diverted to the coffers of Britain's army in the Peninsula, the money allowed Wellington to pay his troops and purchase provisions from the Portuguese and Spanish peasants in whose territory he was campaigning. This gave the British a decisive advantage over the French, the majority of whom were tied up protecting exposed lines of communication against the depredations of local guerrillas, enraged by Napoleon's preference for 'living off the land'.

With the outbreak of the War of 1812, Dixon's job had become more complicated. As the American flour Wellington had previously relied on was now unavailable, the rear-admiral had been ordered to send Chilean grain to Europe – an apparently simple task which would have unforeseen complications. Dixon also had to contend with swarms of American privateers harassing British merchant shipping off the Brazilian coast and in recent months his station had been threatened by the presence of at least three US men-of-war. In December USS *Constitution* and USS *Hornet* had narrowly missed capturing HMS *Bonne Citoyenne*, a lightly-armed sloop carrying one of the crucial bullion shipments to Wellington's troops. The Americans had gone on to destroy HMS *Java* off Salvador before disappearing without trace. Meanwhile, with Dixon absent escorting the *Bonne Citoyenne* to safety with the only ship on his station capable of besting the Americans, the 74-gun HMS *Montague*, USS *Essex* had been sighted off the Island of Saint Catherine's by a Portuguese sloop. HMS *Cherub* and *Raccoon* had set off in pursuit, but their efforts had proved fruitless. Aside from sending a certain Captain John Helt and several other prisoners into Rio on parole, the *Essex* had not been heard from since.[9]

Thus had matters stood until 3 June when Dixon had received a letter from Captain Peter Heywood of the frigate HMS *Nereus*, at anchor off Buenos Ayres. Contained was intelligence forwarded from British merchants in Valparaiso stating that the *Essex* had arrived on 15 March. They added that the Americans intended 'to take and destroy the English whalers' working the coast before '[running] across the Pacific to India, where [it is said] ... she is to join the *Constitution* and *Hornet*, who were to go thither from the coast of Brazil with orders to destroy, but capture nothing'. The merchants also mentioned contradictory rumours that stated that the *Essex* intended to return 'back round Cape Horn and touch at the mouth of the [River] Plate and on the coast of Brazil again on her return to America'. The mention of British whalers was of particular concern to Dixon.

On 30 April he had received orders to send HMS *Cherub* and *Raccoon* into the Pacific to protect this all-important trade. Preoccupied with the threat posed by USS *Constitution*, the rear-admiral had ignored the missive and kept his sloops on the Brazilian coast instead. Their Lordships had been most displeased, but the *Phoebe*'s unexpected arrival presented Dixon with an opportunity to make amends.[10]

By the end of June, having consulted with Captain Hillyar and Messers MacTavish and McDonald, Dixon came up with a plan. The *Phoebe*, *Raccoon*, *Cherub* and *Isaac Todd* would sail for the Pacific under Hillyar's command. Such a squadron would be more than capable of dealing with the *Essex* as well as completing the Admiralty's 'secret' mission. Dixon even factored in the worst-case scenario of the poor-sailing *Todd* not making it round Cape Horn, by specifying that the stores and personnel she carried – crucial for establishing a British base on the Columbia River – were to be distributed amongst the fleet. Meanwhile, the imminent arrival of HMS *Porcupine* with the long-delayed Brazil convoy would enable Dixon to send another shipment of specie (£16,000 in bullion and £60,000 in Brazilian diamonds) to England, while the return of HMS *Montague* would provide a strike force in the event any American cruisers were still lurking off the Brazilian coast.[11]

The Phoebes spent nearly a month at Rio. On 12 June the lower rigging was set up and the hold cleared to receive supplies. The next four weeks saw hard biscuit, coal, fresh beef, live bullocks, barrels of suet, raisins, cocoa, lime juice, salt pork and fresh vegetables, bags of bread and casks of flour, vinegar, split peas, oatmeal, rice, tobacco and spirits brought out from the victualing office and stowed below. Boat parties, watched by Lieutenant Burrow's marines, filled the ship's water casks at the streams spilling into Guanabra Bay or gathered firewood from the forests and twigs to make brooms to sweep the decks, while Cooper James Fullarton, a 23-year-old from Montrose, knocked up barrels to replace those that had rotted through and the caulkers and carpenter's crew, having received new saws and files and a boatload of tropical hardwood from Dixon's warehouse, readied the *Phoebe* and *Isaac Todd* for sea. On 14 June the *Phoebe*'s surgeon, Jason Smith and his assistant, Adam Simpson, checked their stores of amputating saws, knives, needles, bone nippers, bandages and cat gut. Two days later a survey was conducted on the ship's sails and rigging. The sailmakers and boatswains from HMS *Cherub*, *Raccoon* and *Montague* brought on board to conduct the process found the frigate's fore and mizzen topgallant sails, the fore and main topgallant studding sails and parts of the upper rigging unfit for further use. That afternoon the *Phoebe*'s ailing boatswain, John Pomfrey, struggled ashore to requisition the supplies Sailmaker Thomas Millery and his associate, Ropemaker George Clarke, would need to make the repairs. On 17 June the yards and spars were blacked.

Sand from Rio's beaches was brought on board as ballast and the carpenter and his crew rowed across the anchorage to make a new jib boom for the *Isaac Todd*.[12]

The *Phoebe*'s officers were occupied with less laborious pursuits. First Lieutenant Ingram took advantage of an English merchant ship's imminent departure to write a letter to his mother Anne; several others visited the waterfall at Tajuca or explored town. In 1808 Rio de Janeiro had been transformed into the hub of the Portuguese Empire with the arrival of the Prince Regent, Dom Joao VI, and 10,000 of his countrymen following the French invasion of his homeland. Nevertheless, Gardiner 'was ... much disappointed ... All which from the ship had the appearance of beauty and grandeur seemed to vanish when I entered the ... city', he explained. The streets were 'narrow and dirty' and there was 'such an intermixture of fine houses and miserable looking shops, that the latter destroy[ed] the effect of the former'. Gardiner found the city's elite 'ridiculous' and 'vain' and abhorred the infamous Valongo Slave Market, where 20,000 human souls were traded each year 'with as much unconcern as a horse or a sheep would be [sold] in Europe'. Rio's churches, on the other hand, were 'neat and richly ornamented'; the city's botanical gardens boasted brilliantly-coloured blooms; and there was a finely situated main square. Paved with granite and fronted by a stone fountain dedicated to the goddess Phoebe, it was open to the east offering stunning views of the anchorage. Dom Joao's tiled Royal Palace stood to the south, while the west was dominated by a whitewashed cathedral rich in gold ornamentation and oil paintings of Christ.[13]

In early June two of the *Isaac Todd*'s mates, demoralised by the situation on board, resigned. Later, during a particularly 'dark night', seven of the *Todd*'s sailors stole one of her boats and deserted. Rear-Admiral Dixon had several others confined on HMS *Montague* to ensure they could not follow suit. The Phoebes were also prone to desertion. On 25 June Midshipman Michael Lane took a party on the jolly boat to the victualing yard to pick up provisions. Having filled up their bags with fresh oranges from the vegetable house, Ordinary Seamen Peter Carlan and Peter Mortraugh, both pressed men from Drogheda, fled into town. The next morning at daylight, Third Lieutenant Jago was ordered to lead a search party, but it was Captain Smith of the *Isaac Todd* who was approached by a Portuguese guard who had apprehended the two men after being tipped off by a British merchant. 'They immediately declared they belonged to the *Phoebe*', Smith recalled. 'Both ... were crying ... and Mortraugh knelt down and begged I would intercede with Captain Hillyar that they might not be punished.'[14]

A court martial took place on HMS *Phoebe* three days later. The men manned the yards to receive Rear-Admiral Dixon, a single cannon was fired and the Union Flag ran up at the mizzen peak to indicate that the trial had begun. Besides Hillyar and Dixon, Captains Tucker, Black and Robert Elliot, the commander of HMS

Porcupine who had arrived with the Brazil convoy and HMS *Montague* on the 13th, were present. The evidence was delivered by Higgins, Jago and Smith and a plea for clemency based on the men's previous behaviour delivered by First Lieutenant Ingram. Within half an hour the officers had made up their minds. 'In consideration of the . . . [prisoners'] former good character', Carlan and Mortraugh were sentenced 'to receive fifty lashes . . . with a cat-of-nine-tails, on their bare backs.' The punishment was relatively lenient. Three other deserters, one from HMS *Raccoon* and two from HMS *Montague*, had been sentenced to 100 lashes each that very morning.[15]

On 1 July Rear-Admiral Dixon placed HMS *Cherub* and *Raccoon* under Hillyar's command. To give him the best chance of intercepting the *Essex*, Hillyar was advised 'to sail to the Southern Pacific . . . Whale fishery from the 17° of South Latitude to the Equator or Gallipegas Islands, cruizing from ten to one hundred leagues from the Land . . . The additional force . . . [of the two sloops] will . . . afford you the double prospect of succeeding on the Service pointed out in your Most Secret Orders'. Dixon's letter closed with a warning.

> This Expedition . . ., I am sorry to say, appears to be . . . generally known and I have no doubt . . . [news] will reach the Western coast of [South] America long before you arrive . . . It must solely depend upon you', he reminded Hillyar, 'to exercise your Judgement and discretion, how far it may be necessary either to take both . . . [sloops] on to the extent of your destination or leave one or both . . . for the purpose of Cruising . . . for the protection of the Whale-fishery.[16]

Dixon's concerns were well-founded. On 27 June Thomas Sumpter, the local US trade consul, had written a report on the comings and goings of the Royal Navy's ships on Dixon's station. Not only did it give details about Hillyar's destination and target, but also listed the ships under his command and their relative strengths. Sumpter dispatched the letter to William Gilchrist Miller, his colleague in Buenos Ayres, who forwarded it to Joel Roberts Poinsett, the trade consul in Santiago. Another copy made its way to the United States where it was published in *Niles' Weekly Register* in September 1813. The first of a series of glowing reports concerning the whereabouts of the US's ever-elusive 'Admiral of the Great South Sea', the article gave the *Essex*'s crewmembers' friends and family the first definitive indication of their loved ones' whereabouts since they had left Delaware eleven months before.[17]

At the beginning of July the British captains made their final preparations for putting to sea. Hillyar had ten sailors pressed from British merchantmen in the bay bringing the *Phoebe*'s complement to 284; Captain Tucker took thirteen Brazilian landsmen on board the *Cherub* and several more were pressed into service on the ever-unhappy *Isaac Todd*. On 3 July Rear-Admiral Dixon received a letter from Percy Clinton Sydney Smythe, Sixth Viscount Strangford, Envoy Extraordinary and Minister Plenipotentiary to His Britannic Majesty at Rio de Janeiro informing him that Peruvian privateers had seized two of the ships Strangford had sent to Chile to purchase flour and grain for the British army in Portugal. The *Boriska*, a Baltimore merchantman granted special license, and the *Hunter*, a British ship, had been detained at Callao and Strangford feared that the *Fama*, the armed Portuguese merchantman he had dispatched on the same mission at the end of 1812, had suffered a similar fate. Having learnt 'that some of his Majesty's ships are about to proceed ... to the western coast of this continent', Strangford asked Dixon to 'give ... [them] orders ... for the purpose of obtaining from ... Viceroy [Abascal] of Peru the restitution of these vessels as well as of their cargoes'. Dixon passed on the request to Hillyar who promised to look into the matter.[18]

The same morning Dom Joao VI visited the *Phoebe* on his royal barge, accompanied by 'several other boats of state'. Hillyar welcomed the regent with a 21-gun salute. After inspecting the men, Joao, a portly 46-year-old, boarded HMS *Montague* to the sound of another royal salute and was bade farewell with a third. The next morning Lord Strangford went on board the *Phoebe* to brief Hillyar on his mission at Callao and at 7 a.m. on 5 July, with all four ships packed with seven months' provisions and the *Isaac Todd* full of shingle ballast in an attempt to improve her sailing, Hillyar gave the signal to weigh. A sea breeze and a flood tide forced the captain to spend the night at anchor. The following day the unfavourable conditions continued and on the 8th a heavy sea poured into the bay causing panic as the ships rolled violently with the swell. That afternoon, as the boats were employed to drag the ships out to sea, Juan Evastine, one of the thirteen local landsmen taken on board HMS *Cherub,* jumped overboard and deserted. On 9 July, the weather turned. With light breezes, the flotilla worked its way out of the harbour under a cloudy sky and, with the ungainly *Isaac Todd* taking the lead, set a course for Cape Horn.[19]

Chapter 6

The Galapagos Islands: USS *Essex*, 11 April 1813 – 9 July 1813

Sped by steady breezes, the *Essex*'s crossing from Payta to the Galapagos took six days. Having learnt that the islands, dubbed *Las Encantadas* ('the Enchanted Ones') by the Spanish, were notorious for dead calms, strong currents and baffling breezes, Porter prepared for independent boat action. The carpenter's crew checked the barge, longboat, yawl and cutter and the three whaleboats acquired from the *Charles* and *Barclay* were in a state of good repair; plans of attack and signals were established; and extra crew were selected for each boat to serve as boarders. Gunners' Mates George Martin and James Steady, the latter newly promoted to replace the disgraced Lawrence Miller, ensured the powder barrels in the magazine were in good condition while the ship's armourer, Bennet Field, checked the small arms. Muskets and pistols were cleaned and oiled and flints checked for signs of wear, while the boarders honed their cutlasses, axes, knives and pikes with a grindstone set up on the spar deck.[1]

On the evening of 16 April, with the breeze reduced to a murmur, Porter had the *Essex*'s lower steering sail partially submerged, creating a sheltered pool in which the men were permitted to swim. Despite the high temperatures, which increased as the *Essex* drew nearer the Equator, spirits remained high. Only two men were on the sick list, one of them Surgeon Miller himself. Besides the advanced liver disease which had been troubling him even before the *Essex* had left the Delaware, Miller had recently begun to suffer from constipation caused by the bad water shipped at Valparaiso. Consequently, he requested a transfer to the *Barclay*, where he believed the 'greater tranquillity' might aid his recovery. Bored with the doctor's constant complaints, Porter agreed.[2]

At 8 a.m. on 17 April, one of the *Essex*'s lookouts sighted land. Believing it to be Hood's Island, a common stopping-place where whalers obtained wood and giant tortoises, Porter had Cowell haul in for a closer look and signalled the *Barclay* to follow. When the low profile of Hood's rose to the west, however, Porter realised his mistake: the first landfall was actually Chatham's Island, the easternmost of the Galapagos. Changing course, Porter arrived abreast of the anchorage off the northwest part of Hood's, well-sheltered in the lee of an offshore atoll, at 7 p.m. and sent Downes in for a closer look in one of the *Barclay*'s whaleboats. Made of light half-inch cedar planks, the whaleboats were sleek craft, designed to ride over the waves rather than cut through them and in three hours Downes returned having found the anchorage empty. Disappointed, Porter hauled off into the wind with the *Barclay* in company and lay to for the night, wary of the offshore reefs marked on Colnett's charts and the strong north-westward currents.[3]

Dawn revealed seven islands in sight. Signalling the *Barclay*, Porter bore away for Charles' Island, another stopping point for his quarry, with a pleasant breeze from the east. Flocks of large, black frigate birds whirled overhead. One was caught by a topman precariously balanced on the main royal yard. At noon the *Essex* hove to off a bay near the northwest point of Charles' Island marked by a ring of high, black ragged rocks known as the Devil's Crown. Scanning the anchorage, the American officers gathered expectantly on the quarterdeck. Yet again they were disappointed. 'We could perceive no vessels', Porter recalled, 'but understanding that [visiting whalers] . . . were in the practice of depositing letters in a box', Lieutenant Downes was ordered ashore once more.[4]

Downes returned three hours later. As well as several pelicans and doves his men had killed with stones and the bloodied body of a large fur seal, the lieutenant brought a number of letters from the post-box. 'There was none . . . of a late date', Porter recalled, 'but they . . . confirmed . . . the practice of vessels . . . cruising among the . . . islands for whales.' Five London and Milford Haven-based whalers – the *Charlton*, *Nimrod*, *Hector*, *Atlantic* and *Cyrus* – had called at the island in June 1812 on their way to Banks' Bay off the Island of Albemarle. All had enjoyed good fortune and the *Atlantic*, captained by Obadiah Wyer, had nearly filled her casks with whale oil. The letters also revealed that several American whalers had been in the vicinity and that the *Perseverance* and *Sukey* had called in. Meanwhile, Captain Randall of the *Barclay* had sent a boat to a beach a mile to the north where his men caught several green turtles. Two were sent across to the *Essex*. Porter found them excellent eating, but the atmosphere on the American frigate was beginning to sour. No fresh water had been found and the men had not expected to be disappointed in their hunt for British whalers twice in a row. Consoling himself with the thought that the third time he was sure to be lucky, Porter pushed on to the Island of Albemarle. With a fine breeze from the east, the *Essex* arrived off the south head early the next morning.[5]

At 9 a.m., with the wind having dropped and the frigate still eight miles off the southern point, Porter rowed ashore in his gig with Purser Shaw. The volcanic peaks of Cerro Azul and Cierra Negra, both over 1,000 metres above sea-level, were covered in dark clouds, raising hopes that fresh water might be found. After two hours, the gig reached a small rocky cove with an excellent landing. Splashing ashore, the crew were confronted with hundreds of sunbathing aquatic iguanas 'of an enormous size and the most hideous appearance' covering every available patch of open ground. Inland, the island was surprisingly verdant. Waist high grasses, thirty-foot trees and thick underbrush grew out of a thin layer of rich volcanic soil. To Porter's disappointment, no streams were visible near the shore and the scree sides of the volcano were too steep to climb. With their principal mission confounded, Porter's men set about the iguanas with their clubs. 'In a few moments [we had] knocked down hundreds', he recalled. Some were put on board the gig along with a solitary penguin. The rest, with several seals, nesting seabirds, green turtles and large crabs, were left where they fell.

Later that morning, the Americans rowed north round the coast for fifteen miles. Cove after cove appeared, but no suitable landing sites were found. The coastline was dominated by 'craggy rocks, against which the sea broke with inconceivable violence'. Sheer cliffs formed of strata of different coloured stone rose several hundred feet into the sky. Brightly-coloured fish swam round the boat and a number of 'enormous sharks ... snapped at ... [the] oars' and had to be repelled with boarding pikes. Five miles before Albemarle's western headland, Christopher's Point, Porter spotted 'a black gravely beach' covered with the remains of a whaling ship which had been wrecked two or three years before. 'She appeared to have gone entirely to pieces ... and some of her copper ... had been thrown a great distance among the rocks by the violence of the sea.'

At 2 p.m., despairing of finding another suitable landing spot, Porter made his way back to the frigate. Two hours later the gig was hoisted aboard and all sail made to the northwest while the *Barclay*, barely visible far astern, struggled to stay in company. After rounding Christopher's Point, Porter intended to sail north across Elizabeth Bay, round Narborough Island, a circular atoll whose turtle-like profile had just come into view, and tack into Banks' Bay, a sheltered cove frequented by sperm whales searching for cuttlefish and squid driven in by the prevailing currents. According to the whale captains Porter had spoken to, between March and July as many as fifteen British and American ships could be found there. While the men butchered and ate the iguanas that Porter's boat crew had killed and the *Essex* sailed northwards up the barren west coast of Narborough, a sense of anticipation built. The Essexes spoke of the prize money they were soon to make, but the weather turned against them. As the sun sank, the breeze fell away. Having reached the midway point of Narborough under the bulk of La Cumbre, a 1,470-metre high volcano, the *Essex* and *Barclay* were becalmed.[6]

Dawn revealed the ships had been swept back round into Elizabeth Bay by a strong current setting in from the north. Growing impatient, at 9 a.m. Porter ordered Lieutenant Downes to row ahead in one of the whaleboats. One hour later a light breeze sprung up, briefly raising the Essexes' spirits, but it proved variable and the frigate made little headway. To the north, Downes was pulling ahead and at noon, as the whaleboat disappeared round the western point of Narborough Island, the wind died away entirely. With no breeze to cool them and not a scrap of cloud to shade them from the sun, the Essexes' misery was complete when the current returned sweeping the frigate back into Elizabeth Bay. After nightfall, the duty officers of the first and middle watches used cloaked lanterns to flash signals to Downes and at 2 a.m. three guns were fired to attract his attention. Shortly afterwards Downes' whaleboat was spotted and the lieutenant, sunburnt and exhausted following his seventeen-hour odyssey, clambered aboard. Although he had managed to work his way into Banks' Bay just before sundown, Downes was unable to say whether any ships had been present: a low haze had been hanging over the water and the bay was fully thirty-five miles across.[7]

The next two days proved an exercise in frustration. What little progress the Essexes made beating their way up the coast of Narborough during the day was countered by the southern current at night and it wasn't until sundown on 23 April that the frigate finally rounded the Turtle's Nose, the northernmost point of Narborough and tacked into Banks' Bay. Spreading out along the yards, the men scanned the water for any signs of the enemy. At length a cry of 'Sail Ho!' went up. For a moment the Essexes thought all their hard work had been rewarded, but the 'sails' proved to be nothing more than white strata in the rock face ahead. For the first time Porter noted 'murmurings' of discontent, but refused to give up hope. Five miles to the east, on the western shore of Albemarle, was a sheltered bay known as the Basin. As it was reputed to contain one of the archipelago's few sources of fresh water, whalers would frequently stop there. Downes was dispatched in a whaleboat without delay. The lieutenant returned at 1 a.m. Although he had seen no vessels and could not be sure of the exact location of the watering place in the darkness, he reported that the Basin would be a good place for the frigate to lay up.[8]

Porter, setting out in his gig at daylight, was equally impressed. Surrounded by high cliffs, the Basin measured 600 metres across at its entrance, widening to 1,000 metres at the head, where a small beach and ravine gave access inland. The water, crystal clear and abounding in fish, was three fathoms deep at the rock face and twelve in the centre and a bottom of fine, black, volcanic sand made it the perfect anchorage. 'We saw . . . green turtle', Porter recalled, 'and on landing found both the sea and land iguanas, lizards, a small grey snake and a variety of birds.' Large trees grew along the ravine, amongst them a species which produced a small, round, green fruit with 'a very aromatic smell and taste'. Knowing it would pique the curiosity of his friend, the Harvard graduate Chaplain David Adams, Porter took a sample before continuing his search. Amongst the undergrowth, he found a bag, 'which, from its appearance, had been there but a very short time; also a fresh turtle shell and bones, as well as those of fish and fresh ashes, where a fire had been kindled'. A few pages of a British political pamphlet were also discovered. Porter's quarry was not far ahead.

The watering place was a disappointment. Half a mile from the Basin's mouth was a crude stone hut surrounded by the skeletons of dozens of giant tortoises. Nearby was a flat rock inscribed with the names of several British and American whaling vessels. On the surface were four small square depressions, seven inches deep, which had been laboriously hacked out with a pickaxe to catch water dripping from the rocks above. When Porter arrived, the holes 'contained only a little stinking brine ... thrown in by the sea'. After waiting an hour, the Bostonian's disappointment grew. 'I am persuaded that no water can ever be found here, except after heavy rains and then only in small quantities ... The whole island [is] ... like a sponge, soak[ing] the moisture from the passing clouds, which serves to keep alive scanty vegetation ... but ... permit[ing] none of it to escape in springs or streams.' Having killed an enormous sea-lion and several seals and filled the gig with 'as many fish as ... [she] could conveniently carry', Porter returned to the *Essex*.[9]

The next morning, as the *Barclay* was spotted coming into the bay, Porter took four boats on a fishing expedition to a partially-submerged cavern on the southwest point of Albemarle. 'In less than half an hour we loaded all our boats with as many fish as they could carry', he recalled. 'The moment the hook was in the water, hundreds of them were seen rushing towards it ... chiefly the black, yellow and red grouper.' A huge black turtle was hooked along with several shags and penguins and that night the Essexes feasted on turtle soup. Prepared by the officer's cook, George Hill, the giant turtle fed Porter and the officers of the wardroom, the open cabin in the stern of the berth deck presided over by Lieutenant Downes, as well as providing 'an abundant meal' for forty-eight other men.[10]

On 26 April the men cleaned and aired the *Essex*. After Captain Randall had reassured Porter that the absence of British whalers most likely meant that they had been swept north out of the bay by the current, the Bostonian ordered Cowell to plot a course for James Island where the old whaling captain claimed fresh water could be found as well as wood and the giant tortoises the Galapagos were famed for. Capable of reaching weights of over 800lbs, these giants made an excellent portable foodstuff. As well as being 'wholesome, luscious and delicate', they contained enough fat of a quality comparable to olive oil so that no extra was required to cook them. Best of all, they carried an internal water supply 'in a bag at the root of the neck' and could be left alive in a ship's hold for eighteen months without suffering any 'diminution in fatness or excellence'. As many of his men had not disembarked since they had left Chester six months before, Porter also intended to grant the ship's company some time on shore.

At 10.30 a.m. the *Essex* and *Barclay* stood out of the bay. Rounding the head of Albemarle, a haze descended, the habitual mid-afternoon calm set in and a strong current swept the ships northeast. Shortly afterwards two more phantom sails were spotted. They proved to be nothing more than sandbanks whose appearance had been strangely transformed by the haze. 'There were few on board ... who did not now despair of making any captures about the Gallipagos Islands', Porter recalled, 'but ... I determined not to leave ... as long as there remained a hope of finding a British vessel among them.' Swept along 'with great rapidity' by the current, the men's frustration grew, their mood worsened by short water rations. The spar deck was so hot it blistered the men's feet and as the days passed with no change, their murmurings became more pronounced. The wood supply was running low and on the 28th the officers' noon longitude readings revealed that the *Essex* and *Barclay* had been carried 200 miles north of their intended destination.[11]

That night Porter lay awake in his cot. Listening to the noises of the ship as the middle watch went about their duties, his thoughts turned to the possibility of mutiny. Twenty-four years earlier, Lieutenant William Bligh of HMS *Bounty* had been cast adrift in a 23-foot open boat. Stranded in the middle of the South Pacific with barely any provisions or equipment, the fact that Bligh survived was testament to his extraordinary endurance and gift for navigation. The mutineers, led by Master's Mate Fletcher Christian, had not been heard from since. An even more terrifying precedent was the fate of Captain Hugh Pigot, commander of the frigate HMS *Hermione* on the Jamaica station. On 20 September 1797, Pigot, a sadistic sociopath who had brutalised his men, had given the fateful order that the last topman down on deck would be flogged. In the scramble that followed, three men fell to their deaths. The next evening the captain and eight of his officers were murdered. The mutineers sailed to the port of La Guaira, nineteen miles northwest of Caracas and handed the frigate to the Spanish, then at war with Britain. In time the *Hermione* was recaptured and twenty-four of her crew were hanged, but the episode still served as a reminder of the dreadful fate that awaited any captain who pushed his men too far.[12]

At daylight Porter was woken by cries of 'Sail Ho!' This time there was no false alarm. 'The stranger proved to be a large ship, bearing west.' The *Essex* gave chase and soon left the *Barclay* trailing behind her. At 6 a.m. two more sail were spotted. Convinced they were British whalers, Porter cleared for action. The men pulled down the partitions on the gun deck and stood ready by the bow chasers and carronades. At 7 a.m. the *Essex* came up with the first stranger. She proved to be the *Montezuma*, a dull-sailing, 270-ton whaler captained by David Baxter, a native of Nantucket who had emigrated to Pitt's colony at Milford Haven with Benjamin Rotch. Originally built in Philadelphia in 1804, the *Montezuma* had been seized for infringing the British East India Company's trading rights in

Asian waters and condemned in London. Since purchased by Rotch, she had been several months in the Pacific by the time the *Essex* intercepted her, had filled 1,400 barrels with oil and was about to head for home. Taking Baxter and his men on board, Porter put a prize crew on the *Montezuma* and continued chasing the other two strangers, both of which were in full flight. Several of the prisoners from the *Montezuma* were Americans pressed into British service. They revealed that the first stranger was the *Georgiana*, a square-rigged vessel of 280 tons with six 18-pounders, four swivel guns and six large blunderbusses mounted on her main deck. She had a crew of twenty-five men and was commanded by Captain William Pitts. The second was the *Policy* of 275 tons. Manned by twenty-five sailors, she was commanded by Captain Joseph Bowman and mounted ten 6-pounders. Both were 'reputed fast sailers' and had many Americans on board.

At 11 a.m., with the *Policy* and *Georgiana* still hull down over the horizon, a dead calm ensued. Porter had the boats lowered and sent fifty men in chase in two divisions: the whaleboat and the second and third cutter were led by Lieutenant Downes; the pinnace, the first cutter and the gig were commanded by Lieutenant Wilmer. The men were armed with muskets, pistols, knives, axes, boarding pikes, clubs and cutlasses. After an hour, Downes' men passed through a mass of 100 giant tortoises thrown overboard from the *Policy* as she had cleared for action. With their necks extended into the air, they bobbed up and down like corks. 'They were the first we had ever seen', Farragut recalled, 'and excited much curiosity.' By 2 p.m. Downes had got within a mile of his quarry. Becalmed a quarter of a mile from each other, the whalers hoisted British colours and fired two guns to windward to show their intention to fight. Downes responded by forming a single division and pulling for the larger vessel, the *Georgiana*, then tracking his movements with two guns. A few yards from her stern Downes hove to and raised American colours on a boarding pike. The sight was met with three cheers. Assured by the whalers that they were 'all Americans', Downes left a few men to take control before rowing on to the *Policy*, then under command of First Mate Marcus Johnson as Captain Bowman was confined to his cabin in ill-health. 'She had one gun run out abaft and 1 in each gangway', Feltus recalled. '[Johnson] hesitated for some time' as the Americans sat off his stern, but when one cocked his musket, he too struck his colours. The Americans pushed past the men at the gangway and surged on board.

After the Americans had hoisted the Stars and Stripes on the whalers, a breeze sprang up. The *Essex* and *Barclay* set sail and the four ships were soon united. The prisoners were taken onto the *Essex* and offered a chance to join the crew. At least three from the *Montezuma*, nine from the *Georgiana* and six from the *Policy* agreed. The rest were confined below decks with the Spaniards taken from the *Barclay* three weeks before while the prizes were searched for supplies. Equipped for a three-year round voyage, they had not yet consumed half their stock. 'We obtained ... abundant ... cordage, canvas, paints, tar and every other article necessary for the ship', Porter recalled. Numerous small arms, gunpowder and ammunition were found, several of the tortoises that had been thrown overboard, many of them weighing over 350lbs, were picked up by the boat crews on their return and Porter purchased Captains Baxter's and Pitt's private supplies of slops, tobacco and spirits. The captures would also result in significant prize money: they were valuable ships, heavily laden with whale oil, but perhaps the most important consequence was a much-needed boost in morale. '[Their capture] convinced us [that] we ought not to despair of success under any circumstances', Porter recalled, 'and that, although the patient and persevering may for a time meet with disappointments, fortune will at length most commonly make amends.'[13]

On 30 April, Porter fitted out the prizes. Midshipman William H. Odenheimer was given command of the *Montezuma* and Midshipman Cowan, who was replaced in the *Barclay* by Midshipman Feltus, was given charge of the *Policy*. Each was provided with a small prize crew and signal book and ordered to keep their men on reduced rations, clear their decks of whaling equipment, bend their light sails, reave their running rigging and keep up with the *Essex* as best they could. In the event of separation two anchorages popular with British whalers on the northern Peruvian coast, the Bay of Tumbez and the Island of La Plata, were assigned as rendezvous. The plundered supplies were used to make minor repairs to the *Essex*. The carpenters worked on the main deck, Master Cowell and his mates oversaw the tarring and overhauling of the rigging, and others painted the frigate's interior. With Surgeon Miller's condition deteriorating, Porter moved him from the *Barclay* to the *Policy* where the bedridden Bowman proved an amiable companion despite his own poor health.[14]

The best of the prizes, the *Georgiana*, was given to Lieutenant Downes. Built for the British East India Company as a packet, she was 'a noble ship' pierced for twenty guns. Porter felt she would make an ideal cruiser and ordered Downes to strip her down. The oil casks were sent on board the other prizes. The tryworks, iron boilers used for reducing the whale oil, were dismantled, along with the cutting stage where the whale's carcass would be brought alongside and the windlass, a giant winch on the bow designed to tear off strips of blubber. Once the work had been done, the *Georgiana* sat higher in the water, improving her sailing and allowing Porter to mount more guns. Between 3 and 8 May, as the flotilla drifted within sight of Wenman's Island, the *Policy*'s ten 6-pounders were hoisted in through the *Georgiana*'s open gun ports, giving Downes a total of sixteen guns besides the four swivels and six blunderbusses mounted on the main deck. The small arms found on the prizes were also taken on board, bulwarks were built for protection and the lieutenant was provided with a crew of forty-one.

Thirty-six were from the *Essex*. The remainder had enrolled from the prizes and Midshipman Haddaway was assigned acting lieutenant. William Kingsbury, the 'trusty old' tar who had restored calm round the Horn, was made boatswain and the disgraced Mr. Miller was charged with maintaining the guns. By the morning of 8 May the work was complete. Porter renamed the sloop USS *Georgiana* and read out her commission. Downes hoisted American colours at the mizzen peak and saluted with sixteen guns.[15]

Informed that at least three more British whalers – the *Rose*, the *Perseverance* and the *New Zealander* – were 'in the neighbourhood', Porter sailed for James' Island that afternoon. Baffling winds and strong north westerly currents continued to frustrate and on the evening of 9 May, after lunar observations had revealed that the flotilla remained as far to the north as it had been on the 29 April, Porter decided to take the *Montezuma*, the dullest sailer, under tow. Once the hawser was attached, it was the turn of the *Barclay* and *Policy* to slow the convoy. That night the *Essex* was obliged to shorten sail to avoid losing sight of them and on the morning of 10 May Porter rowed across to the *Barclay* to ensure Feltus had set as much canvas as she could carry. The flotilla spent the next two days beating to windward with little to show for their efforts until the lookouts sighted an island on the weather bow at 4 p.m. on 12 May. That evening the current swung round to the southward and by daylight the *Essex* was just four leagues from land.[16]

Dominated by a central vegetation-covered height, sloping down to long, low points and fine sandy beaches, the island possessed 'a very agreeable and inviting appearance', especially as the *Essex*'s water supplies were running low and the men had been so long at sea. Porter 'at first supposed it to be James' Island, as did all the prisoners who were acquainted with its appearance; but they all declared, that ... they could not recollect the sandy beaches and fine bays with which this appeared indented'. A thick fog confused the matter and, as Colnett's charts proved unhelpful, Porter signalled the *Georgiana* to conduct a reconnaissance. As Downes set sail, a breeze sprung up from the northward accompanied by a strong current and Porter took advantage to take his dull sailers to the south towards Hood's Island. A boat was lowered with instructions for the *Georgiana* to continue on her course then look into Banks' Bay before rendezvousing with the *Essex* at either Hood's or Tumbez on the coast of Peru. Downes continued to the southern point of the landmass, which was found to be Indefatigable Island, while the *Essex*, *Barclay*, *Policy* and *Montezuma* proceeded southeast.[17]

At noon, as the fog lifted, the Essexes spotted Charles' Island to the south-southwest. Bearing away, at 4 p.m. Porter dropped anchor in eight fathoms in the bay where he had stopped four weeks before. With the *Barclay*, *Policy* and *Montezuma* at anchor between the *Essex* and the beach, Porter was rowed ashore to see if any letters had been left at the post-box since his last visit. None were found, but a water cask and barrel of bread which the Americans had noticed on their last visit had been taken, fresh tracks were visible on the beach leading to the post box, a deep impression had been made in the sand and some rope, which appeared to be of British manufacture, was found. Deducing that the visitors had pressed on for the whaling grounds at Banks' Bay, Porter reasoned that they were sure to fall into Downes' hands. In the interim he would remain at Charles' Island. His men could get some shore leave and he would have a chance to find the spring that his informants had assured him was in the interior.[18]

The next morning Porter, Randall and Feltus took two boats and two empty ten-gallon kegs and rowed to the western point in search of the spring. Having narrowly avoided being driven onto a hidden rock by the swell, the Americans landed at a black sand beach and dragged their boats ashore. There they found 'fresh embers and [the remains of] a tortoise, which had not been killed ... more than two days [before]'. At the edge of the beach, a well-trodden path cut eastwards across the dunes. Following it, Porter found 'a pair of mockasons, made of English canvas and a tortoise shell containing about two quarts of English barley'. After crossing a series of low, barren hills and lava fields dotted with withered trees, they reached the spring. Porter thought 'the water ... excellent'. While the kegs were filled, the men went in search of giant tortoise. Thirty were turned onto their backs, but the men were only able to carry one, 'selected ... for his antiquated appearance', back to the boats. 'His weight was exactly one hundred and ninety seven pounds', Porter recalled, 'but he was far from being considered of a large size.'

The trip proved exhausting. After manhandling the kegs to the beach, it was 'necessary to ... raft [them] ... to the ship, a distance of six miles, through a high sea and sometimes against rapid currents'. Realising it would be impractical to water the ship in this way, Porter came up with a plan B. 'Well knowing the roving disposition of seamen, I determined to let a party go on shore to amuse themselves', he explained, 'believing, if water was to be found within two or three miles of us, it would be discovered ... On their return at night I was not disappointed.' Half a mile inland the hollows in a lava field had been filled with rainfall. Though brackish and 'filled ... with slime and insects ... it was [deemed] a treasure too precious to lose'. Over the next few days, work parties filled 200 ten-gallon kegs – enough to keep the *Essex* and her prizes at sea for two weeks.[19]

The Essexes enjoyed their stay at Charles' Island. When not employed watering or wooding the ship, the men were allowed ashore in shifts 'to take a run'. While the mess cooks gathered driftwood and thorn scrub to make a fire, their companions fished, hunted and foraged for prickly pears. Giant land tortoises were caught and birds trapped by the dozen. The former were roasted whole in their shells. The latter were made into potpies. In the evening, the men sat round bonfires on the beach and returned to the ships at nightfall. The midshipmen divided their time between playing amongst the sand dunes and studying under Chaplain David Adams. Farragut thought his time on Charles' Island 'among the happiest days of [his] . . . life'. After the pressures of the shipboard routine, the young officers in the making could behave like children again.[20]

At 3 a.m. on 15 May, USS *Georgiana* sailed into Post Office Bay. Weighing anchor near the *Essex*, Lieutenant Downes made his report. While navigating a two mile wide channel between Indefatigable and Duncan Island on 12 May, he had come perilously close to the rocks and had spent the best part of the next twenty-four hours tacking away from the lee shore. The following evening, finding himself in the vicinity of Charles' Island, Downes had decided to stand into Post Office Bay in the hopes of meeting a British whaler. That afternoon Porter dispatched Downes to Albermarle in pursuit of the whaler which he suspected had recently called in at Post Office Bay. The lieutenant was ordered to return to Charles' Island 'as soon afterwards as possible' and look for further instructions buried in a bottle at the foot of the post-box should Porter be obliged to leave the anchorage in the interim. As the *Georgiana* set sail, Porter proposed that Chaplain Adams should survey Indefatigable Island. Having a keen interest in medicinal plants, Adams was delighted. By 4 p.m. he had filled the two whaleboats assigned to him with a week's provisions and selected Midshipman Odenheimer and several men to accompany him. Adams was ordered to return within six days.[21]

Over the next few days Porter had the whalers' hulls and cabins and the *Essex*'s bends and upper works repainted. When he returned to the mainland he intended to sell his prizes to the highest bidder: an improvement in their appearance would command a higher price. Meanwhile, the men continued to explore. Midshipman Feltus found the remains of a vegetable garden once belonging to an Irish castaway by the name of Patrick Watkins and the tomb of a former crewmember of the *Georgiana* was also discovered. 'The spot', Porter recalled, 'was shaded by two lofty thorn-bushes, which afforded an agreeable shade . . . [It] became the favourite resort of our men at their meals. The pile of stones . . . served them . . . for table and seat . . . and [they] quaffed many a can of grog to his poor soul.' On 16 May Feltus discovered two large caverns near the spring. 'The bottom [and] sides were quite black & looked as if they were smoked', he recalled, '[and] in the bottom there appeared to be a quantity of ashes.' Another afternoon, Farragut and Porter went fishing off the Devil's Crown. 'As we approached', the former recalled, 'a number of seals were . . . making for the water . . . the men . . . singled out a fine fellow and beat him over the head with oars and boat hooks, but . . . [to] no avail . . . Finally, one of the sailors succeeded in getting hold of his tail; but he dragged the whole crew . . . into the water. The Captain fired at the seal when he freed himself from the men but he sank out of sight.'[22]

On 20 May, Adams and Odenheimer returned from Indefatigable Island. Indulging his 'zeal for promoting geographical ... knowledge', Adams had measured the latitude and longitude of the principal points and had enjoyed fine views across the archipelago from the summit of its 864-metre high volcano. Wood and giant tortoises had proved abundant. In the fertile southern half, specimens measuring over five and half feet had been found. In terms of practical discoveries, the trip had been less successful. Surrounded by dangerous inshore reefs, Indefatigable offered no suitable anchorage and no fresh water had been found. Adams' most interesting discovery was made on his return to Post Office Bay. While rowing across the channel on the night of 19/20 May, the Americans had passed within a mile of a strange ship heading for Albemarle. In the moonlight Adams could see she was triple-masted and bore a tier of guns. From the outline of the works on her deck, she seemed to be a whaler.

On hearing the news, Porter was caught in two minds. Part of him wanted to pursue the stranger. From the chaplain's description, he thought she might be the *Charlton*, a 274-ton British whaler mounting ten guns, which would make a fine addition to Porter's growing fleet. On the other hand, Downes could probably deal with the stranger on his own. Besides, Porter's chief concern was fresh water and the only sure way to secure it was to return to the mainland. At midday, the Blue Peter was hoisted. While the men returned to the ships, Porter, Gamble and Shaw climbed some heights to see if they could spot the stranger. It proved an arduous undertaking. 'After crawling through prickly-pear trees and scrambling over loose lava, which tore our shoes ... we ... arrived', the captain recalled, 'exhausted with thirst, heat and fatigue, at the summit.' One hundred and twenty metres above sea level, the view was 'extensive', but no sails were in sight. Porter decided to head for Tumbez on the Peruvian coast without delay. Leaving a letter in a bottle buried under the post box informing Downes of his intentions, on the morning of 21 May Porter gave the order to stand out of Post Office Bay.[23]

The voyage to Peru was more difficult than Porter had anticipated. Sailing southwest to round Charles' Island, on the 22nd the *Essex* was obliged to take the *Montezuma* in tow. The next day the ships tacked to the northeast under grey skies. With a good breeze from the southward, they sighted Hood's Island at 11.30 a.m. Porter decided to square away for the bay on the island's northeast side in the hope of making new prizes, but towards evening the wind dropped and a current swept the ships towards the rocks on the southeast point. On the evening of the 24th Captain Randall on the *Barclay* noted a festering slick of whale oil, offal, blood and guts. Feasted on by birds, sharks and scavenging fish, the putrid raft was a sure sign that whalers were nearby. At midnight the flotilla was so close to the rocks that Feltus could hear the breakers and Porter ordered the *Montezuma* cast off for fear that she would drag the *Essex* to her doom. That night the current intensified. The ships managed to tack away from danger, but by daylight had been swept back to Charles' Island. Frustrated, Porter changed his plan once more. 'I determined to bear away, look into the harbour of Charles' Island and proceed from thence to the ... Cocos [an island chain 400 miles to the northeast known for its fresh water], looking into Banks' Bay in my way.' It seemed likely that there were several potential prizes in the vicinity. If Porter caught them they might offer the possibility of fresh water, while if he left Downes to his own devices, the lieutenant ran the risk of being outgunned.[24]

That morning the long-suffering Doctor Miller passed away. 'It was supposed that the danger ... of going on ... [the rocks] the preceding night ... tended greatly to hasten his death', Porter recalled. Out of respect for his station, Miller was placed in a coffin and the funeral delayed until a suitable landfall could be made. Doctor Hoffman was promoted to the rank of acting-surgeon and that afternoon, the *Essex* hove to off Post Office Bay where Porter sent a boat ashore with an updated message for Downes. The next day, with Miller's corpse ripening, a funeral was improvised on the *Policy*. Porter and all his senior officers attended. After Chaplain Adams had read a brief service, the body was committed to the deep.[25]

On 27 May the flotilla drew parallel with the southernmost point of Albemarle. Porter ordered the ships to spread out to maximum signalling distance to conduct a sweep through the whaling grounds. With the *Essex* towing the *Montezuma* in the centre, the *Barclay* stood to the starboard while the *Policy* sailed off the frigate's larboard quarter. At 9 p.m., after a sudden illness of just two hours' duration, Quarter Gunner Benjamin Geers became the seventh Essex to die during the voyage. While the others had all been victims of illness or accident, there was some indication that Geers's death could have been the result of foul play. 'He complained of a violent pain in his breast', Porter recalled, 'was constantly calling for water and died in violent convulsions, frothing very much at the mouth.' Some suspected he had committed suicide by ingesting arsenic, but Porter could not believe that such an apparently 'happy and contented' man would take his own life.[26]

Sailing north across the western limits of Elizabeth Bay, on 28 May the flotilla skirted Narborough Island and by noon could see the northern head of Albemarle beyond the Turtle's Nose. At 4 p.m. a lookout spotted a strange sail making northwest. Casting off the *Montezuma*, Porter gave chase, leaving the prizes behind him and by the time the sun began to dip, he could see the stranger 'standing from us with all the sail she could crowd'. Aware that the chase would change course to elude him during the night, Porter pushed on until 9 p.m. then hove to while his prizes re-joined. That night the *Montezuma* sailed seven miles to the northwest before heaving too. The *Barclay* was sent the same distance to the east, while the *Essex* remained stationary. At dawn the *Montezuma* signalled a sail to the northward and the chase resumed. At sunset, with the *Essex* rapidly gaining, the stranger hauled close on a wind to the eastward, hove about and boldly stood towards her pursuer. An British ensign flew from her stern flagstaff and a pendant from her main peak.

The stranger's audacity gave Porter pause to doubt. With his crew distributed amongst the prizes, the *Essex* could barely muster 200 men. Nevertheless, she was more than a match for any ship that the British had in the Pacific. Ordering his gun crews to their stations and the marines to the tops, Porter brought the *Essex* broadside-on, hoisted British colours and hailed the stranger through his speaking trumpet, inviting her captain to come on board. He duly complied. Introducing himself as Obed Wyer, he identified his ship as the *Atlantic*, a vessel belonging to the London firm of Enderby and Sons. Just then a second sail was sighted. Lieutenant McKnight was given command of the prize and Porter set sail northwest in pursuit. The *Atlantic* proved a fine sailer. Despite having no studding sails bent, she kept pace with the *Essex* and shortly after dark, guided by their night-glasses, Porter and Downes closed to within striking distance of the stranger. She proved to be the *Greenwich*, also owned by Enderby and Sons and armed with ten guns. Firing a shot across her bows, Porter forced her to heave to. Her captain, John Shuttleworth, having been drinking heavily throughout the pursuit, was reluctant to go on board the frigate without knowing her identity, but a second shot, fired between his masts and the threat of a broadside to follow convinced him.[27]

One hundred miles to the east, Downes was similarly engaged off James' Island. Recognising the *Georgiana* as a fellow British whaler, Captain Charles Hamon of the *Catherine* and Captain Monroe of the *Rose*, eight-gun whaling ships of 270 and 220 tons respectively, approached without suspicion. By the time they realised their mistake, Downes had sent two boats to board them and took both prizes without a shot being fired. The *Hector*, a French-built ship of 270 tons, eleven guns and a crew of twenty-five which Downes spotted later that afternoon, put up more resistance. Coming up after dark, Downes hesitated before attacking: the *Hector* had a 'warlike attitude', which had initially made the Americans think that she might be a Spanish sloop of war; and, having dispatched a proportion of his men to man his prizes, the lieutenant only had twenty 'men and boys' on board the *Georgiana*. Nevertheless, he trusted in his men's 'bravery' and, heaving to in a raking position off the *Hector*'s stern, demanded her surrender. Joseph Richards, her captain, responded by clearing for action, prompting Downes to fire a single 18-pounder. Punching through the *Hector*'s stern in a shower of razor-sharp splinters, the ball crashed along her gun deck and when Richards tried to flee, Downes fired five raking broadsides in quick succession. Two of the *Hector*'s twenty-five crew were killed and four others were wounded. The whaler's standing and running rigging were cut to shreds and the main topmast crashed down onto the deck. Richards struck his colours and Downes took his third prize of the day.[28]

On Sunday 30 May Porter redistributed his men. Of the 319 sailors who had left the Delaware River seven months before, seven had died and sixty-three had been sent home as prize crews on the HMP *Nocton*, the *Elizabeth* brig and USS *Georgiana*. Two had deserted at Saint Catherine's and one had been left at Valparaiso. Fifty-two new crewmembers had been recruited from the whaling ships the *Essex* had intercepted or captured, giving Porter a total of 298 men to divide between six ships. Two hundred and forty-five remained on the *Essex*, Midshipman Odenheimer stayed in command of the *Montezuma* with ten men, Feltus and six others stayed with Captain Gardner on the *Barclay* and Midshipman Cowan and his crew of ten remained on the *Policy*. Lieutenant McKnight was given a crew of twelve for the *Atlantic* and Lieutenant Gamble was put in charge of the *Greenwich*. Although Porter had confidence in the marine's resolve and his ability to enforce discipline, due to Gamble's lack of nautical knowledge, he was assigned two reliable old salts as mates amongst his crew of fourteen.[29]

The *Atlantic* and *Greenwich* proved fine additions to the fleet. The former had been constructed in France, was a fast sailer with sleek lines and, at 350 tons, was the largest ship the Americans had taken so far. The *Greenwich* had been built on the River Thames in 1799. Both had holds full of whale oil, over 800 giant tortoises gathered at James' Island and abundant supplies of cordage, canvas, paint, tar and slops. Most importantly, the *Atlantic* had 20,000 gallons of water. Combined with the supplies acquired at Charles' Island, Porter now had enough to last 100 days. Less welcome was the ever-growing number of prisoners. With the capture of the *Greenwich* and *Atlantic* their numbers had swelled to eighty men. In exchange for full provisions, some agreed to serve as sailors on the understanding that they would not take part in combat and would later be discharged as prisoners of war. The rest were kept confined and placed on reduced rations. The captains of the *Atlantic* and *Greenwich*, Obed Wyer and John Shuttleworth, would prove particularly troublesome 'guests'.[30]

Born in 1769 in Nantucket, Wyer was one of dozens of islanders who chose to work for the British. Having left his wife Anna and three children in Nantucket, he had emigrated to England where his whaling experience on board the *Fame* between 1804 and 1806 had secured him the captain's birth on the *Atlantic*. Sailing from Portsmouth on 12 November 1812 in company with the ill-fated HMS *Java*, Wyer had narrowly missed an early encounter with the *Essex* at Porto Praya in December, before parting company with HMS *Java* shortly after crossing the line. While the frigate had gone on to meet Commodore Bainbridge's USS *Constitution* off Salvador on 28 December 1812, Wyer had rounded the Horn alone. Stopping at

Concepción to refit, the *Atlantic* had sailed north to the Galapagos where she had been busy whaling and gathering tortoises until Wyer had had the ill-fortune to run in with Porter while making his way to Banks' Bay. As Porter had been flying British colours, the Nantucketer was only too happy to provide his host with all the intelligence he had at his disposal. Porter was outraged. How could a fellow American possess such a 'corrupt heart'? Introduced to the captains of Porter's other prizes, Wyer was soon 'undeceived' as to which nation had captured him. He 'gave full vent to [his] anger and indulged in the most abusive language', Porter recalled, 'lavishing . . . the most scurrilous epithets and giving me appellations that would have suited a buccaneer'. Captain Shuttleworth proved equally insulting and Porter decided to punish both men. Although his memoirs do not reveal his exact methods, the whalers were so humbled as a consequence that Porter boasted that they 'would have licked the dust from [his] feet, had it been required for them to do so'.[31]

Freed of his obligation to secure fresh water supplies, Porter decided to continue cruising the Galapagos. With the *Montezuma* towed by the *Essex*, the *Barclay* by the *Greenwich* and the *Policy* by the *Atlantic*, on 31 May, the flotilla beat southwards out of Banks' Bay. Contrary currents made rounding the southernmost point of Albemarle impossible, despite the wind being consistently in their favour and on 4 June, Porter was obliged to tack to the northwards. Two days later the fleet sailed past Narborough once more. At 1 p.m. the crew of the *Barclay* hooked a large loggerhead turtle. Two hours later a volcano on Albemarle threw up a dense column of smoke and after nightfall, as a sulphurous stench spread across the ocean, the sky was lit up by an eruption. The next morning a breeze sprung up from the southeast. Sick of battling the currents, Porter changed his mind once again and decided to set sail for the coast of Peru. That afternoon the flotilla passed to the north of Abington Island, one of the smallest of the archipelago. Setting a course due east, by the morning of 8 June the Americans had left the Galapagos behind them.[32]

The flotilla took six days to reach the mainland. Porter conducted as wide a sweep as possible, but no more prizes were found. As the six ships neared the coast on 13 June, the skies clouded over and in the morning the lookouts sighted land on the weather bow. On the 16th they reached the Island of La Plata, a desolate pirates' haunt said to have played host to Francis Drake's *Golden Hind*. Porter was disappointed. 'On every part [it] was perpendicular and inaccessible', he recalled, '[and] the surf [was] beating with great violence on the south and west sides.' Running along the shore, 'innumerable shoals of . . . whales', were sighted, 'all going with great rapidity to the northwest'. Even the most experienced whalers on board '[had] never before . . . seen them in such numbers'. The next morning Porter ran in and hove to. Signalling his two fastest prizes, the *Atlantic* and *Greenwich*, to chase a stranger spotted to the east, he took two whaleboats in to reconnoitre the island. 'No animals or their traces were discovered', Porter recalled, 'and the whole island was the most desolate imaginable.' After leaving a message in a bottle on the offchance that Downes would pass by, Porter returned to the *Essex* to find the *Greenwich* and *Atlantic* at anchor with the other prizes. The chase had proved to be a Spanish brig from Panama.[33]

The flotilla reached the Bay of Guayaquil on 19 June. Passing the Island of Santa Clara or Dead Man's Island, they swept on to the mouth of the River Tumbez, a whalers' rendezvous on the southern extremity of the bay. A mile offshore, the *Essex* anchored in five and half fathoms at 8 p.m. In contrast to the desolate aspect of the Galapagos and La Plata, the bay was teeming with life. Deer and wild turkey inhabited the thickly-wooded shoreline. Sharks, fish, water snakes, giant oysters and alligators measuring up to sixteen feet in length populated the muddy waters. The whole was alive with the buzz of mosquitoes and a variety of brightly plumaged birdlife. Porter was reminded of the Mississippi. Having spent the years of 1808 to 1810 chasing French, Spanish and American smugglers through the fever-ridden creeks and bayous as the commander of the naval station at New Orleans, it was an area he knew well. That night, as bumboats swarmed around the American ships, another accident occurred. While furling the mainsail, a 32-year-old quarter gunner, John Rodgers, 'the best seamen in ... the ship' despite his 'great ... fondness for rum', fell to the deck, shattering his skull on the very spot where Samuel Groce had split his head open five months before. Rodgers died instantly and was buried in a simple grave the next morning.

Anxious that the local Spanish governor, resident several miles up the river at the town of Tumbez, might react badly to his arrival, Porter asked Captain Randall of the *Barclay* to act as his ambassador. Furnished with a 'handsome present' and an invitation for the governor to dine on board the *Essex* as an honoured guest, Randall set out at first light on 20 June. Although hazardous, the bar of the Tumbez River proved passable at low tide and by 1 p.m. Randall was heading upriver. Porter sent another boat 120 miles to the northeast to Guayaquil to find purchasers for his prizes. On board were the Spaniards who had been taken prisoner out of the *Barclay* off Callao. Not wishing to complicate matters during his negotiations with the governor of Tumbez, Porter felt it was better to 'get ... them out of the way'. While awaiting Randall's return, the Essexes wooded and watered the ships. Several boats were swamped crossing the bar and a number of rafts were broken up and the water casks they were carrying lost, but not a single man was drowned. Feltus spent the afternoon gathering oysters on the river bank and Porter and Farragut went alligator hunting. Singling out a fifteen-foot giant, 'nearly as large around as a flour-barrel' and 'of the most hideous appearance',

Porter shot it through the hip joint of its fore leg. 'The ball ... penetrated [its] heart' and killed the beast instantly.[34]

On 22 June Randall returned. From the *Essex*'s quarterdeck, Porter observed four strangers alongside the whaling captain, one of whom was dressed in uniform. To a nine-gun salute, which startled the roosting birdlife, the governor, his godfather, his son and the local collector of customs, were welcomed on board. 'Although the appearance of the whole was as wretched as can ... be imagined, policy induced ... [Porter] to show them every attention'. For the next nineteen hours, much to the crew's amusement, the Spaniards were treated as honoured guests. Gifts worth $100 were presented, Porter accepted an invitation to visit the governor's house and, in exchange for a commission of $200 per ship, the custom's collector agreed to travel to Guayaquil to broker the sale of the prizes. 'The prospect ... kept the poor man restless the whole time he was on board', Porter recalled.[35]

The next day, the governor returned to Tumbez. Leaving Lieutenant James Wilson in charge of the *Essex*, Porter followed at daybreak the next morning accompanied by Randall, Purser Shaw and several heavily-armed men. Frequently stopping to avoid half-submerged logs, the journey took five hours. The humidity was appalling and the mosquitoes a constant annoyance. The land on either bank was low, muddy and 'covered with rushes, reeds and mangroves'. The town, built six miles upriver, consisted of seventy reed huts constructed atop four foot high stilts. At the governor's house, distinguished only by its white-painted interior, his mulatto wife was preparing a meal. '[It was a] wretched place', Porter recalled, '[but,] the inhabitants gave me the most friendly reception, every where [they] invited me into their huts, where hogs, dogs, fowls, jackasses, men, women and children, were grouped together and from whence ... I was always glad to make my escape, on the account of the innumerable swarms of fleas with which they were infested.' Having distributed a number of silk shawls as presents and received 'a pair of fowls, a half dozen ... eggs, a few oranges, watermelons, [and] goats' in return, Porter was rowed back downriver. Although the Bostonian had felt distinctly uneasy in Tumbez and was concerned that the governor might attempt to detain him, he left Purser Shaw to 'procure a supply of fruit and vegetables for the crew'.[36]

On his return, Porter found Lieutenant James Wilson hopelessly drunk. The lieutenant had been arrested on at least two previous occasions during the early part of the voyage for violent and offensive conduct, but had been forgiven due to his 'many good qualities . . ., goodness of heart' and the intercession of his fellow officers. This occasion, however, Porter judged to be different. Wilson had been drinking with Captain Shuttleworth of the *Greenwich*, a self-confessed enemy of the Americans. Wilson had also been acting as officer of the watch. On being informed he was under arrest, the lieutenant 'sprung up' from his cot and 'seized a pistol'. Porter wrestled the weapon from his grasp, only for the lieutenant to grab another and threaten to blow his own brains out. Having disarmed him a second time, Porter had Wilson confined to his cabin. His sea chest was searched for further weapons and an armed marine placed outside his door. That afternoon Porter initiated a reshuffling of assignments. Lieutenant McKnight returned to the *Essex* and Sailing-Master Cowell and Midshipman Cowan were appointed acting Third and Fourth Lieutenants respectively. Midshipman Odenheimer rejoined the frigate as acting sailing master in Cowell's stead, Chaplain Adams was appointed prize commander of the *Atlantic* to replace McKnight and Midshipmen Clarke, Ogden, Gray, Isaacs and Conover, boys of no more than twelve to fifteen years of age, were given command of the *Montezuma* and *Policy* supported by senior sailors 'in whom [Porter] could confide'.[37]

As the days passed with no word from Purser Shaw, Porter grew increasingly concerned. Although the Spanish had insufficient naval forces in the area to seriously trouble the Americans, men onshore made easy targets. One of Porter's prisoners, a whaler's mate, had already disappeared, presumably having fallen victim to local robbers, a loss which prompted Porter to order his boat parties to carry arms at all times and around the same time a letter of unmistakably threatening tone was received from Brigadier Juan Vasco y Pascual, the governor of Guayaquil. After dashing Porter's hopes of selling his prizes, Pascual advised the Bostonian that the sooner his flotilla left Peruvian shores the better.[38]

On 24 June three strange sails hove into the bay. In the aftermath of Pascual's letter, the Americans were nervous and opinion as to the ships' identity was divided. 'As they approached with apparent caution', Porter recalled, 'many on board conjectured them to be enemies, [while] I believed it to be lieutenant Downes in the *Georgiana*, with two prizes.' Porter was proved correct and the new arrivals 'were greeted by three hearty cheers'. Since taking his prizes, Downes had decided to use the dullest sailer, the 220-ton *Rose*, as a cartel to rid himself of seventy-five prisoners. After her oil and guns had been thrown overboard, she had been dispatched to Saint Helena and Downes had proceeded with the *Hector* and the *Catherine* to Tumbez.[39]

With nine ships now under his command, Porter decided to split his forces. The *Essex* would continue the hunt for British whalers, while the least seaworthy of the prizes would be sent to Valparaiso where Porter hoped they would find buyers willing to defy Viceroy Abascal of Peru. The new plan prompted yet more reshuffling of personnel. The *Atlantic*, which was both a faster sailer and a larger ship than USS *Georgiana*, was converted into Downes' new cruiser. The First Lieutenant and his men spent the next few days shifting the cannon out of the latter into the former, which was renamed USS *Essex Junior*. By the time they had finished, she mounted twenty guns and Porter increased the crew to sixty men. Richard Dashiel, the oldest of Porter's midshipmen, was made the *Essex Junior's* acting sailing master and Downes was given William Kingsbury, the 'trusty old son of Neptune' who had acted so decisively during the storm of 3 March, as his acting boatswain. Chaplain Adams was given command of the *Georgiana*, which was converted into a twenty-gun store ship; Farragut was put in charge of the *Barclay* and Feltus was given command of the *Montezuma*.[40]

On 27 June Porter discharged his prisoners. A burden in terms of provisioning, they also posed a security risk. On condition that they would not serve against the United States until properly exchanged, the eighty men were provided with three boats to take them to Tumbez. In his journal, Porter made great play of his magnanimity towards his prisoners ('even to that renegade Wyer and captain Shuttleworth'). Such claims were contradicted by later British reports, however. As well as claiming that Porter frequently had his prisoners whipped or put in irons, they also maintained that they were held in 'the greatest distress' and abandoned 'in danger of being starved to death'.[41]

On the 28th and 29th, Porter was joined by two new recruits. Exactly how Ordinary Seaman Isaac Coffin, whom Porter would later describe as 'a lazy negro', or John Hughes, a thirteen-year-old ship's boy from England, came to be at Tumbez is unclear. Judging by the former's surname, he may well have been a slave or servant of one of the Coffin clan, a prominent whaling family from Nantucket in command of at least three whaling ships (the *Fame*, the *John Jay* and the *Monticello*) then in the Pacific. Perhaps he had deserted, along with Hughes, from his master's ship at Tumbez. Another possibility is that the new recruits had deserted from the *Seringapatam*, *Charlton* or *New Zealander*, British whalers which had left the bay for the Galapagos just a fortnight before the Americans' arrival. Porter learnt that their captains had decided to join forces for mutual protection and was keen to set off in pursuit. The *Seringapatam* would make a particularly fine prize. Teak-built and originally owned by Tippu Sultan of Mysore, at 350 tons and armed with fourteen guns, she was the finest English whaler in the Pacific.[42]

The only thing keeping Porter from leaving was the continuing absence of Mr Shaw. Although he had succeeded in buying provisions from the governor, the purser had been unable to procure a boat to bring them downriver. Learning of the cause of the delay, Porter sent for Shaw and decided to cut his losses. At 5 a.m. on 30 June, once the purser had boarded, all nine ships of the flotilla unmoored and stood out of the Bay. Stretching away to the westward they sailed 100 leagues offshore to the easterly Pacific trade winds. Porter sent Carpenter Langley on board the *Essex Junior* to help build up her defensive breastworks and on 4 July celebrated the thirty-seventh anniversary of the declaration of independence.

With a generous issue of spirits, 'the day was spent in the utmost conviviality' and the Pacific echoed to the thunder of numerous salutes. By the 9th Carpenter Langley had completed his work and Porter split his forces. Under convoy of the *Essex Junior*, the *Hector, Catherine, Policy, Montezuma* and *Barclay* were to proceed to Valparaiso. Downes was ordered to send the *Policy*, which he had had filled with whale oil taken out of the other prizes, to the United States, to find buyers for the other ships and to purchase spirits and other supplies with four thousand dollars taken from HMP *Nocton*, before rendezvousing with the *Essex* at either Hood's or Charles' Island in the Galapagos or the Marquesas, an inhabited archipelago some three thousand miles to the west. At 8 a.m. on 9 July, the two fleets parted company.[43]

Chapter 7

In the Footsteps of Robinson Crusoe: HMS *Phoebe*, 10 July 1813 – 6 October 1813

After leaving Rio de Janeiro on 9 July 1813, the *Isaac Todd* and HMS *Phoebe*, *Cherub* and *Raccoon* made good progress. Sailing before 'a fine breeze from the N[orth] and the E[ast]', on Sunday 11 July, while Hillyar performed his customary double divine service, they sailed 150 miles southwest. Spirits were buoyant. The sky was a brilliant blue. Albatrosses and pinladas circled overhead and Gardiner anticipated a quick passage round the Horn. On the 12th, Captain Tucker of the *Cherub* read the Articles of War. The thirty-six points, instigated by Parliament in 1749, covered all the behaviour the Royal Navy deemed unacceptable, from petty theft, drunkenness and insolence to mutiny, striking a senior officer and desertion. For minor offences, men could be put in irons, have their grog ration stopped or reduced, be assigned to clean the heads or lose their rating; troublesome midshipmen could be suspended from the shrouds or receive an impromptu 'cobbing' from their peers. The ultimate punishment was to be hung from the yardarm, but by far the most commonly employed, and the one to which Captain Tucker resorted that morning, was the cat-o-nine-tails. Tied to the grating and stripped of his shirt, Able Seaman Johnathon McCarthy was given thirty-six lashes for drunkenness and insolence.[1]

Despite such occurrences, the *Cherub* was a relatively happy ship and the 38-year-old Tucker a strict yet popular captain. Most of the crew had served under him in the fever-ridden West Indies on his previous command, HMS *Epervier*, and had requested a transfer to HMS *Cherub* when Tucker had been reassigned in February 1809. The sloop had seen action at the reduction of Martinique and the capture of Guadeloupe, before returning to Portsmouth yard in September 1812 where the crew had been given a month's leave of absence while the *Cherub* had her copper bottom scraped clean. By the time Tucker was ready to depart to join Manley Dixon's South American station, the entire crew had reported for duty, a circumstance so rare that Port-Admiral Sir Richard Bickerton had written an extraordinary report to the Admiralty.[2]

While Tucker was highly professional, several of those who served under him were not. The *Cherub* had a high percentage of landsmen and many of the more experienced crewmembers had poor disciplinary records. Tucker's junior lieutenant, John Belcher, was of particular concern. Commissioned by Dixon two months before, Belcher was a beneficiary of the Royal Navy's most enduring weakness: the habit of promoting undeserving men with 'interest' over those with genuine ability and he would prove eminently unsuited to the rigours of life at sea.[3]

On the same day McCarthy received his lashes, Captain Hillyar opened his third packet of sealed orders. '[I] found I was to proceed to the N[orth] W[est] coast of America, to dispossess the Americans of their settlements on the River Columbia', Hillyar recalled, 'and on [my] return ... to call at the different ports [of South America] for treasure that might be destined for England, limiting [myself] ... to such a quantity of specie as would have [me carry] 12,000l for the freight.' That afternoon, in accordance with Manley Dixon's instructions, Mr. John McDonald of the North West Company transferred to the *Phoebe* from the *Isaac Todd*. Slinging his cot in the confines of the gun deck, McDonald was joined by his consort, Jane Barnes, six of the Canadian *voyageurs* and Naukane, a chief from Hawaii who was familiar with the difficulties of crossing the bar of the Columbia River.[4]

At 1 p.m. Hillyar signalled for Captains Tucker, Black and Smith to join him in his great cabin. Over dinner, they discussed possible rendezvous points should the ships become separated. The first agreed upon was off the shore of Eastern Patagonia, midway between the South American mainland and the Falkland Islands; the second was the Pacific Island of Juan Fernandez, a Spanish colony 700 miles off the Chilean coast; the third was the Island of Cocos close to the Equator; the fourth was the mouth of the Columbia River. Hillyar stressed the importance of sailing along the routes frequented by British whalers: their protection was second only to the destruction of Fort Astoria in his overall aims and he questioned his fellow captains on the charts and navigational equipment they had on board. The response was disappointing. Aside from a general map of the Pacific which Hillyar had received from the Admiralty, they were bereft of guidance. '[We had no charts] of the Falkland Islands, Cape Horn or any port on either side of the continent beyond the Brazil coast', Hillyar recalled; 'one sloop [was] absolutely without chart or timekeeper' and Captain Smith of the *Isaac Todd* had forgotten to bring written directions regarding the entrance to the Columbia River.[5]

That afternoon, Hillyar informed his men that they were heading round the Horn and into the Pacific. As such a long cruise 'gave opportunities for their improvement', he announced that he would be holding literacy classes and would organise religious instruction. Sixty of the crew were found to be unable to recite the Lord's Prayer and the illiterate were taught to form letters out of sand on the deck.[6]

On 13 July the weather deteriorated. The northeasterly breeze that had driven the flotilla south from Rio came round to the west and increased to a hard gale. Hillyar signalled his fellow captains to heave to and the day was spent exercising the great guns while the marines fired at marks suspended from the yards. 'The second day', Gardiner recalled, '[the gale] moderated, but the weather became very unsettled and we made but little progress.' The sky clouded over and the convoy covered no more than twelve miles. On the 15th Purser Surflen issued a ration of the tobacco he had purchased at Rio (a commodity on which he was allowed 10 per cent commission). The men chewed it or smoked clay pipes on the forecastle, the only place on the ship where such a potentially hazardous pastime was allowed.[7]

July 19th brought strong gales and heavy squalls. The sea ran high and lightning struck the waves as the men secured the booms and boats and lashed the guns to the hull. At 1.30 a.m., while the *Isaac Todd* veered crazily off to the northwest, a heavy sea stove in one of the *Phoebe*'s main deck ports, deluging the men in icy water. After daybreak the sprit sail was carried away when the frigate dived into the ocean off the back of a particularly high wave. On 20 July HMS *Raccoon*'s main staysail was blown to pieces. A new one was rigged but destroyed later that afternoon. The next day the wind moderated and the *Isaac Todd* re-joined the flotilla, but on the 27th the gales returned. Over the next two days, the *Phoebe* fired signal guns every hour to keep the convoy together as a thick fog descended and visibility decreased to a few dozen yards. The precautions proved in vain. On the 29th the *Isaac Todd* disappeared from sight. 'The next day we stood on under easy sail in expectation of seeing her', Gardiner recalled, '[but] she did not ... make her appearance, [and] we made sail [that afternoon] ... heartily glad we were rid of such a troublesome companion.' Writing a report in his great cabin, Hillyar suspected that the *Isaac Todd* had parted company 'by design'.[8]

By 1 August the albatrosses and pinladas had begun to desert the flotilla and the temperature was dropping daily. Hail fell as the Phoebes sounded in 63 fathoms with fine, grey sand. To protect the watch, Hillyar had 'a kind of tent shelter' constructed, the heads were sealed with shutlead and a set of extra gunport covers were lashed securely on top of the half ports to prevent the worst of the rain from penetrating. The 4th saw another round of punishments carried out on HMS *Cherub*. James Davidson was given a brutal forty-eight lashes for drunkenness, Thomas Pearson received twenty-four for the same and Thomas Greenalgh got twelve for disobedience of orders. On the 10th, during a downpour of rain and hail, Jesse Settition, also of HMS *Cherub*, was given thirty-six lashes for being drunk on duty and that afternoon the three ships passed to the west of the Falklands and drew within sight of Staten Island. '[It] is one uninterrupted mass of rocks and mountains', Gardiner noted, 'without the least sign of vegetation and . . . almost entirely covered in snow.' Later the man at the masthead thought he had sighted a sail, but it turned out to be an isolated rock formation off the island's eastern point around which a rapid current occasioned a heavy swell.[9]

On 14 August, with the flotilla 250 miles southeast of Cape Horn, the temperature plummeted to minus 16°. Hillyar ordered the watch to be kept constantly moving to avoid frostbite. 'In a few hours the ship was at the water mark completely encrusted with ice', Gardiner recalled. 'Every sea added a new coat, till it became of such thickness as entirely to conceal the figure head. Madam Phoebe I am convinced was never before decked with so white a garb.' The following day divine service was performed as the ships beat over 100 miles to the southwest. At noon the sun broke through the clouds and the temperature rose to seven degrees. That afternoon Surgeon Christopher O'Brien of HMS *Raccoon* recorded the travails of one of his patients, Able Seaman Jas Mortens. A former whaler, Mortens had deserted at a Pacific port in South America and made an epic journey overland across the continent before volunteering on board the sloop at Rio de Janeiro. Mortens was suffering from 'a total loss of appetite, a great dejection of spirits . . . [and] a growing pain across his abdomen', a condition O'Brien termed 'Atrophia' and attributed to a long residence in a warm climate. Confined to his hammock, Mortens was given opiates to relieve the pain.[10]

On 18 August the ships became separated in the fog. Through the firing of signal guns they were reunited the next day and on the morning of the 20th Hillyar exercised the great guns. That afternoon the caulkers worked on the main deck and the next day the lookouts sighted the islands of Diego Ramirez, due south of the Horn. Schoolmaster Philip Brady made two sketches, the first from the southeast eighteen miles from the islands, the second due south from fifteen. On the verge of entering the Pacific, Gardiner felt disappointed that the passage had proved so unremarkable. 'The doubling of this cape has generally been considered as a tedious and often a dangerous undertaking', he mused, 'yet I cannot but think that it has been a little misrepresented. Of the former we had but little reason to complain, of the latter we saw none . . . That we had an excellent passage I will readily allow, but travellers and voyagers, like poets, have their licences and here I think they have exceeded their bounds.'[11]

On 25 August, judging he had made sufficient westing, Hillyar ordered Acting Sailing Master Miller to set a course for Juan Fernandez. With a good breeze filling their sails, the ships made excellent progress, covering well over 100 miles per day. Following a discussion with John McDonald and Naukane, the Hawaiian pilot who had previously sailed the Columbia River, Hillyar reached a decision which would radically alter the course of the *Phoebe*'s mission. Having learnt that there was unlikely to be sufficient water over the river bar to allow a frigate to pass in mid-winter, he determined to send HMS *Raccoon* to capture Fort Astoria while the *Phoebe* and *Cherub* remained in the Pacific to search for the *Essex* and protect the South Seas whaling trade. 'I shall ... govern myself as by information I gain', he noted in his journal, 'and [patrol on the] track ... most likely to find the enemy frigate.'[12]

On 6 September the bad weather that Gardiner had expected to meet at Cape Horn caught up with the flotilla. The storm was presaged by fresh breezes and squalls. Building through the afternoon, they prompted the Phoebes to shorten sail, but it wasn't until the early hours of the next morning that the full fury of the weather was unleashed. At 1.30 a.m. strong gales pounded the ships, breaking the frigate's main topsail brace. The topmen raced up the rigging to make running repairs, but a second squall tore away the blunt and spilling lines, the sail was split across its length and 100 yards of canvas was blown into the sea. At 3 a.m., with the *Cherub* and *Raccoon* lost from sight, the main deck was swamped by a giant wave which washed away the whole of the gangway stations and the foresail was torn from the second reef.[13]

The next morning 'the weather was materially altered'. The deck thermometer recorded 20° and moderate southerly breezes sped the flotilla on its way. At first light on 10 September the island of Más Afuera was sighted and later Juan Fernandez hove into view. Under reefed topsails, the *Phoebe*, *Cherub* and *Raccoon* beat their way around the easternmost point and stood into Cumberland Bay, the anchorage where Commodore Anson's storm-battered, scurvy-ridden fleet had recuperated seventy-two years before. At 6 p.m. Hillyar ordered two guns fired to call a local pilot and, with several men employed blacking the boats and Sailmaker Millery busy making repairs to present as fine an appearance as possible for the Spaniard who had come on board, the *Phoebe* tacked into the bay, coming too with the best bower in 57 fathoms at midnight.[14]

'At daylight the next morning, we were welcomed with a distant view of the spot so celebrated in the romance of Robinson Crusoe', Gardiner recalled. Framed by craggy mountain tops, the highest of which, Los Innocentes, rose to over 1,524 metres, Juan Fernandez made a spectacular sight. Under the volcanic peaks were high windswept valleys covered in scrub. Beneath grew a forest from which tumbling rivers made their way down to the lower slopes, crowned with three batteries overlooking the island's only village, a collection of one hundred single-room mud huts situated in a green valley. The thatched roofs put Gardiner in mind of those he had seen at Madagascar in 1811. The only buildings of note were the governor's house, a chapel built two years before the *Phoebe*'s arrival and a square fort on the western side of the bay, where eighty poorly-armed soldiers manned fourteen ill-mounted cannon and a mournful-looking gallows stood in a parade ground inside the low walls.[15]

All morning the ships continued working their way into the bay. Bedevilled by squalls blowing down from the mountains interspersed by infuriating calms, it wasn't until late that evening that the *Phoebe* came to in 47 fathoms in an exposed position two miles off shore. The next day bumboats surrounded the British flotilla. '[They sold] junk beef', McDonald recalled, 'and some milk tasting and smelling [of] garlic.' At noon captains Hillyar, Tucker and Black, John McDonald, Purser Surflen and the *Phoebe*'s surgeon, Jason Smith, were rowed ashore. 'We were met by two fat priests', McDonald recounted, 'who hugged and kissed us ... [and] conducted us to Government House.' On the balcony the British party were presented to the Governor, the 59-year-old Lieutenant Colonel Manuel Santa María de Escobedo Baeza. Also present were his wife and four 'beautiful daughters'. As Santa María could speak neither English nor French and McDonald's and the British officers' Spanish was limited, Ligorio Philips, the Phoebe who had been born in Tenerife, was brought ashore to act as a translator. Santa María then offered everything in his assistance to help his guests. The news that the *Essex* had left Valparaiso in March was confirmed and more recent reports, brought to Juan Fernandez a few days before by a Spanish brig, stated that the Americans had since taken several prizes, some of which had been spotted cruising off Valparaiso as recently as 23 August. Hillyar also learnt of the insurrections in Chile and the ongoing struggle against Loyalist Peru. Baeza was sympathetic to the patriot cause.[16]

The flotilla stayed at Juan Fernandez for six days. The boats brought oxen and sheep from the village, filled the water casks onshore and gathered wood while a detachment of red-coated marines stood guard. Sailmaker Millery made repairs, the coopers knocked up new barrels to replace those which had rotted through, the butchers slaughtered the oxen and the cooks doled the meat out to the messes along with string bags full of boiled turnips which grew wild onshore. All was made more difficult by the exposed nature of the anchorage. High winds, gusting down from the mountain tops, roared across the bay and on 13 and 14 September the *Cherub* and the *Raccoon* were blown out to sea. While the latter was regaining the anchorage, the *Phoebe* lost her stream anchor: the hawsers chafed through by the rocks. Two of the frigate's boats dredged the bay to recover it. That afternoon squalls blowing off the shore caused violent breakers to pound the beach and the *Phoebe*'s launch was driven onto the rocks. Her stern post and hull were damaged, but no lives were lost.

Early on the 16th, Hillyar took advantage of a lull in the weather to tow the ships closer in shore. The *Phoebe* came to with the small bower in 34 fathoms half a mile from the beach and the sloops anchored nearby. That afternoon, while the carpenter and his crew repaired the launch and the rest of the Phoebes stowed the hold or fished for bream and cod, five of the Brazilian sailors who had volunteered on the *Cherub* deserted. John Bates, a nineteen-year-old ordinary seaman from London who had been a Phoebe since before the Battle of Tamatave and Arthur Willis, a 28-year-old taken onto the frigate from the *Salvador del Mundo* at Plymouth, snuck down to the after hold and stove in the head of one of the pipes of wine purchased at Tenerife. By the time the crime was discovered, the pipe was 'totally leaked out' and both men were paralytic. Surflen charged the cost against their wages and the master at arms put them in irons.[17]

Meanwhile, the officers stretched their legs on shore. Gardiner, a keen student of fortification, inspected the town's defences and noted that the peach trees planted by Commodore Anson had thrived. Several others visited the caves on the far side of the island once inhabited by Alexander Selkirk, a cantankerous Scottish pirate castaway on the island in 1704 long before the Spanish had colonised it. Surviving for four years by hunting feral goats, Selkirk was picked up by another British privateer and his story later inspired Defoe to write *Robinson Crusoe*. The Phoebes found three caves 'in which his name is still to be seen cut in the rock'.

The highlight of the young officers' stay was meeting Santa Maria's youngest daughter, the beautiful María Isabel. A few days before the British left, she accompanied her father on board the *Phoebe* as Hillyar's guest. Gardiner was amongst those chosen to escort them on board. 'In course of conversation ... [she] was asked how she liked being on an island, which at her age (about 19) without amusement or society, could not be supposed to be very agreeable' the midshipman recalled. 'She did not ... hesitate, but turning to her Father with a smile on her countenance, said, "She was happy to be any where with him." An answer so unexpected and which at the same time portrayed so much virtue and good sense, could not be disregarded by any of the company and only left us to regret that so fair a jewel, which would be an ornament to any society, should be concealed in such an unfrequented abode.'[18]

On the morning of 18 September signals were hoisted to warn the officers to retire on board. John McDonald, Takuane and the Canadian *voyageurs* moved their belongings from the *Phoebe* to the *Raccoon*, the boats were hoisted and at 3.30 p.m. the flotilla weighed anchor and sailed north. Over the next two weeks they made excellent progress towards the Equator. 'During the whole of this run we ... were not once becalmed', Gardiner recalled. 'What is more remarkable we had no rain, although the sky was almost continually clouded ... [and we] were ... refreshed by a steady and most delightful breeze.' The day after leaving Juan Fernandez, the flotilla entered the southeast trades. That afternoon the *Phoebe*'s topmen set the gallant studding and fore topsails and on the 21st the *Phoebe* covered 220 miles in twenty-four hours, before altering course to the north-northwest to run parallel with the South American coastline.[19]

On 22 September John Bates and Arthur Willis, the two seamen who had stolen wine from the *Phoebe*'s after hold, were given thirty-six and twenty-four lashes respectively. Private Thomas Presser received two dozen for disobedience and Private John Eves was given the same for theft. Over the next five days Captains Hillyar and Tucker exercised their great guns and small arms and on the 23rd the Phoebes practised with live ammunition, firing three broadsides into the Pacific. Midshipman Lane was discharged into HMS *Raccoon* to bring Captain Black's complement up to strength before he separated, while the carpenter and armourer constructed a new carriage and ring bolts for one of the sloop's cannon. On 25 September Quartermaster John Williams, a 47-year-old from Memmell in Prussia who had fought at Trafalgar, was given twenty-four lashes for drunkenness and demoted to able seaman. Two days later the *Raccoon*'s jolly boat and gig were hoisted onto the *Phoebe* for repairs.[20]

On 29 September, with the flotilla 100 miles west of Lima, a stranger was spotted on the larboard bow. Shifting the starboard studding sails and hauling to the westward, Hillyar gave chase. The stranger hoisted Spanish colours and hove to at midday. She proved to be a Spanish brig from Guayaquil bound for Lima. Her captain revealed that 'the *Essex* had been in the bay of Guayaquil two months since ... and had there landed a number of South Sea-men'. Learning that the prisoners had been 'in great distress', Hillyar decided to sail for Tumbez without delay 'to relieve them as well as gain [further] information'. Over forty-eight hours, the flotilla progressed 300 miles and on 2 October, having exchanged final telegraphs wishing each other good luck, the *Raccoon* sailed north for the Cocos Islands, while the *Phoebe* and *Cherub* stood in for land.[21]

Chapter 8

A Matter of Honour: USS *Essex*, 9 July 1813 – 2 October 1813

On the morning of 9 July 1813, four days after his twelfth birthday, Midshipman Farragut's 'day of trial . . . arrived'. One hundred leagues off the South American mainland, Farragut had been granted his first independent command: the *Barclay*, the New Bedford whaler Porter had liberated from Peruvian privateers over two months before. Such an occasion would normally have been cause for celebration, but Farragut had serious concerns. With the *Essex* and her armed consorts, the *Greenwich* and *Georgiana*, disappearing to the east and the *Essex Junior* and the rest of the prizes making sail to the south for Valparaiso, the *Barclay* would soon be isolated in the vastness of the Pacific Ocean. To make matters worse, the whaler's former captain, the 61-year-old New Englander, Gideon Randall, had been in command nearly as long as Farragut had been alive. The whaler was damned if he was going to stand aside while some wet-behind-the-ears 'nutshell' took over his ship. 'I was a little afraid of the old fellow', Farragut admitted, 'but the time had come for me at least to play the man, so I mustered up courage and informed [him] . . . that I desired the main topsail filled away, in order to close up with the *Essex Junior*. He replied that he would shoot any man who dared to touch a rope without his orders . . . then went below for his pistols.' Determined not to be intimidated, Farragut ordered his right-hand man, a fellow Essex assigned to help the young midshipman, to fill the sail. 'He answered with a clear "Ay, ay, sir"' and by the time Randall re-emerged, Farragut had the confidence to threaten to have him thrown overboard if he appeared on deck with his pistols again.[1]

The rest of Farragut's voyage proved uneventful. Headed by Downes in the *Essex Junior*, the convoy (the *Barclay*, *Policy*, *Montezuma*, *Hector* and *Catherine*) sailed south for Valparaiso. The first seven days brought fresh breezes interspersed with squalls. On 10 July Downes took the *Montezuma* in tow and seven days later a violent gust blew away part of the latter's standing rigging. Two days of dead calms followed. Towards the end of the month the fleet was forced to repeatedly tack into the wind and on the 29th a breeze sprung up out of the northwest. With all sail set, the convoy cut swiftly east-southeast and on 3 August Midshipman Feltus set the *Montezuma*'s studding sails. Flying before the wind, the convoy made Juan Fernandez on the 8th, a little over a month before Captain Hillyar would arrive, and four days later sighted Valparaiso. At 5 p.m. the following afternoon, the Americans dropped anchor in twenty-five fathoms in the bay.[2]

Over 1,000 miles to the north Captain Porter's voyage had been more eventful. Standing in for the continent until Downes' flotilla had disappeared, on 9 July the *Essex*, *Georgiana* and *Greenwich*, made for the Galapagos Islands. Porter was keen to follow-up intelligence he had received at Tumbez: three armed British whalers, the *Seringapatam*, *Charlton* and *New Zealander*, had set sail for the archipelago a fortnight before. 'On the 12th [July], I made Charles' Island', Porter recalled, 'and hove to for the night.' The next morning, a boat was sent into Post Office Bay to leave a note for Downes should the lieutenant pass that way. The papers Porter had previously found in the post-box had been removed along with some water kegs and firewood that the Americans had left on their last visit. Freshly-butchered tortoise shells and recently-used fire pits convinced Porter his quarry could not be far away.[3]

That afternoon the flotilla sailed for Banks' Bay. With a volcano on Charles' Island erupting behind them, they arrived off the southern head of Albemarle at midnight and hove to until the morning, the rocks of the island's southern flank illuminated by the pyrotechnic display eighty miles to the east. On 14 July, Porter sailed northward. As the *Essex* rounded the headland, it became apparent that the volcanoes on Narborough and Albemarle had also been active since their last visit. '[The former] appeared to have undergone great changes', Porter recalled. 'There were no less than four craters smoking ... and [another] ... on the south part of Albemarle', prompting the Bostonian to speculate that there must have been 'a submarine connection between them'. At 11 a.m. three 'fine, large ships' were sighted standing on a wind up Banks' Bay. Porter gave chase to the stranger in the centre. The others split up. One headed to the west and the other made east towards Albemarle, while the chase flew northwards. With the *Essex* leaving her prizes in her wake, the stranger who had stood in for Albemarle tacked to windward, threatening to cut off the *Greenwich* and *Georgiana*. Looking back, Porter nodded in approval as Lieutenant Gamble, in command of the *Greenwich*, hove to for the *Georgiana* to come up. Once the lieutenant had taken on board extra crew, he tacked and closed towards the aggressive stranger.

Early that afternoon Porter caught up with the chase. She proved to be the British whaling ship *Charlton*, of 274 tons and ten guns. Once she had struck her colours, Porter sent a boat across to take possession and brought her captain, Sinclair Halcrow, on board for interrogation. '[He] informed me, that the ship now to windward was the *Seringapatam* ... commanded by William Stavers and that the other [then fleeing to the west] was the *New Zealander*.' Armed with eight guns, the latter was owned by Benjamin Rotch. The *Seringapatam* was more of a concern. Gamble had ten guns to Stavers' fourteen and his ship was marginally smaller than the Englishman's. Stavers was also more experienced and had a reputation for aggression. Having already taken the US whaleship *Edward* off Cape Horn in May, Stavers was keen to give the Americans another bloody nose.

Far to windward, Porter watched as the *Greenwich* closed to cannon shot. The first three broadsides, fired at long range through the *Seringapatam*'s sails and rigging, did little damage, but 'when [Staver's] tacked', Surgeon's Mate Alexander M. Montgomery recalled, 'Captain P. became more anxious than ever.' If Gamble tacked at the same time, the *Seringapatam* would have an opportunity to rake the *Greenwich* as her bow swung level. If the marine waited the tables would turn. "Now Mr. Gamble", Montgomery heard Porter whisper, 'If you will only stand on five minutes and *then* tack, I will make you a prince.' Gamble did just that. The *Greenwich* swung round, her bow passing through the wind and opened fire as she came broadside-on to the *Seringapatam*'s bow. In a shower of splinters and torn canvas, the balls passed through the whaler's spars, rigging and sails, crippling her in an instant. Porter was 'much pleased'. After a futile attempt to flee, Stavers hove to and surrendered. Porter left Gamble to secure the prize and the *New Zealander* was taken without difficulty an hour later.[4]

That evening Porter had the *Seringapatam*'s thirty-one crew and the American prisoners they had taken off the *Edward* brought on board the *Essex*. When Porter demanded to see Staver's letter of marque, the Englishman panicked. He had left London before the United States had declared war and had not taken the trouble to obtain one. Despite Staver's insistence that the *Seringapatam*'s owner, William Mellish, Tory MP for Middlesex and Deputy Governor of the Bank of England, had no doubt since forwarded the document to Lima, Porter had him put in irons under the half-deck and warned him that he would face the hangman's noose on arrival in America like a common pirate. Porter then attempted to induce Staver's crew to join the *Essex*. At least five agreed and in total seventeen men signed up from the three prizes. Amongst them was William Worth, a member of a prominent whaling family from Nantucket who would go on to make several notable discoveries in the Pacific, and a feeble-minded twenty-year-old Scot who had served on the *Seringapatam* named John Swayne. As the latter left Porter's cabin clutching his signing-up bonus, Stavers cursed him as a 'bad fellow' and promised he would have his revenge.[5]

That evening Porter set a course for James' Island, a regular haunt for British whalers that offered considerable resources. The Bostonian had intended to reorganise his flotilla at anchor off shore, but his plans were thwarted by the contrary currents. Swept northwest, by noon on 19 July, the flotilla was at a latitude of 2° 8' North, 200 miles north of its destination. Judging the *Charlton* to be the dullest sailer, Porter determined to rid himself of her by using the whaler as a prisoner cartel. Her captain, Sinclair Halcrow, was reinstated on the condition that he took Porter's forty-eight prisoners directly to Rio de Janeiro. Halcrow and Captain Dunamon of the *New Zealander* – amongst those released – swore an oath to this effect, but some of the prisoners proved reluctant, fearing that they would be impressed into the Royal Navy as soon as they arrived. 'They were very solicitous that I would allow them whale-boats', Porter explained, 'and let them take their chances ... declaring that any fate would be preferable to ... servitude in his majesty's navy.' Despite his sympathy towards their plight, Porter refused, 'lest it ... be supposed I had turned them adrift in the middle of the Pacific'. That afternoon, once her stores had been removed onto the *Georgiana*, the *Charlton* set sail and was soon out of sight.[6]

In the third week of July the *Seringapatam* was fitted out as a man-of-war. The *Essex*'s gunner and carpenter and their crews dismantled the whaler's tryworks, raised her bulwarks and mounted eight more cannon on her spar and gun decks. Master's Mate James Terry was put in charge, while Purser Shaw was given command of the *New Zealander*. Both were ordered not to separate from the fleet. Meanwhile, Porter's new recruits were assigned roles on the *Essex*. John Swayne, the ex-*Seringapatam* who had provoked Stavers' wrath, was appointed to the main top. When being escorted to the heads to relieve himself, Stavers caught sight of the Scot grinding an edge on his cutlass at the armourer's whetstone. 'I hope you don't intend to use that against your own countrymen', he remarked. 'The Scotch and the English ha[ve] not yet settled it', Swayne replied, 'and as I am a Scotchman I have as good a right to fight for the Americans as for the English.' Stavers was furious.[7]

Without the dull-sailing *Charlton*, the flotilla began to make progress and at dawn on 22 July Porter found himself midway between Culpepper and Wenman's islands. Two days later, with the current once more pushing his fleet to the westward, Porter decided to send the *Georgiana* to the United States. Her cargo of whale oil would fetch up to $100,000 on the east coast and as she would arrive during the unpredictable weather of winter she would have a reasonable chance of breaking the British blockade. Porter was also worried about the unsettling presence of William Stavers. The former captain of the *Seringapatam* was 'a man of great cunning and considerable observation' and, following Porter's threats to see him hang, had little to lose. The longer Stavers remained, the more likely he would find a way of fomenting revolt or forwarding information to the enemy. Dispatching the *Georgiana* would also allow Porter to rid himself of James Wilson. Since his attempted suicide, the lieutenant's mood had stabilised and he had acted with 'great activity and bravery' on board the *Greenwich* during Gamble's fight with the *Seringapatam*. Nevertheless, Porter felt it was only a matter of time before he reoffended. Placing Wilson in charge of the returning ship was a face-saving solution. A final motivation for the *Georgiana*'s dispatch was that several crewmembers' year-long service contracts were soon up for renewal. Unlike the tars of the Royal Navy, who were obliged to serve as long as Britain remained at war, US sailors were free to leave once their contracts had expired. 'With this [in mind]', Porter 'permitted ... those' concerned to depart, but 'had the great satisfaction to observe but little desire on the[ir] part.' With her crew made up, the *Georgiana* departed on the 25th, 'giving ... a salute and three cheers at her departure'.[8]

The following morning, Porter redoubled his efforts to reach James' Island. On 27 July the northern headland of Narborough was sighted and the next morning, while the flotilla lay becalmed off Redondo Rock, a sail was spotted to the east. Porter shuffled out along the footrope beneath the topgallant yard to get a better view. Believing her to be a British whaler, the Bostonian gave chase, but with the westerly current against him, the stranger soon dropped over the horizon. The next morning she was sighted 'to the northeast ... standing on a wind ... across [the Americans'] bows'. At 9 a.m., seven miles distant, the stranger hoisted American colours and laid on all sail in flight, heading for Abington Island, fifty miles northeast. Porter set his studding sails and used his drags to bring the *Essex* to within four miles at which point the stranger got his boats out to tow his ship. Porter ordered Lieutenant McKnight and Mr. Bostwick, the ship's clerk, to take a whaleboat and the gig and row ahead of the whaler. Both carried marksmen to drive the British from their boats. The whaler's captain refused to be beaten. Running two light cannon out on his forecastle, he kept up a steady fire on the American boats, forcing McKnight and Bostwick to keep their distance. With both ships becalmed and the Essexes too exhausted to continue working their drags, Porter decided to lower all his boats and surround the stranger. After firing a few guns, the whaler struck his colours at dusk, but set all sail when a breeze sprung up from the eastward. Firing at McKnight and Bostwick as she swept past, the stranger disappeared into the night.[9]

With light and baffling winds and a strong lee current, it wasn't until dawn on 4 August that James' Island's red-black cinder cliffs were sighted. By noon the fleet was beating up the eighteen-mile-wide channel that separated it from Albemarle and at 2.30 p.m. the *Essex* came to anchor in six fathoms in the main bay a quarter of a mile from the beach. With the stranger still at large, Porter ordered the *New Zealander*, *Greenwich* and *Seringapatam* to anchor in line across the bay to prevent any ship moving inshore of them, while the *Essex*'s pinnace and cutters were lowered and rigged and kept on constant patrol.[10]

The fleet remained at James' Island for sixteen days. The *Essex* took on water and supplies from her prizes, the carpenters repaired the boats and Sailmaker

Captain David Porter (1780–1843). Portrait in oils possibly by John Trumbull. US Naval Academy Museum, Annapolis, Maryland.

 A controversial, hot-headed character, Porter saw action in the Caribbean, the Pacific and the Mediterranean. As well as serving his native United States, the Bostonian was employed by the Mexican Navy and later worked in Istanbul as US trade consul to the Ottoman Empire.

USS *Essex*. Watercolour attributed to Joseph Howard. Peabody Essex Museum, Salem, Massachusetts.

A 32-gun frigate launched in 1799, the *Essex* carried a complement of 315 men and boys. She served in the Indian Ocean during the Quasi-War with France, becoming the first US navy vessel to cross the Equator and round the Cape of Good Hope, and in the Mediterranean during the First Barbary War.

David Glasgow Farragut (1801–70). Portrait in oils. William Swain. National Portrait Gallery, Washington.

Pictured above as a 38-year-old on his way to becoming the United States' first admiral, Farragut participated in the *Essex*'s Pacific cruise as an eleven-year-old midshipman. Brave and resourceful, he was memorably referred to as 'three pounds of uniform and seventy pounds of fight'.

Commodore John Downes (1786–1854). Portrait in oils. Canton Historical Society, Massachusetts.

Downes served as Porter's First Lieutenant. Efficient and reliable, he had proved his bravery during the First Barbary War and, despite humble beginnings, would rise to the rank of commodore.

The LIBERTY of the SUBJECT.

The Liberty of the Subject [the Press Gang]. **Caricature. Print. W. Humphrey & James Gillray, 1779, National Maritime Museum, Greenwich, London.**

Impressment was viewed as a necessary evil by the Admiralty. Without it the Royal Navy would not have been able to meet its country's demands. Nevertheless, the press remained controversial at home and was also a major cause of the War of 1812.

THE ESSEX CAPTURING THE ALERT.

The Essex *capturing the* Alert. Taken from *Our Country in War* by Murat Halstead (1998).

Porter captured the 20-gun *Alert* **on 13 August 1812 while returning from a Caribbean commerce-raiding mission. As the United States' first success over a British ship of war, the capture won Porter numerous plaudits, but was later overshadowed by a string of single-ship frigate victories.**

Capture of *La Néréide* by HMS *Phoebe* on 20 December 1797. Oil on canvas. Thomas Whitcombe. National Maritime Museum, Greenwich.

With a career spanning some twenty years, the 36-gun HMS *Phoebe* was one of the Royal Navy's most successful frigates. She saw action in the French Revolutionary War, the Napoleonic Wars and the War of 1812. Her crews would receive six clasps to their General Service Medals.

Captain James Hillyar (1769–1843). Miniature. Artist unknown. National Maritime Museum, Greenwich.

Eleven years Porter's senior, Hillyar was vastly experienced. Calm and calculating where the Bostonian was impetuous, his measured approach would prove superior in Valparaiso Bay.

Allen F. Gardiner (1794–1851). Taken from *The Story of Commander Allen Gardiner, R.N*, sixth edition, John W. Marsh and W. H. Stirling (London, James Nisbett & co. 1883).

An educated and observant midshipman, Gardiner compiled a journal of his impressions during the *Phoebe*'s voyage. Although originally intended for publication, it remained unknown to naval historian for some time.

Signatures of Captain James Hillyar and the *Phoebe*'s First Lieutenant, William Ingram. Taken from the *Phoebe*'s Muster Roll, ADM 36/16809, National Archives, Kew.

Although no portrait of Ingram could be sourced, his signature appears several times in the primary sources. 'A tall, handsome man', the lieutenant became engaged during the voyage, but was mortally wounded in Valparaiso Bay.

Portsmouth Point. Hand-coloured Etching. Thomas Rowlandson. 1811. National Maritime Museum, Greenwich.

Rowlandson's caricature, depicting the crew of a man-of-war saying their farewells, gives an idea of the atmosphere at Portsmouth in the age of sail. The *Phoebe* resupplied here before embarking on her Pacific cruise.

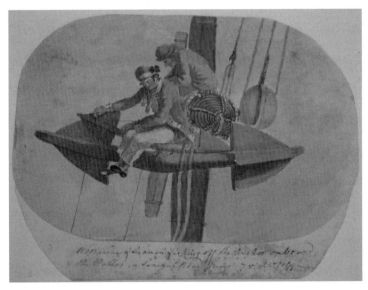

'A Marine & Seaman fishing off the Anchor on board the *Pallas* in Senegal Road, jany 1795.' Watercolour. Gabriel Bray. National Maritime Museum, Greenwich.

This intimate scene provides an unusual glimpse of shipboard life in the Royal Navy during the age of sail.

Saturday Night at Sea. **George Cruikshank. 1841. National Maritime Museum, Greenwich.**
　　This image gives an impression of the confined nature of life below decks. Note the mess
table suspended from the deck above and the guns tightly stowed.

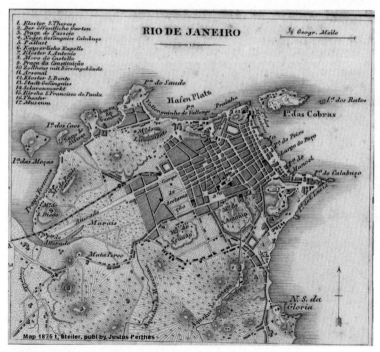

A nineteenth-century map of Rio de Janeiro.
　　Rio was the headquarters of the Royal Navy's Brazil Station and a major stopping-off
point on the *Phoebe*'s cruise. Note the Valongo Slave Market at number 14 and the main square
near number 5.

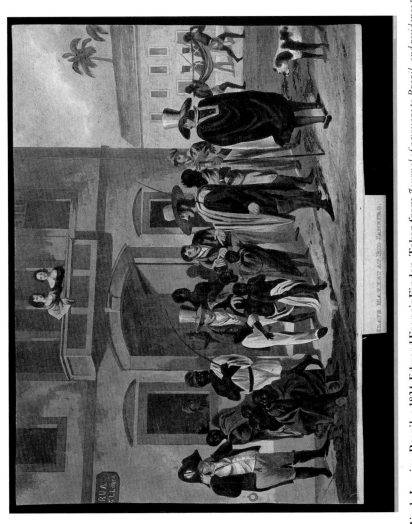

Slave Market in Rio de Janeiro, Brazil, c.1824. Edward Francis Finden. Taken from *Journal of a voyage to Brazil, and residence there . . .* by Maria Graham (London, J. Murray, 1824).

Midshipman Gardiner, a budding evangelical and the product of emancipation-era England, was appalled by the scenes at Valongo, one of the principal slave markets in the Americas.

Vista de la Bahia de Valparaiso. 1830. Copy of a lithograph by E. Dumont. Museo Histórico Nacional de Chile.

By the early nineteenth century, Valparaiso was one of the most important ports in the Southern Pacific. As the Chilean patriots distanced themselves from Spain, the port saw the arrival of an increasing number of foreign merchants, whalers and men of war.

Lima, Plaza de Armas. 1854.

In the early nineteenth century, Lima was still the hub of Spanish South America. Several officers from HMS *Phoebe* visited the city and its environs in December 1813.

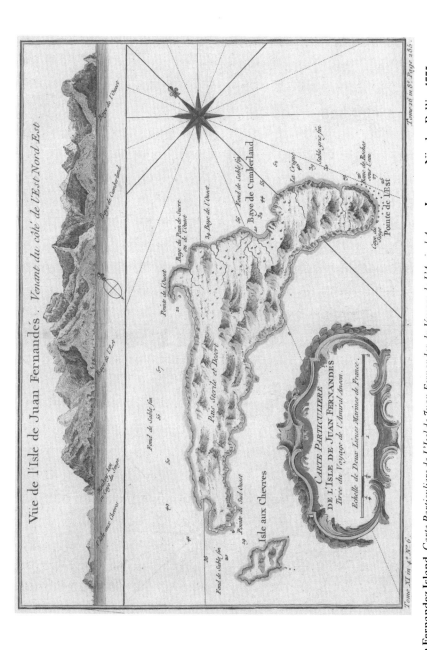

Vüe de l'Isle de Juan Fernandés. *Venant du côté de l'Est Nord Est*

Tome XI in 4.° N.° 6.

Tome 26 in 8.° Page 265.

CARTE PARTICULIERE
DE L'ISLE DE JUAN FERNANDES
Tirée du Voyage de l'Amiral Anson.

Echelle de Deux Lieues Marines de France.

Juan Fernandez Island. *Carte Particuliere de L'Isel de Juan Fernandez du Voyage de L'Amiral Anson.* Jacques Nicolas Bellin. 1775.

Juan Fernandez Island had been a popular provisioning point for pirates, whalers, privateers, men of war and explorers since the sixteenth century. In 1741 Admiral Anson called in having rounded Cape Horn, as did the *Phoebe* in 1813.

Engraving. 1744. *Taken from Relacion histórica del viaje a la América Meridional* by Antonio y Jorge Juan de Ulloa.

Chile was the breadbasket of the Spanish Pacific colonies. By the second decade of the nineteenth century, however, stirrings of independence had begun to reduce inter-colonial trade.

'*At daylight we saw a shoal of sperm whales.*' Drawing. Perry G. Wing. 1854. New Bedford Whaling Museum, Massachusetts.

Whaling was big business. With the Americans looking to gain hegemony, the British Pacific whaling fleet made an attractive target, both financially and strategically, for the USS *Essex*.

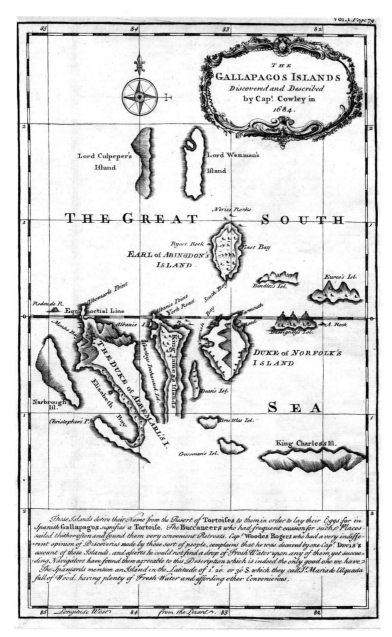

Map of the Galapagos Islands. 1684. Taken from *A Chronological History of the Discoveries in the South Sea or Pacific Ocean* by **James Burney**.

   The inaccuracies in the map above illustrate Captain Porter's frustrations when attempting to navigate the archipelago in 1813. Dead calms, changeable currents and unpredictable winds added to his difficulties.

Draw by Capt Porter   Engraved by W. Strickland

Mouina.
Chief Warrior of the Tayehs.

Mouina. Chief Warrior of the Tayehs [*sic*]. Engraved, c.1813, by William Strickland. Taken from *Journal of a Cruise made to the Pacific* by David Porter.

The Taeehs of Nuka Hiva were initially Porter's allies and Mouina took part in several joint operations against his tribe's traditional enemies, the Happah. The relationship later soured.

Marquesan War Canoe. Engraved, c.1813, by William Strickland. Taken from *Journal of a Cruise made to the Pacific* by David Porter.

Porter's first raid against the Typees, the largest tribe on Nuka Hiva, was led by the USS *Essex Junior*, accompanied by four ship's boats and twenty Marquesan war canoes.

Commodore Porter off Nuka Hiva. Engraved, c.1813, by William Strickland. Taken from *Journal of a Cruise made to the Pacific* by David Porter.

The *Essex* is depicted at anchor in Port Anna Maria alongside her prizes. Fort Madison can be seen on the hilltop to the left and the Taeeh settlement is on the right.

USS Essex vs *HMSs Phoebe and Cherub*. Engraved, c.1813, by William Strickland. Taken from *Journal of a Cruise made to the Pacific* by David Porter.

Porter's depiction of the battle gives the impression that the *Cherub* (far right) was closely engaged. From an examination of the primary sources it is apparent that this was only the case at the beginning of the engagement.

View of Valparaiso Bay. 2015. Author's collection.

The anchorage where the *Essex* and her prizes moored is to the left of the picture. The battle took place beyond the first point on the right.

William Morgan's General Service Medal. Image taken from DNW Auctioneers website. http://www.dnw.co.uk/

Known to his shipmates as the 'Methodist Parson', Morgan was a marine who ran the *Phoebe*'s lower deck prayer meetings. He saw action at Tamatave as well as Valparaiso Bay, rising to the rank of corporal before being dismissed 'unserviceable' due to 'wounded thighs' in December 1814.

H	K	F	Courses	Winds	Sigh	Rem^ks &c^a Monday 28th March 1814

P.M. Continued

At 4.10, made Signal to prepare to Anchor with Springs. — Up Courses. — Came on board the Essex's Boat with M^r O Brien 1st Mate, & Mr Porter and Boats Crew of the Phœbe. — Essex ahead one Mile; Standing towards her Quarter. — Emp^d ranging Cables and preparing Springs, as we drew into the Bay; Ship broke off in the Squalls, so as to prevent us bringing the Enemy to close Action, as we intended. — At 4.20, having fetched as near as the Wind permitted, commenced firing about half Gun-Shot off, St Antonio S W½W 5 Miles, Close to us on the Starboard Quarter. — Enemy red^d our fire with his aftermost Guns & Stern Chasers. — At 4.40, very near the Shore, ceased firing; Wore round & came to the Wind on the larboard Tack Mainsail much cut, Jib-boom badly wounded Fore, Main, & Mizen Stay. Shot away, and other Rigging damaged. — Emp^d repairing damages. — At 4.50 Tacked Ship, furled the Mainsail. — At 5 hailed the Cherub, informed him of our intending to Anchor, and ordered him to keep under Weigh. — At 5.35 Commenced firing with the Bow Guns on the Enemy which was returned. — Light Airs inclinable to Calm. — At 5.50 the Enemy cut his Cable, Set his Jib Fore Topsail & Foresail; Wind becoming light & Variable, endeavoured to keep our broadside to bear on the Enemy. — At 6 the firing was hot

Master's Log Book, HMS *Phoebe*. Entry for 28 March 1814. Taken from ADM 52/4236, National Archives, Kew.

Sailing Master Miller's entry for the Battle of Valparaiso is particularly detailed. Alongside the *Cherub*'s log book, the reports written by Captain Hillyar, and the accounts penned by Midshipmen Gardiner and Thornton Junior and Lieutenant Sampson, it provides a counterbalance to the US accounts previously relied on.

IN MEMORY OF
THE
OFFICERS AND SEAMEN SLAIN
ONBOARD THE U.S. FRIGATE
ESSEX IN THIS HARBOR IN
AN ENGAGEMENT WITH H.B.M
FRIGATE PHOEBE AND BRIG CHERUB
MARCH 28 1814
LT. JAMES P. WILMER
LT. JOHN C. COWELL

REUBEN MARSHALL GUNNER
FRANCIS BLAND Q MASTER
HENRY KENNEDY BOSN MATE
WILLIAM SMITH BOSN MATE

COMMANDING OFFICER CAPTAIN DAVID PORTER
SHIP MOTTO "FREE TRADE AND SAILORS' RIGHTS"
KILLED OR DIED
  FROM WOUNDS   58
  MISSING   31
  WOUNDED   65
  TOTAL CREW   255

Memorial to the USS *Essex*, 2015. Author's collection.

The memorial above stands on a hill overlooking Valparaiso Bay in the Cementario de los Disidentes. The site office also records the burials of Sailing Master Cowell and First Lieutenant William Ingram. Their resting places can no longer be found.

Navarro fixed the rigging, sewed a new main-topsail for the *Essex* and made 'a considerable quantity of cordage from old rope'. Others scrubbed the seaweed and barnacles from the frigate's hull and rowed her powder supply ashore for 'sunning and sifting'. Nearly a third was too damp to use, perhaps as a result of the rudder coat being ruptured whilst rounding the Horn. The rest was packed in new barrels and the deficiency made up with supplies from the prizes. The *Seringapatam* was cleared of 'cumbrous articles' and painted with a broad yellow streak around her hull to resemble the *Essex*, while the frigate's appearance was 'changed entirely' and the *Greenwich* was given 'the aspect of a sloop of war'. Those not thus employed were allowed ashore in shifts. Four boatloads were landed daily. Some explored for water, others served as shepherds for the fleet's flock of sheep and goats or laid in a stock of giant tortoises.[11]

Formed by volcanic eruption, James' Island was made up of mountains of cinder and ash. In places a thin soil supported straggling shrubs and the odd tree. Elsewhere were fields of sharp lava which ruined the men's shoes. Far from being the paradise of 'delightful groves' and 'rivulets of water' which James Colnet had described on his visit twenty years earlier, Porter found it to be a sterile land. His men were unable to find any water even though the island abounded in animal life. Sea iguanas basked on the rocky shores; their land-dwelling cousins roamed the interior; flamingos and teal 'of an excellent quality' inhabited a salt lagoon just beyond the beach; the specie of dove which had proved such easy game on Charles' Island was readily found; and pelicans, boobies, mocking birds, falcons and petrels and a small snake were seen. Giant tortoises were present in large numbers, especially round a beach to the northeast, where the females laid their eggs. The Americans took twenty to thirty a day, weighing on average 60lbs. Stacked on their shells on the *Essex*'s quarterdeck under an awning put up to provide shade, they were left for four days to void their stomachs before being stowed in the hold. In total fourteen tons were taken on board. Adding to the Essexes' ecological crimes, one morning the goatherd found that his charges had absconded along with the sheep. 'Several persons were sent in different directions, for two or three days, to search for them', Porter recalled, 'but without success.'[12]

Early on the morning of 10 August two of Porter's most promising young officers fought a duel, the reason for which is unknown. Lieutenant Gamble of the marines, the tough disciplinarian who had recently distinguished himself in his first sea battle, and Acting Fourth Lieutenant John S. Cowan, a 21-year-old native of Baltimore, met, along with their seconds just beyond the beach as their comrades slept on. Aside from pointing out the fact that the combat took place without his knowledge, the only detail Porter added in his journal was that on the third fire, Cowan was shot dead. 'A neat and simple structure', consisting of a post on which a bottle was suspended, was constructed to mark the spot where he fell by Lieutenant McKnight.[13]

On 20 August Porter set sail for Banks' Bay. Arriving two days later, he left his prizes at anchor within the Basin with orders to establish a signalling post onshore and await his return, before setting out on a final, solitary cruise of the archipelago on the 24th. Heading south, the *Essex* sailed between Narborough and Albemarle. Seal played around her as she passed. Porter spent four days beating round the southern point against a rapid current until the wind hauled to the southward on 29 August and swept the frigate round. Two days later Porter called in at Charles' Island to leave a letter informing Downes to rendezvous with the fleet at the Basin. The next day, at Stephen's Bay, the men gathered prickly pear to turn into jam and hunted turtle and seal. The former were stowed as provisions, the latter were skinned for moccasins and hats. Others went inland and found a lagoon alive with teal and plover. None were caught, however, as Porter had banned the use of gunpowder to preserve supplies. On 7 September the *Essex* reached Hood's Island. Having filled the hold with fish and taken fifty tortoises, which were 'very fat and delicious', Porter left another note for Lieutenant Downes and sailed on.[14]

Three thousand miles to the south-southeast, Downes was preparing to set sail from Valparaiso. The situation in Chile had changed since his last visit. A state of open warfare existed with royalist Peru; and the task force which Abascal had dispatched under Brigadier Antonio Pareja had become increasingly active in the south. Although the royalist advance had been halted following the strategically indecisive Battle of San Carlos, fought near Chillan on 15 May 1813 and the patriots had managed to recapture the port of Concepción, the Carrera brothers were starting to lose the support of their more conservative backers. The cracks in the coalition were beginning to show.[15]

Valparaiso had been in a state of high alert since April 1813. Instructed to build a navy to counter the depredations of the Peruvian privateers, Governor Lastra had purchased the *Colt*, the American brig that the Essexes had seen in March and another armed US merchantman named the *Pearl*. The ships, which largely retained their original crews, were renamed the *Potrillo* and *Perla* and on 2 May sailed out to attack the *Warren*, a blockading Peruvian privateer which also had a largely American crew. The encounter ended in disaster. No sooner had the *Perla* closed to within cannon range than her crew switched sides. Joining forces with their compatriots in the *Warren*, they captured the *Potrillo* and sailed to Callao with their prize.[16]

By the time of Downes' arrival, Valparaiso had the mentality of a city under siege. Commerce had ground to a halt, factionalism had turned the inhabitants against one another and rumours of an imminent royalist assault abounded. Although the Americans' reception was friendly, it proved impossible to sell the prizes and a storm on 14 August saw the *Policy* and *Montezuma* collide after the latter had dragged her anchor. Two of her 4-pounders were lost overboard and the crew were forced to cut two cables. Downes' men spent the next four weeks stripping their prizes and purchasing supplies. Having sent the *Policy* to the United States as instructed, the lieutenant chose to leave the rest of the prizes in Valparaiso and return to the Galapagos with the *Essex Junior* to rendezvous with Porter as arranged.

At some stage during their stay, the Americans learnt of President Madison's re-election. They also heard of the capture of HMS *Macedonian* by USS *United States* and of the victories of the US sloops-of-war *Wasp* and *Hornet* over HMS *Frolic* and *Peacock*. Downes also received a letter for Porter from William Gilchrist Miller, the American vice trade consul at Buenos Ayres, explaining that HMS *Phoebe*, *Cherub* and *Raccoon* and an unnamed 20-gun storeship had left Rio de Janeiro in July 1813 'in pursuit of the *Essex*' and the lieutenant gathered further intelligence from the ships anchored in port. The US whalers *Lima*, *Chili*, *William Penn*, *Charles* and *George* were all seeking shelter from Peruvian predators as were two English merchantmen, the *Emily*, which had arrived with a cargo of firearms for the Chilean patriots on 25 June and the *Mary-Ann*, a 'richly-laden' former East-Indiaman bound for England. While Captain Dart of the *Emily* kept his intentions a secret, Downes overheard the captain of the *Mary-Ann* explaining he intended to sail the Marquesas before rounding the Horn, a piece of intelligence Porter would find particularly interesting. On 8 September the *Essex Junior* set sail accompanied by the whalers *Policy*, *Chili*, *George*, *Lima* and *William Penn*. Once out of sight of Valparaiso, the whalers stood southwards for Cape Horn, while the *Essex Junior* stood north-northwest. Downes planned to follow the Peruvian coast up to Callao before turning west for the Galapagos.[17]

Leaving Hood's Island on 13 September, Porter ran down for Charles' Island, before sweeping on to the southernmost point of Albemarle. The next morning a stranger was spotted to the south. 'On going aloft with my glass, I could perceive that she was ... under very easy sail', Porter recalled, '[and] apparently lying to.' With the stranger directly to windward, Porter was determined not to panic her into flight. 'I ... directed the fore and main royal-yards to be sent down', he explained, 'and the masts to be housed, the ports to be shut in and the ship to be disguised ... as a merchantman and kept plying to windward ... under easy sail.' By noon the Americans had closed to within five miles. Their quarry was in the process of cutting up a sperm whale and 'from her general appearance', seemed to be the same ship that had recently eluded the Americans near Abington Island. With the *Essex* four miles off, the stranger took flight, but it was too late. 'After firing six or eight shot', Porter recalled, 'she bore down under our lee and struck her colours.' To the Bostonian's delight, she was indeed the ship that had previously escaped: the *Sir Andrew Hammond*, a 301-ton whaler of thirty-one crew and twelve guns registered to William Mellish, the same merchant-cum-politician who had owned the *Seringapatam*.[18]

After taking possession, Porter had his new prize searched for supplies. As well as an abundance of beef, pork, bread, water and wood, the whaler was carrying 'two puncheons of choice Jamaica spirits', a particularly welcome addition as the Essexes had been without liquor since the celebrations on 4 July. Another valuable commodity was the freshly-butchered strips of unrefined spermaceti blubber covering the main deck. Informed that they would produce as many as ninety barrels of oil worth $2,000–$3,000, Porter ordered Chaplain Adams and a prize crew of former whalers 'to try out and stow away the oil with all possible expedition'.[19]

The *Essex* and *Sir Andrew Hammond* arrived in the Basin on 15 September. Having grown 'heartily tired' of such a 'desolate and dreary place', where the only occurrence of note was the nightly wailing of a nearby sea-lion colony, the men celebrated the frigate's return. Their joy was complete when the recently captured Jamaican spirits were doled out, but Porter's indulgence backfired. 'Whether it was the great strength of the rum or the length of time they had been without, I cannot say; but our seamen were so much affected ... that many were taken to their hammocks perfectly drunk; and ... there was scarcely a seaman in the ship but what was in some degree intoxicated.' Discipline suffered as a result. James Rynard, the rabble-rousing quarter-master who had come to prominence after the *Essex* had left Porto Praya eight months before, was the chief culprit. 'I had directed him to proceed to superintend some duty on board one of the prizes', Porter recalled. 'He appeared ... somewhat intoxicated and insolently told me he had not been sent from the ship in a proper manner ... I directed him to stay aft on the quarter-deck until he was sober. He attempted, however, ... to rush by me. His dinner was taken on deck to him by his messmates; this he threw overboard in the presence of the officer of the deck and at the same time demanded ... to go below.' Porter had Rynard put in irons and decided to discharge him from the service. 'I ... directed the purser to make out his accounts and send him on board the *Seringapatam*, until we should arrive at some place where he could be put on shore.' The incident had a beneficial effect. 'It rendered every man in the ship sober, attentive and active in the discharge of his duty and assiduous to please.'[20]

With his authority reasserted, Porter considered his next move. The *Essex* was in need of careening. Her copper bottom was coming away and the hull was alive with barnacles and seaweed. A second issue was the rats infesting the hold. 'They had increased so fast as to become a most dreadful annoyance' and were 'destroying ... provisions, eating through ... water casks . . ., getting into the magazine and destroying ... cartridges ... and occasioning considerable destruction of ... clothing, flags, [and] sails.' A safe spot, with access to fresh water and provisions and far from passing British cruisers, was required to remedy these problems. With indiscipline increasing, Porter also wanted to give his men some well-earned recreation. The Marquesas Islands fit the bill. Over 4,000 miles west of the Galapagos, they were suitably remote while the attentions of the local women, famed for what Western sailors considered loose morals, would provide the men with the tonic they required.[21]

With Downes' deadline of 2 October approaching, Porter prepared for sea. The *New Zealander* was re-caulked, the *Sir Andrew Hammond* painted and 'put in order', the sailors re-assigned amongst the prizes, and the supplies and provisions, including the tortoises taken from Hood's Island, redistributed. By 28 September, the work was finished and attention turned to the lookout post on the hill to the north of Banks' Bay. Two days later the *Essex Junior* was spotted and at 3 p.m. Downes anchored alongside the flotilla. The news from Valparaiso soon spread round the fleet. While the men celebrated the United States' naval victories, they also no doubt piqued Porter's pride. The latest captures meant that the Bostonian was in an unenviable minority of active US frigate captains yet to take a major prize. Also of interest was Downes' report on the British squadron bound for the Pacific. Porter had met Captain Hillyar while on service in the Mediterranean in 1807. If the Bostonian could take the *Phoebe*, the feat would be even more impressive than the captures made by his peers. A final note of interest was the intelligence concerning the *Mary-Ann*. The news hardened Porter's resolve to make the Marquesas his next destination. At 5 p.m. on 2 October, the six-ship flotilla sailed out of Bank's Bay.[22]

Chapter 9

Tragedy at Tumbez: HMS *Phoebe*, 3 October 1813 – 10 December 1813

At daylight on 3 October 1813 the lookouts on HMS *Phoebe* and *Cherub* sighted land. Cape Blanco, a sheer sandstone cliff with 'a bold shore' rising out of the azure blue of the Pacific, put a homesick Gardiner in mind of Cornwall's Lizard Point. At 8 a.m., with the ships running northwest along a low, sandy coast, backed by the distant Andes, a stranger was spotted in shore. Two shots from the *Phoebe*'s bow chasers brought her to and a boat was sent across to board her. She proved to be a Spanish brig from Panama bound for Paita. At 10 a.m. the flotilla made all sail and Hillyar mustered his men for divine service. Seven hours later, noting the colour of the water had changed, the *Phoebe*'s deck officer sounded in five fathoms with a muddy bottom. Hauling off shore, the ships ran out to sea, before dropping anchor at 6 p.m. in ten fathoms. That evening Hillyar held divine service for the second time. The Cherubs, once again, were left to their own devices.[1]

At 6 a.m. the next day the signal to weigh was raised at the *Phoebe*'s masthead. Intending to run up to the Island of the Dead for supplies, Hillyar sailed north sounding in 11 to 16 fathoms. At 10 a.m. a boat tested the current which was found to set three-quarters of a knot to the south and that afternoon, with the ships still a few leagues from their destination, a boat was observed off the weather bow. Firing a gun to signal for a pilot, Hillyar tacked and at 4 p.m. hove to as a local fisherman was brought on board. 'We were informed that [the Island of the Dead] was not inhabited', Gardiner recalled, 'and that from that station it would be difficult to bear out of the bay with the sea breeze.' Advised that 'the best anchorage ... was off the River Tumbez', Hillyar spent the next two hours beating up towards the river. At 6 p.m., a league from the bar where the sea broke 'with great violence', the ships moored in seven fathoms, the *Phoebe* with an open hawse to the westward holding her against the surge of fresh water rushing out to sea. That evening the pursers checked their biscuit stores. The *Phoebe* had sixty-nine days' supply remaining while the *Cherub* had forty-eight, prompting Hillyar to put both ships on half rations.[2]

The next morning, with the equatorial light streaming in through the stern windows, Hillyar wrote to Brigadier Juan Vasco y Pascual, the governor of Guayaquil. The letter asked about the Englishmen 'Porter had made prisoner, biscuit & news'. The ships' boats were lowered and sent in shore to gather fresh water. Approaching at low tide between two exposed shoals, the men sounded the river mouth before rowing two miles upstream where Gardiner found a spot with 'clear and excellent' water. When they returned to the bay that afternoon, the tide had come in and the shoals were covered with violent breakers. The first boats passed safely, but at 8.15 p.m. the last was flipped and its crew thrown into the surf. 'All [were] providentially saved', Gardiner recalled and by sunset had reached the ships where Third Lieutenant Jago and Purser Surflen congratulated Gardiner on his safe return.[3]

The next morning the boats watered and gathered firewood while one proceeded thirteen miles upriver to purchase oxen, fruit and vegetables at Tumbez. On the *Phoebe*, Sailmaker Millery and his crew repaired an awning which stretched from the rigging over the frigate's deck. That afternoon the wood and water was stowed and at sunset the boat from Tumbez returned. As well as oxen and vegetables, she carried a solitary Englishman found at the village, perhaps one of Porter's captives who had been released on parole. 'The accounts given us by the Spanish brig [on 29 September] respecting the enemy were now authenticated', Gardiner recalled.

> The *Essex* had been here in the latter end of ... [June], but they could not give us any certain information concerning their subsequent proceedings. It was however generally supposed that she was either at the Gallipagoes or cruising to the windward off the coast of Chili. They had expected us here for some time and orders had been issued all along the coast to supply us with every provision. The greater part of the prisoners [which Porter had released at Tumbez on 27 June] ... had been sent to Lima, a number had volunteered on board a Spanish Privateer and a few yet remained at Guayaquil.[4]

On the morning of 7 October Gardiner visited Tumbez. A local carnival was taking place and the Indians had dressed up 'in a most singular and ridiculous manner, with silk mantles, feathers in their heads, silver caps on their knees, & looking glasses on their breasts. Some wore masks', the midshipman recalled, 'others had their faces painted ... [and] all held in the left hands a little effigy of a woman, probably the Virgin Mary. Thus equipped, they formed several companies and went about the town performing, rather than dancing to the sound of a drum and fife, which were both played by one man ... To this simple music they moved round in a circle, keeping tune with their feet and exerting every limb with an expression and grace, which we little expected to find among these rude people.' Gardiner was also struck by the mother of the town's priest, 'a fine, interesting, old woman' who was 'extremely grateful' for a gift of 'a few Spanish Testaments and other religious books' Hillyar had sent to her son.[5]

After purchasing oranges, limes, pumpkins and potatoes, Gardiner and his companions rowed back to the bay early the next morning. October 9th dawned bright and clear. The *Phoebe*'s butcher slaughtered two oxen. The men received fresh beef with their vegetables and a few got a prized piece of liver. At 7 a.m. a boat was sent to Tumbez to settle the accounts. Intending to combine the trip with a spot of fowling upriver, Third Lieutenant Jago finished his morning prayers and set off with Purser Surflen. It was a decision which would cost the devout young Devonian his life. Half an hour after leaving the frigate, his boat was swamped on the bar. The officer of the watch immediately sent the rest of the *Phoebe*'s boats to aid the men struggling in the surf. Most of the crew were saved, but Jago, Surflen and Joseph Findley, an eighteen-year-old from Yorkshire who was amongst the men pressed at Plymouth in February, were lost. The boats dragged the riverbed for their bodies, but it was thought the tide had carried them out to sea and at sunset the search was called off. That night there was considerable speculation as to the cause of the deaths. 'Whether they were drowned or eaten by the Alligators is uncertain', one officer opined. '[As] several of these frightful creatures were seen … basking … in the sun and both these gentlemen being good swimmers, one may be led to conclude they reached the shore only to die a more wretched death.'[6]

At 11 a.m. the next morning Hillyar remembered the dead at divine service. That afternoon a brig arrived from Guayaquil to sell fresh fruit and Hillyar made three promotions. Nicholas Nickenson, captain's clerk, was made acting purser, Henry J. Gardner, the *Phoebe*'s nineteen-year-old master's mate from Ayr, was made acting Third Lieutenant and Samuel Thornton Junior, a sixteen-year-old First Class volunteer, was raised to the rank of Ordinary Seaman. Thornton's promotion saw his pay increase from £9 per year to £1 5s 6d a month, not that he needed the money. As the third and youngest son of the MP for the County of Surrey, Director of the Bank of England and Governor of Guy's Hospital and the Russian Company, Thornton was rich by any standards. Having turned down the chance to follow his older brothers to Trinity College and his mother's plans for him to enter the ministry, he had joined HMS *Amazon*, a 38-gun frigate commanded by Captain William Parker, at the age of eleven. As well as witnessing the celebrated destruction of a French convoy near the Penmark Rocks, Thornton had taken part in several cutting-out operations with another young officer who would go on to join the *Phoebe*, First Lieutenant William Ingram. He had then joined the *Armide*, another 38-gun frigate, before being transferred to the *Phoebe* shortly before her current cruise. Like many of the younger crewmembers, the sixteen-year-old messed with Gunner Lawson in the gunroom. Thornton could not have wished for a more experienced mentor. A veteran of fifteen years' service, Lawson had been bloodied at the Battle of the Nile aboard HMS *Swiftsure* and had fought at Cape Ortegal and the Basque Roads. Despite the discrepancies in their age, experience and background, a friendship had blossomed which would last until the end of Lawson's days.[7]

On 11 October the *Phoebe*'s new purser was put to work. As Surflen's replacement, the Admiralty would hold Nickenson financially responsible for the ship's supplies, so his first order of business was to conduct a general survey. Touring the hold with a hooded lantern while the purser and master of HMS *Cherub* acted as witnesses, Nickenson noted that the *Phoebe* held 18,584lbs of bread, 1,496 gallons of wine, 2,009 gallons of spirits, 816 pieces of salt beef, 616 pieces of salt pork, 674lbs of suet, 1,370lbs of cocoa, 100 barrels of oatmeal, 1,100lbs of rice, twenty barrels of pumpkins, 5,750lbs of sugar, 830 gallons of vinegar, 130 bushels of peas, 1,712lbs of tobacco, 336lbs of raisins, eighteen barrels of punch, twelve live oxen, 100lbs of fresh vegetables, 200 oranges and thirty-five bottles of lime juice.

That afternoon another brig arrived from Guayaquil. On board was Señor Villanueva, aide of the governor of Guayaquil, who informed Hillyar that the *Essex* had called in five weeks previously, having taken thirteen prizes. In contrast to local opinion, which held that Porter had returned to the Galapagos Islands, Villanueva believed the Americans had set out for home via Valparaiso. With Villanueva were four of Porter's former prisoners, all that the authorities at Guayaquil had been able to muster. After being questioned, two of them, being 'on their beam-ends' as naval parlance would have it, chose to join up. Both were rated able seamen. Charles Turner, a 22-year-old from Rotherhithe, Surrey, had been captured on board the *Greenwich* on 29 May.[8]

The next day Lieutenant Burrow of the marines wrote to Edward Jago – also an officer in the Royal Navy – informing him of his brother's death. The letter praised Nathaniel's character and devotion to God. Later a dispatch from Guayaquil arrived overland, informing Hillyar that the *Essex*, in company with seven armed ships, had been fired on by shore batteries at Callao eighteen days before. Even though more of Porter's ex-prisoners were *en route* from Guayaquil and only 2,200lbs of biscuit had been taken on board, Hillyar decided to proceed to Lima without delay. As well as ascertaining if the rumours of Porter's presence were true, the English captain had to fulfil the promise he had made to Lord Strangford concerning the British ships detained by the Peruvian authorities. *En route* he determined to pass by the bays 'where whalers generally fish' in the Galapagos. With the entire Peruvian coast closed to the *Essex*, the islands were the only place Porter could resupply. That night the Blue Peter was raised, the boats were hoisted and the Cherubs and the Phoebes prepared for sea. The gun crews were put through their paces and Lieutenant Burrow's marines practised firing musket volleys from the deck. At 8.30 a.m. the next morning, setting the courses and driver, Hillyar stood out to sea with the tide. With Jago's and Surflen's bodies left behind, their comrades 'took [their] leave of . . . [Tumbez], with emotions scarcely to be described'.[9]

The voyage to the Galapagos was a pleasant one. 'We had constantly a fine steady breeze', Gardiner recalled, 'and the most delightful weather.' Hillyar used the time to prepare for battle. The *Cherub*'s gunner turned the powder in the magazine, extra shot were hauled out of the *Phoebe*'s hold and every day the ocean echoed to the sound of live drill with the great guns. On 17 October Lieutenant Burrow wrote a second letter to Edward Jago, enclosing a copy of Nathaniel's will and explaining that he had been chosen as the executor. Over the next forty-eight hours the ships covered over 200 miles, sailing steadily to the northwest and on the morning of the 19th, the *Phoebe* sounded in 100 fathoms, indicating her imminent arrival at the islands. At 11 a.m. Ordinary Seaman Christopher Lambert, a twenty-year-old from Wexford who had fought at Tamatave, was punished with thirty-six lashes for striking a senior officer. The following day, as the ships altered course due west, Manuello Antonio, one of the Portuguese sailors who had volunteered on the *Cherub* in Rio de Janeiro, was given twelve lashes for fighting.[10]

Lookouts sighted the southernmost part of Albemarle at 4 p.m. on 21 October. As the ships passed to windward, Schoolmaster Brady made three sketches of the island. The first, drawn twenty-four miles to the south-southwest, showed thick black smoke spewing from a volcano on the southernmost point. As the ships beat up towards the island Captain Tucker punished two more seamen, Jonathon Lamb and Joseph Haimsely, with thirty-six and twelve lashes respectively for insolence to a superior officer, and at 5.15 p.m. Hillyar hove to five miles off Banks' Bay. The next morning, guided by Able Seaman Charles Turner, the former *Greenwich* taken on board at Tumbez, the ships ran into Elizabeth Bay. 'This is the general rendezvous for all the Whalers in these seas', Gardiner explained, 'but we found it quite deserted as the greater part of them had been captured . . . all the Capes and headlands we passed had very much the same appearance, rising inland to a great height and shelving gradually towards the sea.' Gardiner was keen to go onshore, but was disappointed. 'Our present situation would not allow of the smallest delay and having . . . [failed to find] our American friends, we hauled to the wind, without even sending a boat onshore and made sail . . . to Lima.'[11]

The fair winds which had carried the British to the Galapagos prevented them from returning to the continent. Blowing down from the Andes, they forced the flotilla to run southward parallel with the coast while the captains continued to prepare for the battle both longed for. The *Cherub*'s gunner turned the powder and made up cartridges, while a party of men beat the iron roundshot with hammers to even out any irregularities and ensure that they would fly true. On 25 October Hillyar and Tucker put their men on two-thirds rations of bread and meat, while allowing extra cocoa to be served. Three days later John Eves, the marine private who had been given two dozen lashes for stealing a pipe of wine at Cumberland Bay, fell overboard. The *Phoebe* hove to, the cutters and jollyboat were lowered, but due to 'the darkness of the night', as Gardiner explained, 'all our efforts to save him were ineffectual'.[12]

The contrary winds continued into November. The *Phoebe* and *Cherub* had long since passed the latitude of Lima, but Hillyar had little choice but to continue running down the coast as the weather deteriorated. Periods of calm were interspersed with violent squalls and heavy showers. On 13 and 14 November, the *Phoebe* was twice taken aback. The sails were plastered against the masts and several of the stays and spars split under the pressure. Wanting the *Phoebe* to look her best for the Peruvian viceroy, Hillyar had the main deck re-caulked; the quarterdeck scraped and painted, the ship's sides scrubbed, the Nelson Chequer on the hull retouched and the gunroom and ship's boats repainted. On 23 November, the men's prayers were answered. With the British ships at the latitude of 26° South, parallel with northern Chile, the wind swung round to the southeast. Piling on all sail, the *Phoebe* and *Cherub* turned north for Lima.[13]

Chapter 10

Death in Paradise: USS *Essex*, 4 October 1813 – 13 December 1813

With fresh breezes blowing from the southeast, on 4 October 1813 the American flotilla left the volcanoes of Albemarle behind. The next day, with the *Greenwich* springing her main topmast, it dawned on Porter that his prizes would cause him considerable delay. Not wishing to miss out on an opportunity of taking the *Mary-Ann*, he ordered Downes to sail ahead, before the 'richly laden' former East Indiaman left the Marquesas for the Atlantic. The next eighteen days passed uneventfully. A steady breeze blew out of the east, and with barely a cloud in the sky the sun beat down on the awnings stretched over the ships' decks and the temperature increased as they sailed westward accompanied by 'vast numbers' of flying fish. With the *Essex* leading, the *Greenwich*, *Seringapatam* and *Sir Andrew Hammond* became strung out behind while the dull-sailing *New Zealander* struggled to keep pace at the rear. A current, surging along at a rate of twenty-five miles a day, aided their progress.[1]

On 15 October, John Hughes, the boy recruited at Tumbez, had his fourteenth birthday, while the men speculated as to their destination. Soon afterwards Porter posted an official communique round the fleet. 'We are bound for the Western Islands, with two objects in view', he announced. 'First, that we may put the ship in a suitable condition to . . . take advantage of the most favourable season for our return home. Secondly, I am desirous that you should have some relaxation and amusement after being so long at sea, . . . If every person exerts himself to carry on the work of the ship . . . I shall allow you time to amuse yourselves on shore . . .' Porter's message had an immediate effect on morale. 'For the remainder of the voyage . . . [the men] could talk and think of nothing else but the amusements and novelties that awaited them in this new world.'[2]

Ever since Captain Cook's voyage to Tahiti in the *Endeavour* in 1771, the islands of the southern Pacific had held a special allure for Western sailors. Stories of their natural abundance and the sexual favours bestowed by their women were the stuff of fantasies. Uninhibited by the Christian West's preoccupation with sin, the Polynesians had a laissez-faire attitude to sex. Outside of the ruling classes, amongst whom issues of succession were paramount, neither pre-marital or extra-marital sex were frowned upon and a woman's choice and quantity of partners was not restricted by social mores or concepts of guilt and shame. From the age of six children of both sexes learned about sexual roles and techniques by direct observation. They were taught that intercourse was a pleasure. Even prepubescent children were not prohibited from indulging; young men were free to openly experiment with homosexuality and transvestitism; nudity was commonplace; couples had intercourse in the same rooms where their families' slept; and children born out of wedlock were readily accepted into society. When Western sailors first encountered South Sea Island societies they quickly took advantage and casual relationships with local women were commonplace.[3]

There was a another side to this island paradise, however. As well as tales of beguiling native women, early travellers to the Marquesas had warned of less appealing native traits. With no concept of private property, the islanders and their visitors had frequently fallen out with Westerners who accused them of theft. On a five-day visit during his second exploratory voyage in 1774, Cook had traded with islanders in the south of the archipelago, only for relations to sour when they began helping themselves to items from the *Resolution*. In the fallout at least one islander was killed. Captain Joseph Ingraham, an American fur trader and veteran of the Revolutionary War, reached the Marquesas on the brig *Hope* in 1791. His subsequent narrative commented on the islanders' habit of wearing jewellery made of human teeth, hair and skulls, leading him to conclude that they indulged in cannibalism. Since such early pioneers, Western visitations had become increasingly common. South Sea whalers regularly called in for provisions and the Marquesas were popular with American and British traders seeking sandalwood. Valued for its perfume when burned, the product, which was abundant on the islands, fetched a high price at the Chinese port of Canton.[4]

On 23 October, the man at the *Essex*'s masthead sighted land. 'A barren lump of rock inaccessible on all sides and about three miles in circuit', Hood's Island, named after Captain Cook's midshipman who had discovered it, had no source of water and was uninhabited. Porter hove to and waited off shore while his prizes came up. An hour later they sailed on for Ua Huka, a larger island just visible on the horizon fifty miles to the northwest. They arrived the next day. 'Its aspect, on first making it, was little better than the [Galapagos]', Porter observed, 'but on our nearer approach, [we could make out] . . . fertile valleys, whose beauties were heightened by the pleasant streams and clusters of houses and groups of natives on the hills inviting us to land.' Rounding the southeast point, the *Essex* came to while her prizes re-joined. Soon a 40-foot dugout outrigger canoe was spotted approaching. On board were eight natives. Copper-skinned, dressed in loincloths and covered in tattoos, they were over six feet tall and heavily muscled. Sitting in the bow whilst his companions paddled, one wore a headdress constructed of large yellow leaves. Although happy to run alongside the frigate, they refused to go on board. With Tameoy, the Tahitian, acting as his translator, Porter assured the islanders he meant no harm and lowered a bucket from the stern containing iron hoops, knives, fish-hooks and other metal articles prized on the islands. The natives were delighted. After taking the gifts they filled the bucket with fish and ornamental coconut fibre belts decorated with pigs' teeth. Repeating the word '*taya*' or friend, they invited Porter to accompany them onshore.[5]

With Lieutenant McKnight positioned beyond the breakers on one of the cutters, Porter was rowed in on his gig with Tameoy and a well-armed crew. A number of natives had gathered on the beach. Dropping their spears and clubs, they swam out and a nervous yet lively trade was conducted. In exchange for metal goods, Porter received breadfruit ornaments and several 'good sized pigs'. Throughout the morning the crowd on the beach steadily increased. Many began to dance and clap to show their appreciation. After two hours, Porter moved on to a nearby cove where fifty natives had gathered. Supposing them important due to their distinctive gorgets, black feather headdresses, whale-tooth necklaces and white paper cloaks, Porter gave them several gifts and Tameoy learnt they were tribal elders, led by Chief Othaûough, whose skin was so covered in tattoos as to appear almost entirely black. Having nothing to offer Porter in return, Othaûough suggested he make use of two attractive sixteen-year-old girls. Porter's journal neglects to inform us whether or not he accepted the offer.[6]

Returning to the frigate, Porter found a crowd of canoes had gathered. Several natives had been on board and 'expressed much surprise at the sight of the goats, sheep, dogs and other animals ... What seemed most to astonish them', Porter recalled, 'was one of the large Gallapagoes tortoises. It seemed as though they could not sufficiently feast their eyes on it: and to view it more at their ease they stretched themselves at full length on the deck.' With nightfall imminent, the natives were told to return to their boats while the Americans sailed round to the southwest point where Porter noted a large bay, secure against the prevailing winds, which faced onto a fertile valley. Offshore, the *Essex* and her prizes hove to for the night.[7]

At daylight the flotilla sailed thirty miles west to Nuka Hiva. The largest island of the archipelago, Nuka Hiva was also the most populous with 40,000 inhabitants divided into three dozen warring tribes. Porter dubbed it Madison's Island in honour of the president. By dawn, the *Essex* had reached Comptroller's Bay, a large, deep-water anchorage on the southeast coast indented with several small coves. '[Each] seemed to afford good landing ... several pleasant villages were situated near the beaches and the houses were interspersed among the trees of the valleys, which appeared highly cultivated and thickly inhabited'. Although several canoes sailed out from the beaches, none dared to approach, prompting Porter to sail west to Port Anna Maria, a bay separated from Comptroller's by a line of red rock cliffs. Flying American colours, the *Essex* arrived at 10 a.m. Two small islands, separated from the mainland by narrow channels barely wide enough for the passage of the natives' canoes, guarded the mouth of the bay, which was flanked by jungle covered mountains and extended four miles inland.[8]

Within minutes of the *Essex*'s arrival, a canoe crewed by three white men was spotted approaching. One was dressed in a loincloth. His skin was deeply tanned and covered in native tattoos. Suspecting him of being a deserter, Porter refused to allow the men to come alongside and the boat returned to the beach and was surrounded by armed natives. Fearing he had thrown fellow white men on the mercy of the savages, Porter led four boats ashore. The natives scattered as they landed and one of the white men approached. To Porter's 'great astonishment', this was John Minor Maury, an eighteen-year-old Virginian and a midshipman in the US Navy. Given a furlough in 1811, Maury had signed up on the *Pennsylvania Packet*, a merchantman involved in the Chinese opium trade. En route, her captain, another US navy officer on furlough named William Lewis, had left Maury and six others on Nuka Hiva to gather sandalwood, promising to return in two months' time. Lewis had since been blockaded by the British at Canton and had left Maury and his companions to their fate. Initially, the castaways had lived well. Befriended by the local Taeeh tribe, they constructed a treehouse concealed on top of four coconut palms accessible only by a rope ladder which was hauled up each night. In the intervening two years, however, five had been killed by the Taeeh's rivals, the Happahs. An aggressive tribe from the far side of the mountains forming the western boundary of Port Anna Maria, the Happahs could field 3,000 warriors compared to the Taeeh's 2,500. The tribes habitually raided each other's villages and plantations. The warfare was low-intensity and intermittent – weeks could pass without a single casualty – but had recently escalated due to the killing of a prominent Taeeh priest. Maury and a man named Baker were the only two Americans to have survived. Once Maury's identity had been vouched for by Lieutenant McKnight, who had formerly served with the Virginian, the two castaways were signed up on board the *Essex*.[9]

The third white man was an English 'beachcomber'. Known as 'Wilson', he had been on the Marquesas for 'many years'. According to Porter, Wilson spoke the local language 'with the same facility as his own and had become in every respect, except in colour, an Indian'. Porter warmed to Wilson. '[He was] an inoffensive, honest, good-hearted fellow', he opined, 'well disposed to render every service in his power ... whose only failing was a strong attachment to rum.' Wilson would prove a valuable ally. 'Without his aid I should have succeeded badly on the island', Porter admitted. 'His knowledge of the people ... removed all difficulties in our intercourse with them ... [and] even the landing of the marines did not seem to occasion any uneasiness.' The natives were particularly delighted by the antics of the marine drummer, William MacDonald, 'and the regular movements of [Gamble's men] occasioned much astonishment. They said they were spirits or beings of a class different from other men.'[10]

Porter's attention was drawn to the mountains. Happah war bands could be seen amongst the trees and the Bostonian learnt that the Taeehs' chief, Gattanewa, was directing the defence from a hilltop stronghold guarding the pass that connected the two tribes' territories. Arranging to have a messenger sent to the Happahs, Porter warned that he would retaliate if any further attacks were made during his stay and assured the Taeehs that he would protect them on condition they never approached the Americans armed. Thus, within minutes of his arrival, Porter had taken sides in an inter-tribal conflict which he knew nothing about.[11]

The American party on the beach soon lost all sense of order. Led away by smiling, scantily-clad, native women, men and officers dispersed into the surrounding woods. 'They had soon made themselves understood without the aid of interpreters', Porter recalled, 'and had wandered to the houses or perhaps the bushes ... to ratify their treaty, the negotiating of which neither cost them much time or trouble.' Far from disapproving of his men's conduct, Porter was keen to join in. 'A handsome young woman, of about eighteen years of age, her complexion fairer than common, her carriage majestic and her dress better and somewhat different from the other females, approached [me]', he recalled. 'Her glossy black hair and her skin were highly anointed with ... cocoa-nut oil and her whole person and appearance [was] neat and comely'. This was Piteenee, Gattanewa's granddaughter. '[She] was held in great estimation', Porter recorded, 'and I felt it would be necessary, from motives of policy, to pay some attentions to a personage so exalted.' Piteenee was unimpressed. 'With a coldness and hauteur which would have suited a princess', she rejected Porter's advances, leaving him to gather his men who were reluctantly rowed back to the *Essex*. Porter intended to stand out to sea for the night, but no sooner had he clambered up the gangway, than he was mobbed by requests for shore leave from his men. Despite unfavourable winds, Porter allowed the crew to kedge the ship in shore. A few hours later, the *Essex* was anchored half a mile from the beach where the natives had gathered once more.[12]

That afternoon the *Essex* was overrun by native women. 'Many ... had been in the habit of visiting [sailing] ships', Porter explained, '[and] had been taught ... some ... words of English, which they pronounced too plain to be misunderstood.' The women were free with their favours. 'Far from seeming to consider ... [sexual relations] an offence against modesty, they seemed to view it only as an accommodation to strangers who had claims on their hospitality ... They attached no shame to a proceeding which they not only considered as natural, but as an innocent and harmless amusement, by which no one was injured . . . With the common sailors and their girls', Porter recalled, 'all was helter skelter and promiscuous intercourse, every girl the wife of every man in the mess and frequently of every man in the ship: each one from time to time took such as suited his fancy.'[13]

Later, a message arrived informing Porter that Gattanewa had returned from the hills. 'To show [his] respect', Porter 'sent him . . . a fine large English sow.' Pleased with the gift, Gattanewa came aboard. Porter could barely disguise his disappointment. '[He was] an infirm old man of seventy years of age, destitute of every covering . . . except a clout about his loins and a piece of palm leaf tied about his head: a long stick seemed to assist him in walking; his face and body were as black as a negro's, from the quantity of tattooing, which entirely covered them and his skin was rough and appeared to be peeling off in scales, from the quantity of kava [an intoxicating root] in which he had indulged.' Porter had one of the great guns fired in the chief's honour, but Gattanewa was more interested in the Bostonian's collection of whales' teeth, an item which the Americans had been informed had considerable worth. Presented with one as a present, Gattanewa insisted that he and Porter exchange names, a Marquesan bonding ceremony, then asked the American to help him defeat the Happahs. 'To the first I immediately consented', Porter recalled, 'but told him . . . that I should not engage in any hostilities, unless the Happahs came into the valley.' At Gattanewa's further insistence, Porter promised to reconsider and the chief retired on shore for the night. Later, the *Essex Junior* was spotted at the head of the bay and that evening Downes came aboard. To Porter's disappointment, the lieutenant informed him that the *Mary-Ann* had been nowhere to be seen.[14]

On the morning of 26 October, Gattanewa sent Porter several small pigs, coconuts and plantains. The *Greenwich*, *Sir Andrew Hammond*, *Seringaptam* and *New Zealander* worked their way into the bay, while Porter constructed a rudimentary encampment on shore where the sailmakers, coopers and carpenters could work. An extensive plain situated between the territories of the Taeehs and Happahs, was selected. It was uninhabited and spotted with sixty-foot breadfruit trees whose canopies provided much-needed shade. The site commanded the countryside and dominated the bay. Guarded by the frigate's marines, the men constructed an outer wall from empty water casks and erected a large marquee in the interior were the ship's sails where taken for repair. With the curious Taeehs crowding round, the *Essex* was hauled in shore to within cannon range, while the prizes were lined up further out in the bay.

That afternoon a Happah war band came down the mountainside and laid waste to a Taeeh orchard of breadfruit trees. Porter fired several signal guns as a warning and raised the cornet from the *Essex*'s masthead to call the men ashore back on board. The noise stopped the Happahs in their tracks and, with Taeeh warriors forming up to counter-attack, they retreated over the mountains. A message arrived shortly afterwards. As the Americans had permitted the destruction of the trees, the Happahs considered them cowards and vowed to return and carry off their sails. In response Porter ordered one quarter of each ship's company to be armed and landed at 4 p.m. each afternoon to guard the camp. The men were to be permitted to 'stroll about the valley and amuse themselves' while ashore. Porter also had a tent erected in the encampment to serve as his personal quarters. He claimed his presence was needed to 'preserve order' and being ashore would improve his health after 'being so long confined to the ship'.[15]

The following morning Porter decided to pre-empt the Happahs' next move. Gattanewa agreed to have a cannon hauled up a nearby mountain to bombard the enemy positions and Downes was ordered to land one of the *Essex Junior*'s 6-pounders. The barrel and carriage were rowed ashore and set up on the beach amongst a crowd of natives who demanded a demonstration. 'First', Porter recalled, 'a shot was fired with the gun, considerably elevated.' The sudden spout of water which marked the roundshot's fall far out to sea was greeted with 'a general shout of admiration ... I then directed the gun to be fired, [so] that the ball might skip along the surface of the water. At every bound [the Taeehs] ... gave a general shout of applause ... last of all, I directed her to be fired with grape-shot, which seemed to afford them more pleasure than all the rest; they hugged and kissed the gun, lay down beside it, fondled it with the utmost delight and at length, slung it to two long poles and carried it toward the mountain.'

That afternoon, a second 6-pounder was set up in the camp and a long swivel gun was mounted on the walls. The ships' masts, spars and sails were taken down and a brick bread oven was constructed from the captured whalers' dismantled tryworks. The *Essex*'s rigging was stripped and replaced and the contents of her hold, storerooms and magazine were transferred to the prizes in preparation for fumigation. Onshore, Cooper Adams began replacing the *Essex*'s water casks, many of which had rotted through, while Carpenter Langley and his crew re-caulked the frigate's seams. At sundown, Feltus wandered through the Taeeh village. A sprawling settlement running the length of the valley, it consisted of several communal feasting halls grouped around a central square. Beyond numerous huts had been constructed around central, coconut wood ridge-poles, reinforced with bamboo frames. For roofing, breadfruit and coconut tree leaves were interwoven to create a rain-proof thatch.[16]

On 28 October Porter was introduced to the Taeehs' chief warrior. A heavily-muscled man of about thirty-five years of age, Mouina had 'an intelligent and open countenance', was over six feet tall and wore a striking scarlet cloak and feathered headdress. 'He had ... left the other warriors in the fortified village' at the mountain pass, Porter recalled, to ask 'me to cause a musket to be fired that he might witness its effects.' Mouina's request proved rather opportune. The Happahs had once more descended from the mountainside and had begun to gather around the American encampment. Several had thrown stones at the tents and although none had dared to enter, Porter felt another show of force was required. Accordingly, he took a musket and fired several shots at a target 'to show them that I never failed of hitting an object the size of a man'. As the Happahs were evidently unmoved, Gamble's marines reduced a barrel to shreds with volley fire and another messenger was dispatched to warn them that the Americans would retaliate should they be attacked. The response was the opposite that Porter had desired. Rather than being reassured by his attempts at negotiation, the Happahs saw it as a sign of weakness. With each passing day, they grew bolder and once again threatened to raid the encampment and make off with the ships' sails. This proved the final straw. With the 6-pounder in place on the mountain top, Porter decided on a pre-emptive strike. If the Taeehs would provide porters to bear their ammunition, Porter promised to send men to attack their rivals the following morning. Gattanewa agreed.[17]

At first light the strike force gathered. Led by Lieutenants Downes and Gamble, it consisted of twenty sailors and twenty-nine marines, each accompanied by a native porter. Several other tribesmen were tasked with carrying provisions and roundshot and powder for the cannon. A number of warriors led by Mouina completed the force. They were armed with coconut-bark-fibre slings, elaborately carved war clubs and two types of spear: light throwing weapons whose tips were designed to break off on impact; and fourteen-foot-long hand-to-hand weapons made from a highly-polished black wood known as *toa*. At 6 a.m. Porter gave the order to move out. No sooner had the men disappeared into the jungle than a breathless Gattanewa begged Porter to arrange a last-minute truce. Suspecting treachery, Porter had him held hostage until the expedition's return. Moments later, a girl ran into camp saying she had seen a party of Happahs approaching. Porter manned the defences with the carpenters, coopers and sailmakers and fired the alarm gun to bring reinforcements ashore. Several minutes passed before a band of warriors was spotted 'skulking among the reeds and grass' on a nearby hill. Elevating the barrel of the camp's 6-pounder, Porter scattered them with a few shots. There was 'no other interruption of alarm during the day'.

Up in the mountain passes, Downes' men had come under attack. With the enemy pelting them with spears and sling stones, the Americans and Taeehs dislodged the Happahs from one position after another with concentrated musket volleys. Mouina was particularly active. Beckoning his companions onwards alongside an exuberant native porter bearing the American flag, he could be seen from the encampment below. Shortly after midday, the Happahs made a final stand in a fortress on the brow of a steep hill. Protected by a breastwork of interlocking tree trunks, the Happahs rained missiles down on their foes from a fighting platform. Downes was struck in the stomach with an oval sling stone. Another American was pierced through the neck with a spear. The Happahs bared their backsides in contempt and the Taeehs began to falter until Downes led a second charge. With three cheers, the Americans rushed into the fort and unleashed a close-range musket volley. One Happah had the top of his head blown off. Four others were mortally wounded, set upon by Taeeh braves and finished off with war clubs. As the survivors fled, the Taeehs dipped the points of their spears in their enemies' blood then plundered a nearby village unopposed before stringing the bodies of their victims between long poles and returning home, weighed down with their booty. Porter ordered Gattanewa liberated and the chief celebrated the victory in the village square.[18]

The next morning Porter entered the Taeeh village with Wilson and a marine guard. Having heard rumours of the natives' predilection for cannibalism, he was keen to ascertain the truth. Five or six hundred villagers had assembled around the dead bodies in the main square. Two priests were leading them in ritual chanting and several warriors were beating out a rapid rhythm on large drums. When the Americans' were discovered, the dead bodies were snatched away. Porter recoiled in disgust and 'directed them . . . to return the[m]'. Guessing at the source of their guest's discomfort, the natives assured him they had had no intention of eating the dead, explaining they wished to offer them up as sacrifices to the spirit of the priest killed prior to the Americans' arrival. Porter 'consented to their request', although a lingering doubt remained.[19]

At 5 p.m. Mowattaeeh, a Happah chief, was received at the American encampment. After berating him for the Happah's hostility, Porter reassured Mowattaeeh of his peaceful intentions and, in exchange for a weekly delivery of hogs and fruit, offered iron 'and other articles as would be most useful to them'. In return, Mowattaeeh promised to rally representatives from all the tribes on the island to help build a more lasting settlement for the Americans. His proposal met with approval and in less than two days envoys had arrived from every tribe with the exception of the Typees, a warlike people of 3,500 warriors who resided at the head of Comptroller's Bay.[20]

Over the next few days the Americans fell into an easy routine. In the mornings and afternoons they worked on the ships and made themselves more comfortable on shore. The brick oven produced enough loaves to feed the entire complement, allowing Porter to preserve his supplies of hard tack. Boatswain Linscott set up a ropewalk to make cables, while the coopers produced barrels and the *Essex*'s hold was cleared. On 1 November the magazine was emptied and the main topmast, which had rotted through, was replaced with a spare which Porter had had the foresight to bring from the United States. Later, the frigate was hauled up onto the beach and careened. With the aid of several Taeehs, who had improvised scrapers from halved coconut shells, her copper bottom was cleared of barnacles and seaweed. Damaged sheets were replaced with others stripped from the prizes and the hull was repainted red and white. Finally, the *Essex* was 'thoroughly smoked'. Large pots filled with charcoal were lit and distributed about the decks. By the time the ship was aired, 1,500 rats had been killed.

At 4 p.m. each day, the Americans ceased work. The men wrestled on the beach, pitched quoits or strolled through the valleys and mountain heights. Others explored the Taeeh villages or amused themselves fishing for 'the large and ravenous' sharks which 'infested' the bay, one of which had 'devoured' a villager not long after the Americans' arrival. At nightfall a quarter of the men were allowed to remain on shore. The rest returned to the ships and every Sunday a gathering took place on the *Essex Junior.* Compared with the typical discipline of navy life, it was a convivial atmosphere and even the prisoners from the *Sir Andrew Hammond* were allowed the freedom of the valley.[21]

Some of the Essexes established relationships with local women. Piteenee, Gattanewa's granddaughter whom Porter had admired on the first day at the beach, accepted one of his junior officers as her partner, much to the captain's annoyance, and the Taeehs began to recognise the Americans as individuals. Some were even dubbed with Marquesan names. Porter became *Opotee*, Downes was *Onou*, Lieutenant Wilmer was *Wooreme* and McKnight was *Muscheetie*.[22]

To protect their innocence, Porter had the young midshipmen and boys separated from the rest of the crew. Under the guidance of Chaplain Adams, they spent their days studying on board the *Sir Andrew Hammond*. Classes focussed on navigation and mathematics, but as Adams was a cultured man, the curriculum may also have included writing, literature and history. Adams displayed a keen interest in the culture of the islands and collected several 'Indian curiosities' during his stay. At 4 p.m. school finished. The youngsters spent the rest of the day rambling on the beach in company with the native boys. 'From them we learned to throw the spear and walk on stilts', Farragut recalled, '[and] the art of swimming. It really appears as natural for these islanders to swim as to eat ... [and] I have often seen mothers take their little children, apparently not more than two years old, down to the sea on their backs, wade deliberately into deep water and leave them to paddle for themselves. To my astonishment, the little creatures could swim like young ducks.'[23]

On 3 November 4,000 natives representing tribes across Nuka Hiva gathered at the American encampment with sufficient building materials to construct a village. To Porter's amazement, by nightfall the settlement was complete. A house for Porter and another for his officers was built, along with a sail loft, a cooper's shop, a hospital, a bake-house, a guard house and a shed for the sentinel to walk under while performing his nightly rounds. Each building was fifty feet in length and connected to the next by a four-foot defensive wall. The whole was laid out in the form of a crescent. Porter was particularly impressed by the natives' organisation. 'Nothing could exceed the regularity with which these people carried on their work', he noted, 'without any chief to guide them, without confusion and without much noise ... Each man appeared to be the master of his business and every tribe appeared to strive [to see] which should complete their house with most expedition and in the most perfect manner. When the village was completed', Porter recalled, 'I distributed among them several harpoons and as usual gave them an opportunity of contending for old iron hoops. All were perfectly happy and contented and it was the cause of great pleasure to Gattanewa and his people that I praised the house they had built above all the rest.'[24]

In November, ten of the Sir Andrew Hammonds plotted their escape. Their leader was Edward Lawson, the ship's first mate. Having bribed two marines charged with guarding the frigate's spirit supply, Lawson had amassed a quantity of rum which he dosed with laudanum, intending to drug the crew of the *Essex Junior*, the only ship ready for sea, and sail to freedom. Although aware of Lawson's plan, Porter lacked evidence and decided only to arrest the British whalers once their guilt had been proved beyond doubt. The two culpable marines, on the other hand, were flogged 'severely', while the rest of Gamble's men were warned to be extra vigilant. Nevertheless, the next evening the marine tasked with guarding the bake-house fell asleep on watch. Furious, Porter shot him through the fleshy part of his thigh. 'If the punishment should appear a severe one', he commented in his journal, 'let those who censure me place themselves for a moment in my situation: I was far from the means of obtaining a judicial enquiry into his offence, which would probably have terminated fatally for him; promptness and vigilance on my part were the only sure guarantees to the success of a cruise so highly important to the interests of my country.'[25]

Porter's problems were compounded by unrest amongst his crew. Having been at sea for over a year, many of their contracts were about to expire, a perennial problem in the US Navy, brought to a head when Quartermaster Robert Dunn threatened to quit. Due to be punished for neglect of duty, Dunn had used the pretext of his contract's imminent expiration to blackmail Porter. If the captain insisted on going through with the punishment, Dunn assured him he 'would never again do duty in the ship'. Porter's reaction was typically uncompromising. Mustering the crew, he ordered Dunn to strip to receive his lashes. 'I assured him', Porter recalled, 'that I should punish him severely ... [then] turn him on shore ... observing that his time was out and it was proper he should have his discharge.' Porter then offered the rest of those whose contracts were up for renewal two options. 'If they wished to enlist again, I would ... give them the usual advance and on a suitable occasion give them three days liberty on shore[;] ... such as refused to enlist, but would bind themselves to do duty, might remain on board till I would have an opportunity of putting them on shore in some civilized place. They should be supplied with provisions; but should be allowed neither pay nor prize-money.' Only one man, 'from some foolish whim', chose the latter. The rest were reenlisted. Dunn, having begged forgiveness, was exonerated of his crime.[26]

Ever since the Happahs' humiliation, an extensive tribute of hogs, breadfruit, sugar cane, taro, bananas and coconuts had been delivered to the American village by the various tribes. The Typees alone were conspicuous by their absence. Having sent a message purporting his desire for peace while at the same time threatening them with destruction, Porter was shocked when the offer was rebuffed and in the second half of November, the Typees made increasingly threatening gestures. In response Porter constructed a fort on a hill dominating the Taeeh valley and the bay. Once the top of the hill had been levelled by native work parties, several empty watercasks were filled with soil and stacked to form a breastwork pierced for fourteen guns. Four small cannon were mounted on the walls. 'All worked with zeal', Porter noted and by 14 November the project was complete.[27]

That afternoon lookouts spotted a sail at the head of the bay. Several signal cannon were fired and the stranger set sail in flight. Boarding the *Essex Junior*, Downes slipped his cables and set off in pursuit. The stranger proved to be the *Albatross*, an American merchantman whose captain, William Smith, was looking to pick up a cargo of sandalwood before returning to Canton. After a short chase, Downes brought him too with a shot across his bows. The ships returned in company, the *Albatross* dropping anchor off the beach at Port Anna Maria at 1 p.m. on 16 November.[28]

In Downes' absence, Porter had Edward Lawson and the nine other poison plotters detained. Lawson was flogged for stealing the rum and one other man was whipped for using 'improper language'. All were put in irons, with heavy bar shot attached and sent ashore on punishment drill to build a stone wall around the perimeter of the village. Six hundred yards long and five feet high, it was an arduous undertaking which would take the prisoners four weeks. Porter and Gamble proved harsh taskmasters. 'We had men to attend us with whips', Lawson recalled, '[and were not] allowed to carry [the bar] shot under our arm, but [were] made to drag it after us.' The only respite was the kind treatment they received at the hands of Lieutenant Downes. The thirty-year-old proved himself 'a generous fellow and did as much as he could to 'alleviate ... the distresses of the prisoners' who 'spoke of him in very high terms'.[29]

On 19 November Porter took it upon himself to begin the American colonisation of the Pacific. Before a crowd of bemused natives the Star-Spangled Banner was raised from the fort's flag post as Porter read the official declaration aloud. 'It is hereby made known to the world', he began, 'that I, David Porter ... have, on the part of the ... United States, taken possession of the island called by the natives Nooaheevah ... Our rights[,] ... being founded on priority of discovery, conquest and possession, cannot be disputed ... the natives ... have requested to be admitted into the great American family, whose pure republican policy approaches so near their own.' The document was witnessed by several officers from the *Essex* and *Albatross*, Nuka Hiva was rechristened Madison's Island and Port Anna Maria was dubbed Massachusett's Bay. A seventeen-gun salute was fired from the fort and returned by the *Essex Junior* and the declaration was buried in a bottle beneath the flag pole whereupon the ceremonials were brought to a close with a toast drunk to 'the prosperity of [the] ... newly acquired land'.[30]

The next week passed quietly. The Essexes stowed the frigate's hold with dried and salted provisions and water, tribute came in from the islanders and Captain Smith of the *Albatross* completed his cargo of sandal wood. Before leaving, Smith purchased four cannon from Porter which he mounted on his ship to afford some protection from the British letters of marque lurking off Canton. Smith also agreed to take Porter's dispatches and several private letters which were sealed in a lead packet which could be thrown overboard should the *Albatross* be captured. One of his men, Benjamin Clapp, decided to stay behind and was later added to the *Essex*'s muster as an acting midshipman and on 24 November the *Albatross* upped anchor and set sail for Canton.[31]

At the end of November Porter turned his attention to the Typees. Not only had they refused to offer tribute, but they had also begun to mock the other tribes for doing so. The amount of goods arriving had diminished as a consequence prompting Porter to realise he would have to take action to remain in control. At 4 p.m. on 27 November, after arranging for a number of native warriors to trek overland to the Typee valley via the mountain passes, Downes took the *Essex Junior* to Comptroller's Bay. Gamble, Doctor Hoffman, Purser Shaw and Gattanewa, Mouina and two Taeeh ambassadors, one of whom was related to the Typees by marriage, were on board. At 3 a.m. the following morning Porter and twenty other Americans followed in four ship's boats accompanied by ten Taeeh war canoes. Kept together by frequent soundings of the warriors' conch horns, the canoes arrived at the Typee landing at sunrise on 29 November where they were joined by the *Essex Junior* and ten Happah canoes. With 'the tops of ... the neighbouring mountains ... covered with the Taeeh and Happah warriors' who had travelled overland, the allied force amounted to 5,000 men. The Typees were nowhere to be seen.

Beyond the beach was a plain extending a quarter of a mile to a swampy thicket. Following a solitary path which led to the Typee village, the Taeeh ambassador advanced under a flag of truce, only to come running back, having been threatened with death if he advanced further. Porter took this as a signal that hostilities had commenced and advanced with thirty-five Americans and a number of warriors led by Mouina. 'We entered the bushes', Porter recalled, 'and were at every instant assailed by spears and stones.' Keeping up a scattered fire at fleeting targets spotted through the undergrowth, the Americans emerged at a small clearing on the bank of a river without loss. A withering hail of missiles was launched from the bushes on the far side. Downes' leg was broken by a sling stone and the Taeehs and Happahs began to desert in droves. Sending Downes back to the boats with Purser Shaw and four men, Porter pushed on. A volley and bayonet charge forced the passage of a steep-sided ford, beyond which the Typees had built a seven foot high barricade from palm trunks flanked by impenetrable thorn bushes. Taking cover behind a fallen log, Porter, Gamble and Hoffman picked off several of the enemy with their muskets, but soon realised they were hopelessly outnumbered and were beginning to run low on ammunition. Gamble and four men were sent to collect more cartridges from the *Essex Junior* while the others kept the enemy at bay. Three more Americans were wounded before Mouina, the only tribesman remaining, begged Porter to retreat. The Bostonian reluctantly agreed. Falling back to the treeline, the Americans turned just as the Typees rushed after them, killed two with a close range volley then pulled back to the beach, boarding their boats as a second wave emerged from the trees.[32]

On his return to Massachusetts' Bay, Porter began planning a second raid. He was determined the Typees would not get the better of him and suspected the Happahs were on the point of changing sides. This time Porter would march across the mountains and attack by land. One hundred and fifty-five Americans set off at 6 p.m. on 29 November led by Taeeh guides. 'We had a fine moonlight night', Porter recalled. Passing by a Happah village, the Bostonian urged his men to stay quiet and 'not a whisper was heard from one end of the line to the other'. Although technically still allied to the Happahs, Porter was worried they might alert the Typees if they learned of his plans. The three-hour trek to the summit was gruelling. 'Our guides marched in front and we followed ... up and down the steep sides of rocks and mountains, through rivulets, thickets and reed brakes and by the sides of precipices which ... caused us to shudder.' Several dropped out *en route*, but by midnight the lights of the Typee villages were visible beneath them and the sound of drums and singing wafted up through the night air. The Typees 'were celebrating the victory they had obtained', Porter recalled, 'and [were] calling on their gods to give them rain, in order that it might render our *bouhies* [guns] useless.' At a narrow ridgeline, Porter gave the order to halt for the night, but no sooner had he drifted off into a restless sleep than the rain poured down in torrents. 'Never ... did I spend a more anxious or disagreeable night', Porter recalled. 'A cold and piercing wind accompanied the deluge .... and chilled us to the heart ... Without room to keep ourselves warm by moving ... we ... anxiously looked for morning.'

At dawn Porter decided to return to the Happah village he had passed the previous evening and rest before pressing home his attack. His men were exhausted and their ammunition needed to be laid out to dry. At first the Happahs proved unfriendly. Food had to be taken by force and the women were nowhere to be seen, but once Gattenawa and Mouina had berated them, the Happah chiefs ordered hogs roasted in covered pits, the women reappeared and the Americans passed the day recuperating their strength. Early the next morning, joined by large numbers of Taeehs and Happahs motivated by the prospect of plunder, Porter pushed on to the ridgeline where he paused to take in the view.

> The upper part [of the Typee valley] was bounded by a precipice of many hundred feet in height, from the top of which a handsome sheet of water was precipitated and formed a beautiful river, which ran meandering through the valley and discharged itself at the beach. Villages were scattered here and there, the bread-fruit and cocoa-nut trees flourished ... plantations laid out in good order, enclosed with stone walls, were in a high state of cultivation and everything bespoke industry, abundance and happiness ... Never ... did I witness a more delightful scene, or experience more repugnancy than I now felt, for the necessity which compelled me to make war against this happy and heroic people.

Descending the mountain, Porter halted where the river met the lower slopes. The Typees shot sling stones over the water, forcing the Americans to shelter behind a series of stone walls, but once Porter had reformed he took the first fortified village with ease. A leading Typee warrior was killed by a musket volley and several others were wounded. The survivors retreated to a series of stone walls on high ground, where they kept up a heavy fire of spear and sling stones. 'Three of my men were wounded', Porter recalled, 'and many of the Typees killed before we dislodged them.' Splitting his force, Porter took several more villages with the main body while 'scouting parties' captured periphery positions before the whole regrouped to advance on the Typee capital. 'The beauty and regularity of this place was such, as to strike every spectator with astonishment', Porter recalled, 'and their grand site or public square, was far superior to any other we had met with.' Smashing the idols with their musket butts, the Americans put the town to the torch, while their

Taeeh and Happah allies plundered the houses and hacked down the breadfruit plantations. His work done, Porter pulled back to the beach, destroying several other villages *en route*, before returning over the mountains.[33]

The Americans arrived at Massachusetts Bay three days and two nights after they had set out. A Happah messenger arrived shortly afterwards to reassert his tribe's loyalty and a humbled Typee delegation appeared the next day. Seated on a throne he had had built in his cabin, Porter received them as a tribal king and demanded 400 hogs as reparations. Over the next few days tribute came in with alacrity. Soon there were too many animals to keep inside the walls. Dozens were hoisted on board the ships, while others, having had their ears marked, were allowed to run free, and the men feasted on pork for days. Meanwhile, Downes and the three wounded sailors recovered. Several others came down with fever induced by their exertions and on 4 December Corporal Andrew Mahon of the marines died. At 11 a.m. the next morning he was buried on shore. All of the Essexes and several natives attended, a flag was lowered over his coffin and a musket volley fired over his grave.[34]

The remainder of Porter's stay at Nuka Hiva was largely without incident. While a division finished the repairs and refitting of the *Essex*, another loaded the whale oil from the *Seringapatam*, *Greenwich* and *Sir Andrew Hammond* onto the *New Zealander* and Porter made several excursions into different parts of the valley. One day he visited a sacred site which stank of the rotting flesh of sacrificed animals and the corpses of enemy warriors. On another occasion, Porter presented several chiefs with breeding pairs of 'superior' English pigs and goats and planted melon, pumpkin, orange, peach and lime seeds as well as setting up pea and bean plantations and sowing several fields of wheat. The latter was particularly valued by the natives, who had acquired a taste for fresh bread. 'They would swim off to the ships, about meal times', Porter recalled, 'in large shoals and wait for the sailors to throw them pieces ... A string of beads, highly as they were valued, could be purchased for a loaf; and chiefs, after walking many miles over mountains to bring us presents of fruit and hogs, would return well satisfied, if I gave them a hot roll from the oven.'[35]

By the end of the first week of December, Porter had decided on his next move. The *Essex* would set sail for South America in company with the *Essex Junior*. The *New Zealander* would be sent back to the United Sates, her hold full of whale oil, while the *Greenwich*, *Seringapatam* and *Sir Andrew Hammond* would remain under the guns of Fort Madison at Massachusetts's Bay. Twenty-three 'volunteers' would be left to watch the ships and guard six of the most problematic prisoners from the *Sir Andrew Hammond*. Amongst the former were at least seven British sailors of dubious loyalty, including Boatswain's Mate Thomas Belcher, whom Porter later described as a 'consummate villain'. Several deserters would also remain, including Isaac Coffin, the 'lazy negro' who had joined the *Essex* at Tumbez. The unhappy task of commanding this motley crew fell to Lieutenant Gamble. Unafraid of using force to maintain discipline, the New Yorker was not a man to be trifled with, as Lieutenant Cowan had learnt to his cost. Gamble was to be seconded by Midshipman Feltus and Acting Midshipman Clapp. They would be responsible for gathering provisions and preparing the ships for sea. If Porter failed to return within five and half months Gamble was ordered to make for the United States as best he could.[36]

While Gamble commanded at Nuka Hiva, Porter planned to cruise off the central Chilean coast between Mocha Island and Valparaiso as long as his supplies held out. Both were popular spots with British whalers, but what the Bostonian was really seeking was a run-in with an enemy man-of-war. Even though the *Essex* was poorly armed compared to the 'super-frigates' which had humbled their foes and single ship combat failed to further the war aims of his country, Porter was desperate to emulate Captains Hull, Decatur and Bainbridge by taking a frigate of his own. HMS *Phoebe*'s arrival in the Pacific appeared to offer the perfect opportunity. In his pursuit of the *Essex*, Captain Hillyar was sure to call in at Valparaiso. When he did, Porter would be waiting for him.[37]

By 9 December the *Essex* was nearly ready for sea. Copious supplies of 'provisions, wood and water' had been loaded, the 'decks [were] filled with hogs'; coconuts and bananas had been strung from the spars in net bags and the hold was crammed with 'dried cocoa-nuts . . . calculated for keeping three or four months'. Porter also found room for a load of sandalwood – its high market value no doubt outweighing the risk of censure for using a state-owned ship for private enterprise. Edward Lawson and his fellow poison plotters were confined below decks while the crew was directed to 'remain on board and work late and early, to hasten the departure of the ship'. Struggling to adapt to the sudden change of routine, that night three men swam ashore 'determined to have a parting kiss'. Porter had them put in irons and flogged severely the next morning. The incident increased the rumblings of discontent. The men complained that 'their situation . . . was worse than slavery' and their desperation was fuelled by the native women gathering on the beach each night to entice them ashore.[38]

The next day Porter set the date of departure for Monday 13 December. The day before, as was customary on Sundays, the men gathered on the *Essex Junior.* There was more than a whiff of mutiny in the air. The ringleader, Robert White, one of the *Essex*'s Englishmen, announced that he had come to a resolution to refuse to weigh anchor. If compelled to do so, he assured his fellows, the crew would mutiny on the third day after leaving the island. The news soon reached Porter. 'I was willing to let them ease their minds by a little grumbling', he recalled, 'but a threat of this kind was carrying matters rather too far.' Calling a general meeting on the *Essex* the next morning, Porter had the men line up on the larboard side of the deck, 'took his cutlass in his hand' and laid it on the capstan. Then, 'though shaking with rage', he 'addressed the crew . . . with forced composure. "All of you who are in favour of weighing the anchor when I give the order, pass over to the starboard side"', he commanded. Every man duly obeyed. Porter then assured them that he would 'put a match to the magazine and blow them all to eternity' should they ever dare to take his ship, before turning his wrath on White. When the Englishman 'tremblingly' denied his accusations, Porter branded him a 'liar' and a 'scoundrel', took up his cutlass and chased him overboard. Throwing himself into the sea, White was picked up by a passing native canoe and soon disappeared into the jungle.[39]

By the afternoon of 13 December all was ready. With the four whalers moored close under the guns of Fort Madison, Porter gave the order to weigh. The marines heaved at the capstan, the cable came dripping up from the seabed and a fiddler struck up the sailors' lament 'The girl I left behind me' as the *Essex* and *Essex Junior* stood out of the bay. Behind the fort's ramparts, Gamble, Feltus, Clapp and their men looked on anxiously, while several native women, lining the beach, burst into tears at their beaux' departure. Somewhere amongst the trees, Robert White and Isaac Coffin must also have had mixed emotions as they watched their comrades set sail while Porter, his head full of dreams of adding his name to the list of US naval captains who had humbled the British, was perhaps the only one present not to share their sentiments to some degree.[40]

Chapter 11

The Valley of the Unknown God: HMS *Phoebe*, 24 November 1813 – 8 February 1814

In the last week of November 1813 HMS *Phoebe* and *Cherub* sailed for Callao. Hillyar ordered his men to paint the ship's sides, and drill with the great guns and small arms was a daily occurrence. On 29 November ordinary Seaman Robert Phelps, a 26-year-old Londoner, was given twenty-four lashes for contempt. The good weather continued and on 3 December, a day of fresh breezes and thick cloud, the ships covered 150 miles. Land was spotted off the bow at 8 a.m. The sighting raised a spontaneous cheer, the men having been on two-thirds rations of bread and salt meat since 25 October. Later, a strange sail was spotted. Lowering the studding sails, the *Phoebe* hove to and Hillyar sent a boat to board her. She proved to be yet another Spanish brig running the coastal trade. Learning that Callao was but a few hours' sail away, Hillyar and Tucker restored full rations and at 3 p.m., as the open roadstead hove into view, pilots were taken on board. The ships worked their way into the harbour, coming to anchor at 6 p.m. in five fathoms half a mile from the shore, their small bowers sunk deep into the muddy bottom.[1]

Two Spanish sloops-of-war preparing for sea and thirty merchantmen were moored in Callao roads. Most of the latter had previously been employed importing corn and cocoa from Chile, but, with the on-going hostilities, had been laid up for months. Moored tight under the guns of the formidable sea defences were three foreign ships which had also fallen victim to the recent political upheavals. The *Hunter* and the *Hector* were British. The *Boriska*, although US-owned, had been chartered by Lord Strangford at Rio to buy Chilean grain for Wellington's troops in the Peninsula. All three had been captured by Peruvian privateers and detained for their involvement in the Chilean trade, a highly contentious decision which Hillyar had been asked to look into. Strangford had been particularly put out by the fate of the *Boriska*: the Viscount had provided her captain with $15,000 only for it to disappear into the pockets of a Peruvian privateer.[2]

To the south of the anchorage were two barren islands providing some protection from the southerly swell. To the east, the flat, open shoreline was framed by the snow-capped heights of the Cordillera de los Andes. Gardiner thought the town 'small, miserable', 'ill-built' and barely worth description. Prior to 1747, when Callao had been devastated by a major earthquake, it had been relatively grand. The ruins of several churches and colonial offices were still visible, but by 1813 the population had fallen to 700 and the town consisted of little more than a line of low mud houses, interspersed with shore defences. To the south stood a square fort named San Felipe. Twin towers rose above four bastions surrounded by a dry ditch. It mounted 120 guns and a half-moon redoubt with twelve cannon was built to the north. Beyond, a series of arid, scrub-covered hills cut by a single road winding northeast, led six miles to the capital of Lima. Its spires were just visible through the evening haze.[3]

On 4 December, the ships' boats went ashore for water and provisions. Hillyar learnt that the report he had heard at Tumbez about the *Essex*'s movements had been 'entirely false. She had been seen off this port about five months ago', Gardiner explained, 'but had sailed from Valparaiso with all her prizes (19 in number) some time since.' The news, the latest in a series of fabrications, rumours and half-truths that the Phoebes had been hearing ever since their arrival in the Pacific, garnered a mixed response on board. As well as being put out that the Americans appeared to have eluded them, the British officers could not help but afford their opponents grudging respect. 'No expedition could have been better planned [than the *Essex*'s]', Gardiner opined, 'or have been crowned with greater success. She came into these seas before the intelligence of the war arrived, captured the greater part of our southseamen and warned all her own off the coast. Had we been here but two months sooner we might probably have put a stop to the whole, but we now gave up all hope of meeting her.'[4]

In early December fourteen British sailors were added to the ships' muster rolls. Four were taken on board HMS *Cherub* from the *Mercurio*, one of the Spanish sloops of war. Jeremiah Ryan, a 22-year-old from Ireland, had been captured on the *Greenwich* on 29 May 1813. Paroled by Porter at Tumbez one month later, he had volunteered on the *Mercurio*, whose captain now allowed him to transfer to Tucker's command. The other three were most likely sailors from one of the three American and British ships detained in port. With no pay or provisions, many had volunteered on passing vessels to avoid starvation. On Sunday 5 December, after Hillyar's customary morning service, seven men signed up on board HMS *Phoebe*. Four were former crewmembers of HMP *Nocton* who had been paroled at Valparaiso nine months before. Two had served on the *Montezuma* and *Atlantic*. The recruits were more than welcome. Although the chances of encountering the *Essex* seemed to be becoming slimmer, Hillyar had made up his mind to return to

England via Valparaiso. He would need all the hands he could muster going back round the Horn.[5]

On 6 December, Joseph Hobbart, a 24-year-old Phoebe from Greenock in Scotland, deserted from the boats. The next day, three men ran from the *Cherub*. All had volunteered at Rio back in June. To make matters worse, it was apparent that the supplies Hillyar had hoped to take on would not be easily procured. While fresh fruit and meat were abundant, the limited supplies of salt meat and biscuit were all needed for the Spanish sloops. Over the next five days the pursers of the *Phoebe* and *Cherub* purchased what they could: water, firewood, limes, oranges and vegetables were stowed and sheep tethered on deck. On a diet of mutton broth, a classic Georgian restorative, most of the men who had fallen ill during the prolonged cruise from the Galapagos 'rapidly recovered', but Bryan Murphy, a 24-year-old landsman from Dublin, was to remain in Surgeon Smith's sick berth under the forecastle for ten days. Meanwhile, the *Phoebe*'s bowsprit was repaired, her decks scrubbed and her rigging blacked and experiments were conducted in preserving the fresh meat. The voyage to England could take months and as the *Phoebe* only had six weeks' supplies of salt provisions remaining, it was vital that more was procured. All attempts to salt the meat failed, however, leading Captain Tucker to adopt a local solution. Cut into thin strips, the meat was hung from the rigging and left to dry in the sun. Once 'as hard as wood', the strips were packed between layers of matting and stored on the main deck about the booms.[6]

By the 9th Hillyar's enquiries had turned up several details about the fate of the detained ships. The *Boriska* had been taken in Chilean waters by a Peruvian vessel named the *Vulture*. Her captain, Don Domingo Amezaga, had treated his prisoners in 'a most brutal manner, plundering the captain ... of all his clothes ... [and] nautical instruments ... and expressing his abhorrence and contempt for the English, their flag & government'. The Hunters, having also fallen victim to Don Amezaga, had been 'kick[ed] ... about' after capture and nine had been forced to join the *Vulture* against their will, while the *Hector*, taken by a privateer operating out of Callao named the *Santa Teresa*, had been stripped 'of nearly all her provisions, water, [and] sails, &c ... and given up in such a deplorable state as to be unfit for her voyage [home]'. Writing to Viceroy Abascal, Hillyar requested 'a resolution of the ship[s] and dollars' and insisted that 'an enquiry ... be made into the conduct of ... Captain ... Amezaga'. The viceroy's reply was evasive: 'Neither in the condemnation of the ... *Boriska*, nor in that of the *Hunter* ... have I had or can I have the last interference', he explained. 'It is an affair which corresponds exclusively to the Marine Department of Callao.'[7]

On 13 December Hillyar had the opportunity of continuing the discussion face-to-face. That afternoon Abascal visited the *Phoebe* to the thunder of four royal salutes accompanied by several attendants and his daughter, María Ramona, 'a pretty young girl, [of] about sixteen'. After dinner the ladies danced with the British officers for two hours in Hillyar's Great Cabin. Gardiner thought the Spaniards 'seemed . . . very much entertained'. With the equatorial light streaming in through the windows, Maria Ramona made a particularly strong impression. Meanwhile, Hillyar and Abascal, 'a fine venerable looking old man' of seventy-one years of age, got down to business. Although Abascal was perfectly polite, he refused to accept responsibility for the detained ships and could only promise to forward Hillyar's requests to the minister of marine. At 5.30 p.m., having invited the British officers to attend a dance at the palace in Lima in a week's time, the Spaniards departed.[8]

The next morning Ordinary Seaman Bryan Murphy was found dead in his hammock, having fallen victim to an unnamed disease. As a Catholic, Murphy was buried ashore in consecrated ground, a dignity normally denied to Protestants visiting Spanish shores. The next week passed routinely. Each morning the ships' boats went ashore. While a party of marines stood guard at the dockside storehouses, they made several runs to the ships with fresh water and supplies. The rest of the men were employed painting the guns and the slides of the carronades and whitewashing the main deck. On 17 December Hillyar received a reply to his enquiries from the Minister of Marine, Don Joshua Pasqual de Vivero. 'The cases [of the *Boriska*, *Hunter* and *Hector*] have been forwarded . . . to the Supreme Government of our Nation [in Cadiz]', Vivero explained, 'where the two Governments [of Britain and Spain] reciprocally may reclaim or give satisfaction to one another, without compromising the statues, rights or . . . respects of each nation . . . in case of any faults being imputed to their respective chiefs they will correct it . . . from this reason . . . there is not the least opening for the discussion . . . of these affairs.'[9]

With that, one part of Hillyar's mission was brought to a close. Another, however, soon presented itself. Abascal's campaign against the Chilean patriots had had mixed results. While the Peruvian privateers had humbled the fledgling Chilean navy at Valparaiso in May and Brigadier Pareja's expeditionary force had initially gained ground in southern Chile, the war had since ground to a stalemate. The royalists were ensconced in the fortified town of Chillán, while the patriots, split between a weakening pro-Carrera faction and those who supported a promising young commander, the bastard son of a former Peruvian viceroy of Irish-Chilean parentage named Bernardo O'Higgins, were unable to dislodge them. With no possibility of help from Spain, Abascal was considering a negotiated settlement with the Chileans and thought Hillyar, a respectable representative of a country with economic interests on both sides, would make the perfect mediator. Once Hillyar agreed and had been furnished with the necessary letters of introduction, Abascal had twelve Chilean patriot officers taken prisoner from *La Perla* at Valparaiso in May put on board the *Phoebe*. Hillyar was instructed to release them on arrival at Valparaiso as a token of the viceroy's pacific intent.[10]

On 20 December a punishment parade was held on board the *Phoebe*. Private Oliver Hardy was given forty-eight lashes for theft and his accomplices, Thomas Brodie and Evan Jones, received twelve each for the same crime, while Able Seaman William James and Thomas Kilby got twenty-four and twelve respectively for disobedience of orders. That afternoon, the men scrubbed their hammocks and washed their clothes while Gardiner and several other officers were rowed ashore to attend the viceroy's party. The young midshipman hired horses and took the road from Callao. After they had passed the pre-Inca ruins of Rimac and the remains of the temple of the Sun, the road grew busy with negro slaves, Indians dressed in ponchos pushing barrows to the market and uniformed dispatch riders who raced past mule-trains laden with fruit, vegetables and poultry, while small two-wheeled carriages known as 'valencins', rattled along the cobblestones carrying hooded female passengers. The road terminated in a Gothic archway set into Lima's walls which led to the grid of city streets. 'Such an entrance', Gardiner recalled, 'agreed with the ideas we had formed of the magnificence of this place.' Lima itself proved a disappointment.[11]

Founded in 1535 by Francisco Pizarro, 'the City of Kings' had been in decline since the mid-eighteenth century due to the growing economic competition from Buenos Ayres and the mining centre of Potosi. Nevertheless, by the time of the Phoebes' visit it was still the largest city on the continent with a population of 50,000 Spaniards, Creoles, blacks, Indians, *mulattoes*, *mestizos*, *quarteroons*, *quinteroons*, *zambos* and *chinos*. Gardiner thought 'the low, square houses in the outer districts had a 'mean . . . shabby appearance'. Their whitewashed walls were peeling. Faded, green balconies jutted over the streets busy with *pulperias* or grog shops, where crowds of half-dressed, drunken negro slaves danced to African rhythms. At the centre of a regular grid of fifty-five streets, the *Plaza Real* was the largest in South America. The cathedral, whose corner stone had been laid by Pizarro himself, stood to the east alongside the Archbishop's residence. The interior walls were draped with velvet and adorned with giant paintings depicting the sufferings of Christ. To the north was the viceroy's palace, 'a shabby building without ornament' whose ground floor housed several cobblers' shops. To the west were the Cablido and prison. To the south a covered stone walkway boasted the city's principal stores and in the centre of the square was a three-tiered fountain. Built in 1650, it was decorated with lions and griffins and surmounted by a five-foot high statue of Fame.

Shortly after midday the British officers arrived at the viceroy's palace for dinner. Gardiner thought 'the apartments . . . ill-furnished', but the lack 'of pomp and magnificence, was more than compensated by the friendly and cordial reception.' After a meal made noteworthy by the Spaniards' poor table manners, the party attended a bullfight in the southern suburb of Rimac. En route they crossed the river of the same name via a stone bridge before passing through 'a grove of large and spreading trees watered on each side by rapid rivulets'. The streets were heaving and there was a great press at each gate. Built of brick with a diameter of 400 feet, the bullring could house up to 10,000 spectators. Five rows of boxes accommodated the most important. The viceroy himself was attended by a strong guard. Gardiner was sickened by what followed: 'The . . . [bullfighters] do not dispatch the . . . [bulls] immediately . . . but to heighten the sport, irritate them almost to madness', he recalled. 'Not contented with seeing . . . [the bull] run through and through with spears and swords, panting for breath and covered with blood . . . they hamstring him . . . then exultingly get upon his back and . . . oblige him to carry them about for several minutes, till by loss of blood he is rendered so weak, as to no longer afford . . . any amusement, when they put an end to his existence.'[12]

On the afternoon of 22 December the *Indespensible*, a British South Sea whaler, arrived at Callao. Her captain, William Bickle, boasted that he was the only British ship to have escaped the *Essex* on the entire coast of Peru. On the *Phoebe*, preparations to put to sea continued. Sailmaker Millery stowed the spare sails in his store room, apples and limes were brought on board and John King, a 28-year-old whaler from Cambridgeshire captured by Porter and released at Tumbez, was added to the frigate's muster roll, bringing her complement to over 300 men. On the 28th Gardiner and several of his fellow officers attended a ball at the viceroy's palace. Refreshed by a range of 'elegant' ices, they did not return to the *Phoebe* until 3 a.m.[13]

On New Year's Eve the viceroy and his entourage were invited to a ball on the *Phoebe*. The frigate was decked up with British and Spanish bunting, candles were lit, an awning rigged across the main deck and Thomas Staines, the trumpeter and the rest of the ship's band, dressed up in their finest clothes. 'After dancing for some time', the British officers were invited to a second ball in Lima. The party proved 'very pleasant' and the revellers 'kept it up till about 5 o'clock in the morning, having according to custom danced out the old year and danced in the new'. 'After breakfast', Gardiner recalled, 'we took a ride in the country and in the evening returned on board.' The men spent the day exercising the frigate's great guns and small arms while Schoolmaster Patrick Brady made a pencil sketch of Callao Bay. Firing practice punctuated the week that followed. Putting his faith in 'Divine Providence', Hilllyar had grown more optimistic about his chances of a run-in with the Americans. Over the course of the next month he would raise his men to a new height of combat readiness.[14]

On 7 January 1814 Francisco Juan, one of the *Cherub*'s dwindling band of Brazilian volunteers, deserted from a boat party. Meanwhile, Gardiner visited the ruins of the mines of Cajamarquilla la Vieja and that evening, as news arrived of the defeat of a patriot army in Upper Peru, Hillyar announced his intention to sail for Valparaiso on the 11th. The next day Ordinary Seamen James Mcafferty, Peter Forsythe and Joseph Clarke ran while assigned to shore duty. A petty officer and a party of marines were ordered to search for them, but no trace was found. The same day two new recruits signed up. Thomas Howard, a 24-year-old from London, and Isaac Scott, a 22-year-old from Newcastle, were rated as able seamen. Both had served on the *Atlantic* until her capture by Porter seven months before. The twelve Chilean prisoners that Abascal had entrusted to Hillyar's care were also admitted as supernumeries, along with two llamas which the viceroy had sent as a gift. The latter proved bad-tempered shipmates and had a habit of hawking mouthfuls of saliva at any crewmember who got too close. Another passenger taken on board was Thomas N. Crompton. A British merchant and supercargo for the armed Portuguese merchantman *Fama*, Crompton loaded large quantities of specie in the *Phoebe*'s hold. Although transporting currency was an added responsibility, it was also a profitable one. In wartime, captains were entitled to a negotiable commission of roughly 3 per cent.[15]

Gardiner spent his last full day in Peru bidding farewell to his friends: 'on the 10th I dined at the palace and in the evening accompanied some of the party to a bull fight'. William Ingram also said his farewells. 'A tall, handsome man', the *Phoebe*'s First Lieutenant had formed an especially close relationship with one of the black-mantled ladies of Lima. Before he departed the couple became engaged. At 5 a.m. on 11 January Hillyar gave the order to weigh. The *Phoebe* unmoored and sailed in company with the *Cherub* and the *Indespensible*, Captain Bickle having taken up the offer of an armed escort to Valparaiso.[16]

Chapter 12

The Standoff, 13 December 1813 – 28 March 1814

On the evening of 13 December 1813, the *Essex* and *Essex Junior* left Nuka Hiva behind. While cutting through a choppy passage between Fatu Uka and Hiva 'Oa *en route* to the South American mainland, Tameoy, the *Essex*'s Tahitian crewmember, had a 'minor altercation' with one of the boatswain's mates. 'This he could not brook', Farragut explained, 'and so jumped overboard.' Although one of the night watch later recalled hearing a loud splash, Tameoy's disappearance went unnoticed until roll call the following morning. 'Whether he took with him an oar or small spar, to buoy himself up; whether he hoped to reach the shore; or whether he determined to put an end to his existence', Porter could not 'pretend to say . . . The distance, however, was so great and the sea so rough, that I [could not] . . . entertain a hope of his surviving.' Farragut also 'thought he had drowned . . . As he was a general favourite . . . it gave' the crew 'great regret'.[1]

The remainder of the voyage was routine. With the *Essex Junior* matching the speed of the frigate, the ships remained in sight of one another throughout and at midday on 18 December had reached 131° West. The men, now numbering 300, 'were exercised at the great guns, small arms and single stick' every day. The practice paid dividends. Years later, with a wealth of combat experience behind him, Farragut maintained that he had 'never been in a ship where the crew of the old *Essex* was represented, but that I found them to be the best swordsmen on board. They had been so thoroughly trained . . . that every man was prepared for such an emergency, with his cutlass as sharp as a razor, a dirk made by the ship's armourer from a file and a pistol' thrust in his belt.[2]

On 12 January 1814 the island of Mocha was sighted. Running northwards parallel to the coast, the next day the ships anchored at Isla Santa Maria, 100 miles to the north. Porter sent the boats to water before proceeding to Concepción where the flotilla arrived on the 18th. Downes performed a reconnaissance, flying British colours while Porter stood off shore. Several British whalers were at anchor, having been detained by the Peruvian royalists who held the port, but as all where under the guns of the shore defences, Porter pressed on to Valparaiso where he 'hoped

... to signalize ... [his] cruise by something more splendid [than capturing mere merchantmen]'.[3]

After a tedious passage, punctuated by Porter's thirty-fourth birthday, the *Essex* arrived on 3 February. Downes was ordered to cruise off shore and intercept any British vessels, while Porter stood in for the roads. The *Hector, Montezuma* and *Atlantic*, which Downes had left behind on his previous visit, were at anchor along with two British merchantmen: the *Good Friends*, commanded by Master N. Murphy and the *Emily*, which the *Essex*'s First Lieutenant had seen in July. Unwilling to risk his ship while American cruisers and Peruvian privateers lurked off-shore, Captain Dart of the *Emily* had remained at Valparaiso in the hope that a British man-of-war would arrive and escort him home. Another of the *Emily*'s complement was Sailing Master George O'Brien. Formerly a lieutenant on HMS *Sparrowhawk*, O'Brien had been dismissed for 'youthful indiscretions'. The arrival of the *Essex* and *Essex Junior* would afford him a way of making amends.[4]

Despite the rise of the Anglophile faction, Valparaiso afforded the Essexes a friendly reception. Porter stayed at the house of Mr. Blanco, a Chilean who had been appointed American trade vice-consul by Joel Poinsett while he played soldier with O'Higgins' and Carrera's troops in the south and on 4 February Governor Lastra and his wife were entertained on board the *Essex*. Porter heard that the British squadron assigned to pursue him had disappeared rounding the Horn, but paid the rumour little heed and invited Lastra, the officers of his government, 'their families and all the other respectable inhabitants' of Valparaiso to a ball to be held on the frigate on the 7th. In the interim, the *Essex* was resupplied, repairs were undertaken and the men allowed ashore by watches. The time passed pleasantly and the day of the ball soon arrived. Chilean and American flags were put up, an awning was strung from the rigging, refreshments were readied in the galley and the decks scrubbed clean. Having anchored the *Essex Junior* in the roads 'so as to save a full view of the sea', Downes was rowed aboard as the guests began arriving. The ball was a great success. 'The dancing continued until midnight', Porter recalled, 'after which Lt. Downes repaired to his vessel, got her under weigh and proceeded to sea.'[5]

The next morning was overcast with moderate breezes. As usual, a third of the Essexes were ashore on leave. At 6 a.m., as the rest of the crew were taking down the decorations, lookouts in the tops cried out an alarm. The moment Porter had long anticipated seemed to have finally arrived. Two unidentified men-of-war were approaching the bay.[6]

HMS *Phoebe* and *Cherub* had taken four weeks to sail from Callao. Hillyar and Tucker had exercised the great guns twice daily until 16 January and once every twenty-four hours thereafter. Aside from the Sabbath, the only day on which the guns had fallen silent was 18 January, when squalls had led to the ports being battened shut. Pistol drill had been initiated two days later. Firing at marks strung up from the spars, those designated boarders had fine-tuned their aim. On the *Cherub*, Tucker had flogged several men for a variety of petty crimes. On the 14th Jonathan Baker had been given twenty-four lashes for neglect of duty and partaking of stolen goods; Thomas Owens and John Rafferty received twelve apiece for disobedience of orders; Johnathan Pitman got twenty-four for drunkenness; and William Lint was punished with thirty-six for theft.[7]

On 24 January, as the *Indespensible* prepared to part company, Hillyar wrote to Secretary Croker. 'I have given convoy to the only British vessel I have heard of on this coast ... on her way to Europe', he began. 'Not being quite satisfied of the final departure of the American frigate ... I propose to proceed to Valparaiso for information previous to ... repassing Cape Horn ... Since my last ... I have experienced much anxiety respecting our separated companion [HMS *Raccoon*], having heard from an American gentleman, that as early as December 1812, accounts had reached New York of two hundred Americans having arrived at the Columbia to strengthen the settlement and that ships had also sailed for the northwest coast a few days previous to the commencement of hostilities with Great Britain.' Although Hillyar believed his mission had been a failure, a small glimmer of hope remained of 'Providence doing some good at Valparaiso ... This is my only present consolation', he confided in Croker, 'for my having been obliged to give up my voyage once promising to be of much usefulness for my country, interesting adventure and personal emolument.'[8]

On 27 January the *Indespensible* parted company. Later Ordinary Seaman James Hedges, a 34-year-old from Windsor who had been with the *Phoebe* since before the Battle of Tamatave, was 'attacked with a swelling in his leg' and was taken to Surgeon Smith's sick berth under the forecastle to recover. The next day Gardiner celebrated his twentieth birthday and on 29 January Captain Tucker had yet another of his men flogged. At some stage during the cruise from Callao, the *Cherub*'s junior lieutenant, the recently-commissioned John Belcher, a favourite of Rear-Admiral Dixon's who had been foisted on Tucker at Rio de Janiero, committed a crime. Although the details are unrecorded, Tucker considered it serious enough to have Belcher confined in his cabin under guard.[9]

On 3 February the swelling on Hedges' leg 'produced a mortification'. Within hours he had passed away. 'His loss was much lamented by all', Gardiner recorded, 'his upright character and good disposition, having endeared him to everyone on board.' Hedges' body was committed to the deep and the next day two Phoebes were flogged for insolence and theft. On the 5th the ships passed Juan Fernandez and changed course for Valparaiso. February 8th began unremarkably enough. At 4 a.m., as the *Phoebe*'s cook, John Dunn, lit the galley stove, the officer of the watch noted that the breeze was moderate and the weather cloudy. Fifty-five minutes later land was sighted and at 7 a.m. a strange sail, believed to be an American sloop, was spotted off the starboard bow. Dressed in a pea-green jacket, Hillyar ordered the cables ranged and the ship cleared for action as the stranger disappeared smartly round Angels Point. Captain Tucker followed suit. With anticipation rising, the *Phoebe* and *Cherub* tacked into Valparaiso Bay.[10]

Downes' signal flag had caused a flurry of activity. On the *Essex* Lieutenant Odenheimer hoisted a cornet; a gun was fired to call those ashore on board; Edward Lawson and the other prisoners were put in irons below decks; the crew cleared for action; and Porter was rowed across to the *Essex Junior* for a better look. Master George O'Brien of the *Emily* lowered a boat, mustered a scratch crew and rowed out towards Angels Point to intercept the strangers and several of the *Essex*'s boats set out from shore. On board the *Essex Junior*, Porter ordered Downes to stand out to the edge of the bay. Peering through his telescope, he judged the new arrivals to be frigates and returned to the *Essex*, leaving Downes with orders to run back into the roads 'and take a position where we could mutually defend each other'. At 7.30 a.m. Porter was back on board. 'I found the ship completely prepared for action', he recalled. 'Every man [was present and] ... at his post ... [and] we had now only to act on the defensive.' According to Farragut, however, not everything was as perfect as Porter had made out. Several of the Essexes had been drinking the previous night and were far from compos mentis. A few were unsteady on their feet and at least one, 'a mere boy', was fighting drunk.[11]

At 8 a.m. the *Phoebe* and *Cherub* rounded Angels Point. Before them was the quarry they had been seeking these past six months. The *Essex*, the *Essex Junior* and three of the prizes Porter had taken were all present. After getting over their surprise, the British officers were delighted and when George O'Brien's boat pulled alongside and Hillyar learnt that a third of Porter's crew were on shore, he decided to bring about an immediate resolution: if the Americans were short-handed, they could be taken by boarding. International convention prohibited Hillyar from firing on an enemy anchored within cannon shot of a neutral coast, but if he could provoke Porter into opening fire first, he would be perfectly within his rights to retaliate. Hauling into the harbour with a moderate wind, Hillyar made for the *Essex*, while Captain Tucker set a course to bring the *Cherub* alongside the *Essex Junior*.[12]

Farragut watched the British approach. Taking a wide berth of the rocks at Angels Point, the ships cut across the harbour and closed from the east. 'The *Phoebe* made our larboard quarter', the midshipman recalled, 'but the *Cherub* fell to leeward about half a mile [away]' where the *Essex Junior* rode at anchor. Putting the frigate's helm down, Hillyar luffed up within fifteen feet of Porter's starboard bow. Contrary to O'Brien's intelligence, the Americans were ready. 'The powder boys [were] stationed with slow matches ... to discharge the guns, [and] the boarders, cutlasses in hand, [were] standing by.' The tension was unbearable. Looking around, Farragut noticed 'the intoxicated youth . . . [He] saw or imagined that he saw, through the [gun] port, someone on the *Phoebe* grinning at him', the midshipman recalled and 'declared with drunken bravado, "I'll stop you making faces".' Grabbing a slow match, he leant forward to fire the nearest gun. With that all hell would have broken loose, but instead he was sent 'sprawl[ing] . . . on the deck' by a well-placed blow from an attentive Lieutenant McKnight.[13]

Fifteen feet away, it was beginning to dawn on Hillyar that O'Brien's intelligence had been flawed. The *Essex* was fully-manned and ready for action. Even though Porter's ship was four feet shorter than the *Phoebe* and not quite as broad, she packed a 676lb punch in weight of broadside compared to the *Phoebe*'s 502lbs. At such short range, the *Essex*'s carronades, which accounted for over 90 per cent of her firepower, could sweep Hillyar's quarterdeck and cause carnage below. Rapidly weighing his options, the Englishman decided to bluff. He raised his speaking trumpet to his lips, casually leant across the taffrail and called out across the water in a 'careless, indifferent manner: "Captain Hillyar's compliments to Captain Porter and hopes he is well."' Porter replied with equal equanimity. '"Very well, I thank you, but I hope you will not come too near, for fear some accident might take place which would be disagreeable to you".' The American punctuated his threat with a signal to his men. Hoisting the kedge anchors up to the yards, they prepared to grapple with the *Phoebe* before boarding. '"Upon my honour Captain Porter"', Hillyar responded, his arms raised in a theatrical gesture of supplication. '"I do not mean to touch you . . . I respect the neutrality of the port, & only came alongside for the purpose of enquiring after your health."' With that the Englishman signalled his men to back the yards. Her sails taut against the masts, the *Phoebe* inched away from the confrontation, her jib boom swinging perilously close to the *Essex*'s yards.[14]

Months later, Porter admitted that at that moment he had been caught in two minds. 'Not a gun from the *Phoebe* could be brought to bear on either the *Essex* or the *Essex Junior*', he explained, 'while her bow was exposed to the raking fire of the one and her stern to that of the other . . . I could have destroyed her in fifteen minutes . . . The temptation was great, but . . . [,] disarmed by these assurances of Captain Hillyar[, I]' delivered another warning instead.[15]

'You have no business where you are', Porter called out. 'If you touch a rope-yarn of this ship, I shall board instantly.' Hailing Downes, Porter ordered him not to fire without command, then signalled his boarders to take to the rigging. To Samuel Thornton Junior, the MP's son, it seemed as if no less than 340 'Yankee warriors . . . armed with Pistols and Cutlasses' filled the *Essex*'s yards. Many recently-recruited whalers recognised former crewmates across the water and Farragut noted Quarter Gunner Adam Roach had taken up a particularly belligerent position, 'exposed ... on the Cat Head ... with every expression of eagerness to ... board'. Slowly, the two ships parted while the shouts and whistles of the crew of the *Emily* and a host of Spaniards gathered on shore carried across the bay. 'The *Phoebe*['s] ... yards passed over ours', Farragut recalled, 'not touching a rope and [at 10.55 a.m.] she anchored [in 16 fathoms] about half a mile astern' – well within range of Hillyar's 18-pounders, yet beyond that of Porter's carronades. Captain Tucker anchored the *Cherub*, which also packed a powerful close-range punch, within pistol-shot of the *Essex*'s larboard bow.[16]

That afternoon the *Phoebe*'s boats went ashore to water while Hillyar reformulated his plan of attack. Instead of prompting a rash confrontation, he would blockade the Americans at the mouth of the bay. First, however, he needed to resupply. The *Phoebe*'s supplies of salt beef in particular were running perilously low. By 4 p.m. ten tons of water and two oxen had been brought on board. One was slaughtered and 129lbs of fresh beef sent across to the *Cherub*. Meanwhile, Downes had moved the *Essex Junior*. Unhappy that the British had gained an advantage by their choice of mooring sites, Porter had his consort 'take a position that would place the *Cherub* between [the *Essex Junior*'s] fire and that of the *Essex*'. Downes followed his orders to the letter. The *Essex Junior* dropped anchor within a few dozen yards of her adversary, 'an arrangement', Porter noted, 'that gave great umbrage to ... Captain Tucker'.[17]

That evening Hillyar interviewed the crew of the *Emily* and Richard Jones, a 25-year-old able seaman from Cornwall, joined the *Phoebe*'s muster. Besides learning of Porter's ill-advised attempt at Pacific colonialism, Hillyar also discovered that several of the Essexes and Essex Juniors were former British whalers captured during the cruise. At sunset the *Phoebe*'s boats were hoisted up and that night, the crews of the *Cherub* and *Essex Junior* exchanged insults across the water. Samuel Thornton Junior considered it 'not unentertaining'. His former shipmate on HMS *Amazon*, the *Phoebe*'s First Lieutenant, William Ingram, was less impressed.[18]

At dawn on 9 February the sun broke through the clouds. The *Phoebe*'s boats, aided by those of the *Emily*, watered while the morning watch mended the frigate's sails. At 8 a.m. the *Essex* hoisted a large white flag at her foretopgallant masthead emblazoned with Porter's motto, 'Sailors' Rights and Free Trade'. 'To counteract this insidious effort to shake the loyalty of thoughtless British seamen', Hillyar had the *Phoebe*'s Saint George's ensign adorned with the slogan 'Traitors offend both God and Country. British Sailors' best Rights'. The Essexes manned their rigging and gave three cheers at the sight. Hillyar had his band strike up 'God Save the King' and his sailors gave three cheers in reply. 'A finer sight never was seen', Thornton opined, 'than after the first stanza ... when we cheered again, & the *Essex* answered our cheers, & struck up the Rights of Man.' This chest-beating went on all day. 'Boats full of liberty men . . . passed us', Hillyar recalled, 'carrying small flags with inscriptions on them, such as "Sons of Commerce, Free Trade", etc'. After circling the British ships, the Americans paraded over Valparaiso's hills.[19]

At noon, to the thunder of a fifteen-gun salute, Governor Lastra boarded the *Phoebe*. Hillyar discharged the patriot prisoners put into his care and Lastra responded by assuring him 'that the [Chilean] government [was] favourable to England' and promised he would do everything in his power to aid him. Hillyar met the courtesy by offering his services as a mediator between the Patriots and Royalists as per Abascal's suggestion 'as soon as he should be freed from the duty of watching the American ships'. According to Samuel Burr Johnston, an American printer and journalist who had arrived with Poinsett to set up the Patriots' first newspaper, Lastra was painfully deferential to the British captain. 'So much so', he wrote, 'that you could even say that [Hillyar] . . . began to govern the country from the moment he dropped anchor in Valparaiso'. Porter agreed. 'When I commanded the most powerful force in the Pacific [in the first half of 1813], all were willing to serve me', he complained, 'but when Captain Hillyar appeared, with one still stronger, it became the great object [of the Chilean government] to conciliate his friendship, by evincing hostility to me.'[20]

Lastra's fawning was a result of the ever-changing situation in Chile. At the start of 1814 the Loyalists had been bolstered by a second task force sent from Peru. Commanded by General Gavino Gainza, it landed at Arauco, where it was reinforced by Mapuche chieftains, before uniting with Antonio Pareja's troops at Chillán and attacking the Patriot lines. To the north, Bernardo O'Higgins' star continued to rise and on 1 February Carrera reluctantly gave his support to the new commander. As a result, the moderates in the Chilean Junta, amongst whom Lastra was a key figure, began to dominate. As far as the British and Americans in Valparaiso were concerned, the upshot was a tendency to favour Britain over a more risky association with the still-emerging United States.[21]

On the afternoon of 9 February Hillyar and Tucker visited Porter at Mr Blanco's house. The convivial atmosphere belied the fact that their two countries were at war. After each paid the other the customary compliments, Porter asked 'whether . . . [Hillyar] intended to respect the neutrality of the port'. The Englishman assured his adversary that he felt 'duty bound in honour to respect it'. The discussion then turned to the captains' recent cruises.

Porter recalled that:

> We talked freely and good humouredly of the object of [Hillyar's]
> coming to [the Pacific] and on my views in coming to Valparaiso. He
> asked me what I intended to do with my prizes; [and] when I was going

to sea ... I told him, whenever he sent away the *Cherub*, I should [set sail and] ... added, that the *Essex* being smaller than the *Phoebe*, I did not feel that I should be justified to my country for losing my ship, if I gave him a challenge, but if he would challenge me and send away the *Cherub*, I would have no hesitation in fighting ... Captain Hillyar ... repl[ied] ... that the results of naval actions were very uncertain: ... the loss of a mast or spar, often turned the fate of the day. He observed, that notwithstanding the inferiority of my ship ... if I could come to close quarters with her carronades, I should no doubt do great execution. On the whole, therefore, [Hillyar said] he should trust to circumstances to bring us together, as he was not disposed to yield the advantage of a superior force ... [and] would ... blockade me until other ships arrived ... As regarded my prizes, I informed him, they were only encumbrances to me and I should take them to sea and destroy them, the first opportunity. He told me I dared not do it while he was in sight. I replied, 'we shall see'.[22]

At 6 p.m. that evening, Richard Mclean, one of the men imprisoned on the *Essex Junior* for the Nuka Hiva poison plot, freed himself from his irons. Dashing up to the waist, he leapt overboard and swam towards the *Cherub*. Captain Tucker had a boat lowered and sent to his aid. Downes responded in kind, but the British proved quicker. Mclean was soon safely on board the *Cherub* and that night was entered onto her muster roll. Stories of Mclean's treatment at the hands of Porter and Gamble soon spread to the *Phoebe*, prompting Hillyar to write to Porter that evening: 'Captain Tucker has been informed', he began, 'that nine of our countrymen are suffering the miseries of close confinement ... under your orders ... aggravated by their being kept in irons. As this mode of treatment is so contrary to ... the usages of honourable warfare, may I beg ... that you will do me the favour to interest yourself in their behalf.'[23]

That night the rival crews once again exchanged insults across the water. 'You Rascals, we've found you at last', yelled a Cherub. 'Yes', an Essex Junior replied, 'you have found the worst job you've had to do since you left England, we will give you [HMS] *Java*'s time for it.' 'The Yankees then struck up a Song', Thornton recalled, '[entitled] Let Britain no longer lay claim to the Seas', which 'was ... answered by Rule Britannia which the whole crews of the *Cherub* & *Phoebe* ... joined in'. As the night wore on, the singing grew more inventive. 'Some of [the songs] ... were of their own composition', Porter recalled. 'Those ... from the *Cherub* were better sung, but those of the *Essex* were more witty and more to the point. The national tune of the yankee doodle was the vehicle through which the crew ... in full chorus, conveyed their ... sarcasms; while "the sweet little Cherub that sits up aloft", was . . . selected by their rivals.' The locals were much amused. Eugenio Santos, a young boy at the time, understood little of what he heard, but as an old man would still remember the nightly choruses of the summer of 1814.[24]

On 10 February while the British boats carried oxen, vegetables and water out to the roads, Hillyar wrote to the Admiralty with barely disguised glee. Several other Phoebes took advantage of the imminent departure of a postal dispatch rider for Buenos Ayres to write to their families, but Lieutenant Ingram decided against it. Despite not having had an opportunity to address a letter home since leaving Rio, the 27-year-old thought he would wait until the battle had been fought so as not to unduly worry his mother, Anne. That afternoon Porter penned a reply to Hillyar's letter of 9 February, justifying his treatment of his prisoners by referencing their attempt to poison his men. The Essexes spent the day unloading the sandalwood and livestock in the frigate's hold onto one of the prizes and at 10 p.m. it was discovered that Lieutenant John Belcher, the *Cherub*'s junior commissioned officer, had escaped from close confinement. A search turned up a note explaining that he '[had] commit[ted] himself to the waves'.[25]

The next day passed peacefully. In the morning the Phoebes washed their hammocks and clothes. The Essexes continued unloading Porter's stocks of sandalwood and hoisted several small guns up onto the booms; while the Cherubs painted their carronades and the *Phoebe* took on 340 bags of bread. William Kirby, an eighteen-year-old midshipman who had been under Hillyar's command since 1812, was transferred to the *Cherub* as Captain Tucker's acting Second Lieutenant to replace Belcher, now listed 'missing presumed drowned' and Samuel Thornton Junior was promoted to midshipman in Kirby's stead. The next morning a white flag was hoisted from the *Essex*'s mizzen top. Since his meeting with Hillyar, Porter had 'secretly resolved to take every means of provoking' his opponent to a single-ship duel and the new banner, emblazoned with the motto 'God, Our Country and Liberty, Tyrants Offend Them', was his latest attempt to circumvent the Englishman's icy resolve. The Phoebes responded with three cheers, promptly returned by the *Essex*.[26]

At some point during the next two days Hillyar was rowed ashore. His first order of business was to set up a signal station on one of the hills to allow regular reports on the enemy's movements to be broadcast out into the bay. Later, Hillyar met with a number of Britons living in Valparaiso: Thomas Crompton, the merchant who had taken passage in the *Phoebe* from Callao; George Cood, a native of Donegal who had been resident since August 1813 and was a supercargo for the *Good Friends*; Andrew Blest, an Irish doctor and Protestant minister who had arrived in 1812 with a consignment of scriptures supplied by the Bible Society in London; and Andrew Munro, a Scottish merchant with a financial interest in the *Emily*. All were concerned by the turbulent political situation in Chile. Forced to remain in port by government order as a means of lessening their risk of capture by American cruisers and Peruvian privateers, the merchants worried that their goods would spoil and wanted Governor Lastra to pay compensation. Having promised to look into the issue, Hillyar proceeded to Blanco's house for another meeting with Porter. The Bostonian asked permission to send his prisoners to England on one of his prizes 'with a passport to secure her from capture; there to take in an equal number of American prisoners and proceed with them to the United States'. Hillyar refused. Besides being contrary to the norms of war, the proposition was entirely in Porter's favour. Not only would it release him from the responsibility of guarding his prisoners, it would also ensure that they could not be released if the cartel was recaptured by the British on the high seas.[27]

During the days that the Royal Navy ships spent in the roads, several of Hillyar's and Porter's junior officers fraternised on shore. A few even struck up lasting friendships. The young British midshipman, Samuel Thornton Junior, and the *Essex*'s schoolmaster-cum-chaplain, David Phineas Adams, realised they had a mutual interest in anthropology and Adams presented Thornton with several of the 'Indian curiosities' he had acquired while at Nuka Hiva. Porter claimed that the frigates' rival boats' crews also mixed in an amicable manner, although Farragut stated 'they invariably fought'. Several were old acquaintances. Jeremiah Ryan, who joined the *Phoebe* at Callao, had served on the *Greenwich* with Lewis Earle, Peter Ripple and John Deacon, all of whom had signed up on the *Essex*; James Tucker and Daniel Smith had served together on the *New Zealander*; and Thomas James of the *Phoebe* and John Powell and Robert Brown of the *Essex* had all sailed on the *Montezuma*. As she was on her way back to England when captured, they must have lived together for at least two years![28]

On 14 February Hillyar completed his supplies. Purser Nickenson purchased 120lbs of white rope which was sent across to the *Cherub* along with barrels of cocoa, dried beef and flour, bags of bread, fresh vegetables and several live oxen. That afternoon Porter promoted John M. Maury, the midshipman who had joined the *Essex* at Nuka Hiva, to acting lieutenant and sent him on board the *Essex Junior* to reinforce Lieutenant Downes. At dawn on the 15th a lookout on the *Essex* observed the local telegraph station signalling a strange sail off shore. 'The morning being calm', Porter decided to test his opponents' readiness. Sending his boats across to the *Essex Junior*, he had the sloop towed out of the bay to reconnoitre. The British failed to react until 9 a.m., when an offshore breeze allowed the *Phoebe* and *Cherub* to set sail in pursuit. Rather than directly following Downes' line, Hillyar set a course which would bring him wide round Angels Point allowing him to pursue the *Essex Junior* while also keeping the *Essex* in sight. By this stage Downes had intercepted the stranger. She proved to be the *Vulture*, the Peruvian privateer which had taken the *Boriska* and *Hunter* to Callao. Downes then tacked and raced back to the bay with the *Phoebe* and *Cherub* coming out into open sea three miles off his larboard bow. Hauling in for the land, Downes passed tight round Angels Point a pistol shot from the rocks. Hillyar signalled Captain Tucker to pursue the American, while he sailed on to investigate the stranger. Tucker tacked and piled on all sail, but the *Essex Junior* slipped back into the roads before the *Cherub* could get within cannon shot. Porter was delighted. If Downes could outrun the British ships, then so could he.[29]

That afternoon, the *Phoebe* and *Cherub* reunited at the mouth of the bay where one of the *Emily*'s boats came out to meet them. On board were six new recruits. Five, including George O'Brien, the former Royal Navy lieutenant, temporarily joined the *Phoebe* from the *Emily*. The sixth was Landsman Daniel Coleman, a deserter from the *Essex* who had been under Porter's command since he had left the Delaware sixteen months before. Exactly how or why Coleman deserted is a matter of speculation. Porter fails to mention the incident. A member of the United States Navy willingly placing himself under British 'tyranny' did not fit the Bostonian's view of the world. Gardiner, on the other hand, hints at an explanation. Coleman, like many 'Americans' in the US Navy, was most likely an Englishman who had once served in the Royal Navy. Having spent two days staring at Hillyar's motto: 'Traitors offend both God and Country', he perhaps felt it time to throw himself on the mercy of his former employers. The alternative – capture after battle – would result in a court martial. Hanging from the yardarm was the punishment for men caught fighting their own side.[30]

The *Phoebe* and *Cherub* spent the next six weeks blockading the Americans. By tacking and wearing dozens of times a day, an exhausting undertaking which First Lieutenant Ingram sarcastically dubbed 'delightful work', they would attempt to maintain a position one to three miles northwest of Angels Point. In theory this would enable Hillyar to keep the *Essex* in sight while also being able to intercept any vessels entering or leaving the bay. In practice blockading was not an exact science, as Gardiner explained, 'we were frequently becalmed and drifted a long way from shore ... on the other hand, it sometimes blew so strong that it was with great difficulty, by carrying a press of sail, we could keep to windward of the port'. The worst case scenario was shipwreck off Angels Point. Able seamen were constantly employed sounding to ensure the British did not meet such a fate.[31]

On 16 February the Phoebes 'agreed to share prize money with the officers and Crew of the *Cherub* during the time both ships remained westward [of] Cape Horn'. That afternoon a Spanish boat, possibly sent by Governor Lastra, warned Hillyar that the *Essex* was preparing to get under weigh. The Phoebes were beat to quarters, but it proved a false alarm. At 2 a.m. on the 19th, Boatswain John Pomfrey, whom Hillyar had 'begged' the Admiralty to appoint an onshore role at Plymouth due to his age and ill-health, 'departed this life'. His body was committed to the deep at 2 o'clock that afternoon. Four hours later the Phoebes and Cherubs exercised their great guns and small arms, an event which would become a daily fixture from then on. On 22 February Captain Tucker sent his boatswain, William Forder, to replace Pomfrey, while John Gillespie, a 41-year-old Phoebe and veteran of Trafalgar was appointed to fill Forder's berth.[32]

That afternoon, while Hillyar and Tucker oversaw gun drill two miles off Angels Point, Porter began to make preparations to put to sea, 'to know the sailing of my ship and that of the enemy'. Two days before he had sent 150 men on board the *Essex Junior*, a fact reported to Hillyar by the crew of the *Emily* and that afternoon Porter took to the hills to study the movements of the British ships and determine the best means of eluding them. The resident British merchants took careful note of Porter's movements. When he moved to a four-gun battery on a bluff to the north of the bay, they grew convinced that he was intending to run for the open sea. At 8.30 p.m. their suspicions seemed to be confirmed. Two blue lights – the signal used to indicate that a ship was about to leave port – were spotted burning on shore.[33]

The *Phoebe*'s and *Cherub*'s lookouts also saw the lights and the ships cleared for action. As the gun crews rushed to their stations and the partitions were stowed, Hillyar flashed a lantern signal to Tucker ordering him to stand close inshore. Both crews passed the hours of darkness in a state of nervous tension. While the topmen tacked again and again to maintain their ships' positions, the gun crews remained below decks, expecting the Americans to slide out of the darkness, their carronades blazing or attempt to elude them by sailing close along the shore. Dawn brought a mixture of relief and frustration. The *Essex* and *Essex Junior* remained at anchor in the roads.[34]

Porter spent the morning of Thursday 23 February paying his debts in town. That afternoon he re-climbed the path to the battery on the bluff, prompting Thomas Crompton to write a letter urging Hillyar to remain on guard. 'I think ... [Porter] intends to weigh out with his parachutes', the merchant warned. 'The governor says he may get out with a strong north wind. If you want anything whatever drop me a line.' At 10 a.m. Crompton sent the note to sea on one of the *Emily*'s boats just as a sudden squall ripped across the bay. With the *Phoebe* and *Cherub* blown six miles out to sea, Porter made his move. The *Essex*'s cable, taken from a prize, was cut and by 10.20 a.m. the American frigate was under weigh. Several miles beyond Angels Point, Hillyar spotted the move, piled on as much sail as he dared and attempted to tack back into the bay. The Phoebes and Cherubs were beat to quarters and the gun deck cleared for action for the second time that day. Porter was delighted. 'I ... ascertained that ... [we] had greatly the advantage and consequently believed I could, at almost any time, make my escape'. Nevertheless, the Bostonian chose to remain. There was still hope that he might provoke Hillyar into accepting a challenge and win everlasting fame. With the *Phoebe*'s mizzen top and fore topsails being torn to shreds by the squall, the *Essex* tacked and returned to the anchorage.[35]

Over the next two days several letters were exchanged between Hillyar and Porter concerning the latter's prisoners and on the morning of 25 February they were released on parole. Hillyar, in return, promised to write to the Admiralty and request that the same number of US prisoners be granted liberty and restored to their homes. At 4 p.m., Porter attempted to provoke Hillyar into action once more. With the British maintaining their vigil three miles off Angels Point, the Essexes towed the *Hector* a mile from shore and set her alight. Her timbers impregnated with whale oil, the 270-ton prize burned for four and a half hours as she drifted across the bay. Blazing debris rained down over the port and she passed within a musket shot of the British and Spanish shipping in the roads. The British merchants were furious. Calling Porter's act a 'gross' and 'shameful' violation of the port's neutrality, they wrote to Hillyar assuring him that he would now be well within his rights to attack the Americans, whether they were within gunshot of the shore or not. Gardiner also felt that Porter had broken the law, while Governor Lastra was 'indignant' and went on board the *Essex* that afternoon 'to let Captn. Porter know that he consider[ed] ... the burning of the English prize ... a complete violation'. At 9 p.m., with her blackened timbers still crackling, the *Hector* sank beneath the waves. Porter felt that his methods were entirely justified. He was convinced that he was beginning to work his way under Hillyar's skin.[36]

At 7 a.m. on Sunday 27 February a dead calm fell over the bay. With the current setting off shore, the *Phoebe* and *Cherub* drifted out to sea and by 11 a.m., as Hillyar gathered his men for divine service, the British ships were fully six miles off Angels Point. At 2 p.m. a westerly breeze picked up. Shaking three reefs out of their topsails, the Phoebes managed to hold their position, but the *Cherub* drifted further northwest. By the middle of the afternoon six miles separated the British ships and at 5.30 p.m. Hillyar fired a gun and hoisted a signal ordering the *Cherub* to sail closer inshore. Misreading the separation as a deliberate act and interpreting the signal gun as a challenge, Porter assumed that Hillyar had finally taken the bait. He ordered the *Essex* and *Essex Junior* to slip their cables and hoisted his motto flags and a jack to all three mastheads. With the offshore breeze behind them, the American ships were soon racing out of the bay.

With the *Cherub* five miles to leeward, Hillyar was faced with a difficult decision. Even given a favourable change in the wind, Tucker could not possibly hope to come up within the next hour and half. This left two choices: either Hillyar could flee, thereby abandoning his mission or he could stand and fight. Despite being outgunned, the Englishman chose the latter. 'We immediately prepared to receive them', he recalled. 'The colours were hoisted, the main topsail backed and the driver brailed up'. As the ship was cleared for action, Hillyar took to the gundeck, 'read prayers ... adapted to the occasion ... [and] admonished the ... [men] to be calm & steady'. He was answered with three cheers. By 7 p.m. the *Essex* and *Essex Junior* were closing rapidly, the frigate racing ahead. Not wanting to give Porter the choice of both 'distance' and 'situation', Hillyar wore to bring his starboard broadside to bear on the *Essex*'s bow. With the helm hard over, the *Phoebe* turned away from the wind. A mile to the eastward, Porter interpreted the movement as an attempt to run down towards the *Cherub* and directed two shot to be fired ahead of the *Phoebe* to bring her to. Hillyar continued wearing, his gun crews rushing across to man the starboard broadside, but before the *Phoebe*'s stern could be brought round into the wind, Porter hauled onto the larboard tack and headed back to port. Hillyar stood after him, but at 8 p.m. the American reached the safety of the anchorage before the *Phoebe*'s shot 'could be expected to produce any material effect'.

With contradictory evidence on both sides, the incident of 27 February is open to interpretation. The Americans claimed Hillyar had run from the fight. Porter was 'extremely indignant' and Farragut was incensed. 'This I consider the 2nd breach of faith on the part of Capt. H', the midshipman wrote. 'By his manoeuvres in both [the incident of 27 February and that which occurred when the two ships had met on the 8] it was evident, he either had not the courage or wanted the good faith of a high toned chivalrous spirit, to act out the original intention.' Both British ships' logs and Midshipman Gardiner, on the other hand, maintained that it was Porter who had fled while Hillyar himself remained characteristically unmoved. 'I should not have thought this circumstance of sufficient consideration to detail to their lordships', he informed Secretary Croker, 'had not Capn. Porter's unkind assertion [made several months later] called it forth.' One consequence was that the British now felt that the Americans had twice breached the neutrality of the port. Interpreting the two shots Porter had fired as an act of aggression undertaken within the extremities of the bay, the feeling that the Americans had no right to claim further protection was rapidly gaining currency.[37]

On the 28th Hillyar and Tucker resumed their positions off Angels Point. There they would remain for the next four weeks. Both practised regular boarding drills by divisions and exercised their great guns and small arms, while a stream of boats came out from the *Emily* with supplies. Occasionally, Porter would attempt to provoke Hillyar into making a mistake. Ordering the *Essex Junior* to sally out to the mouth of the bay, he had her towed in again as soon as the British reacted.[38]

Meanwhile, in the Chilean south, the Peruvian-backed Royalists were gaining the upper hand. At the end of February, under pressure from General Gainza, O'Higgins abandoned his base at Talca; on 3 March a Loyalist column occupied the town after massacring the garrison and the next day Royalist guerrillas captured José and Luis Carrera. The news caused panic in Santiago. A *Cabildo Abierto*[39] vested power in Governor Lastra with the title of Supreme Director while O'Higgins rallied his troops and attempted to bar Gainza's route north. One consequence was that on 8 March Lastra left for the capital, appointing the 32-year-old Captain Francisco de Formas as governor of Valparaiso in his stead. An ineffectual leader, Formas had gained a reputation for cowardice when serving the Carreras and proved unable to assert his authority. With a power vacuum in Valparaiso, Hillyar and Porter were free to act as they chose.[40]

On 9 March the Essexes printed a letter in the local newspaper, the *Aurora*. 'The sons of liberty and commerce on board the saucy *Essex* ... present their compliments to their oppressed brother tars, on board the ship whose motto is too tedious to mention', it began. '[We] hope ... [you] will put an end to all this nonsense of singing, sporting, hunting and writing, which we know less about than the use of our guns. Send the *Cherub* away, we will meet your frigate and fight you, then shake hands and be friends ... if we take you, we shall respect the rights of a sailor, hail you as brethren whom we have liberated from slavery and place you in future beyond the reach of a press gang.'[41]

The next day Gardiner responded in verse:

> To you, Americans, who seek redress,
> For fancied wrongs from Britons you've sustained;
> Hear what we Britons now to you address,
> From malice free, from blasphemy unstain'd;
> Think not, vain boasters, that your insidious lay,
> Which calls for vengeance from the Almighty God Can
> from their duty Britons lead away,
> Or path of honor which they have always trod.
> No-Your vile infamy can never fail,
> To excite disgust in each true Briton's heart;
> Your proffered liberty cannot avail,
> For virtue is the sons of Albion's crest.
> Our God, our king, our country and our Laws,
> We proudly reverence like Britons true;
> Our captain who defends such glorious cause,
> Meets due respect from all his grateful crew.
> When to the battle we're by duty called,
> Our cause, like Britons, bravely we'll maintain;
> We'll fight like men whom fear ne'er yet appall'd,
> And hope, AMERICANS! you'll do the same.
> Your vile letter, which on board, was brought,

We scorn to answer, tho' with malice frought;
But if, by such foul means, you think to make
Dissentions rise our loyalty to shake,
Know then we are Britons all, both stout and true,
We love our king, our country, captain too;
When honor calls, we'll glory in his name,
Acquit like men and hope you'll do the same.[42]

On 12 March there was another dead calm. With the *Phoebe* and *Cherub* maintaining position off the point with their stream anchors, Porter decided to attempt a nighttime cutting-out operation. After dark ten boats filled with heavily-armed men set out with muffled oars. They were spotted in the roads, however, and a message dispatched to Hillyar warning him of the imminent attack. The *Phoebe*'s and *Cherub*'s cutters were lowered to tow the ships, thus preventing them from being a sitting target, while the men armed themselves. As the Americans approached, Porter overheard a conversation on the *Phoebe*'s quarterdeck and learnt that his plan had been discovered. Ordering the boats to return to port, he left the British to ponder another American attempt to violate Chilean neutrality.[43]

In mid-March the war of words intensified. The British labelled their enemies 'Blackguard[s]' and damned them for writing 'Blasphemous productions'. The Americans responded in kind. Both sides alleged the other had fled on 27 February and on 15 March rumours reached Hillyar that Porter had accused him of cowardice. His honour besmirched, at 5 p.m. the British captain ordered Ingram to row to the *Essex* under a flag of truce 'to ascertain the truth'. Porter admitted he had called Hillyar a coward, 'and still thought [him] so. [Ingram] then stated', as Porter recalled, 'that Captain Hillyar had entrusted him to tell me, that his firing a gun and hoisting the flag [on 27 February], was not intended as a challenge, but as a signal to the Cherub.' Porter dismissed the explanation, insisting that all who had witnessed the event agreed that Hillyar had deliberately shied away. 'Again [Ingram] ... assured me of the mistake;' Porter recalled, 'adding, that Captain Hillyar was a religious man and did not approve of sending challenges.' Having long since established his reputation for bravery, as the First Lieutenant explained, Hillyar intended to adhere to 'an implicit obedience to his orders to capture the *Essex*, at the least possible risk to his vessel and crew'.

Although Ingram followed Hillyar's orders, he did not concur with his strategy. Yet to win his laurels on the field of battle, the First Lieutenant was as keen as Porter to establish his martial reputation. Combined with his 'manly, frank and chivalrous bearing[, this sentiment] quite won the hearts of' the American officers who had gathered in Porter's cabin. Warming to his audience, Ingram professed that 'it would be the happiest moment of his life', if the *Phoebe* were to prove victorious and he was ordered 'to take ... [the *Essex* as a prize] to England', but only if she was taken 'in equal fight'. Porter's reply matched his guest's in chivalry. 'If such an event had to occur', the Bostonian stated, 'he knew of no British officer to whom he would more readily yield his honour.' It was a sentiment with which Farragut and the rest of the American 'officers and crew sincerely coincided'.[44]

A day of squalls followed Ingram's visit. The *Phoebe* and *Cherub* struggled to maintain their stations, but on 18 March the breeze moderated, allowing the British ships to take on canvas, cannon balls, twine, rope and hides. The next day a dead calm prompted Hillyar and Tucker to deploy their stream anchors and that night the British boats rowed guard. The next morning, after divine service, Hillyar received a letter from Thomas Crompton. Having travelled to Santiago, the merchant had learnt that the Carrera brothers had been placed under arrest and that a ship from Guernsey, recently arrived at Buenos Ayres, had brought news from Europe. Dresden and Leipzig had been taken from the French; Marshal Davout was cut off in Hamburg; Soult had been defeated by Wellington; the British were laying siege to Bayonne; and Napoleon was in Paris in a desperate attempt to conscript a further 350,000 men. Less encouragingly, fifteen French frigates were rumoured to have escaped the blockade at Brest and the US Navy was boasting of having captured a British East Indiaman with $2 million on board.[45]

That night the *Phoebe*'s and *Cherub*'s boats rowed guard duty in shore. As well as ensuring that no American boats slipped by, they were charged with keeping an eye on the *Essex*. If she were to sail, they were to purse her at a distance and light blue flares to attract Hillyar's attention. On the *Phoebe* Lieutenant Ingram wrote to his mother. 'I have a presentiment that this will be the night', he began, '[and] knowing how uncertain the fate of war is ... it is my first prayer to the almighty that he will endow me with that courage becoming my situation and protect me through the battle ... Should it be his divine will to take me from this world through the mercy of our blessed saviour [I pray] to have all my various sins forgiven [and] that he will protect my beloved mother, sister & brother.' At the foot of the letter Ingram composed his will. All his possessions and future pay and prize money were left to his mother, to divide up amongst herself and his siblings, aside from 'four or five pounds' which he owed to 'Mr George of Plymouth' and £400 which he bequeathed to 'Miss Slade' – presumably the young lady to whom he had recently become engaged. Lieutenant Burrow of the marines and Acting Third Lieutenant Henry Gardner served as witnesses.[46]

Despite Ingram's 'presentiment', the night passed uneventfully and dawn revealed the Americans ships remained in the roads. That morning James Tucker, a 28-year-old able seaman from Portsmouth who had joined the *Essex* after being captured from the *New Zealander*, 'made his escape' and signed up on board the *Phoebe*. On 19 March Hillyar received another letter from Crompton. The merchant had learnt 'that the *Tagus* Frigate had arrived off Montevideo bound around Cape Horn in search of the ... *Essex*'. The news dramatically altered the dynamic at Valparaiso. If Porter continued to delay, he ran the risk of his enemies being reinforced. Paradoxically, the Phoebes and Cherubs, unwilling to lessen their share of the potential prize money, were equally keen to bring the contest to a conclusion.[47]

Over the next three days both sides' preparations gathered pace. The British were hampered by a series of squalls interspersed by calm weather when the stream anchors were employed. The gunners turned their powder supplies, while the crews chipped the rough edges from the roundshot. Each night boats, supplied with blue signal flares, went in shore to watch the Americans and both Hillyar and Tucker exercised their great guns twice daily while the marines fired at targets suspended from the yards. Porter, meanwhile, was taking every volunteer he could get. On 26 March Samuel Burr Johnson, the American newspaperman, was signed up as the *Essex*'s lieutenant of marines. In the second week of March, Joel Poinsett, the American trade consul who had been fighting with the patriot armies in the south, returned to Valparaiso. As well as confirming the imminent arrival of the *Tagus*, he also heard rumours that two more British frigates were *en route* and that HMS *Raccoon* was expected to call in at Valparaiso on her way home. The odds were stacking ever further in Hillyar's favour. Porter had run out of time.[48]

Chapter 13

The Battle, 27–28 March 1814

On the morning of 27 March 1814 Porter informed Downes he intended to sail early the next day. While Porter drew the *Phoebe* and *Cherub* out to sea, where the *Essex*'s superior sailing would place her beyond Hillyar's reach, the *Essex Junior* was to escape to the north. The ships would make for a pre-arranged rendezvous before returning to Nuka Hiva, provisioning and sailing for the Horn. After nearly a year and a half at sea, the Americans were heading home. That evening Purser Shaw was sent into town as a decoy where he would remain until the ships had sailed in an attempt to convince Hillyar that the *Essex* was not yet ready for sea.[1]

After nightfall Porter deployed his second *ruse de guerre*. John Maury, acting First Lieutenant on the *Essex Junior*, was ordered to take the fastest boat and slip past the British crew rowing guard. The first part of his instructions successfully completed, Maury turned northwest and heading up the coast beyond Point Piedra. Shortly after midnight he lit several blue flares. Hillyar and Tucker were both taken in. Believing the lights to be a signal from their own boat indicating that the *Essex* had put to sea, they cleared for action and gave chase. At 1 a.m., as the British ships closed with fresh breezes, Maury lit another flare, flashed a signal light and fired a rocket into the darkness. He then spun his boat around and returned to the anchorage as fast as he could.[2]

Hillyar was beginning to smell a rat. At 1.30 a.m. he ordered a signal lantern flashed to the north and when no answer was forthcoming, became convinced he had been duped. Shortening sail, he hauled to the larboard tack and ordered Tucker to follow him back to the bay. The British were in a race against time. Worried that the *Essex* and *Essex Junior* were escaping, Hillyar had his men tack and wear repeatedly, beating southwards against the wind. At 1.40 a.m. the frigate's main topsail split under the pressure. Racing up the ratlines, the men replaced it and by 4 a.m. the *Phoebe* had regained her station off Angels Point. Unsure if his enemies had fled, Hillyar faced an agonising two-and-a-half hour wait until dawn.[3]

Porter had spent the night preparing for sea. Final checks were made to the sails and rigging and Edward Lawson and the other poison plotters were transferred to the *Essex Junior*. In the small hours, when the decoy boat returned, Porter summoned Maury to his cabin. Informed that the British were still several miles to leeward, the captain sped up his preparations, but at 6.30 a.m. first light revealed the British ships in their customary position off Angels Point. Porter was as surprised as Hillyar was relieved.

By noon the sun had burnt through the cloud cover and the wind was blowing ever stronger out of the south southwest. Not wishing to lose another sail, Hillyar ordered his men to take down the royal yards and close reef the topsails. Five miles to the east, Porter followed suit. That afternoon the weather deteriorated and by 2 p.m. fresh gales interspersed with heavy squalls were tearing across the bay.

At 2.45 p.m. a particularly violent squall struck the *Essex*. Her top and mainsails taut under the pressure, the frigate tore her larboard cable and began dragging her starboard anchor across the bay. With the rest of his cables stowed on the orlop deck, Porter had no choice but to put to sea. Ordering Downes to send a boat to take Poinsett on shore, he cut his remaining cable, set the topgallant sails and sailed westwards out of the roads. Downes followed once the trade consul had been taken ashore. By now a crowd of locals had gathered on the hills to watch the drama develop and George O'Brien, who had been working on shore with the *Phoebe*'s cutter, had himself rowed out to the British ships with Mr N. Murphy, the master of the *Good Friends*. Both were desperate not to miss out on the action. Porter, meanwhile, was set upon a perilous course. Trusting on his ship's superiority when hauling close to the wind, he took a line tight round the rocks off Angels Point, intending to run into the open sea to the south before the British could get within range.

At 3.05 p.m. Hillyar ordered his men to give chase and clear for action. '[The topmen] immediately made all sail', Gardiner recalled, while the boatswains beat to quarters. The wardroom partitions were pulled down, the officers' furniture stowed below the waterline, the men's mess tables were hoisted to the ceiling and tied off and their hammocks tightly rolled into dense tubes, taken to the quarterdeck and secured round the bulwarks to provide extra protection. The decks were covered in sand to soak up the blood; livestock were hurled overboard; a net, known as a *sauve-tete*, was rigged to catch any blocks shot out of the tops; and the boats were lowered and towed astern. On the gun deck the men opened the ports, removed the tompions, allowing them to hang by the muzzles and hauled at the breeching ropes to run out the guns. Shot, wadding, matches, match tubs, powder horns, sponges, hand spikes and worms were laid out; Gunner Lawson made up fresh cartridges in the magazine, while Surgeon Smith and his assistant, Adam Simpson, readied knives, bandages and bone saws in the cockpit.

At 3.10 p.m. the *Essex* luffed round Angels Point, the wind howling round the rocks from the open sea. With his mainmast creaking under the pressure, Porter ordered the topgallant sails taken in. The topmen clambered up the ratlines, edged along the spars and gathered in the courses, but the order had come too late. 'Scarcely had the ... sails been clewed down, when a squall struck the ship.' Resigning themselves to losing the sail, the topmen let the halyards slip through their fingers, but the yards jammed. The *Essex* heeled over with the strain. With waves crashing over her gunwales, for a moment it seemed as if she might founder. Then, with a terrible splintering, the lower cap snapped and the main topmast, trailing ropes and torn canvas, crashed into the sea, pitching Ordinary Seaman Samuel Miller and Able Seamen Thomas Browne into the brine. As they struck out for the ship's lifebuoy, the *Essex* righted and sailed on. Realising he could no longer escape, Porter decided to return to the roads. Dragging the wreckage of the maintop and mainsail through 225 degrees, he wore the ship and hauled to the wind on the starboard tack. The debris was cut away, but the frigate was crippled and driven north eastwards by the gale. At 3.20 p.m. Porter gave up on his attempts to regain the roads and bore up for a small bay on the far side of Point Piedra instead. As a Spanish 24-pounder had been set up on a bluff to the east, the bay was technically neutral ground. Whether Hillyar would respect the convention remained to be seen.

As the *Essex* struggled eastwards with the *Essex Junior* in her wake, Hillyar moved in for the kill. Lieutenant Burrow noticed Miller and Browne clinging to the *Essex*'s lifebuoy as the *Phoebe* swept past, but Hillyar was in no mood to delay. At 3.30 p.m. a Saint George's Ensign bearing the motto 'God & Country, British Best Rights, Traitors offend both' was hoisted on the *Phoebe*'s main. The *Cherub* did likewise. Hillyar then went down to the gun deck to address his men. Samuel Thornton Junior thought his captain's icy demeanour 'peculiarly impressive ... [He] implored the Divine assistance in [his crew's] endeavours', the sixteen-year-old recalled, 'after which he addressed them in a short but spirited speech which concluded with these words, "Do your duty my Lads & you can't be afraid."' After giving the watchword as 'God Save the King!', Hillyar returned to the quarterdeck to a rousing three cheers.

At 3.40 p.m. the *Essex* anchored with her best bower in 9½ fathoms half a pistol shot from shore. Seeing his opponents raising their banners, Porter ran up three White Ensigns over his usual motto flags and gave the order to clear for action. The partitions were knocked out and the guns run out of the ports. Chaplain Adams joined Doctor Hoffman, the acting surgeon and his mate, Alexander Montgomery, in the cockpit while those on the quarterdeck watched the British ships' casual approach. Some believed themselves safe, protected by Chilean neutrality, yet Farragut thought it 'evident ... the enemy ... intended to attack ... We made arrangements to receive him as well as we possibly could', he recalled. 'Springs were got on our cables [to turn the frigate broadside on] and the ship was ... prepared for action ... Even to my young mind', he continued, 'it was perceptible in the faces of those around me ... that our case was hopeless ... [but] it was equally apparent that all were ready to die at their guns rather than surrender.'

At 3.50 p.m. Hillyar signalled his intention to fight at anchor off the *Essex*'s stern to the *Cherub*. The topmen took in the courses, the frigate inched closer under topsails, while the waisters prepared to deploy the springs. One mile from Point Piedra, O'Brien and Murphy caught up. As they scrambled aboard, their boat was swamped by a wave. At 4.00 p.m. the *Phoebe* entered the bay. Hillyar was about to deploy his anchor and spin on his cables to rake the *Essex* when a squall blew in from the south. The *Phoebe* was blown alongside the *Essex*'s larboard quarter about half a gun shot off while the *Cherub* sailed round onto the Americans' starboard bow. At 4.10 p.m., his efforts to close to pistol-shot having been frustrated, Hillyar opened fire. On the gun deck, the command was repeated by Lieutenant Pearson and Acting Lieutenant Gardner to their divisions, the gun captains pulled their lanyards and the frigate's starboard broadside rippled flame. The cannon leapt back on their breeching ropes and thirteen 18-pound roundshot hurtled towards the *Essex*. Five minutes later, Tucker fired a volley of grape from his 32-pounder carronades.

On the *Essex* the men fell in droves. Roundshot smashed through the hull, tore the rolled hammocks from above the bulwarks and burst in the windows of the great cabin. Skipping along the gun deck they disabled several carronades, scything off ring bolts and carrying away tackle and blocks. Others killed or maimed the crews while grape shot swept the quarterdeck. Employed as 'Captain's aid', Farragut was 'sickened' to see 'a boatswain's mate [named Henry Kennedy]' killed beside him. 'His abdomen was taken entirely out', he recalled, 'and he expired in a few moments.' Lieutenants McKnight and Odenheimer busied themselves returning fire. Loading the carronades on the larboard quarter, the only ones which could be brought to bear, with round and grape, they alternated their fire between the British hulls and rigging while Acting-Lieutenant Burr formed a squad of marines on the quarterdeck to snipe at the British officers. Porter was trying to get a spring rigged to his anchor cable to bring his broadside into action. Acting Sailing Master Barnewall and Boatswain Linscott attached a hawser to the anchor ring, but before it could be fastened to the capstan and hauled taut, it was shot through by the *Phoebe*'s long 18s. At 4.20 p.m. Barnewell and Linscott tried again, while lieutenants McKnight and Odenheimer ran three long 12s out of the stern ports. Hauling them down the centre of the gundeck, their crews opened fire.

Half a gunshot away, the British were also suffering. Captain Tucker had received a 'severe contusion' to both legs soon after firing his first broadside. Whipping across the quarterdeck, the roundshot had also hit several marines. Private William Derbyshire was killed. Corporal John Edwards and Ernest

Rafferty suffered minor injuries and joined their captain on Surgeon Ramsey's operating table in the cockpit below. In Tucker's absence the sloop drifted to leeward and passed out of carronade range. The *Phoebe* was also in difficulties. Burr's marines were peppering the forecastle, spar and quarterdeck. Seven 32-pound shot had hulled the frigate between wind and water and several others had drilled through the waist. The sails and rigging had been badly torn by grape and the *Essex*'s long 12s were bringing accurate fire down on the frigate's quarterdeck. Hillyar was concerned. The *Phoebe* was being blown close to shore, his shot appeared to be producing 'no visible effect' and, despite the fact that his gun captains had demonstrated accurate fire in cutting both of the Americans' springs, the close range seemed to be playing towards his opponent. At 4.30 p.m. Hillyar ceased fire and gave the order to wear.

Porter was pleased with the opening exchanges. Considering his disadvantageous position, the first twenty minutes had gone well. Both the *Phoebe* and the *Cherub* had received damage to their sails and rigging; although Captain Tucker had remerged from the cockpit, his sloop's 'top-sail sheets were flying away' and the frigate's mainsail was 'much cut', her jib boom was 'badly wounded' and her fore, main and mizzen stays had been 'shot away'. To make matters worse, just as the *Phoebe* was coming to the wind on the larboard tack, a shot from one of the *Essex*'s long 12s 'passed through several folds of . . . [her] mainsail'. Given the strong winds howling out of the south, the course could not be reset for several moments and with the jib similarly disabled, the *Phoebe* drifted out of contact while firing 'a few random shot'. As Hillyar was forced to admit, 'appearances were a little inauspicious'.

The *Essex* had also received her fair share of damage. Over a dozen roundshot had gone through her hull, 'the gaff, with the ensign and motto flag at the mizzen, had been shot away', a number of guns had been disabled and 'several men had been killed and wounded', the majority in the first ten minutes before McKnight and Odenheimer had deployed the long 12s. In the cockpit, Doctors Hoffman and Montgomery and the 'indefatigable' Chaplain Adams were already up to their elbows in gore. Acting Lieutenant Cowell, who had been hit in the breast and his assistant Edward Barnewall, soon regained their positions on the quarterdeck, but others were killed by flying splinters while under the surgeons' hands. Nevertheless, Farragut thought they had 'suffered less than might have been expected' and the officers and men 'were nowise discouraged', as Porter recalled. 'All appeared determined to defend their ship to the last . . . and to die, in preference to a shameful surrender.' A second ensign was 'made fast in the mizzen rigging . . ., several jacks were hoisted in different parts of the ship' and Porter had a third spring attached to the anchor cable. Tying it off at the capstan, the marines hauled the *Essex* broadside on. The Americans were ready for the second round.

To the north the British were making repairs. In a feverish ten minutes, spare courses were set, torn rigging spliced and new spars hoisted to replace those damaged in the tops. At 4.40 p.m., Hillyar tacked and the *Phoebe* turned through the wind to face her opponent. The mainsail was furled and Tucker was signalled to come within shouting distance. Putting his speaking trumpet to his lips, Hillyar announced his intention to close to within long-range of his 18-pounders, anchor on a spring cable and pound the Americans into submission, while the *Cherub* was to keep under weigh 'and take a convenient station for annoying' the enemy. First Lieutenant Ingram was appalled. Believing 'it was deliberate murder to lie off at long range and fire at [the *Essex*] like a target', he 'begged [his] Captain ... to bear down and board [her]' instead. Hillyar was unmoved. He refused to risk the lives of his men to satisfy a youngster's lust for glory and at 4.50 p.m. the *Phoebe* began her second, measured approach towards the *Essex*'s starboard quarter.

By now a crowd of locals had gathered on the bluff to watch the battle. As well as the nine daughters of Antonio Carrera, a cousin of José Miguel who owned a nearby hacienda, Acting Governor Formas and Joel Poinsett were present. At some stage, the American trade consul asked the acting governor to order his artillerymen to engage the British ships for contravening Chilean neutrality. With the United States' influence declining with every shot, Formas refused to act.

At 5.00 p.m. the wind dropped, a phenomenon Gardiner put down to the heat of the firing and it wasn't until 5.25 p.m. that Hillyar could reengage with a pair of forecastle-mounted long 9s. Returning fire with the long 12s on his quarterdeck, one of Porter's first shots struck the *Phoebe*'s taffrail. A cloud of jagged splinters scythed across the quarterdeck. One tore open William Ingram's scalp. With blood gushing from the wound, the young First Lieutenant was carried below.

The *Phoebe*'s fire, combined with the occasional shot from the *Cherub*'s two long 9s, was also causing casualties. Acting Lieutenant Cowell was shot through the leg. Rather than being taken below, he insisted on being 'placed on the coamings of his hatchway, where he continued to give his orders'. By 5.15 p.m., seeing 'no prospect of injuring [the enemy] without getting under weigh and becoming the assailant', Porter ordered his men to set any sail they could. The task proved nigh-on impossible. 'My top-sail sheets and haliards were all shot away, as well as the jib and fore-top-mast-staysail-halliards', Porter explained, but 'after many ineffectual attempts' the flying-jib was hoisted. Ordering his cable cut, Porter bore down on the *Phoebe* to board her.

With the *Cherub* unable to close due to the 'light and baffling winds', the *Phoebe* was taking all the Americans' fire. A single 12-pounder had hulled her three feet below the waterline, the carriage of a 9-pounder bow chaser had been destroyed, one of the small-bore carronades in the tops had had its slide smashed, the fransom bolt on a gun deck 18-pounder was damaged and the main-masthead was 'badly wounded' below the first quarter. Three able seamen had been killed. Several others, including two marine privates, had been badly wounded and carried below and Ingram was barely conscious and still bleeding from his wound. Nevertheless, 'the Almighty disposer of events' seemed inclined to grant Hillyar victory. The *Essex* was crippled and although Tucker was taking little part in the fight, despite 'using every exertion', the *Essex Junior*, at anchor four miles to windward, was equally ineffective. While Porter could only fire a few long 12s, the *Phoebe* remained broadside-on. Double-shotting, the gun crews began hulling the *Essex* with every shot.

By 5.30 p.m., American casualties were mounting. 'The decks were . . . strewed with dead', Porter recalled, 'and our cockpit filled with wounded'. Farragut, racing round like 'Paddy in the cat-harpins', witnessed several fall. 'While . . . standing near the Captain, just abaft the mainmast', he recalled, 'a shot came through the waterways and glanced upward.' Four men, stood by the side of the gun, were killed instantly. The last was struck in the head. His brains smattered Porter and Farragut with gore. Unable to wear with just the one sail set, the *Essex* was drifting backwards towards the *Phoebe*, exposing the stern guns to her fire. At least ten of the men crewing them were killed and a dozen wounded, but by constantly replacing those that fell, lieutenants McKnight and Odenheimer were able to return the British fire.

By 5.45 p.m. it was clear that Porter's attempt to run aboard the *Phoebe* was futile. Although victory was now beyond his reach, the Bostonian refused to countenance surrender and decided to run his ship aground instead, thus allowing his men to escape capture. Luck had deserted him, however. With the *Essex* just a musket shot from shore, the wind began blowing off the land and swung the frigate's bows round to face the *Phoebe*, exposing her to a 'dreadful raking fire'. John Hughes, the fourteen-year-old boy recruited at Tumbez, had his right leg fractured; John Glasseau, a young Scot who had been with the *Essex* since the Delaware, was hit in the right shoulder with grape; and Able Seaman John Alvison was drilled through the body with an eighteen pound roundshot. He expired with the words '"free trade and sailors' r-i-g-ht-s" . . . quivering on his lips'. Manning the bow guns, a young Scot named Thomas Bailey had his leg shot off close to the groin. 'He used his handkerchief as a tourniquet' and, bidding farewell to his messmates, leaned on the sill of the port and threw himself overboard. Acting Lieutenant Cowell had fainted from loss of blood and been carried below, while Edward Barnewall, his assistant, had been hit for a second time and joined his superior in the cockpit. Farragut, meanwhile, continued to lead a charmed life. 'An old quarter master, named Francis Bland, was standing at the wheel when I saw a shot come over the fore-yard in such a direction that I thought it would strike him or me' he recalled. 'I told him to jump, at the same time pulling him toward me . . . [but] the shot took off his right leg.'

At 5.50 p.m. Lieutenant Downes arrived from the *Essex Junior*. '[As] he could be of no use to me', Porter recalled, 'I directed him to return to his . . . ship, to be prepared for defending and destroying her in case of an attack. He took with him several of my wounded, leaving three of his boat's crew on board to make room for them'. Downes' acting lieutenant, William Kingsbury, was amongst those who 'had insisted on 'shar[ing] . . . the fate of his old Ship'. Downes also took some specie to the *Essex Junior*. Having captured considerable treasure during the cruise, Porter was determined it would not fall into Hillyar's hands. The Bostonian then had one last attempt at confounding his enemy ordering Lieutenant Wilmer to deploy the sheet anchor with a spring in an effort to turn the *Essex* broadside on. No sooner had the young lieutenant succeeded, however, than he was knocked overboard by a splinter and drowned.

By 6.00 p.m. the situation on the *Essex* was appalling. 'Many of my guns had been rendered useless by the enemy's shot', Porter recalled, 'and many . . . had their whole crews destroyed'. The hold was filling with water, fires had broken out both forward and aft and loose cartridges were exploding on the gun deck. Daniel Gardner was 'blown up with powder', 'flames were bursting up each hatchway' and several men's clothes were set ablaze. Some were stripped by their comrades while William Kingsbury leapt overboard to douse the flames. Others continued to fall victim to the *Phoebe*'s guns. William Whitney, captain of the foretop, had his thigh broken and was wounded in the side; Peter Coddington was hit in the head; John Ripley, having lost a leg, apologised to his comrades that he could be no more use and hopped out of the bow port; and Able Seaman John Lazarro had his leg pierced with a dozen shards of shrapnel when the gun he was serving was struck by an 18-pound shot. To make matters worse, the cable Wilmer had set had parted and the *Essex* was drifting away from the shore.

By 6.10 p.m. discipline had collapsed. Lieutenant Odenheimer had hidden deep in the hold and Quarter-Gunner Adam Roach had deserted his post. Found 'skulking on the berth deck', he was chased by Able Seaman William Cole dragging the 'shattered stump' of one of his legs behind him. Hearing of the incident, Porter ordered Farragut to execute Roach before his example spread, but the quarter-gunner escaped on the ship's pinnace with six others before the midshipman could reach him. Moments later, Farragut saw 'the Captain of the gun directly opposite the hatchway . . . struck full in the face by an eighteen pound shot . . . [He] fell back on me', the twelve-year-old recalled, '[and] we tumbled down the hatch together. I struck on my head and . . . he fell on my hips'. As Farragut returned to the quarterdeck, Porter was knocked down by a shot passing narrowly overhead. Fortunately for the Bostonian, the only injury received was to his hat.

At 6.15 p.m. Porter convened an officers' meeting on the quarterdeck. Lieutenant McKnight and Carpenter Langley were the only ones able to attend. '[The former] confirmed the report respecting the condition of the guns on the gun-deck', Porter recalled, '[and] I was informed that the cock-pit, the steerage, the ward-room and the birth-deck, could contain no more wounded ... and ... unless something was speedily done ... the ship would ... sink from the number of shot holes in her bottom.... [Langley] ... informed me that all his crew had been killed or wounded and that he had been once over the side to stop the leaks, when his slings had been shot away and it was with difficulty he was saved from drowning.' Seeing no other options left open, Porter decided the game was up and gave the survivors permission to abandon ship. Roughly eighty men complied. The *Essex*'s three remaining boats were soon full. The rest leapt overboard. Braving the icy water and strong currents, they struck out for the beach three-quarters of a mile away.

At 6.20 p.m. Porter gave the order to strike. The ensign was hauled down, but as a motto flag was still flying, the Phoebes fired 'several more broadsides'. Meanwhile, Farragut was ordered to ensure Lieutenant Odenheimer had destroyed the ship's signal book. 'I could not find him ... for some time', he recalled, 'but at last saw the [book] ... lying on the sill of a port and dashed it into the sea.' Farragut and Midshipman Isaacs then began throwing small arms overboard to prevent them falling into enemy hands, while Porter destroyed several parts of his journal and the ship's log and muster roll. All the while the *Phoebe*'s shot came crashing in. Four men were killed at Porter's side after the order to strike and eleven others fell below decks. Eventually, a man was ordered to scramble up the rigging and haul down the offending banner. 'A shot took him, Flag & all, just as he was in the act of striking it', Samuel Thornton recalled. It was 6.30 p.m. The Battle of Valparaiso was over.

Blinking through the gun smoke, their ears ringing from repeated concussion, it took the Phoebes a moment to realise they had won. Hillyar ordered the small bower deployed to stop the frigate drifting further off shore, had the sails furled and sent Second Lieutenant Pearson and Acting Midshipman Thornton with twenty men and two petty officers to take possession of the prize. 'Nothing was to be seen all over [the *Essex*'s] decks, but dead, wounded & dying', Thornton recalled. 'We threw 63 overboard ... & there were several wounded that it would have been a mercy to do the same to. One poor fellow, who had his thigh shot off, managed to crawl to a Port, & tumble himself into the water.' Several others decided to take their own lives. Dressing himself up in 'a clean shirt and jerkin', Able Seaman Benjamin Hazen, a married man from 'Groton[,] ... addressed his remaining mess-mates ... telling them he could never submit to be[ing] a prisoner of the English, [and] threw himself into the sea', while Ruff, Lieutenant Wilmer's 'negro boy, deliberately jumped [overboard] and was drowned'. After berating Porter for allowing his men to flee the ship, Lieutenant Pearson demanded the Bostonian's sword. 'That sir', Porter replied, 'is reserved for your master.'

Meanwhile, the eighty Essexes who had abandoned ship were struggling to reach shore. One of the three boats launched had swamped under the frigate's stern drowning all on board, while the pinnace, 'in the most deplorable condition', was intercepted by a British boat. Several dead were lying in the bottom and of the seven survivors, two were seriously wounded. The third boat reached the shore. The swimmers were also 'struggling'. The officer of a British boat had his crew rescue as many as they could safely take on board and promised to return for the others. 'When the men in the water expressed their doubts that the promise would be kept, a British sailor jumped … into the water … "I will remain with you," he promised, "if they forget you they will not forget me."' Nine swimmers were rescued. Thirty-one others drowned. With the muster roll destroyed and Porter unwilling to provide details, estimates of those who reached the shore vary. Hillyar believed that thirty to forty men made it. Those that were uninjured, such as John Swayne, the twenty-year-old Scot who had served on the *Seringapatam*, disappeared into the scrub-covered hills. The rest were carried to the Hacienda de la Viña del Mar, where they were treated by Antonio Carrera's nine daughters. With 'scarcely a square inch of his body which had not been burned', William Kingsbury was amongst the fortunate recipients of their charity.

At 7 p.m. Porter was rowed on board the *Phoebe* with a number of his officers and crew while a boat sent by Captain Tucker took several others to the *Cherub*. Porter was in tears as he surrendered his sword and told Hillyar of the 'brave fellows' killed after he had struck. The British captain countered by stating that the men who had fled the *Essex* at the moment of her surrender should have been his prisoners. Porter insisted he had been forced to give the order to save them from the fire on the gundeck and Hillyar decided not to press the point further. In the *Phoebe*'s cockpit, Surgeon Smith cared for the wounded. Eight men awaited his attention, the most pressing case being Lieutenant Ingram. The 27-year-old remained unconscious and little hope was held out for his recovery.

On the *Essex* the prize crew were already making repairs. The shot holes below the waterline were plugged, cables were bent to the anchors and a jury mast rigged. In the cockpit, the grim work of Doctors Hoffman and Montgomery went on. Splinters were pulled from sucking flesh wounds; cuts bandaged; burns doused with ointment. Forty-four limbs were amputated with knives and bone saws and thrown through the ports. The stumps were cauterized in the fire and bound. Farragut grew 'faint and sick' at the sight. Collecting himself, the twelve-year-old asked after the shipmates he had seen fall. Quartermaster Francis Bland had bled to death for want of a tourniquet, while Acting Lieutenant Cowell 'had lost a leg just below the knee'. Doctor Hoffman had wanted to amputate as soon as he had been bought in, but Cowell had insisted on waiting his turn. 'One man's life is as dear as another's', the father of two from Marblehead, Massachusetts had explained. 'I would not cheat any poor fellow out of his turn.'

At 8 p.m. Farragut was rowed to the *Phoebe*: 'I went on board ... and was ushered into the steerage ... [and] was so mortified at my capture, that ... I laid down and gave vent to my tears.' In the cockpit, Ingram was close to the end. At midnight, as the baffling winds that had marked the day settled to a dead calm and a thick fog descended, the frigate let go her stream anchor in 34 fathoms and the 27-year-old 'was ... happily released from his pain'.[4]

Chapter 14

The Aftermath, 29 March 1814 – 25 December 1814

At 6 a.m. on 29 March 1814 the fog lifted and the *Phoebe*, *Cherub* and *Essex* stood in for Valparaiso Roads. An hour later Hillyar, whose conduct towards his prisoners had been 'delicate and respectful' from the start, invited Porter and Farragut to join him for breakfast. The former accepted, but Farragut declined, saying his 'heart was too full' to eat. 'Never mind my little fellow,' Hillyar replied, 'it will be your turn next perhaps.' 'I told him I hoped so', Farragut recalled, 'and left the cabin to keep from crying in his presence.' At 9 a.m. the ships sailed into the bay. While the *Cherub* stood off and on, watching the *Essex Junior* lingering off shore, the *Phoebe* and *Essex* came to in the roads.[1]

That morning the American officers were allowed to go into town on parole. Porter hired a 'comfortable' room as a hospital and had his wounded transferred ashore. The Cherubs spent the morning making repairs, while Hillyar enquired about more permanent accommodation for his prisoners. While they remained on board, the Americans posed a security risk as well as preventing repairs being carried out to the lower decks. The *Sacramento*, an old Spanish merchantman, was hired and that afternoon all ninety-three unwounded prisoners were sent on board. Gardiner was given a detachment of Royal Marines to guard them. Afterwards, Captain Tucker, having recovered somewhat from his contusion, returned to his station, beating up and down in the bay watching the *Essex Junior*, while the Phoebes sent a sheet anchor and cable to the *Essex* to allow her to be moored.[2]

At 10 a.m. the next morning, Ingram's body was carried ashore. With the *Phoebe* firing minute guns in his honour, a detachment of marines escorted his coffin to the Governor's castle where his funeral took place. All the surviving American officers and a number of the *Essex*'s crew were present as well as 'the greater part of the [*Phoebe*'s] company'. Hillyar performed a service, many 'manly tears' were shed and Gardiner composed a poem to mark the occasion.[3]

That afternoon, Hillyar wrote to Secretary Croker informing the Admiralty of his success, while Farragut attended to the American wounded. 'I volunteered my services to the Surgeon, as an assistant', the twelve-year-old recalled, 'and was given charge of all such patients as required plastering and rubbing. These consisted of those burnt and bruised.' William Kingsbury remained 'deranged for some days' but would ultimately recover, while Acting Lieutenant Cowell was less fortunate. Having insisted on waiting his turn before going under the knife, he had lost so much blood that his condition was deteriorating daily. Farragut found the job exhausting: 'I rose at day light and spread a bolt of linen into plasters, by 8 o'clock got my breakfast and then went to work on my patients [for the rest of the day].' The doctors were also assisted by the 'ladies of Valparaiso . . . Without their aid', Porter opined, 'many [more] would have died.'[4]

Over the next few days, many of the combatants began to reflect on the battle. Honour gained and lost was assessed and blame apportioned. Porter, blind to his own responsibility, believed Hillyar had acted dishonourably on two counts. First, by attacking him within gun shot of the shore and second, by engaging while the *Essex* was at a disadvantage. These, from Porter's point of view, were compounded by the fact that the English captain had consistently refused an 'honourable' single-ship duel in the weeks beforehand. 'The blood of the slain must be on . . . [Hillyar's] head', Porter judged, 'and he has yet to reconcile his conduct to heaven, to his conscience and to the world.' Gardiner noted that 'what little honour . . . [the *Phoebe*] may have gained . . . will no doubt be detracted' by the fact that the *Cherub* was also present, even though Tucker had 'only had an opportunity of giving . . . one broadside', while Hillyar, predictably, attributed his victory to the 'providence' of 'the Almighty disposer of events'. Samuel Thornton Junior felt the Phoebes had done their 'business very well' and dubbed his superior Sir James, 'in anticipation of the Baronetage' he felt sure Hillyar would be granted.[5]

Farragut provided the most detailed post-mortem: 'I consider that our original and greatest error was in attempting to regain the anchorage [after the main topmast had gone by the board off the Point of Angels]', he opined.

> Being greatly superior to the enemy in sailing qualities, I think we should have borne up and run before the wind. If we had come into contact with the *Phoebe*, we should have carried her by boarding, if she avoided us, as she might have done by her greater ability to manoeuvre, then we could have taken her fire and passed on, leaving both vessels behind, until we replaced our topmast, by which time they would have been separated . . . the *Cherub* being a dull sailer. Secondly, when it was apparent to everybody that we had no chance of success [in the battle beyond Point Piedra], the ship should have been run ashore, throwing her broadside to the beach, to prevent raking and fought as long as was

consistent with humanity and then set on fire. But, having determined
on anchoring we should have bent a spring to the ring of the anchor,
instead of the cable, where it was exposed and could be shot away as
fast as put on. This ... would have given us, in my opinion, a better
opportunity of injuring our opponents.[6]

As March turned to April, with the *Essex Junior* and *Cherub* continuing to eye
each other off shore, the *Phoebe* underwent repair. Her main yard was overhauled,
the mainmast was fished and the rigging, fore and aft, was re-spliced and knotted
where the *Essex*'s shot had cut through. The caulkers resealed the hull and in
early April the guns were shifted to one side and the frigate careened, allowing
the carpenter and his crew to plug the eight 32-pounder shot holes between wind
and water and the single 12-pounder one below the waterline. The starboard
billboards and bolsters and three chain plates and dead eyes were replaced, a new
slide was made for the damaged carronade in the tops and the hammock boards,
quarter galley and lashes were repaired. On 18 April, the *Phoebe* received a fresh
coat of paint while the gunner fixed the transom and transom bolt on the damaged
18-pounder and repaired the axletree of one of the long 9s.[7]

The *Essex* also underwent repairs. On 4 April the *Cherub*'s carpenters went
aboard to speed up the process. Their first job was to clear the hull of roundshot.
According to Carpenter Langley's report '[they] were planted so thick ... they
could not be well counted, but [were] supposed to [number] ... upwards of
200 ... through the larbrd. side below the spar deck'. The head had been shot
away, the bulwarks on the larboard side of the forecastle destroyed, the stern
'much shattered', the pumps had been rendered useless, the bowsprit was 'much
damaged', seven of the ship's structural knees had been cut in two and the booms,
spars and masts had been 'crippled'. Thirteen guns on the larboard side had been
disabled. Several had had their carriages shattered; others had their barrels or
muzzles split or had lost their fighting bolts, britchings, eye bolts, blocks, ring
bolts or tackles. Two starboard guns needed repair and the sails and rigging were
shredded.[8]

On 5 April the *Essex Junior* surrendered. Hillyar, Porter and Downes agreed
that the sloop should be disarmed and serve as a prisoner cartel to take the
Americans home on parole on condition they would be exchanged for British
prisoners of equal rank. The deal suited both sides. Porter was desperate to get
back to the United States and acquire a new command, and Hillyar wanted to
get his ships and specie back to Britain safely. Once she had come to anchor,
English and American ensigns were hoisted on the *Essex Junior* and over the next
few days the guns and stores were hoisted out. The *Cherub* also anchored and
Hillyar persuaded Tucker to rest for a few days in town. 'His wounds though not

dangerous confine him to his cabin', he explained in a letter written to Croker that afternoon, 'and quiet is necessary for his restoration to health.'[9]

The *Essex Junior*'s surrender brought an end to the saga of the poison plotters of Nuka Hiva. The former Sir Andrew Hammonds were released in exchange for eleven American seamen as well as Lieutenant McKnight, Midshipman Lyman and Chaplain Adams, whom Hillyar agreed to transport to England or any intermediate point in between. Edward Lawson and the others signed up to serve on the *Phoebe* and their stories of Porter's tyrannical conduct soon spread. Three other Britons also signed up that afternoon. All may well have been former crewmembers of the *Essex* who had swum ashore and hidden in the aftermath of the battle, but only one, the Scot John Swayne, was foolish enough to give his real name. Admitting his recent service with the enemy, Swayne insisted he had only served under duress and had taken the first opportunity of running.[10]

By the end of the first week of April, all Hillyar's immediate concerns had been taken care of. 'Our wounded are doing well', he informed Croker, 'and our damages will soon be repaired. We have much reason to be grateful to Divine Providence for this and many other proofs of goodness manifested to us.' Hillyar's anxieties as to the completion of his original mission had also been eased: Porter had informed him that the 'fort' belonging to the American Pacific Fur Company at the mouth of the Columbia River was a purely civilian concern and its capture would pose no problem whatsoever to a man-of-war. By 7 April Hillyar directed all his energies to preparing his ships for sea. The *Cherub*'s boats swept the bay for the anchor that Porter had slipped on the day of the battle and thirteen locals were employed to help resupply the ships. Water and provisions were taken on board, including 392lbs of fresh cheese. Shore duty brought the risk of desertion and on 11 April Thomas Banks, who had joined the *Phoebe* at Lima on 5 December, ran from the launch and was not heard of again.[11]

On 13 April HMS *Tagus* arrived. One of ten 36-gun Fifth Rates ordered by the Admiralty in 1812 in response to the threat posed by the US, the *Tagus* had been laid down in August and launched within the year. Her captain, Philip Pippon, had sailed from Falmouth with a convoy for Brazil on 7 December 1813 with orders to proceed to the Pacific in search of the *Essex*. Aside from being pine-built, a policy which traded structural strength for rapid construction, the *Tagus* was also one of the first British warships to be fitted with iron water tanks, thus not only saving time in provisioning, but also improving the crew's health. Pippon's arrival and the news that HMS *Raccoon* was unlikely to face any difficulties at the River Columbia, freed Hillyar of any further responsibilities in the Pacific. As his commission pre-dated Pippon's, he ordered the *Tagus* to cruise the Sandwich Islands in search of American merchantmen. The *Cherub* would be dispatched to hunt down Lieutenant Gamble's detachment at Nuka Hiva and the *Phoebe* would return home.[12]

Once news of Hillyar's decision spread his officers began to enjoy their time on shore. Midshipman Thornton of the *Phoebe* and Chaplain Adams of the *Essex* took up the friendship that had been interrupted by the recent hostilities, others went hunting for black swans which bred around a lagoon ten miles to the southeast, while Gardiner explored Valparaiso. 'The town is a poor shabby place', he opined, '[and] built without any degree of regularity.' The male inhabitants were 'hospitable' yet 'indolent', the women 'pretty' and with a happy predilection for Englishmen, despite the disapproval of their ever-present chaperones. Gardiner admired the fertility of the land, the quality of the local bread and the beauty of the sunsets, whose fading rays lit up the distant Andes 'cover[ing] their hoary heads with a mantle of gold'.[13]

Hillyar had more serious business to attend to. As well as attempting to secure compensation for the British merchants whose ships and cargoes were languishing in Valparaiso Roads, the English captain had to fulfil his promise to Viceroy Abascal. On 15 April, leaving the *Phoebe* in charge of Lieutenant Pearson, he set out for Santiago accompanied by several servants, a numerous mule train and John Barnard, the *Emily*'s teenage supercargo and pioneer of Anglo-Chilean trade who would serve as the captain's guide and translator. Packed amongst Hillyar's baggage were several of Andrew Blest's Protestant bibles which Hillyar intended to distribute on his travels. The journey to the capital took two days. The party crossed the fertile plains of the Chilean breadbasket, before ascending the 609m-high Cuesta de Zapata. At Santiago Supreme Director Lastra asked Hillyar to travel to the south to negotiate peace between the opposing generals at 'the seat of [the] war'. Borne by a four-horse carriage and escorted by a troop of cavalry, Hillyar was welcomed at General Bernardo O'Higgins' headquarters near the town of Talca on 26 April with an artillery salute. The entire patriot army had been formed up to receive him.

Since the fall of Talca, the situation had stabilised. Both the Patriots and Loyalists had exhausted their men and materiel in a series of skirmishes. With Gainza unable to move further north and O'Higgins incapable of forcing his retreat, a stalemate had ensued and the need for some sort of accommodation between the armies was evident. 'The Spaniards, naturally jealous, & suspicious, were fearful', Gardiner explained, 'lest some other power should take a part in their quarrel & thus in some measure weaken their interest in this part of the world, while the revolutionists ... were continually dunn'd with the [allied] successes [against the French] in old Spain, from whence they soon expected their enemies would receive ... reinforcement.' After presenting Abascal's terms to O'Higgins, Hillyar visited the Loyalist camp. A series of negotiations between

Gainza and O'Higgins followed, with Hillyar ever-present, culminating in the signing of the Treaty of Lircay on 3 May. While allowing a degree of Chilean autonomy, it stipulated that the colony would remain within the Spanish Empire and have to sacrifice the national flag. In return, the Peruvians would withdraw and Chile would be permitted to open its ports to international trade. Hillyar relished his role in the process. 'I cannot give a just idea of my personal feelings on this very interesting termination of my effort', he wrote to Croker on 11 May, 'they were the most heart elating I ever experienced.'[14]

There had been several developments in Valparaiso in Hillyar's absence. On the afternoon of 18 April, having transferred eight men and one petty officer to the *Essex*'s prize crew, the *Cherub* sailed for Nuka Hiva. Four days later, Acting Lieutenant John Cowell died. Although Porter had departed for Santiago, the majority of the British and American officers and men attended his funeral as well as a number of locals. On 26 April ninety-three prisoners were transferred on board the *Essex Junior* from the *Sacramento*. Fifty-two were rowed across from the *Phoebe* while Porter and the other American officers left their lodgings in town and went on board. With the sloop's departure for the United States on the 27th, only eleven of Porter's men remained in town. Already exchanged, Lieutenant McKnight, Midshipman Lyman and Chaplain Adams would sail to England on board the *Phoebe*, a measure deemed necessary by prize law as the *Essex*'s papers had been 'lost' during the battle. Eight others, including seamen William Cole and William Whitney, were too badly wounded to travel.[15]

On 7 May Hillyar returned to Santiago. With everything proceeding smoothly in Valparaiso, he stayed in the capital to take up the British merchants' case with the government and celebrate the peace. On the 10th he was granted the freedom of the city and attended a Te Deum in the cathedral and a party in Government House before watching a firework display that lasted 'three successive nights'. On 13 May Hillyar placed an advert in the *Monitor Araucano* announcing the *Phoebe*'s imminent departure and informing all merchants that 'her register for transporting specie is open'. Two days later Hillyar took part in a procession with the 'supreme director, clergy, [and the] chief officers of the state'. Passing between a double line of troops and the King's Colours, the dignitaries entered the cathedral, where an address was given. Hillyar was gratified to hear himself mentioned by name. Further meetings at Government House followed before Hillyar left for Valparaiso on 17 May. Once he departed the Evangelical tracts which he had 'promulgated with so much assiduity ... were ... collected by order of the [Catholic] bishop and publically burnt'.[16]

When news of the peace reached Valparaiso, spontaneous celebrations broke out. Gardiner, who had been transferred to the *Essex* as part of her seventy-strong prize crew under Lieutenant Pearson, noted that 'the joy and satisfaction seemed to be general: the Royalists who had been confined were liberated & Viva el re[y] Viva la patria was echoed in every direction, even by many who had before been adherents to the opposite party'. In the midst of the celebrations, William Carter, the *Phoebe*'s master at arms, deserted and on 17 May the fort hoisted Spanish colours and fired a salute which was returned by the three British frigates in the bay. Hillyar arrived on the 19th. Greeted by Governor Formas and a party of mounted officials on the outskirts, he rode into town with the church bells ringing in his honour and fireworks fizzing overhead. 'I had the satisfaction of witnessing ... the pleasing effects of returning tranquillity', he wrote to Secretary Croker. 'Many respectable officers, [whom,] when I had left [had been] prisoners, were enjoying the blessings of liberty ... ships that were dismantled when I quitted the port, were loading and nearly ready for sea; stores were emptying their long enclosed contents and commercial bustle and cheerfulness had succeeded the ... anxiety and inactivity attendant on a calamitous war.'[17]

On 21 May HMS *Briton*, a 38-gun Fifth Rate of the *Leda* class, arrived in Valparaiso. 'She ... had [also] been sent round [the Horn] in search of the *Essex*', Gardiner recalled, 'which it was supposed in England had escaped us. Had they come out before all the [whaling] trade was destroyed, they might have been of some service, but John Bull like, after the horse is stolen, he keeps the stable door shut.' Hillyar ordered the *Briton*'s captain, Sir Thomas Staines, to join the *Tagus* in a cruise of the Sandwich Islands. Over the next ten days, while the new arrivals watered their ships, two more Phoebes deserted and on 24 May a strong northerly gale brought a heavy sea into the bay. The bad weather delayed the *Briton*'s watering and blew two merchantmen on shore. Over the next week the eight wounded American prisoners Porter had left behind were brought on board the *Phoebe* along with the American officers due to travel to England while the *Tagus* and *Briton* received thirty Spanish Loyalist officers to repatriate to Peru. On 30 May Gardiner went on shore for the last time. '[I took] leave of Valparaiso & all my friends in this part of the world', he recalled, 'not ... I must confess, without some regret as it was in all probability the last time I would ever see them.' That afternoon, after Hillyar had ordered the frigate unmoored, Able Seaman John Peters deserted and Joseph Waple, one of the wounded American prisoners, went over the side and swam for shore.[18]

At 7 a.m. on 31 May the *Phoebe*, *Briton*, *Tagus* and *Essex* warped out of the harbour. On arrival off Juan Fernandez on 5 June the *Tagus* and *Briton* sailed north for Callao, *en route* to the Sandwich Islands, while the *Phoebe* and *Essex* turned south for the Horn. Beset by bad weather, for the next seven days Hillyar and Pearson lit their stern lanterns to ensure that they remained in company. For the *Essex*, the voyage proved particularly arduous. 'Our masts & rigging were greatly damaged', Gardiner recalled, 'our ship leaky and our whole crew, officers included, only amounted to seventy; fifteen of whom, from sickness were rendered useless'. On 25 June the ships changed course to the northeast. The next forty-eight hours saw them cover over 300 miles and on the morning of the 27th they entered the Atlantic. Early July saw the ships averaging 8 knots as they made for Rio de Janeiro, the *Phoebe* tacking occasionally to allow the *Essex* to catch up.[19]

On 9 July, after seventy-three days at sea, the *Essex Junior* arrived off New York. Despite the cramped conditions, the voyage had passed smoothly. The winds had been in the Americans' favour, they had rounded the Horn with ease under topgallant steering sails and the ship was abundantly supplied. Porter spent the voyage writing face-saving reports while Farragut attended the wounded. At Sandy Hook, the *Essex Junior* fell in with HMS *Saturn*, one of the 58-gun *rasée* Fourth Rates the Admiralty had ordered cut down from old 74s as part of their strategy to counter the threat posed by the American 'super-frigates'. Operating as part of the New York blockading squadron, the *Saturn*'s captain, James Nash ordered Porter to heave to and sent a boat aboard. 'Nash ... treated me ... with great civility', Porter recalled. '[He] examined the papers of the *Essex Junior*; furnished me with late newspapers; and sent me some oranges – at the same time making offers of his services.' Two hours later, as the ships stood in on the same tack and Porter, perusing the press, learnt of the bitter turn the war had taken, the situation soured. '[I] was again brought to', Porter explained, 'the papers [were re]examined and the ship's hold overhauled by a boat's crew and officer ... It was added that Captain Hillyar had no authority to make such arrangements ... and that the *Essex Junior* [must] be detained.' Porter was not about to allow such an insult to go unchallenged. Declaring himself no longer bound by the terms of his parole, he began plotting his escape.

The next morning, with the *Essex Junior* close under the *Saturn*'s lee forty miles off the eastern point of Long Island, Porter boarded one of his whaleboats and began pulling for shore. Leaving Downes in charge of the *Essex Junior*, the Bostonian ensured it remained between himself and the *Saturn* for as long as possible, but his escape was soon discovered. The *Saturn* beat to quarters, wore round under the *Essex Junior*'s stern and gave chase. 'Fortunately ... a thick fog came on', Porter recalled, 'upon which I changed my course and entirely eluded further pursuit.' Less fortunate, Downes was retaken at 11 a.m. as the fog lifted. Once the cartel's crew had been inspected and the passport that Hillyar had issued was re-examined, the British admitted they had made a mistake and the Americans were allowed to proceed. The *Essex Junior* drew a salvo from a nervous shore battery as she approached New York Harbour that evening, 'but the ship was not struck by a single shot' and Downes anchored safely on the morning of 23 July. Porter, meanwhile, had reached the village of Babylon on Long Island and was proceeding overland to New York.[20]

On 14 July electrical storms and heavy seas hit the *Phoebe* and *Essex* off the River Plate estuary. Despite having a rotten bowsprit, the latter 'met with no accident', while the *Phoebe*'s mizzen staysail was split and blown away. Hillyar also found that his main topsail log lines had been 'eaten through and much damaged by rats' and at 12.30 a.m. on the 15 July the *Phoebe* 'shipped a heavy sea' which washed the jolly boat from the stern davit 'and ... carried away the larboard gangway'. On the morning of 20 July Hillyar spoke the *Fanny*, a British merchantman bound for Buenos Ayres, whose captain told him of Wellington's victory at the Battle of Toulouse and the advent of general peace in Europe. 'This welcome news ... was ... received with ... joy and enthusiasm', Gardiner recalled. 'Like an electric shock it passed almost instantaneously from one [man] to another.'

A week later the ships arrived at Rio de Janeiro. Hillyar received a letter from the Admiralty approving his decision to pursue the *Essex* and on 29 July Manley Dixon came on board. After promoting Pearson to the rank of commander, he gathered the ship's company and read the declaration of peace between Britain and France. The crew 'mannd [the] Yards and gave three cheers' in appreciation.

Over the next few weeks, while awaiting the construction of a new bowsprit, the *Essex* underwent further repair. On July 4 Admiral Dixon purchased the frigate for the Royal Navy 'at six pounds sterling per ton', a price Chaplain Adams considered a 'small valuation' and a new captain, Thomas Morgan, took command. The next day 'a hundred and seventy men were sent on board from the different ships' in the harbour. Amongst them were thirty-four Phoebes, several supernumeries Hillyar had picked up at Valparaiso and Callao and Midshipman Gardiner, who 'had the good fortune' to be appointed Second Lieutenant. In the meantime the British officers had plenty of time to become reacquainted with Rio. Gardiner 'was forcibly struck with the appearance of the place which seemed far to exceed the description I gave on our first arrival. It was then a mean and shabby looking place, but was now a large & handsome city. Such is the effect of comparison, by which all our judgements, however erroneous, must be formed. In the former instance we had come from England in the latter from Chili.'

In mid-August Dixon received word that HMS *Nereus*, a 32-gun frigate stationed in the River Plate since 1811, was to call at Rio *en route* for England. As she was carrying large quantities of specie, it was decided that Hillyar should wait for her before making his return. The delay proved too much for Lieutenant McKnight and Midshipman Lyman. Desperate to reach the US before the war ended, they were granted permission to travel on board the *Adonis*, a Swedish merchantman which left for England on 22 August. Twenty-three days later HMS *Phoebe*, *Essex* and *Nereus* set sail, with Gardiner 'not a little rejoiced at having our head again turned towards Old England'. The monotony was broken on 16 September when they fell in with a strange sail. Not recognising her white ensign, Hillyar brought her to. She proved to be a French merchantman bound for the West Indies and flying Bourbon colours, a flag rarely seen on the high seas since the French Revolution twenty-five years before. On 10 October, the frigates passed HMS *Alpheus* convoying several merchantmen to Brazil. Two weeks later a homebound convoy from the East Indies which had sailed via Saint Helena was sighted and on 12 November, after enduring a week of contrary winds, the frigates sighted Lizard Point. The next afternoon, seventeen months and twenty days since Hillyar and his men had left home waters, the frigates anchored in Plymouth Sound.[21]

Epilogue: Loose Ends, 7 July 1814 – 14 August 1870

The men of the *Essex* received a hero's welcome. On 7 July 1814 Porter was saluted by swivel guns, musketry and cannon as he made his triumphant procession from the village of Babylon to Brooklyn, New York. Having crossed the East River in the steamboat ferry *Nassau*, he found Downes and the rest of the men who had made the passage from Valparaiso awaiting him. The *Essex Junior* had already been sold to the US Navy for $25,000 and crowds of cheering townsfolk had flocked to the quayside. News of Porter's epic cruise, printed in *Niles' Weekly Register*, had preceded his arrival. Converted into a much-needed hero for a public tired of war and starved of good news, Porter's carriage was mobbed. The crowd unhitched the horses and bodily pulled it to City Hall. Porter was overwhelmed. 'The reception ... made an impression on my mind, never to be effaced', he recalled.[1]

By 20 July, however, the Essexes were broke. Frustrated in their applications for back pay, they wrote to Porter who forwarded their requests to William Jones, the new Secretary of the US Navy. Compared to the glacial processes of the British Admiralty, Jones moved swiftly and within five days Porter had received an advance of $30,000 to be divided amongst himself and his crew. Several wounded men also applied for pensions: on 29 July William Kingsbury, whose burns had resulted in his being 'deprived of the perfect use of both his hands', was granted $10 per month, while the Armourer, Bennet Field, who had had his left leg amputated above the knee, was awarded a monthly payment of $18 on 7 August. The *Essex*'s officers, meanwhile, were busy seeking promotion. On 19 July two of the frigate's midshipman travelled to Washington to personally plead their cases and Lieutenant Maury wrote to the Secretary of State, James Monroe, requesting his commission be backdated.[2]

On 27 August another celebration was held in New York. Gathering at the Battery with colours flying, the Essexes proceeded to Tammany Hall led by Commodore Decatur's band where an 'elegant dinner' was served. *Niles' Weekly Register* recorded that no less than 184 former crewmembers attended, amongst them several men who had been wounded. Porter's reception at Philadelphia was even more enthusiastic. Passing down streets thronged with cheering crowds, he accompanied the mayor to Mansion House Hotel and was carried inside to a series of huzzahs. Afterwards Porter and Farragut returned to Chester where the captain was reunited with his family and introduced to his second son, David Dixon, who had been born eight and half months after the *Essex* had departed.[3]

Porter's next port of call was Washington. Taken to dinner at the White House by Secretary Jones, he regaled President Madison with stories of his exploits in the Pacific. Porter also enjoyed an alcoholic reunion with Commodore Bainbridge before resurfacing in New York on 22 August where he learnt that the British had landed 4,000 troops under Major-General Robert Ross just north of the Potomac River which were marching on Washington. With the bulk of its regulars deployed on the Canadian front, the American army was hopelessly unprepared. Militia and auxiliary units were mobilised and Porter was asked to gather his former crewmates and set out for the capital. Arriving at Baltimore on the 27th, the Bostonian learnt he was too late. After a desultory defence, Washington had been occupied by the British. Ross burnt several public buildings, including the White House, and two partially-constructed men-of-war were destroyed in the naval yard. One of them, a 44-gun frigate named the *Essex*, had been destined as Porter's next command.

Marching south from Washington, the British stopped at Alexandria, where Ross had arranged to rendezvous with the Royal Navy flotilla based in Chesapeake Bay. While the British gathered tribute from the townsfolk, who had surrendered without a shot being fired, Porter took 500 sailors and marines downriver to cut off their retreat. A barely believable incident followed. Dressed in civilian clothes and accompanied by one other naval officer, Porter rode up to the docks at Alexandria to perform a personal reconnaissance. Spotting a young British midshipman supervising the loading of boats at the quayside, Porter charged down to take him prisoner, but was thwarted when the cravat by which his companion had bodily hauled the terrified young officer off his feet broke in his hands. From 1 September to 6 September Porter and his men manned a land battery overlooking a bend in the Potomac River. Aided by local militia, they engaged the British as they sailed back to Chesapeake Bay, resulting in two dozen killed and wounded on both sides.[4]

The arrival of the Phoebes at Plymouth, by contrast, was a rather low-key affair. The American war had always been a sideshow for the British and although the dramatic capture of USS *Chesapeake* in June 1813 had fired the public's imagination, interest had since waned. Hillyar's clinical victory at Valparaiso lacked the romance of Broke's and his success was overshadowed by peace with the French. While Hillyar would be made a Companion of the Order of the Bath in June 1815 along with 500 other navy and army officers, no official celebrations were held. Instead, the captain spent mid-November writing reports detailing his cruise and defending his actions against the vitriol he knew would be forthcoming from Porter, while his crew fought an army of rats which had been multiplying since infesting the frigate at Valparaiso. On 4 December the entire company was rowed ashore to a local church to give 'thanks to the almighty god for their safe deliverance back to their native country'.[5]

Two days later the seemingly inevitable arguments over the division of prize money began. Learning that Manley Dixon had claimed a share as flag officer in charge of the South American Station, Hillyar protested that as the *Phoebe* had been 'exclusively under Admiralty Orders', the money should not be paid. More secure was Hillyar's commission on the specie he had carried back from South America. With 'rather more than Twenty Thousand Pounds on board in . . . bullion and precious stones . . . received at Lima, Valparaiso and Rio de Janiero', Hillyar's cut would amount to some £600, equivalent to three and a half years' of a captain's pay.[6]

In the first week of December Hillyar wrote to the Admiralty supporting several of his men's claims for promotion. Nicholas Nickenson, the *Phoebe*'s acting purser, was praised for his 'most active and most useful employment on deck during the action with the *Essex*'; and acting master Miller was lauded for making the 'fullest exertions' after Lieutenant Ingram had been hit. As a result, in 1816 Miller was appointed sailing master on HMS *Minden*, a 74-gun Third Rate, aboard which he would take part in the Bombardment of Algiers later that year.[7]

In mid-December 1814, John Stavers visited the *Phoebe*. The former captain of the *Seringapatam* had spent the best part of the last twenty-one months at sea. As a prisoner on USS *Georgiana*, he had sailed from the Galapagos on 25 July 1813 for the United States only to be liberated on 28 November by HMS *Barossa* in the Caribbean. Stavers had then made his way back to England, still piqued by the fact that at least five of his crew of thirty-one had joined the *Essex* within days of his surrender despite his promise that he would have them prosecuted for treason. Sixteen months later in Plymouth, as he looked through the *Phoebe*'s muster roll, one name stood out. When Able Seaman John Swayne was summoned to Hillyar's Great Cabin, Stavers recognised the Scot immediately. 'After looking at him, [he] asked [Swayne] if he knew him . . . [Swayne] replied, yes . . . [Stavers] then added, that he was come to be as good as his word.'[8]

On 19 December, while Stavers began the long process of putting his case against Swayne to the Admiralty, the *Essex* was condemned as unfit for further service despite the time and money spent on her repair. 'She was therefore sent to Ham[o]aze', the Royal Dockyard at Plymouth, 'where she was constantly visited by carpenters and draftsmen . . . endeavouring to procure her model.' This was another part of the Admiralty's attempt to deal with the threat posed by the United States Navy. As well as initiating both short and long-term modification and building programmes specifically aimed at countering the 44s, the Admiralty systematically examined the US warships the Royal Navy had captured. Although they considered the *Essex* strong, weatherly, capacious and an easy seaboat, the draftsmen concluded, however, that little could be learnt that was applicable to the particular limitations of Royal Navy frigate design.[9]

On 27 December Corporal William Morgan's Royal Marine career came to a close. After serving on HMS *Phoebe* for eight years, ten months and seven days, the 'Methodist Preacher' was dismissed as 'unserviceable' due to 'wounded thighs'.[10]

By the end of 1814 the war with America was drawing to a close. Although negotiations, held in Ghent since August, had initially made little progress, both sides had since dropped all problematic stipulations and the talks were showing signs of bearing fruit. The United States had been economically crippled by the war. The Royal Navy blockade had resulted in the capture of 20,000 American seaman and 1,407 merchant ships and had driven insurance premiums to unmanageable levels; amphibious raids in Chesapeake Bay and up the Penobscot and Connecticut Rivers had resulted in the occupation of large swathes of north-eastern Maine, the destruction of several smuggling towns and the burning of Washington D.C. In the Federalist states of New England there were calls for secession. Many US merchants were happy to supply the Royal Navy with provisions; traitors helped the British select targets for raids; while in Nantucket, whalers begged to be allowed to make an independent peace. The land war in Canada had ground to a stalemate and, after the glory days of 1812 and the first half of 1813, even the naval war had soured for the Americans. USS *Essex*, *Argus*, *Frolic*, *Syren* and *Rattlesnake* had all been captured and the majority of the remaining warships were bottled up in their home ports.

The British public, exhausted by twenty-two years of conflict with Revolutionary and Napoleonic France, was equally tired of war. Overconfidence resulting from the easily-won victory at Washington led the British to defeat at Baltimore, where Major-General Sir Robert Ross was killed and his troops pushed back in disarray by determined US resistance. Despite the success of the convoy system, American privateers were taking a heavy toll on British merchantmen, especially in the economically vital area of the West Indies whose vociferous merchant class and their allies in Parliament, the sugar lobby, brought their political influence to bear in the push for peace. There was also a need to refocus on Europe. With Napoleon exiled in Elba, the priority was to secure a favourable Continental peace. The American war was a drain on Britain's financial and military resources at a time when her efforts needed to be directed towards the Congress of Vienna. Accordingly, on 24 December peace was secured. The Treaty of Ghent restored relations between the two nations to the *status quo ante bellum*. The US had failed to achieve any of its stated reasons for going to war.

As the treaty was not ratified by the Senate until 18 February 1815, further humiliations resulted on both sides. On 8 January an army of British veterans fresh from victory in Europe was decimated by a ramshackle force led by future US President Andrew Jackson at New Orleans. One week later USS *President*, one of the original six frigates commanded by the darling of the US Navy, Commodore Stephen Decatur, was taken off New York.[11]

Back in Plymouth, the *Phoebe* was also called into action. Following a report that the only two American frigates still eluding the Royal Navy, USS *Constitution* and *Congress*, were patrolling the English Channel, Hillyar set sail in pursuit on 26 January alongside the 74-gun HMS *Centaur*, the *Hyperion* frigate and several sloops of war. Although no sign was seen of the enemy, on the *Phoebe*'s return the first distribution of the prize money due for the capture of the *Essex* was paid. As captain, Hillyar was entitled to £619 17s; Lieutenants Pearson and Price received £132 15s 6d; Lieutenants Burrow and Sampson of the marines, Surgeon Smith and Gunner Lawson were paid £61 19s 2d; the midshipmen and petty officers got just over £23 per man; while the ordinary and able seaman were paid £7 13s 6d. While Hillyar's share was equivalent to roughly three years' salary, the £5 2s 4d paid to the landsmen was only a little over four months' pay.[12]

In February 1815 Napoleon escaped from exile on Elba. HMS *Phoebe*, back in home waters following a dash to Bermuda in hunt of US privateers, played a minor role in the drama that ensued. On 17 June, as Wellington prepared to take on Napoleon at Waterloo, Hillyar sailed from Plymouth with twenty French Royalist officers and 8,000 pairs of shoes. After landing her cargo in France, the *Phoebe* helped blockade the coastline. Napoleon was still at large and in early July Hillyar was ordered to search all American vessels as intelligence had been received that the former Emperor was planning to escape to the United States. Napoleon's plans were thwarted, however and on 15 July he surrendered. Taken to Plymouth aboard HMS *Bellerophon*, he went into exile on Saint Helena.[13]

By 5 August HMS *Phoebe* was back at Plymouth. With rumours abounding that the crew would be paid off, there was a celebratory mood. The Phoebes spent the next two weeks stripping the ship to her bare bones. The guns were hoisted out along with the contents of the warrant officers' store rooms; the rigging was dismantled and the masts and bowsprit lifted out by sheer hulk; hundreds of barrels of provisions were removed along with bags of bread and coal and tons of foul-smelling shingle ballast. On 28 August, once the crew had washed the decks one final time, a Royal Navy commissioner came on board with clerks from the Treasury and Navy Board carrying chests of notes and coins. The men were mustered and called forward one by one, cap in hand, to be awarded their back pay. Afterwards, they were free to leave. Having endured the discipline and tedium of shipboard life for up to a decade, most were delighted. The ship's commissioned officers, on the other hand, had mixed feelings. With the inevitable downsizing of the armed forces, many faced an uncertain future on half pay. Lieutenant Charles Sampson hoped to gain a commission in the Royal Artillery, but admitted his chances were slim. That evening, Hillyar closed the ship's log and the commissioning pennant was hauled down from the jackstaff at the stern. After twenty years' near-continuous service, the *Phoebe* was no longer a man-of-war.[14]

Nearly 3,500 miles across the Atlantic, on 29 August Lieutenant John Gamble arrived home. The odyssey the 24-year-old New Yorker and the twenty-eight men under his command had endured had all the hallmarks of a nightmarish Pacific adventure. Within two hours of the *Essex* and *Essex Junior* disappearing round the headland of Port Anna Maria on 13 December 1813, Gamble's situation on Nuka Hiva had deteriorated. First, the Taeehs began pilfering small items from the village stores. His attention occupied transferring the whale oil from the *Seringaptam* and *Greenwich* to the *New Zealander* in preparation for her departure to the United States, Gamble did not react until 15 December when he ordered a musket volley fired over the heads of a group of natives who had set fire to some grassland close to the camp. Three days later, when squalls resulted in two of Gamble's ships parting their cables, the lieutenant had six of the *Seringapatam*'s cannon mounted behind the breastwork of Fort Madison.

That afternoon, Tameoy, the Tahitian who had gone overboard from the *Essex*, stumbled into camp. After falling into the water, he had been drawn under the keel and by the time he had surfaced the *Essex* had disappeared. Striking out for shore, he had been washed up on the beach two days later. The Taeehs, meanwhile, were growing increasingly aggressive. On 22 December a group descended from the mountains to raid the Americans' stores. Forty hogs were killed and several others were stolen. Gattanewa, the Taeehs' ageing chieftain, was sympathetic to Gamble's plight, but had little control over the rebels and the lieutenant's threats met with a contemptuous response. The time for pre-emptive action had arrived.

On the morning of 24 December the opportunity arose. Learning that several armed tribesmen had gathered on a hill overlooking the camp, Gamble stationed three men on board the ships with directions to fire their cannon when indicated. Arming the rest of his men, he sallied out. 'When we had arrived within a quarter of a mile [of the hill]', Gamble recalled, 'a signal [was] made for the artillery to be discharged. The shot tore up the earth near where the savages had taken a stand … and … so terrified them that … they fled to the mountains.' Following up their initial success, the Americans took the rebels' base and recovered a number of stolen hogs. Gamble also secured several hostages whom he confined on the ships and a promise of future tribute was extracted. Two days later, her hold filled with 1,950 barrels of whale oil, the *New Zealander* set sail for the United States commanded by Master's Mate John J. King.

Revolting natives were just one of the problems Gamble faced. The longer he remained on Nuka Hiva the harder it became to keep his men in check; the six prisoners Porter had left behind proved particularly difficult; Wilson, the British beachcomber-cum-interpreter, was believed to be passing information to the natives; salt provisions were running low; fresh food was becoming more difficult to procure from the tribesmen; and the gardens planted by Porter had been invaded by ravenous ants. Gamble's response was to impose an ever more draconian regime. The lash was frequently employed and a sunset curfew was strictly adhered to. January brought heavy rain and electrical storms. Two men caught sleeping on watch were flogged and deprived of their rum ration and on 22 January 1814, during a surprise inspection, Midshipmen Feltus and Clapp discovered a number of women on board the *Seringapatam*. Gamble was furious. The men and three of the women were flogged and cast onshore. The next day the grog ran out.

On 7 February Gamble took the *Sir Andrew Hammond* on a tour of the windward islands of the Marquesas in search of food. Leaving Feltus and Clapp in command at Fort Madison, he procured forty hogs, six dozen fowls, 'a quantity of fine bread-fruit, two bushels of sweet potatoes and many other articles' at the island of Dominica and on his return to Port Anna Maria on 16 February, was delighted to find that all was well. The first lettuces were being harvested, while the melon and cucumber crops promised to offer up 'a profusion . . . in the course of two or three weeks'. The good atmosphere continued for twelve days. The Americans busied themselves on shore, wooding the ships and knotting yarns to make ropes for the rigging, but on 28 February John Witter, a marine private from Germany, was caught by a heavy surf and drowned. Witter had been reliable and trustworthy and Gamble felt as if 'one of his main supports had fallen from him'.

On 6 March Isaac Coffin deserted. Forming a search party, Gamble found him dozing in a Happah hut, had him clapped in irons and given a brutal sixty lashes the next morning. Appalled, a group of nearby natives 'gave evident signs of their conviction, that such conduct . . . was illiberal and unjust'. Over the next two weeks Gamble's problems intensified. With provisions strictly rationed, Able Seaman John Robertson was punished for stealing. The crew were growing increasingly embittered and the situation reached boiling point on 18 March. Given first watch on the *Greenwich*, at 12.30 a.m. Able Seaman Thomas Welch released Coffin and Robertson from their irons, loaded one of the ship's boats with arms, ammunition and supplies and rowed across to the *Seringapatam* where he was joined by Private Peter Swook. The mutineers then scuttled the 'fastest pulling' of the ship's boats to prevent pursuit and rowed off into the night. Gamble did not note their absence until 2.30 a.m. With no way of knowing the direction they had taken, he was unable to pursue.

In late March, forced to countenance the thought of Porter failing to return, Gamble ordered the ships readied for sea. By the end of April his preparations were coming to a close, but the men's discontent had reached fever-pitch. On 3 May Gamble discovered that a boat-sail had been stolen from the stores and the next day learnt that thirteen men intended to desert. Inspired by one or two old hands and six of the prisoners from the *Sir Andrew Hammond*, they planned to sail for the British colony of Australia. All were British and their ringleader, Boatswain's Mate Thomas Belcher, was considered a 'consummate villain'. Gamble had the small arms gathered and stored on board the *Greenwich* in response, but by 6 May 'matters wore an alarming aspect'. The 'sudden change in the countenances of the men, plainly indicated, that an awful explosion was soon to take place'.

At 2 p.m. the next day, having gone on board the *Seringapatam* to oversee the stowage of the oil tanks, Gamble, Clapp and Feltus were set upon by 'six or seven' men. Knocked down, their hands and legs were bound and they were thrown down to the berth deck. The scuttle was nailed shut and two armed guards placed over them. The mutineers hoisted the British flag, spiked several of the *Greenwich*'s and *Sir Andrew Hammond*'s guns as well as those remaining in the fort and took all the powder and small arms on board the *Seringapatam*. At 6 p.m., once Robert White, the man Porter had expelled from the *Essex* on 13 December, had been brought on board increasing their numbers to fourteen, the mutineers began working their way out of the bay.

At 8 p.m. a shot was heard from the birth-deck. Either 'by accident or design', Lewis Ronsford, one of the former prisoners of war, had shot Gamble through his left heel. One hour later the worst of the ship's boats was lowered and Gamble, Feltus and Clapp bundled on board along with William Worth and Richard Sansbury, two seamen who had remained loyal. They were given two muskets and a keg of cartridges before being turned loose three miles out to sea. The pull back to the bay proved exhausting. With the boat slowly filling with water, 'Midshipman Clapp was employed incessantly in bailing' and Gamble, 'weakened by loss of blood', was obliged to steer, while Feltus and the others 'exerted themselves at the oars'. After two hours they reached the *Greenwich* where they passed an anxious night.

Gamble and his men spent the next day ferrying supplies from the *Greenwich* to the *Sir Andrew Hammond*. The lieutenant proposed setting sail for the Sandwich Islands with the northerly trades before they were overrun by the natives, but Feltus and four others had learnt that Wilson had been plotting against them and wanted to search his hut to see what supplies they could secure. At 11.30 a.m., with the *Sir Andrew Hammond* moored in deep water, Feltus's party went ashore.

One hour later, Gamble spotted their boat surrounded by natives in the surf and began firing the ship's cannon at the village to provide a distraction. Moments later, two Americans were seen swimming towards the ship. Taking the remaining four men in a boat to pick them up, Clapp left Gamble alone on the *Sir Andrew Hammond*. In his haste, the young midshipman had failed to notice two native war canoes bearing down on his boat. 'At this critical moment', Gamble recalled, 'I went on one foot from gun to gun, moving each, so as to bear upon the canoes, which were several times driven back to the shore.' Aided by the covering fire, Clapp rescued the swimmers. 'One of the[m] . . . was . . . almost senseless', Gamble recalled, 'having had his skull fractured by a blow with a war club.' The other was exhausted after spending 'some time' in the water, while Feltus and two others had been bludgeoned to death on the beach. At sundown, having set the *Greenwich* on fire, Gamble had the *Sir Andrew Hammond*'s cable cut and the eight survivors, six of whom were sick or wounded, stood out of the bay.

Over the next two weeks, the *Sir Andrew Hammond* stood northwards with the trade winds and on the 23 May, to Gamble's 'great joy', made the island of Owhyhee of the Sandwich group. After receiving supplies from the natives and aid from several American merchant vessels around the archipelago, on 13 June Gamble's luck ran out. Following a brief chase, the *Sir Andrew Hammond* was captured by HMS *Cherub*, which Hillyar had dispatched to Nuka Hiva two months before and on 22 June was dispatched with a prize crew to Rio along with the *Charon*, another American prize Tucker had taken in the islands. Midshipman Clapp sailed in the *Sir Andrew Hammond* 'for the purpose of condemning her in the vice-admiralty court', but Gamble was kept on board the *Cherub*. Tucker then cruised the Sandwich Islands until 16 July, after which he sailed round the Society Islands for several weeks, before heading for Valparaiso. On the *Cherub*'s arrival on 23 September, Gamble found that about twenty Essexes were still in town, presumably the remains of those who had abandoned the frigate shortly before Porter's surrender. Several others had enlisted in the patriot army at Santiago.

Chile was in turmoil once again. The truce that Hillyar had negotiated had not been ratified by Abascal; the Royalists and Patriots were skirmishing in the south; and Valparaiso was alive with intrigue. 'So awful, indeed, had the crisis become', Porter later learnt, 'that lieut. Gamble was earnestly advised to repair on board the *Cherub*, for the sake of ensuring the safety of his person.' In early October news reached town of a Patriot reversal. The Royalists were on the verge of capturing Santiago and a new Spanish governor arrived in Valparaiso soon afterwards.

On 15 October HMS *Tagus*, *Briton* and *Raccoon* arrived. The frigates brought news from Nuka Hiva: one of the men Gamble had thought killed on the day of his departure had actually escaped into the mountains and been given sanctuary by an aging chieftain, Fort Madison and the American encampment had been destroyed and the four men who had deserted on 18 March had been seen at the island of Tahuata. One of them, Private Peter Swook, had signed up on board the *Briton*. The rest had decided to remain. After leaving Nuka Hiva, the *Briton* and *Tagus* had happened across the island of Pitcairn. Surprised to find it so far from the position marked on their charts, the British officers' astonishment had grown when the occupants of a canoe which had come out to meet them answered their enquiries in English. These were the descendants of Fletcher Christian's mutineers who had cast Captain Bligh loose in the South Pacific. It was the end to a mystery which had perplexed the Royal Navy since 1789.

The *Raccoon*, for its part, had had an unhappy voyage since parting from the *Phoebe* and *Cherub* in October 1813. Following an accident during gun drill which had killed eight and wounded twenty including John McDonald, one of the North West Company representatives, Captain William Black had proceeded to the Columbia River only to find the American trading post had already been bought by the British-owned Hudson Bay Company. The *Raccoon* had knocked off her false keel and started several planks from the bow in grounding on the bar on her way back out of the river and had had to call in at San Francisco, California for repairs.[15]

Following Gamble's return to the US on 27 August 1815 (after a mid-Atlantic transfer from the *Cherub* onto an American merchantman), the only officers from the *Essex* left unaccounted for were Lieutenant McKnight and Midshipman Lyman. Their voyage from Rio to Falmouth on the Swedish brig *Adonis* had passed without particular note until 9 October 1814, when the *Adonis* was obliged to heave to by an armed stranger. It transpired she was USS *Wasp*, a sloop-of-war commanded by Master Commandant Johnston Blakeley which had scored a series of successes since setting sail from Portsmouth, New Hampshire on a commerce-raiding cruise on 1 May. As well as capturing twelve merchantmen, Blakeley had defeated three British ships of war. Learning that McKnight and Lyman were aboard, Blakely offered them the chance of joining him. The two officers accepted and the *Wasp* set sail southwards. There were no further confirmed sightings of Blakeley's command. What happened remains a mystery, but it seems likely that she foundered in a storm and was lost with all hands.[16]

The fourteen men who had taken the *Seringapatam* from Gamble on 7 May 1814, reached Port Jackson, Australia on 1 July. Their arrival was reported in *The Literary Panorama and National Register*, whose editor noted, in stark contrast to Porter and Gamble's views, that the men's story afforded 'a most praiseworthy instance of what bravery and resolution, governed by prudence and decision can accomplish'. The men, the *Panorama* continued, had been 'treated with a cruelty scarcely ever known to have been practised among enlightened nations ... they were wrought in heavy irons, exposed to every privation and doomed to linger in miserable captivity; but with a spirit peculiar to the sons of Britain, they bore their sufferings with resignation, watching an opportunity to effect their deliverance from their unfeeling tyrants; and ... were at length happily furnished with an opportunity ...' Former Boatswain's Mate Thomas Belcher and his companions had touched at Otaheite before sailing for Australia. Travelling to Sydney, Belcher attempted to secure an award for the salvage of the *Seringapatam* from the Court of the Vice-Admiralty, but the case was referred to London, prompting Belcher and his fellows to sail for England aided by one of the most formidable whaling captains of the era, the Massachusetts-born Eber Bunker.[17] The last of Belcher's former crewmates were not to reach home until June 1816.

Having been deemed in too serious a condition to undertake the voyage back round the horn on the *Essex Junior*, eight of the *Essex*'s ratings had been left at Valparaiso. Although four had since died, in early 1816 William Cole, Joshua Wipple, Peter Coddington and William Whitney had recovered sufficiently to set sail. Once their vessel had arrived at New York, Cole applied for his navy pension. He secured it on 9 July 1816.[18]

On 13 September 1815 the second distribution of the prize money for the capture of the *Essex* was paid at No. 22 Norfolk Street, Islington, London. Hillyar received £299 2s 9d. The payments awarded to the lower ranks fell proportionately. £1 8d was paid to the ship's boys.[19]

In late December 1815 John Swayne was summoned to the High Court of the Admiralty. Sir Christopher Robinson, the King's Advocate, presented the case to the jury. Thomas Jervis, King's Counsel, then examined Captain Stavers who told the story of the *Seringapatam*'s voyage from her departure from England in March 1812 to her capture off the Galapagos Islands in July the following year. Stavers explained how Swayne had taken a bounty to serve under Porter, how he had sworn that as a Scotsman he was free to fight the English if he so chose and how he had answered to his name at the *Essex*'s daily roll call. Edward Lawson, the former master of the *Sir Andrew Hammond*, also gave evidence, stating that he had known the Scot when he had served on the *Seringapatam* and had been surprised to see him on board the *Essex* at the time of the *Sir Andrew Hammond*'s capture. The final witness for the prosecution was John Hamilton, the *Phoebe*'s assistant clerk, who testified that he had been present when Swayne signed up on board the *Phoebe* at Valparaiso after the battle of 28 March.

In his defence, Swayne assured the court he had never raised his hand against his countrymen. He claimed he had been on board the '*Little Essex*' at the time of the battle and had therefore not taken part. Captain Hillyar testified 'to ... [Swayne's] general good conduct while on board the *Phoebe*, but [stated that he] considered him rather silly in his demeanour and of exceeding weak intellect'. The jury delivered a verdict of guilty, while recommending 'the Prisoner to mercy on account of ... Hillyer['s]' evidence. The judge, Sir William Scott, sentenced Swayne to death, but the punishment was later commuted to transportation for life and in November 1816, Swayne boarded the *Morley* transport with 174 others bound for New South Wales. He arrived safely after a six-month voyage and was forwarded to Parramatta for distribution. Seven years later Swayne appears as the convict servant of one Henry Russell of the Field of Mars before disappearing from the historical record forever.[20]

In Britain the War of 1812 soon faded into obscurity. The Battle of Waterloo, Napoleon's subsequent exile and the Congress of Vienna fully occupied the public imagination. Aside from a few calculating heads in the Admiralty, who would take great pains to learn the lessons of 1812 and 1813, the war with America was swiftly forgotten. In the United States the opposite was true. Taking advantage of the vacuum of interest across the Atlantic, President Madison's Republican administration created its own version of events for posterity, their motivation political necessity. The war had divided the country into two camps. The Federalists, their power base in New England dominated by a merchant class whose economic interests centred round oceanic trade, had firmly opposed the war which Madison's Republicans had prosecuted. With the peace, it was necessary for the Republicans to paint the conflict in positive colours. In this way they would not only maintain public support, but would also be given ammunition to belittle their opponents and label them cowards, collaborators and defeatists.

Such reinvention was no easy undertaking. Madison had failed to achieve any of his war aims; the matter of impressment and international maritime rights remained unresolved; the Indians who inhabited the border regions with Canada and received support from the British remained as bellicose and anti-union as ever; the US economy had been crippled and her armed forces had suffered several humiliating reverses. In spite of this, the conflict was widely viewed as a victory. Painted as the second war of independence, it was seen as the moment when the country finally emerged from Britain's shadow and became a major player on the international stage. The early naval triumphs in the Atlantic and those later won on the Great Lakes were trumpeted along with Jackson's victory at New Orleans. The reverses were downplayed or re-imagined as heroic failures or moral victories snatched against impossible odds or blamed on conspiratorial, weak (and preferably Federalist) scapegoats within US society.

These misconceptions were aided by several factors. Having endured so many hardships, the people wanted to believe the war had been worthwhile. The time delay in transatlantic communication led to a fortuitous misunderstanding of cause and effect and the Republicans' version of events was given space to thrive by British indifference. Although the Battle of New Orleans took place after the signing of the Treaty of Ghent and therefore had no impact on negotiations, as news of the peace reached the US after the publication of Jackson's victory dispatches, it was widely believed the defeat had forced the timorous British to sue for peace. The frigate victories of 1812 and 1813 were also little understood. Popular belief was that they had come about due to superior US seamanship and valour or the notion that while the oppressed British tars laboured under the lash and therefore had little personal interest in victory, the American sailor was motivated by higher ideals. The cold truth of weights of broadside, hull thickness, wood density and crew size were overlooked as was the fact that the British had grown complacent about victory having spent the best part of the last twenty-five years fighting a demoralised and unprofessional enemy who believed himself defeated before even leaving port.[21]

The *Essex*'s Pacific cruise played a role in Madison's mythologising. An official court of enquiry to look into the loss of the frigate, scheduled for August 1814, was postponed due to the pressures of the war. Later, despite protocol and somewhat suspiciously, the process was abandoned and Madison chose to glorify Porter's actions instead. 'The loss [of the *Essex*]', he assured Congress, 'is hidden in the blaze of heroism with which she was defended. Captain Porter ... maintained a sanguinary contest against two ships ... till humanity tore down the colours, which valour had nailed to the mast. This officer and his comrades have added much to the rising glory of the American flag; and have merited all the effusions of gratitude, which their country is ever ready to bestow, on the champions of its rights and of its safety.' This unquestioning hagiography was supported by Porter's *Journal of a Cruise Made to the Pacific Ocean*, published in 1815. Detailed, entertaining, energetic and ambitious, the book was also biased, self-serving, selective in its coverage and shied away from inconvenient truths. The Bostonian overlooks no opportunity to contrast the cruelty of his opponents towards their men with the near-universal enthusiasm with which he claimed his own sailors took to their work. Hillyar is held culpable for the *Essex*'s defeat for refusing to accept Porter's honourable challenge to single-ship combat despite the fact that by doing so the British captain would have sacrificed every advantage he had held. Porter is also consistently coy as to his own failings. His use of the lash is never directly referred to; he claimed to have treated his prisoners well throughout, despite considerable evidence to the contrary; and the fact that he sacrificed the success of his mission and his country's prime interests to his own yearnings for personal glory is unacknowledged.[22]

Equally questionable are Porter's conclusions as to the success of his mission: 'I had completely broken up the British navigation in the Pacific', he claimed in his *Journal*, 'the vessels which had not been captured by me, were laid up and dared not venture out. I had afforded the most ample protection to our own vessels ... The valuable whale fishery there, is entirely destroyed and the ... injury we have done ... may be estimated at two and a half millions of dollars.' Such claims fail to stand up to close scrutiny. Although the *Essex* was successful in capturing British whalers, the damage had little permanent effect and it wasn't until the mid-1830s that the US gained hegemony in the South Seas whaling trade. Only one of the twelve ships taken, the *Atlantic*, reached the US (as the *Essex Junior*). With the exceptions of the *Montezuma*, which is believed to have been sold at Valparaiso and the *Rose* and *Charlton*, which were used as prisoner cartels in the Galapagos in mid-1813, the rest were destroyed or retaken by the Royal Navy. The *Hector* and *Catherine* were burnt at Valparaiso; the *Seringapatam* was retaken by mutineers and prisoners of war; the *Greenwich* was burnt at Nuka Hiva; the *Sir Andrew Hammond* was captured by the *Cherub* off the Sandwich Islands; the *Georgiana* was retaken by HMS *Barossa* in the Caribbean; the *Policy* was retaken off the coast of North America by HMS *Loire* and *Ramillies*; and the *New Zealander* was retaken by HMS *Belvidera* one day shy of reaching New York. Equally dubious are Porter's claims that his cruise obliged the Royal Navy to divert resources worth $6 million to hunt him down. While it is true that HMS *Briton* and *Tagus* were dispatched for that purpose, the *Phoebe*, *Cherub* and *Raccoon* had all been destined for the region long before the Admiralty was even aware of Porter's presence.

Paradoxically, the haste with which Porter's journal was edited and published – a fact influenced by political concerns – led to the book containing some rather embarrassingly naive confessions which the Bostonian's detractors would later delight in using against him. Chief amongst them were Porter's reflections on the destruction he had inflicted on Typee territory on 1 December 1813. 'When I had reached the summit of the mountain [on my return from the mission]', Porter had written, 'I stopped to contemplate that valley which, in the morning, we had viewed in all its beauty, the scene of abundance and happiness. A long line of smoking ruins now marked our traces from one end to the other; the opposite hills were covered with the unhappy fugitives and the whole presented a scene of desolation and horror.' Such passages and those that detailed the Essexes' sexual adventures, caused outrage on both sides of the Atlantic. *The Quarterly Review*, the house journal of Lord Liverpool's Tory Ministry, denounced Porter as a pirate in a venomous 31-page attack published in early December 1815; William James, Britain's pre-eminent contemporary naval historian, dismissed Porter's writing as 'filth and falsehood'; while *The Salem Gazette* claimed that Porter should have been court-martialled 'for laying ... waste [to Nuka Hiva] by fire and sword and slaughtering the natives'.[23]

Porter's post-war career was equally controversial. In 1815 he was one of three veterans appointed to the Board of Navy Commissioners by President Madison. He took to the role with enthusiasm. Based in the Navy Building just to the west of the White House, the board ensured that control of the service was no longer the exclusive domain of politicians. Porter oversaw improvements to the navy's yards, ships and guns and tried to regulate the officer class through the implementation of service-wide standards and training programmes. Although some reforms were successful, such as the imposition of an examination for would-be midshipmen, the board's attempts to close inefficient naval yards were thwarted by local mercantile and political interests. It proved equally impossible to weed out the undesirable elements from the officer class. During the seven years he held the post, Porter also struggled on a personal level: his attempts to aid José Carrera when the former Chilean president visited the US in 1816 to seek support were undone by a lack of financial backing and political interest; in 1820 Commodore Stephen Decatur, Porter's friend and colleague, was killed in a duel while Porter was serving as his second; a year later Carrera, who had returned to South America after eleven frustrating months in the US, was shot by an Argentine firing squad; and in 1822 Porter's hand was crippled when an innovative gunlock exploded during a trial. Even more debilitating were the Bostonian's financial woes: the costs of a mansion he had built to keep up with Washington's high rollers spiralled out of control; his farming projects and business schemes backfired; and his ever growing family heaped pressure on his beleaguered finances. Porter's salary of $3,500 proved inadequate. The prize money he had accumulated during the war was soon spent and he fell into debt to a range of individuals including his former First Lieutenant John Downes.

By 1822 it was clear that Porter's financial situation was untenable. Resigning as Commissioner, he accepted command of the US Navy's West Indies Squadron. The situation in the Caribbean was chaotic. Unwilling to accept the political changes that had taken place in South and Central America, Spain continued to fight her former colonies. Venezuela, Colombia and Mexico responded by unleashing swarms of privateers. With the British and French having already dispatched squadrons to convoy their countrymen through the troubled waters, it was Porter's job to protect US bottoms. He achieved some initial success, but the privateers soon learnt that they could evade Porter's ships by sailing into Spanish waters where international regulations forbade the Americans from pursuing. Porter grew increasingly frustrated and a series of embarrassing incidents followed. First Porter fell out with some of his own officers and later had a run in with the British authorities with whom he was nominally allied. Then in 1824, Porter made an armed landing at the port of Fajardo on the Spanish colony of Puerto Rico, having learnt that the local authorities were in cahoots with the South American privateers. The incident led to Porter's recall. At first the authorities were content with a mere court of enquiry, but Porter's undisguised contempt led to his court martial in July 1825 for disobedience of orders and insubordinate conduct unbecoming an officer. Found guilty on both charges, Porter was suspended without pay for six months. Although the punishment was lenient, Porter's pride would not permit him to accept it. Resigning his commission, he sought employment abroad.

In 1826 Porter was appointed commodore of the Mexican Navy. Arriving to much fanfare in Veracruz accompanied by his 21-year-old nephew and namesake, Lieutenant David H. Porter and two of his sons, Porter's new post began promisingly. The recently appointed US Minister to Mexico, Porter's friend, Joel Poinsett, helped the commodore navigate his way through Mexico's murky political waters, but the men under his command proved less amenable. The rank and file of the Mexican Navy was ill-disciplined and poorly-trained, while many of the officers were ex-Royal Navy. Unsurprisingly, a mutual antagonism soon developed. Nevertheless, Porter captured several of Spain's commercial vessels, but in 1827 courted controversy once again. By using the US territory of Key West, Florida as a base for raids against Cuban shipping, Porter came close to causing an international incident and was ousted from the territory by the US at the end of the year.

Moving his fleet to Veracruz, Porter's limited success continued, but in February 1828 his most effective ship, the 22-gun brig *Guerrero*, was captured by the *Lealtad*, a Spanish 64. The *Guerrero*'s captain, Porter's nephew, David H., was 'cut in two' by a cannonball after striking his colours. Later that year Porter's pay began to dry up as the Mexican government fell into bankruptcy; in June Porter's favourite son, twelve-year-old Thomas, died of yellow fever; in October, after being bitten by a tarantula, Porter's health went into decline; and at the end of the year news arrived of his wife's alleged infidelities. 1829 saw political upheaval in Mexico and in 1830 the incoming government deemed a Blue Water navy a luxury beyond its means. Out of a job, Porter returned home.

The following year, thanks to the influence of his friend, President Jackson, Porter was appointed charge d'affaires to the Ottoman Empire, a post upgraded to minister resident in 1839. Aside from two brief visits home, Porter spent the rest of his life in Constantinople. Enjoying a luxurious lifestyle and the personal friendship of Sultan Mahmud II, the Bostonian mellowed and found a certain inner peace, although the years were also marked by continuing financial problems. His attempts to claim his back pay from the Mexican government met with disappointment: he was forced to sell his Washington mansion and his debt began to spiral out of control. Meanwhile, Porter's family grew increasingly distant and his relationship with his wife, Evelina, deteriorated into one of mutual suspicion and hatred. By 1832 Porter's health was also in decline. A long illness followed and he died on 3 March 1843 of 'perdicarium and pleura'. USS *Truxtun* was sent to take his remains back to the US. Porter was afforded a lavish funeral by the navy and had a monument erected in his honour.[24]

James Hillyar's post-war career was considerably more serene. After being paid off in August 1815, he returned to Tor House, the family home built within sight of the Royal Navy yards at Hamoaze, before moving to the Continent. Two more children were born to Hillyar and his wife Mary, but his frequent applications for active service went unanswered until 1830 when he was given command of the 74-gun HMS *Revenge*. After commissioning his ship at Plymouth in November, Hillyar joined a squadron engaged in monitoring the French siege of Antwerp before being appointed to command the First Rate HMS *Caledonia*, which cruised off the River Tagus in Portugal in 1832. Arriving back at Plymouth the following year, after recovering from a 'severe bout of pneumonia', Hillyar was paid off once more. It would prove his last active employment.

In 1834 Hillyar was named Knight Commander of the Royal Hanoverian Guelphic Order. Soon afterwards, he was honoured with an English knighthood and on 4 July 1840 was advanced to Knight Commandership of the Order of the Bath. In his latter years, Hillyar divided his time between his wife and six children and the Naval and Military Bible Society. By the late 1830s he had become an active committee member and gave a key address in 1837 in which he recalled his time in the Pacific with the *Phoebe*. In the same year, due to the Royal Navy's practice of maintaining all former officers of post rank on the promotion ladder, Hillyar was appointed Rear-Admiral of the Blue. The following June he was advanced to the White Flag, a post he held until his death at Tor House on 10 July 1843. Although Hillyar's funeral was private, in keeping with 'his unobtrusive character[,] ... many of his brother naval officers, several of the neighbouring gentlemen, with a large number of the inhabitants of Torpoint ... assembled at the church, to pay a last tribute ... All the shops ... were closed ... [and] the pall was supported by four Warrant Officers, who had served with the deceased ... when ... he [had] captured the *Essex*.'[25]

Two of Porter's subordinates on the *Essex* went on to enjoy notable naval careers. In 1815 John Downes took part in the Second Barbary War as the commander of the 18-gun brig sloop USS *Epervier*. As the North African states had once again taken to attacking US merchantmen in the Mediterranean, on the conclusion of the conflict with Britain, Congress ordered two naval squadrons to sail to the region. Downes played an active role in the conflict, being involved in the capture of two Algerian vessels, before Commodore Stephen Decatur brought the war to a negotiated close with the US guaranteed full shipping rights. Downes was promoted to captain in 1817 and the following year took command of USS *Macedonian*. Setting out on a three-year cruise of the Pacific, a region still troubled by the wars of South American Independence, Downes took advantage of his position to act as a banker to South American privateers, taking at least

$2.6 million in specie on board the *Macedonian* over the period, some of which he syphoned off for his own personal use.

From 1828 to 1829 Downes served as Commodore of the Mediterranean Squadron and from 1832 to 1834 commanded the Pacific Squadron. The latter role saw him court controversy once more. In response to an attack on a US merchantman off Sumatra, Downes was ordered to 'inflict chastisement' on the pirates that infested the coast. In command of USS *Potomac*, he attacked several native fortresses and destroyed the town of Kuala Batee. The *Potomac* then circumnavigated the globe, only the second US warship to do so, calling in at the Hawaiian Islands and Valparaiso before returning to Boston in May 1834. Downes was severely criticised for his actions in Sumatra, but avoided official censure due to the support of President Jackson. Nevertheless, the *Potomac* cruise was to prove his last active service afloat. From 1837 to 1842 and 1859 to 1852 Downes commanded the Charlestown Navy Yard in Boston. He died in 1854 at the age of 68.[26]

Downes' career was eclipsed by that of David Glasgow Farragut. In 1815 he also served in the Second Barbary War and in 1822, after being promoted to lieutenant, joined the West Indies squadron operating in the Caribbean. Two years later Farragut was given his first command: the three-gun schooner USS *Ferret* was part of the Mosquito Fleet, its mission to chase privateers and pirates into the inshore creeks where they sought refuge. Once Porter arrived to take command of the station, Farragut was transferred to USS *Greyhound*. Later, he saw two stints of service on the Brazil station and briefly took part in the US–Mexican War of 1846 to 1848, before being assigned to set up the navy's first Pacific base on Mare Island, twenty-five miles northeast of San Francisco, in 1854. After five years, Farragut returned to the east coast to take command of USS *Brooklyn*, a state-of-the-art steam-powered sloop of war.

It was the American Civil War which saw Farragut rise to prominence. Although a long-term resident of Norfolk, Virginia, Farragut opposed secession and offered his services to the Union on the outbreak of hostilities in 1861. The following year he was appointed commander of the Gulf Blockading Squadron, operating off the mouth of the Mississippi. In April, after running past Forts Jackson and St. Philip, he took New Orleans and was promoted to rear-admiral as a result, the first time such a high rank had existed in the US Navy. On 5 August 1864, Farragut won a second decisive victory at the Battle of Mobile Bay. Despite the waters being heavily mined, Farragut steamed in at full speed, overran Forts Morgan and Gaines and defeated the Confederate squadron under Admiral Franklin Buchanan. After the war Farragut was made a full admiral. He remained on active duty for life and commanded the European Squadron from 1867 to 1868 from his flagship, the steam frigate USS *Franklin*. Farragut died of a heart attack in 1870 at the age of 69.[27]

Allen Francis Gardiner of the *Phoebe* also enjoyed a colourful post-war career. Transferred out of the *Essex* after she was decommissioned, Gardiner's acting promotion to lieutenant was confirmed by the Admiralty in December 1814. The following year he served on the Sixth Rate HMS *Ganymede*, then employed cruising the Channel. Like many of his former comrades, Gardiner spent several years on half pay, before being assigned to the 60-gun HMS *Leander* in 1819. Having narrowly avoided shipwreck off Madeira, the *Leander* sailed via the Cape of Good Hope to Trincomalee. The following year Gardiner transferred into HMS *Dauntless* and sailed to Madras, Penang, Malacca, Singapore, Manilla and Macao. After being refitted, the *Dauntless* proceeded to Port Jackson, New South Wales and on to Chile and Peru, before returning to China via the Marquesas and Tahiti. Invalided out of the ship for poor health, Gardiner returned to Portsmouth in October 1822. During his travels on the *Dauntless*, he had made the acquaintance of several Protestant missionaries in Asia and had 'steadily set his face towards the service of God'.

In July 1823, Gardiner married Julia Susanna Reade. He was called back to service the following year as second lieutenant on HMS *Jupiter*, a 60-gun Third Rate serving on the Halifax station. 1825 saw Gardiner receive his first independent command, the 12-gun HMS *Clinker*. The following year, the *Clinker* was paid off at Portsmouth and Gardiner was promoted to the rank of commander. Although he made several more applications for employment, the *Clinker* proved to be his last ship. The next nine years saw Gardiner's wife's health decline and she died in 1834 along with one of the couple's five children. Afterwards, Gardiner turned to missionary work. Travelling to Africa, he founded the Zulu country's first missionary station at Port Natal, but his efforts were ultimately frustrated by the outbreak of war between the Zulus and the Boers. In 1836 Gardiner married for a second time. His new wife, Elizabeth Lydia and her children, accompanied Gardiner to Chile two years later where he preached to the still-independent Mapuche Indians to the south of the Biobio River. In 1844 Gardiner joined the Patagonian Missionary Society and spent the next six years travelling and preaching in Tierra del Fuego, northern Chile and Bolivia.

In 1850, having received a donation of £1,000, Gardiner set out for Tierra del Fuego to establish a mission with six other volunteers. They were dropped off at Picton Island on 5 December with two small boats and six months' supplies. The natives proved hostile, the country barren and conditions appalling. Heavy snow fall, treacherous currents and storms confined the men to a short area of coastline and with further supplies detained at the Falklands for want of a suitable ship, by May 1851 they were beginning to starve. The lack of provisions was exacerbated by frequent thefts committed by Indians, sickness took hold and, despite several successes at fishing, hunting and trapping game, the men's health rapidly declined.

On 29 June John Braddock was the first to die. The next casualties were recorded on 23 and 26 August. On 6 September, Gardiner, believed to be the last survivor, wrote his final words: 'I neither hunger nor thirst, though five days without food! Marvellous loving kindness to me a sinner! – Your affectionate brother in Christ, Allen F. Gardiner.'[28]

Gardiner's former crewmate, Samuel Thornton Junior, also served on the East India Station. From 1814 until 1819 he was a midshipman on HMS *Cornwallis*, 74, *Iphigenia*, 42 and *Minden*, 74, before joining HMS *Conway*, 26, as an acting lieutenant for six months. In 1821, Thornton was transferred to the *Liffey*, a 50-gun ship commanded by Commodore Charles Grant on which he saw action in the First Anglo-Burmese War. Thornton distinguished himself on 11 May 1824 at the capture of Rangoon, being the first to hoist a British flag on a captured enemy fort and in 1825, having transferred to the *Alligator*, 28, was present at the taking of Donoobew and commanded the ship's cutter during the boat operations against Maha Bandoola. The following year Thornton was promoted to captain and given command of the *Slaney* of 20 guns. Although he would remain on the navy list and would eventually reach the rank of rear-admiral, the *Slaney* was Thornton's final official posting.

In 1830 Hillyar allowed Thornton to join him on HMS *Revenge* as a volunteer for a five-month cruise, after which he settled down to an early retirement. In 1833 Thornton published a history of the East India Company and was married to Emily Elizabeth Rice seven years later. The couple had five children, one of whom, Percy Melville Thornton, went on to write a rambling family memoir which recorded a little of his father's later years, much of which was spent with former comrades reliving the glory of his active service days. 'One of my earliest recollections', Percy Thornton wrote, 'is that of Gunner Gilbert Lawson of the victorious *Phoebe* coming to 12 Upper Gloucester Place' for the annual reunion his father held on 28 March. 'I do not think my father saw him after 1848, as he (Gunner Lawson) died two years later and at his death, left his old friend and messmate [i.e. Samuel Thornton] . . . a copy of Captain David Porter's "Cruise in the Essex" . . . which concluded with an account of the conflict with the *Phoebe*. Mr Lawson also left his two South Sea war clubs.' Thornton was unimpressed by Porter's memoir. He died in 1859 at the age of sixty-two.[29]

Less is known of the post-war careers of the rank and file of the *Essex* and *Phoebe*. A handful of the former can be traced via their pension records. William Kingsbury claimed his $10 per month at the Navy Office in Washington until 1823; John Lazaro received $5 per month in New York until 1825; while John Hughes, probably the last surviving crewmember, was still collecting $8 per month on his ninety-third birthday on 15 October 1882. Only one Phoebe was admitted to the Royal Hospital in Greenwich. John Crooney, who had served on the frigate at Trafalgar as well as at Valparaiso Bay, was sixty-five when he became an in-pensioner in 1838. He was also amongst the twelve ex-crewmembers to receive their General Service Medal for the action against the *Essex*, issued by the Admiralty in 1848. Sailing Master John Miller and Charles Rawdon, a Third-Class Boy in 1814, both received a second bar for their service at the Bombardment of Algiers in 1816; Josh Manning, Patrick Condon and the 'Methodist parson', William Morgan, received three bars: one for the Battle of Tamatave and one for the capture of the island of Java, both in 1811, as well as the third for the action of 1814; while Stephen Laura was awarded five. The former captain of the foretop was given one for each of the single-ship actions he had taken part in: against the *Néréide* in 1797, the *Africaine* in 1801 and the *Essex* in 1814; and two for the Battles of Trafalgar and Tamatave.[30]

Outside of the archives, little physical evidence of those that fought the Battle of Valparaiso remains. Hillyar rests beneath a simple headstone in a churchyard at Anthony, Cornwall and there is a memorial to Captain David Porter in Woodlands Cemetery, Philadelphia. Erected in a dappled glade, an obelisk mounted on a plinth bears an inscription eulogising the Bostonian's colourful career. Perhaps the most moving tribute is to be found in the Cementario de Disidentes in Valparaiso. Founded in 1825, the cemetery sits atop one of the less visited of the port's iconic hills and commands spectacular views of the bay where the battle was fought in 1814. Inside the whitewashed walls, far from the hustle and bustle of the students and tourists who frequent Chile's second most populous conurbation, an American memorial records the names of the fifty-eight crewmembers of the *Essex* who lost their lives. Two gold plaques recall visits in 1991 and 2012 by the crew of the USS *Underwood* and the Daughters of 1812 respectively. Elsewhere lie the remains of William Ingram. In the 190 years that have elapsed since his body was transferred to the cemetery from the fort where he was originally buried, his grave has received few visitors. Lost amongst hundreds of other weather-beaten headstones whose inscriptions have long since been rendered illegible, it is now all but impossible to find.

Notes

Introduction

1. General histories on the growth of the Royal Navy include N. A. M. Rodger's *A Naval History of Britain*, 2 volumes, London: Penguin, 2004 & 2006, and Ben Wilson, *Empire of the Deep: the Rise and Fall of the British Navy*, London: Weidenfield & Nicholson, 2013. For more detail on the late eighteenth and early nineteenth centuries see Brian Lavery, *Nelson's Navy*, London: Conway Maritime Press, 2012; N. A. M. Rodger's *The Wooden World: Anatomy of the Georgian Navy*, London: Fontana, 1998; and Bernard Ireland, *Naval Warfare in the Age of Sail*, London: Harper Collins, 2000.
2. In the mid-seventeenth century an ox which cost £5 in Virginia could be sold for £25 in Barbados.
3. On the triangular trade see Ian W. Toll, *Six Frigates*, London: Penguin, 2007; Matthew Parker, *The Sugar Barons*, New York: Walker, 2011; and Simon Schama, *Rough Crossings*, London: BBC Books, 2005.
4. See Tim McGrath, *Give me a Fast Ship: The Revolution at Sea*, New York: New American Library, 2014, and Wilson, *Empire of the Deep*.
5. Andrew Lambert, *The Challenge: Britain Against America in the Naval War of 1812*, London: Faber & Faber, 2012, p. 19.
6. See Frank Lambert, *The Barbary Wars: American Independence in the Atlantic World*, New York: Hill & Wang, 2007, and David Long, *Nothing Too Daring*, Annapolis: Naval Institute Press, 1970, pp. 22–32.
7. Andrew Lambert, *The Challenge*, pp. 14, 26.
8. Toll, *Six Frigates*, pp. 290–302; Andrew Lambert, *The Challenge*, pp. 7–9.
9. Toll, *Six Frigates*, p. 305.
10. Toll, *Six Frigates*, pp. 324–8; Andrew Lambert, *The Challenge*, pp. 41–3.
11. Andrew Lambert, *The Challenge*, pp. 2–6.
12. Toll, *Six Frigates*, p. 355.
13. Ibid, p. 332.
14. Toll, *Six Frigates*, pp. 337–54; Andrew Lambert, *The Challenge*, p. 79.
15. Toll, *Six Frigates*, pp. 359–60.

Chapter 1

1. David Porter, *Journal of a Cruise Made to the Pacific Ocean, by Captain David Porter in the United States Frigate Essex, in the Years 1812, 1813 and 1814*, 2 volumes, New York, 1822, Vol. 1, p. 57 ; George E. Darlington, *Recollections of the Old Borough of Chester from 1834 to 1850*, Delaware County Historical Society, 1917; Toll, *Six Frigates*, p. 97.

2. *Niles' Weekly Register,* Baltimore, 6 August 1814; Donal O'Sullivan, *The USS Essex in Ireland: A Dún Laoghaire Connection with a Forgotten War,* http://dlharbour.ie/owp-content/uploads/2013/04/The-Convict-Hulk-Essex.pdf.

3. Long, *Nothing Too Daring,* pp. 3–7.

4. Toll, *Six Frigates,* pp. 112–20; Long, *Nothing Too Daring,* p. 8.

5. *The History of the War, Between the United States and Great Britain, Which Commenced in June, 1812 and Closed in Feb. 1815, Containing the Correspondence . . .,* Hartford: William S. Marsh, 1815, p. 208; Loyal Farragut, *The Life of David Glasgow Farragut, First Admiral of the United States Navy, Embodying his Journal and Letters,* Memphis: General Books LLC, 2012, p. 7; Porter to Hamilton, Chester, 2 October 1812, reproduced in *The Naval War of 1812: A Documentary History,* Vol. 2, Washington D.C.: Naval Historical Centre, 2011, pp. 505–6.

6. Porter to Bainbridge, Valparaiso, 23 March 1813, reproduced in *The Naval War of 1812,* pp. 688–9; Porter, *Journal,* Vol. 1, pp. 1–3.

7. Porter to Hamilton, Chester, 2 October 1812, *The Naval War of 1812,* pp. 505–6; Porter, *Journal,* Vol. 1, p. 3.

8. Porter, *Journal,* Vol. 1, p. 3; for background of Feltus see *The Naval War of 1812,* p. 688.

9. Porter, *Journal,* Vol. 1, p. 14. Although drunkenness was rife throughout both the British and US navies of the period, it appears that the *Essex* was a particularly alcoholic ship. The sources make numerous references to Porter's drinking, Lieutenant Wilson was eventually dismissed for alcoholism and even the eleven-year-old Midshipman Farragut indulged. Perhaps the only teetotaller on board was Midshipman Henry Warren Ogden, a young man from a deeply religious New Jersey family whose abstinence Farragut refers to in his memoirs.

10. Porter to Bainbridge, 8 September 1812, at the mouth of the Delaware, *Naval War of 1812,* pp. 468–9; Long, *Nothing Too Daring,* pp. 38–9; Bruce Linder, *Tidewater's Navy: An Illustrated History,* Annapolis: Naval Institute Press, 2005, p. 53.

11. Royal Navy sailing report on the *Essex,* Ralph Delaware Paine, *The Ships and Sailors of Old Salem, Massachusetts,* Berwyn Heights, MD: Heritage Books Inc., 2007, pp. 196–217; on the *Essex*'s armament see William James, *The Naval History of Great Britain: From the Declaration of War by France, in February 1793, to the Succession of George IV, in January 1820,* London: Harding, Lepard and Co., 1826, Vol. 6, p. 123; Porter to Hamilton, Chester, PA, 12 October 1812, reproduced in *The Naval War of 1812,* Vol. 3, pp. 528.

12. John G. Cowell to Paul Hamilton, 24 September 1812, quoted in Christopher McKee, *A Gentlemanly and Honorable Profession: The Creation of the US Naval Officer Corps, 1794-1815,* Annapolis: Naval Institute Press, 1991, pp. 314–15.

13. See *The Naval War of 1812,* Vol. 1, p. 170.

14. For a list of those who sailed on the *Essex* see Porter, *Journal,* Vol. 1, pp. 4–12; on Sweeny see Porter, *Journal,* Vol. 1, p. 48; on Witter see Porter, *Journal,* Vol. 1, p. 193; on White see Porter, *Journal,* Vol. 1, pp. 138, 199; on Belcher see Porter, *Journal,* Vol. 1, pp. 197–8; on Glasseau or Glasser, see Farragut, *The Life of David Glasgow Farragut,* quoted in *The Naval War of 1812,* Vol. 3, p. 757; on Almy see *The Old Dartmouth Historical Sketches, Numbers 1 to 15,* Cornell University, 1903, p. 134; on Ruff see Farragut, *The Life of David*

Glasgow Farragut, p. 14; on Holmes see Porter, *Journal*, Vol. 1, pp. 14 and 22 and Henry P. Johnston (ed.), *The Record of Connecticut Men in the Military and Naval Service of the War of the Revolution 1775-1783*, Salem: Higginson Book Company, 1995, p. 599.

15. Surgeon Edward Cutbush to Hamilton, New Castle, 16 November 1812, reproduced in *The Naval War of 1812*, Vol. 7, pp. 590–2; Porter, *Journal*, Vol. 1, p. 3.

16. Feltus, *Journal*, entries for 24 and 25 October 1812; David Porter, *Constantinople and its Environs in a Series of Letters, Exhibiting the Actual State of the Manners, Customs and Habits of the Turks . . .*, New York: Harper & Brothers, 1835, p. 10.

17. Porter, *Journal*, Vol. 1, pp. 2–3.

18. Ibid, p. 3.

19. Ibid, p. 13.

20. Ibid; Feltus, *Journal*, entries for 4 and 5 November 1812; for games played see Robert Hay, *Landsman Hay*, Barnsley: Seaforth Publishing, 2010, p. 75.

21. Porter, *Journal*, Vol. 1, pp. 13–14; Toll, *Six Frigates*, pp. 369–70.

22. Feltus, *Journal*, see entries for 10 and 11 November 1812; for a discussion of gun drill see Roy and Lesley Atkins, *Jack Tar: The Extraordinary Lives of Ordinary Seamen in Nelson's Navy*, London: Abacus, 2008, pp. 271–3; also see Lavery, *Nelson's Navy*, pp. 172–8.

23. Porter, *Journal*, Vol. 1, p. 14.

24. Ibid, pp. 14–15.

25. Ibid, p. 15; Feltus, *Journal*, entry for 23 November 1812. On Kingsbury see War of 1812 Pension Files, US Navy, Surnames K, at http://www.fold3.com/image/314284970/.

26. Porter, *Journal*, Vol. 1, p. 15; Feltus, *Journal*, entries for 24, 25 and 26 November 1812.

Chapter 2

1. Porter, *Journal*, Vol. 1, p. 16; Feltus, *Journal*, entry for 27 November 1812; for a near-contemporary description of Porto Praya see John Purdy, *Memoir, Descriptive and Explanatory, to Accompany the Charts of the Northern Atlantic Ocean*, London: R. H. Laurie, 1853.

2. Charles W. Moore, *The Freemasons' Monthly Magazine*, Boston: Hugh H. Tuttle, 1854, Vol. XIII, pp. 348–9; M. Bancroft, J. Wiley and G., C. and H. Carvill, *The American Monthly Magazine*, New York: New York Public Library, 1836, Vol. II, pp. 73–5.

3. Porter, *Journal*, Vol. 1, pp. 20–1; Feltus, *Journal*, entry for 27 and 28 November 1812.

4. Porter, *Journal*, Vol. 1, p. 21.

5. Long, *Nothing Too Daring*, pp. 3–4.

6. Porter, *Journal*, Vol. 1, p. 38. Porter is coy about the punishment he dished out to the drunkards. Although no official records survive, twelve lashes was customary for such an offence. During a previous command (USS *Enterprize*), Porter had ordered fifteen of his crew of 113 (or 13.3 per cent) to be flogged between 21 August 1805 and 17 November 1806. Five were punished twice, one was flogged three times, the average number of lashes given was twelve and the maximum twenty-four. In his memoir, Porter failed to detail the punishments he applied during the cruise from the Delware. Nevertheless, flogging was common in the US Navy and all commanding officers employed it. While

Thomas Truxtun only used the lash as a last resort, William Bainbridge was notorious. In the Mediterranean in 1800 he hit a sailor so violently with his sword that the man's skull was fractured and he was sent into violent convulsions. Porter's use of physical punishment fell somewhere in between.

7. Porter, *Journal*, Vol. 1, p. 18; Feltus, *Journal*, see entry for 29 November.

8. Porter, *Journal*, Vol. 1, pp. 19–20.

9. Ibid, p. 20; for the identities of Porter's servants see ibid, pp. 234–5.

10. Ibid, pp. 24–5 and 27–8; Porter to Hamilton, *Essex* at Sea, July 2 1813, reproduced in *The Naval War of 1812*, pp. 696–7; on Adams see McKee, *A Gentlemanly and Honorable Profession*, pp. 197–8.

11. Porter, *Journal*, Vol. 1, pp. 22–6.

12. Ibid, pp. 25–8; Feltus, *Journal*, entries for 5, 6 and 7 December 1812.

13. Porter, *Journal*, Vol. 1, p. 28.

14. Toll, *Six Frigates*, pp. 190–8 and 261–2; William Ray, *Horrors of Slavery or the American Tars in Tripoli*, Troy, 1808, p. 105.

15. Porter, *Journal*, Vol. 1, p. 32; Feltus, *Journal*, entry for 12 December 1812; see also entry for prisoner John Williams (roll no.14573), ADM 103/466; and Finch to Hamilton, reproduced in *The Naval War of 1812*, p. 684.

16. Feltus, *Journal*, entries for 12 and 13 December 1812; Porter, *Journal*, Vol. 1, pp. 34–6; on the movements of the British ships under Hall Dixon's command see Gerald S. Graham (ed.), *The Navy and South America, 1807-1823, Correspondence of the Commanders-in-Chief on the South American Station*, London: Navy Records Society, 1962, pp. 76–121.

17. Porter, *Journal*, Vol. 1, pp. 35–7.

18. Ibid.

19. Ibid, p. 39.

20. Ibid, pp. 41–3; Feltus, *Journal*, entries for 25, 26 and 27 December 1812.

21. Porter, *Journal*, Vol. 1, pp. 43–4; Feltus, *Journal*, entry for 29 December 1812; on John Bagnell (prisoner roll no.1202) see ADM 103/466; on Charles T. Clarke and the fate of the *Elizabeth*, see The Naval War of 1812, p. 690 and Effie Gwynn Bowie, *Across the Years in Prince George's County*, Clearfield Company, 2010.

22. Porter, *Journal*, Vol. 1, pp. 44–6; Feltus, *Journal*, entries for 30 December 1812 and 1, 2 and 3 January 1813.

23. Porter, *Journal*, Vol. 1, pp. 46–8; Feltus, *Journal*, entries for 4 to 12 January 1813.

24. Porter, *Journal*, Vol. 1, pp. 48–9 and 238; Feltus, *Journal*, entry for 12 January 1813.

25. Although banned in the Royal Navy by Admiralty order in 1806, Running the Gauntlet was used in the US service at the time. On Porter's methods of punishment see McKee, *A Gentlemanly and Honorable Profession*, Table 10, pp. 480–1; J. Shillibeer, *A Narrative of the Briton's Voyage to Pitcairn's Island, Including an Interesting Sketch of the Present State of the Brazils and of Spanish South America*, London: Law and Whittaker, 1817, pp. 72–3: 'American Capture Retaken', *The Literary Panorama and National Register*, New Series, Volume the Second, 1817; a report on the court case of John Swayne in *The Bury and Norwich Post*, 27 December 1815.

26. Porter, *Journal*, Vol. 1, pp. 41–58 and the appendix entitled *Explanation of the Sketch of the Islands of St. Catherines and Alvardo*, found after p. 243.

27. Ibid.

28. Porter, *Journal*, Vol. 1, pp. 49–54; Feltus, *Journal*, entries for 20, 21 and 22 January 1813. On the *Essex*'s boats see Portia Takakjian, *Anatomy of the Ship: The 32-Gun Frigate Essex*, London: Conway Maritime Press, 1990.

29. Porter, *Journal*, Vol. 1, p. 55.

30. Porter, *Journal*, Vol. 1, pp. 55–9; Porter to Hamilton, *Essex* at Sea, 2 July 1813, reproduced in *The Naval War of 1812*, pp. 696–7; James Hughes to Secretary Crowninshield, 18 February 1815, reproduced in *The Naval War of 1812* and the accompanying footnotes, pp. 771–2; Feltus, *Journal*, entry for 25 January 1813.

31. See *The Naval War of 1812*, p. 683; George C. Daughan, *The Shining Sea: David Porter and the Epic Voyage of the USS. Essex during the War of 1812*, New York: Basic Books, 2013, pp. 83–5.

32. Porter, *Journal*, Vol. 1, p. 57.

Chapter 3

1. On Hillyar see *Colburn*'s *United Service Magazine and Naval and Military Journal*, 1843, Part III, pp. 271–85; also Richard Blake, *Evangelicals in the Royal Navy, 1775-1815: Blue Lights & Psalm Singers*, Woodbridge: Boydell Press, 2008, pp. 185–6 and 240; on Scargill see the ship's muster and pay rolls – ADM 37/4380, ADM 35/3677 and ADM 36/16809; for attire of sailors and officers in the Royal Navy see Lavery, *Nelson's Navy*, pp. 104–8, 134 and 203–4.

2. Rif Winfield, *British Warships in the Age of Sail, 1793-1817: Design, Construction, Careers and Fates*, Barnsley: Seaforth, 2008, p. 147; James, *The Naval History of Great Britain*, p. 470.

3. For the crew of the *Phoebe* see the ship's log and muster and pay rolls – ADM 1/1947, ADM 37/4380, ADM 35/3677 and ADM 36/16809. Also note the Hillyar's official dispatches following the Battle of Tamatave, reproduced in *The London Gazette*, Issue 16540, 12 November 1811; and see National Archives, Trafalgar Ancestors Online http://www.nationalarchives.gov.uk/trafalgarancestors/default.asp .

4. On Ingram see *Owemoigne Baptisms 1752 to 1812* - http://www.opcdorset.org/OwermoigneFiles/OwermoignBaps1752-1812.htm and *Owermoigne Wills* http://www.opcdorset.org/OwermoigneFiles/OwermoigneWills.htm ; also see Thornton to Thornton, Valparaiso Bay 12 April 1814, reproduced in Allen Gardiner, *Hunting the Essex: A Journal of the Voyage of HMS Phoebe 1813-1814 by Midshipman Allen Gardiner*, John S. Rieske (ed.), Barnsley: Seaforth, 2013, pp. 130–5; on Jago see Cornwall Council Archives, X807, documents 2 to 4; on Gardiner see John Marsh, *A Memoir of Allen F. Gardiner, Commander R.N.*, London: James Nisbet & Co., 1857; on Samuel Thornton Junior see Percy Melville Thornton, *Some Things we have remembered: Samuel Thornton, admiral, 1797-1859*, London: Longmans, Green & Co., 1912. On captains' habits of recruiting like-minded officers see Michael Lewis, *A Social History of the Navy 1793-1815*, London: George Allen & Unwin, 1960, p. 72.

5. Blake, *Evangelicals in the Royal Navy*, p. 240; ADM 37/4380; see also archive catalogue notes for Morgan's medal http://www.dnw.co.uk/

6. On Miller see Hillyar to Croker, HMS *Phoebe* at Portsmouth, 5 December 1814, ADM1/1950; on Laura (or Laurie) see ADM 36/16809, ADM 37/4380 and Kenneth Douglas-Morris, *The Naval General Service Medal Roll, 1793-1840*, Andrews UK Ltd., 2012, p. 112.

7. Hillyar to Croker, HMS *Phoebe* at Sea, 28 December 1812, reproduced in *The London Gazette*; and Hillyar to Croker, 28 December 1812, ADM 1/1947.

8. Ommanney & Druce (Prize Agents) to Croker, reproduced in *The London Gazette*, issue 16703, page 337; Hillyar to Croker, 8 January 1813, Plymouth, ADM 1/1947; Hillyar to Croker, ADM 52/4236; Midshipman Robert Gordon to his mother, quoted here http://www.invaluable.com/catalog/viewLot.cfm?afRedir=true&lotRef=221ac52304&scp=c&ri=308

9. *Colburn*'s *United Service Magazine and Naval and Military Journal*, 1843, Part III, pp. 271–85.

10. *Phoebe*'s Log, ADM 51/2675; Paul Chamberlain, *Hell Upon Water: Prisoners of War in Britain, 1793-1815*, Staplehurst: Spellmount, 2008, pp. 58–9.

11. *Phoebe*'s Log, ADM 51/2675; on a ship's routine in home port see Adkins, Lesley and Roy, *Jack Tar: Life in Nelson's Navy*, New York: Little, Brown Book Group, 2009, pp. 153–93, and William Robinson, *Jack Nastyface: Memoirs of an English Seaman*, London: Chatham Publishing, 2002, pp. 87 and 96.

12. ADM 51/2675; Hillyar to Croker, 12 February 1813, ADM 1/1947; ADM 37/4380; on the colour scheme of Trafalgar ships see Basil Hall (ed.), *The Letter of Private Wheeler, 1809-1828*, Gloucestershire: Windrush Press, 1999, p. 46.

13. ADM 51/2675; on Pomfrey see Hillyar to Croker, Plymouth, 14 January 1813, ADM 1/1947 and *An Alphabetical List of the Pursers, Gunners, Boatswains and Carpenters of His Majesty's Fleet, with the Dates of their First Warrants*, London: S. Brooke, 1813, p. 185; on Brady see Hillyar to Croker, 19 January 1813, ADM 1/1948; on schoolmasters' pay, conditions and duties see Lavery, *Nelson's Navy*, pp. 104 and 326–7.

14. ADM 51/2675; on victualing at Plymouth see Lavery, *Nelson's Navy*, pp. 236 and 241–4; ADM 37/4380; on Surflen see *An Alphabetical List of the Pursers, Gunners, Boatswains and Carpenters...*, p. 62; *The Courier*, London, 12 February 1812; and *The Morning Post*, London, 2 May 1814.

15. ADM 36/16809; ADM 37/4380; on a seaman's entry on board ship see Lavery, *Nelson's Navy*, p. 129; for Jackson's donation to his mother see ADM 27/18.

16. On the *Phoebe*'s band see Thornton to Thornton, Valparaiso Bay 12 April 1814, reproduced in Gardiner, *Hunting the Essex*, pp. 130–5; and Hillyar to Croker, off Valparaiso, 28 February 1814, ADM 1/22.

17. ADM 51/2675; Lavery, *Nelson's Navy*, pp. 230–4; on the *Isaac Todd* see Keith H. Lloyd, 'Voyage of the *Isaac Todd*', *Oregon Historical Quarterly*, Winter 2008.

18. ADM 52/4236; on Hillyar's orders, see his coded journal, contained in Hillyar to Croker, HMS *Phoebe*, 22 October 1814, ADM 1/1948.

19. Lloyd, 'Voyage of the Isaac Todd'; on the 'Old China Trade' see Eric J. Dolin, *When America First Met China: An Exotic History of Tea, Drugs and Money in the Age of Sail*, New York: Liveright, 2012.

20. ADM 52/4236; Adkins, *Jack Tar*, pp. 209–11.

21. Gardiner, *Hunting the Essex*, p. 34.

22. Marsh, *A Memoir of Allen F. Gardiner*, pp. 5–6.

23. ADM 52/4236; On Smith see ADM 37/4380 and *The London Gazette*, 12 November 1811, Issue 16540, p .2185.

24. ADM 52/4236; Lavery, *Nelson's Navy*, pp. 172–8.

25. See (online) *Dictionary of Canadian Biography* http://www.biographi.ca/en/bio. php?BioId=36672 and http://www.biographi.ca/009004-119.01-e.php?&id_nbr=4580; see McDonald, *Autobiographical Notes* reproduced in L. R. Mason, *Les Bourgeois de la Compagnie du Nord-Ouest, Recits de Voyages, Lettres et Rapports Inedits Relatifs au Nord-Ouest Canadien*, Quebec: de L'Imprimierie Generale, 1890, pp. 43–8.

26. ADM 52/4236; Lavery, *Nelson's Navy*, pp. 139–40 and 326–7; National Archives, Trafalgar Ancestors Online http://www.nationalarchives.gov.uk/trafalgarancestors/default.asp .

27. ADM 52/4236; Hillyar to Croker, Spithead, 13 March 1813 and Hillyar to Croker, Spithead, 16 March 1813, both in ADM 1/1947; On Barnes see *Dictionary of Canadian Biography* http://www.biographi.ca/en/bio.php?BioId=36672;

28. *Naval Chronicle* 29, 1813, p. 242; *The Times*, London, 20 March 1813. Both quoted in Stephen Budiansky, *Perilous Fight: America's Intrepid War with Britain on the High Seas, 1812-1815*, New York: Vintage Books, 2011, pp. 187–8.

29. ADM 52/4236; ADM 37/4380.

30. ADM 52/4236.

31. ADM 52/4236; Gardiner, *Hunting the Essex*, p. 34; Captain Salt to Croker, 30 March 1813, HMS *Unicorn* at Sea, reproduced in *The European Magazine and London Review*, Vol. 63, Philological Society of London, 1813, p. 529.

32. ADM 52/4236; Gardiner, *Hunting the Essex*, pp. 34–5.

33. ADM 52/4236.

34. Burrow to Jago, HMS *Phoebe* at Sea, 17 October 1814, Cornwall Council Archives, X807, document 4.

35. ADM 52/4236.

36. ADM 52/4236; Gardiner, *Hunting the Essex*, pp. 35–6; for contemporary descriptions of Tenerife see John Payne, *Universal Geography, Formed into a New and Entire System, Describing Asia, Africa, Europe and America . . .*, Dublin: Z Jackson, 1794, p. 679; and John Purdy, *Memoir Descriptive and Explanatory, to Accompany the New Chart of the Atlantic Ocean . . .*, London: Whittle and Holmes Laurie, 1812, pp. 112–13.

Chapter 4

1. Porter, *Journal*, Vol. 1, p. 61; Feltus, *Journal*, entry for 25 January 1813.

2. Porter, *Journal*, Vol. 1, pp. 62–3.

3. Ibid, pp. 63–4.

4. Ibid, p. 65; Feltus, *Journal*, entries for 4 to 10 February 1813.

5. Porter, *Journal*, Vol. 1, p. 66; on Tameoy (Tamaha) see ibid, p. 118; Farragut, *The Life of David Glasgow Farragut*, p. 11; and the footnotes on p. 748 of *The Naval War of 1812*. On Cowell see H. Niles (ed.), *Niles' Weekly Register – Supplement to Vol. VII, from September 1814 to March 1815*, Baltimore, 1815, p.29.

6. Porter, *Journal*, Vol. 1, pp. 66–9; Feltus, *Journal*, entries for 13 and 14 February 1813.

7. Porter, *Journal*, Vol. 1, pp. 69–71; Feltus, *Journal*, entry for 14 February 1813.

8. Porter, *Journal*, Vol. 1, pp. 70–1; Feltus, *Journal*, entry for 15 February 1813.

9. Porter, *Journal*, Vol. 1, pp. 71–3; Feltus, *Journal*, entries for 18 and 19 February 1813. On Porter's wounds see Long, *Nothing Too Daring*, p. 21.

10. Porter, *Journal*, Vol. 1, pp. 72–7.

11. Ibid, pp. 77–8 and 80; Feltus, *Journal*, entry for 28 February 1813.

12. Porter, *Journal*, Vol. 1, pp. 78–9; Feltus, *Journal*, entries for 2 and 3 March 1813; Farragut, *The Life of David Glasgow Farragut*, p. 7.

13. Porter, *Journal*, Vol. 1, pp. 79–80 and 92; Feltus, *Journal*, entries for 3, 4 and 5 March 1813; Farragut, *The Life of David Glasgow Farragut*, p. 7.

14. Porter, *Journal*, Vol. 1, pp. 84 and 87; George Malcolm Thompson, *Sir Francis Drake*, Suffolk: Chaucer Press, 1972, pp. 118–19; on Mocha Dick see Jeremiah N. Reynolds, *Mocha Dick: Or, The White Whale of the Pacific*, Michigan: 1932.

15. Porter, *Journal*, Vol. 1, p. 85.

16. Ibid, pp. 85–6; Farragut, *The Life of David Glasgow Farragut*, pp. 7–8; Feltus, *Journal*, entry for 7 March 1813; Porter to Hamilton, *Essex* at Sea, 2 July 1813, reproduced in *The Naval War of 1812*, pp. 696–7.

17. Porter, *Journal*, Vol. 1, p. 89; Feltus, *Journal*, entry for 8 March 1813.

18. Porter, *Journal*, Vol. 1, p. 90; Feltus, *Journal*, entry for 10 March 1813.

19. On South Pacific whaling see Edouard A. Stackpole, *Whales & Destiny: The Rivalry between America, France and Britain for Control of the Southern Whales Fishery, 1785–1825*, The University of Massachusetts Press, 1972; Porter, *Journal*, Vol. 1, pp. 181–5. For details of the *Comet*'s voyage see *Transcript of the Voyage of the Comet*, National Maritime Museum, Greenwich, LUB 38/10.

20. Porter, *Journal*, pp. 91–3.

21. For contemporary descriptions of Valparaiso see George Vancouver, *A Voyage of Discovery to the North Pacific Ocean and Round the World in the Years 1790-95*, London: Robinson, 1798, pp. 400–40; Thomas H. Bennett and Washington Chase, *A Voyage from the United States to South America Performed During the Years 1821, 1822 and 1823 . . . in a Nantucket Whaleship*, The Herald Press, 1823, pp. 22–42; John Miers, *Travels in Chile and La Plata*, Vol. 1, Oxford, 1826, pp. 446–53.

22. Porter, *Journal*, Vol. 1, pp. 91–3. On the *Colt* see Charles Lyon Chandler, *Inter-American Acquaintances*, Sewanee, TN: 1917, pp. 133–4.

23. Porter, *Journal*, Vol. 1, p. 94; Farragut, *The Life of David Glasgow Farragut*, p. 8; Feltus, *Journal*, entry for 14 March 1813.

24. Porter, *Journal*, Vol. 1, p. 94.

25. For a brief overview on the Wars of Independence see John Charles Chasteen, *Americanos: Latin America's Struggle for Independence*, Oxford: Oxford University Press, 2009; and John Fletcher, *The Wars of Spanish American Independence*, Oxford: Osprey, 2013.

26. For a more detailed look at the move towards independence in Chile see Simon Collier, *Ideas and Politics of Chilean Independence 1808-1833*, Cambridge: Cambridge University Press, 1967.

27. Porter, *Journal*, Vol. 1, pp. 94–6.

28. Porter, *Journal*, Vol. 1, pp. 96–100. On Poinsett see James Fred Rippy, *Joel R. Poinsett: Versatile American*, Whitefish, MT: Literary Licensing, 2012.

29. Porter, *Journal*, Vol. 1, pp. 94–6.

30. Ibid; Farragut, *The Life of David Glasgow Farragut*, p. 15.

31. Porter, *Journal*, Vol. 1, pp. 97–9 and 107.

32. Ibid, pp. 97–101; Feltus, *Journal*, entries for 18 to 21 March 1813.

33. Porter, *Journal*, Vol. 1, pp. 100–1; Feltus, *Journal*, entries for 21 and 22 March 1813.

34. Porter, *Journal*, Vol. 1, pp. 102, 105–6; Feltus, *Journal*, entry for 22 March 1813. For a reference to the English merchants' letter see Graham (ed.), *The Navy and South America*, document 67b, p. 92.

35. Porter, *Journal*, Vol. 1, pp. 102–4; prisoner list ADM 103/466; on Langley's promotion see *The Naval War of 1812*, p. 742; Porter to Bainbridge, Valparaiso, 23 March 1813, reproduced in *The Naval War of 1812*, pp. 696–7.

36. Porter, *Journal*, Vol. 1, pp. 102–3; Feltus, *Journal*, entry for 24 March 1813.

37. Porter, *Journal*, Vol. 1, pp. 108–10; Farragut, *The Life of David Glasgow Farragut*, p. 8; Feltus, *Journal*, entries for 25 and 26 March 1813; on West see National Maritime Digital Library http://nmdl.org/aowv/whvoyage.cfm?VesselNumber=677 ; on the *Nimrod* and Perry see Jane M. Clayton, *Ships Employed in the South Sea Whale Fishery from Britain: 1775-1815: An Alphabetical List of Ships*, 2014, p. 183; on the *Charles* and Gardener see Federal Writers Project, *Whaling Masters*, Wildside Press LLC, 2009, p. 136.

38. Porter, *Journal*, Vol. 1, pp. 108–10; Farragut, *The Life of David Glasgow Farragut*, p. 8; Feltus, *Journal*, entries for 25 and 26 March 1813; on Bly see Stackpole, *Whales and Destiny*, pp. 340–3.

39. Porter to Abascal, USS *Essex* at Sea, 26 March 1813, reproduced in *The Naval War of 1812*, p. 692.

40. Porter, *Journal*, Vol. 1, pp. 111–12; Feltus, *Journal*, entry for 27 March 1813.

41. Porter, *Journal*, Vol. 1, pp. 115–19; Feltus, *Journal*, entries for 27 March 1813 to 4 April 1813.

42. Porter, *Journal*, Vol. 1, pp. 115–17; Feltus, *Journal*, entries for 4 and 5 April 1813.

43. On Randall see Writers Project, *Whaling Masters*, p. 228; Maritime Digital Library entry; Barney Genealogical Record http://www.nantuckethistoricalassociation.net/bgr/BGR-o/p415.htm#i12459; and Farragut, *The Life of David Glasgow Farragut*, p. 9.

44. Porter, *Journal*, Vol. 1, pp. 119–21; Feltus, *Journal*, entries for 5 and 6 April 1813.

45. Porter, *Journal*, Vol. 1, pp. 121–3; Feltus, *Journal*, entries for 9 and 10 April 1813.

46. Porter, *Journal*, Vol. 1, pp. 125–6; Feltus, *Journal*, entry for 11 April 1813.

Chapter 5

1. ADM 52/4236; log of the *Ocean* East Indiaman, British Library, L/MAR/B/222R; John McDonald, *Journal*, entry for 11 April 1813, reproduced in Alexander Henry and David Thompson, *New Light on the Early History of the Greater Northwest*, Cambridge: Cambridge University Press, 2015, p. 762n. For contemporary descriptions of Santa Cruz see John Payne, *Universal Geography*, p. 679; and John Purdy, *Memoir Descriptive and Explanatory, to Accompany the New Chart of the Atlantic Ocean . . .*, London: Whittle and Holmes Laurie, 1812, pp. 112–13. On Nelson's attack on Santa Cruz see Colin White, *1797: Nelson's Year of Destiny*, Stroud: Sutton Publishing, 1999.
2. ADM 52/4236; Gardiner, *Hunting the Essex*, pp. 34–7; McDonald, *Autobiographical Notes*, pp. 45–6.
3. ADM 52/4236; Gardiner, *Hunting the Essex*, pp. 37–8; log of *Devaynes* East Indiaman, British Library, L/MAR/B/223F.
4. ADM 52/4236; Gardiner, *Hunting the Essex*, pp. 38–9. The 1798 Convoy Act forbade merchantmen from sailing alone, a precaution which greatly reduced the number captured in the opening years of the Revolutionary War. Some captains chose to break the rules, however, by slipping ahead as the convoy neared its destination. Fines or imprisonment were sought by Lloyd's of London, the largest naval insurer, to punish those who transgressed but the financial benefit accrued from getting a jump on the competition were a considerable lure.
5. ADM 52/4236; Gardiner, *Hunting the Essex*, pp. 38–40; L/MAR/B/223F; L/MAR/B/222R. On Staines see The National Archives Trafalgar Ancestors search engine.
6. ADM 52/4236; L/MAR/B/223F; L/MAR/B/222R.
7. ADM 52/4236; *Phoebe*'s pay roll, ADM 35/3677; ADM 37/4380; Hillyar's Journal, ADM 1/1950. On the pay of an able seaman see Lavery, *Nelson's Navy*, pp. 326–7.
8. ADM 52/4236; Gardiner, *Hunting the Essex*, pp. 41–2. On the activities of the *Cherub* and *Raccoon* see Manley-Dixon to Croker, HMS *Cherub*, Rio de Janeiro, 9 June 1813, reproduced in Graham (ed.), *The Navy and South America*, p. 90. For a contemporary description of Rio de Janeiro see John Luccock, *Notes on Rio de Janeiro and the Southern Parts of Brazil; taken during a Residence of Ten Years in that Country*, London: Samuel Leigh, 1820.
9. Graham (ed.), *The Navy and South America*, pp. 76–90; Lambert, *The Challenge*, pp. 277–9. For an overview of Anglo-Portuguese relations and the effect on Brazil of the Napoleonic Wars see Laurentino Gomes, *1808 – The Flight of the Emperor: How a Weak Prince, a Made Queen and the British Navy Tricked Napoleon and Changed the New World*, Connecticut: Lyons Press, 2007.
10. Graham (ed.), *The Navy and South America*, pp. 87–92.
11. Ibid, pp. 93–6; McDonald, *Autobiographical Notes*, p. 46.
12. ADM 52/4236.
13. Shillibeer, *A Narrative of the Briton's Voyage*, p. 14; Last Will and Testament of Lieutenant William Ingram, PROB 11/1567; Gardiner, *Hunting the Essex*, pp. 42–4.

14. ADM 52/4236; Graham (ed.), *The Navy and South America*, pp. 93–5; Court Martial of Carlan and Mortraugh, 29 June 1813, HMS *Phoebe* at anchor off Rio de Janeiro, ADM 1/5346.

15. ADM 1/5346.

16. Dixon to Hillyar, 1 July 1813, Rio de Janeiro, reproduced in Graham (ed.), *The Navy and South America*, pp. 99–101.

17. *Niles' Weekly Register*, volume 5, 1814, p. 29.

18. ADM 37/4380; Muster roll of HMS *Cherub*, ADM 35/3411; Strangford to Dixon, 3 July 1813, reproduced in Graham (ed.), *The Navy in South America*, pp. 101–2.

19. ADM 52/4236; Gardiner, *Hunting the Essex*, p. 44; *A Gazeta do Rio* (Rio de Janeiro Gazette), 10 and 14 July 1813.

Chapter 6

1. Porter, *Journal*, Vol. 1, pp. 125–6; Feltus, *Journal*, entries for 11 to 15 April 1813.

2. Porter, *Journal*, Vol. 1, p. 126; Feltus, *Journal*, entry for 16 April 1813.

3. Porter, *Journal*, Vol. 1, pp. 127–8; Feltus, *Journal*, entry for 17 April 1813.

4. Porter, *Journal*, Vol. 1, pp. 128–9; Feltus, *Journal*, entry for 18 April 1813.

5. Porter, *Journal*, Vol. 1, pp. 129–35; Feltus, *Journal*, entries for 18 and 19 April 1813.

6. Porter, *Journal*, Vol. 1, pp. 135–9; Feltus, *Journal*, entries for 19 and 20 April 1813.

7. Porter, *Journal*, Vol. 1, pp. 139–40; Feltus, *Journal*, entries for 20 and 21 April 1813.

8. Porter, *Journal*, Vol. 1, pp. 140–1; Feltus, *Journal*, entries for 20 to 24 April 1813.

9. Porter, *Journal*, Vol. 1, pp. 141–4; Feltus, *Journal*, entries for 23 to 24 April 1813.

10. Porter, *Journal*, Vol. 1, pp. 144–5; Feltus, *Journal*, entries for 24 to 25 April 1813.

11. Porter, *Journal*, Vol. 1, pp. 146–8 and 151; Feltus, *Journal*, entries for 26 to 28 April 1813.

12. Porter, *Journal*, Vol. 1, pp. 148–9. On the *Bounty* see Caroline Alexander, *The Bounty: the True Story of the Mutiny on the Bounty*, New York: Harper Perennial, 2004. On HMS *Hermione* see Dudley Pope, *The Black Ship*, Barnsley: Pen & Sword Military Classics, 2003.

13. Porter, *Journal*, Vol. 1, pp. 149–51; Feltus, *Journal*, entries for 29 and 30 April 1813; Farragut, *The Life of David Glasgow Farragut*, p. 8; Porter to Hamilton, US Frigate *Essex* at Sea, 2 July 1813, reproduced in *The Naval War of 1812*, pp. 694–7. For further details on the British whale ships *Montezuma* and *Georgiana* see Clayton, *Ships Employed in the South Seas Whale Fishery*, pp. 126–9 and 175–6; Washington Irvine, *The Analectic Magazine*, Vol. 6 (1815), pp. 450–1; and John Dodson, *English Admiralty Reports: Reports of cases argued and determined in the High Court of the admiralty ... 1811-1822*, New York: Little, Brown, 1853, pp. 397–402. On the prisoners who joined the *Essex* from the prizes see ADM 103/466 and the lists of casualties on the *Essex* in Porter, *Journal*, Vol. 1, pp. 234–41.

14. Porter, *Journal*, Vol. 1, pp. 151–3; Feltus, *Journal*, entries for 30 April and 1 May 1813.

15. Porter, *Journal*, Vol. 1, pp. 153–4; Feltus, *Journal*, entries for 1 to 8 May 1813; Farragut, *The Life of David Glasgow Farragut*, p. 8. On the workings of whale ships see Nathaniel Philbrick, *In the Heart of the Sea: the Epic True Story that Inspired Moby Dick*, New York: Harper Perennial, 2005, pp. 55–7.

16. Porter, *Journal*, Vol. 1, p. 155; Feltus, *Journal*, entries for 9 to 12 May 1813.

17. Porter, *Journal*, Vol. 1, pp. 155–8; Feltus, *Journal*, entries for 12 to 13 May 1813.

18. Porter, *Journal*, Vol. 1, pp. 158–9; Feltus, *Journal*, entries for 12 to 13 May 1813.

19. Porter, *Journal*, Vol. 1, pp. 159–61 and 179; Feltus, *Journal*, entries for 14 to 15 May 1813; Farragut, *The Life of David Glasgow Farragut*, p. 8.

20. Porter, *Journal*, Vol. 1, pp. 162–4; Farragut, *The Life of David Glasgow Farragut*, pp. 8–9.

21. Porter, *Journal*, Vol. 1, pp. 161–2.

22. Porter, *Journal*, Vol. 1, pp. 162–4; Feltus, *Journal*, entries for 14 to 16 May 1813; Farragut, *The Life of David Glasgow Farragut*, p. 9.

23. Porter, *Journal*, Vol. 1, pp. 164–7 and 176.

24. Porter, *Journal*, Vol. 1, pp. 165-7.

25. Ibid, p. 168; Porter to Hamilton and Porter to Bainbridge, 2 July 1813, US Frigate *Essex* at Sea, reproduced in *The Naval War of 1812*, pp. 694–7.

26. Porter, *Journal*, Vol. 1, p. 169; Feltus, *Journal*, entry for 27 May 1813.

27. Porter, *Journal*, Vol. 1, pp. 169–70; Feltus, *Journal*, entry for 28 May 1813; Farragut, *The Life of David Glasgow Farragut*, p. 9. On the *Atlantic* and *Greenwich* and Wyer and Shuttleworth see Clayton, *Ships Employed in the South Sea Whale Fishery*, pp. 65 and 132–3 and Porter, *Journal*, Vol. 1, pp. 172–4.

28. Porter, *Journal*, Vol. 1, pp. 198–9; Feltus, *Journal*, entry for 25 June 1813; Porter to Hamilton, 2 July 1813, US Frigate *Essex* at Sea, reproduced in *The Naval War of 1812*, p. 697.

29. Porter, *Journal*, Vol. 1, pp. 174–5. On prisoners who joined the *Essex* see ADM 103/466 and the lists of casualties on the *Essex* in Porter, *Journal*, Vol. 1, pp. 234–41.

30. Clayton, *Ships Employed in the South Sea Whale Fishery*, pp. 65 and 132–3.

31. Ibid, and Porter, *Journal*, Vol. 1, pp. 172–4. On Wyer also see http://www.geni.com/people/Obed-Wyer/6000000021470063486.

32. Porter, *Journal*, Vol. 1, pp. 174–7; Feltus, *Journal*, entries for 6 and 7 June 1813.

33. Porter, *Journal*, Vol. 1, pp. 186–90; Feltus, *Journal*, entries for 8 to 18 June 1813.

34. Porter, *Journal*, Vol. 1, pp. 190–3; Feltus, *Journal*, entries for 19 and 20 June 1813. On Porter's time in New Orleans see Long, *Nothing Too Daring*, pp. 36–56.

35. Porter, *Journal*, Vol. 1, pp. 191–2; Feltus, *Journal*, entry for 22 June 1813.

36. Porter, *Journal*, Vol. 1, pp. 192–4.

37. Ibid, pp. 194–6; Long, *Nothing Too Daring*, p. 100.

38. Porter, *Journal*, Vol. 1, pp. 196–7.

39. Ibid, pp. 197–9; Feltus, *Journal*, entries for 24 and 25 June 1813; Farragut, *The Life of David Glasgow Farragut*, p. 9.

40. Porter, *Journal*, Vol. 1, p. 200; Feltus, *Journal*, entries for 26 to 29 June 1813.

41. Porter, *Journal*, Vol. 1, p. 200; ADM 103/466. For British verdict on Porter's treatment of prisoners see Dixon to Staines, La Ceres, Rio de Janeiro, 24 March 1814, ADM1/22 and Shillibeer, *A Narrative of the Briton's Voyage*, p. 72.

42. On Coffin see *Naval War of 1812*, p. 773, fn 2. On Hughes see War of 1812 Pension Files, US Navy, Surnames H, at http://www.fold3.com/image/314284970/

43. Porter, *Journal*, Vol. 1, pp. 200–2; Feltus, *Journal*, entries for 1 to 9 July 1813.

Chapter 7

1. ADM 52/4236; HMS *Cherub* log, ADM 51/206. On the Articles of War see Lavery, *Nelson's Navy*, pp. 203, 208, 209 and 216.
2. On Tucker's background and his time in command of HMS *Cherub* see F. Jeffries (ed.), *The Gentleman's Magazine*, Volumes 192–3, July to December 1852, pp. 529–30.
3. HMS *Cherub*'s muster roll, ADM 35/3411.
4. Henry Colburn (ed.), *Colburn's United Service Magazine and Naval and Military Journal*, Part 3, 1843, p. 279; ADM 52/4236; John McDonald, *Journal*, entry for 10 July 1813, p. 762.
5. ADM 52/4236; ADM 51/206; Hillyar to Black and Turner, HMS *Phoebe* at Sea, 12 July 1813, National Maritime Museum Archives, AGC 23/7.
6. Blake, *Evangelicals in the Royal Navy*, pp. 185–6.
7. ADM 52/4236; ADM 51/206; Gardiner, *Hunting the Essex*, p. 45; Lavery, *Nelson's Navy*, p. 211.
8. ADM 52/4236; ADM 51/206; Log of HMS *Raccoon*, ADM 51/2765; Gardiner, *Hunting the Essex*, pp. 45–6; McDonald, *Journal*, entries for 20, 23, 29 and 30 July 1813, pp. 762–3; Hillyar's Coded Journal, Hillyar to Croker, HMS *Phoebe*, 22 October 1814, ADM 1/1948. The *Isaac Todd* eventually arrived at her destination off the mouth of the Columbia River on 23 April 1814. After delivering the supplies and men she was carrying, she sailed for China and eventually returned to England with a hold full of tea for the East India Company.
9. ADM 52/4236; ADM 51/206; ADM 51/2765; Gardiner, *Hunting the Essex*, pp. 46–7; McDonald, *Autobiographical Notes*, p. 47.
10. ADM 52/4236; ADM 51/206; ADM 51/2765; Gardiner, *Hunting the Essex*, pp. 47–8; Hillyar to Croker, 22 October 1814, ADM 1/1950; Christopher O'Brien's Medical Report, ADM 101/116/1.
11. ADM 52/4236; Gardiner, *Hunting the Essex*, p. 48; Philip Brady sketches, ADM 344/2696; McDonald, *Journal*, p. 763.
12. ADM 52/4236; McDonald to Hillyar, HMS *Phoebe* at Sea, 26 August 1813, ADM 1/1948; Hillyar's Coded Journal, ADM 1/1948.
13. ADM 52/4236; ADM 51/206; ADM 51/2765; Gardiner, *Hunting the Essex*, p. 48.
14. ADM 52/4237; Gardiner, *Hunting the Essex*, pp. 48–9.
15. Gardiner, *Hunting the Essex*, pp. 49–52.
16. ADM 52/4237; McDonald, *Autobiographical Notes*, pp. 47–8; Gardiner, *Hunting the Essex*, pp. 50–6; Hillyar to Croker, 22 October 1814. ADM 1/1950; Colburn (ed.), *Colburn's United Service Magazine*, Part 3, 1843, p. 279. On Baeza see http://www.genealog.cl/Chile/S/SantaMaria/. The fact that he was sympathetic towards the patriots is attested to by his subsequent arrival in Valparaiso and Gardiner's comments, Gardiner, *Hunting the Essex*, pp. 113–14.
17. ADM 52/4237; ADM 51/206; ADM 51/2765; ADM 37/4381.
18. Gardiner, *Hunting the Essex*, pp. 50–6.

19. ADM 52/4237; Gardiner, *Hunting the Essex*, pp. 56–7; McDonald, *Journal*, p. 763.
20. ADM 52/4237; ADM 53/291.
21. ADM 52/4237; Gardiner, *Hunting the Essex*, pp. 56–7; Hillyar's coded journal, ADM 1/1948.

Chapter 8

1. Farragut, *The Life of David Glasgow Farragut*, p. 9.
2. Feltus, *Journal*, entries for 10 July 1813 to 14 August 1813.
3. Porter, *Journal*, Vol. 1, pp. 201–2.
4. Ibid, pp. 202–4; Montgomery to Gamble, United States Frigate *Essex*, off Albemarle Isle, 15 July 1813, reproduced in *The Memorial of Lieut. Colonel J. M. Gamble, of the United States' Marine Corps, to Congress, 1828*, New York: George F. Hopkins, 1828, p. 4; Feltus. *Journal*, entry for 30 September 1813. On the *Seringapatam*, *New Zealander* and *Charlton* see Clayton, *Ships Employed in the South Sea Whale Fishery*, pp. 216–17, 180 and 85–6; http://www.1812privateers.org/Great per cent20Britain/owners.pdf. On the *Seringapatam*'s voyage also see *Lloyd's List*, London, 18 June 1813; *The Bury and Norwich Post*, 27 December 1815; *The Literary Panorama and National Register*, London: C. Taylor, 1815, pp. 802–3. On Stavers see Colburn (ed.), *Colburn's United Service Magazine*, London: Hurst and Blackett, 1862, Part 3, p. 127.
5. Porter, *Journal*, Vol. 1, p. 204; *Bury and Norwich Post*, 27 December 1815; ADM 103/466. On Worth also see http://www.angelfire.com/ks/hagenswain/oswain8.html. On Swayne also see *Bury and Norwich Post*, 27 December 1815.
6. Porter, *Journal*, Vol. 1, pp. 204–5.
7. Ibid, p. 205; *Bury and Norwich Post*, 27 December 1815.
8. Porter, *Journal*, Vol. 1, pp. 201 and 207.
9. Ibid, pp. 208–11.
10. Ibid, pp. 211–14.
11. Ibid, pp. 213–15.
12. Porter, *Journal*, Vol. 1, pp. 215–24.
13. Ibid, pp. 221–2; Niles (ed.), *Niles' Weekly Register*, Vol. 7, September 1814 to March 1815, p. 23; Shillibeer, *A Narrative of the Briton's Voyage*, p. 31. Such contests were common among the young officers of the United States Navy. At least thirty-six were killed in eighty-two duels between 1798 and 1848, half of the fatalities occurring before 1815. Congress passed a law forbidding the practice amongst civilians in 1806, but it was not banned in the US Navy until almost sixty years later. The 'honour code' was held in high esteem by the naval establishment, many of whom had partaken of 'grass before breakfast' themselves and, as the majority of encounters took place overseas, government influence was slight. The causes of duelling were often out of all proportion with the results. One gentleman lying to or raising his hands against another was sufficient and when alcohol was combined with high spirits and testosterone, challenges could be sparked by 'insults' of comic triviality. On one occasion an officer was said to have fought another for entering the ship's wardroom wearing a hat; another demanded satisfaction when a shipmate spilled some water on a letter he was writing; a third resulted from an argument as to

whether a bottle was green or black. Although Porter held duels to be a 'disgrace ... [to] human nature', he had been raised to see them as part of the service's culture and had acted as a second to Marine Captain James McKnight, the father of one of his lieutenants on his current cruise, in Italy in 1802. In the light of such precedents, it is unsurprising that the Bostonian not only failed to punish Gamble for Cowan's death, but also omitted to name him as the culprit in his memoirs. For more on duelling in the US Navy see McKee, *A Gentlemanly and Honorable Profession*, pp. 403–6.

14. Porter, *Journal*, Vol. 1, pp. 225–34.
15. Collier, *Ideas and Politics of Chilean Independence*, pp. 98–9.
16. Chandler, *Inter-American Acquaintances*, pp. 133–4; Rosario Orrego de Uribe (ed.), *Revista de Valparaiso, Periódico Quincenal*, Numero 1, Valparaiso: Tornero y Letelier, 1873, pp. 163–4.
17. Porter, *Journal*, Vol. 1, pp. 239–41; Porter, *Journal*, Vol. 2, pp. 1–2; Feltus, *Journal*, entries for 13 August 1813 to 10 September 1813. On the *Emily* see Moisés Hasson Camhi, *Viaje y Migración de los Blest en los Albores de la Independencia*, available online at http:// www.irlandeses.org/wp-content/uploads/2012/10/6-Viaje-y-Migraci%C3%B3n-de-los-Blest-en-los-Albores-de-la-Independencia.pdf; *El Monitor Araucano*, Tomo 2, No. 24, 1 March 1814 and Tomo 1, No. 36, 29 June 1813.
18. Porter, *Journal*, Vol. 1, pp. 234–9. On the *Sir Andrew Hammond* see Clayton, *Ships Employed in the South Sea Whale Fishery*, p. 219; James Jay Mapes, *The Working Farmer, Devoted to Agriculture*, Vol. 3, New York: Longett, 1852, p. 133, and http:// www.1812privateers.org/Great%20Britain/owners.pdf.
19. Porter, *Journal*, Vol. 1, pp. 234–9.
20. Ibid.
21. Ibid, pp. 236–41.
22. Ibid, pp. 239–41; Feltus, *Journal*, entries for 30 September 1813 to 3 October 1813; Farragut, *The Life of David Glasgow Farragut*, p.10.

Chapter 9

1. ADM 52/4237; HMS *Cherub*'s Log, ADM 53/291; Gardiner, *Hunting the Essex*, pp. 57–8.
2. ADM 52/4237; ADM 53/291; Gardiner, *Hunting the Essex*, pp. 58–9; Hillyar to Croker, 22 October 1814, ADM 1/1950; Hillyar Coded Journal, Hillyar to Croker, HMS *Phoebe*, 22 October 1814, ADM 1/1950.
3. ADM 52/4237; Gardiner, *Hunting the Essex*, pp. 59–66; Hillyar Coded Journal, Hillyar to Croker, HMS *Phoebe*, 22 October 1814, ADM 1/1950.
4. ADM 52/4237; Gardiner, *Hunting the Essex*, pp. 59–60.
5. Gardiner, *Hunting the Essex*, pp. 61–6.
6. ADM 52/4237; Gardiner, *Hunting the Essex*, p. 66; Shillibeer, *A Narrative of the Briton*'s *Voyage*, p. 26; Burrow to Jago, HMS *Phoebe* at Sea, 17 October 1813, Cornwall Council Archives, X807, document 4.
7. ADM 52/4237; ADM 53/291; ADM 37/4380. On Thornton and Lawson also see Percy Melville Thornton, *Some Things We Have Remembered: Samuel Thornton, Admiral,*

1797-1859, Percy Melville Thornton, 1841-1911, London: Longmans & Green, 1912, pp. 16–23, 30 and 32.

8. ADM 52/4237; ADM 53/291; Hillyar Coded Journal, Hillyar to Croker, HMS *Phoebe*, 22 October 1814, ADM 1/1950. On Turner and Cummings see ADM 37/4380 and ADM 103/466.

9. Burrow to Jago, HMS *Phoebe* at Sea, 12 October 1813, Cornwall Council Archives, X807, document 2; ADM 52/4237; ADM 53/291; Hillyar Coded Journal, Hillyar to Croker, HMS *Phoebe*, 22 October 1814, ADM 1/1950; Gardiner, *Hunting the Essex*, pp. 67–8.

10. ADM 52/4237; ADM 53/291; Hillyar Coded Journal, Hillyar to Croker, HMS *Phoebe*, 22 October 1814, ADM 1/1950; Gardiner, *Hunting the Essex*, pp. 67–8.

11. ADM 52/4237; ADM 53/291; Hillyar to Croker, 22 October 1814, ADM 1/1950; Gardiner, *Hunting the Essex*, pp. 68–9; P. Brady sketches, ADM 344/2366.

12. ADM 52/4237; ADM 53/291; Gardiner, *Hunting the Essex*, pp. 69–70.

13. ADM 52/4237; ADM 53/291.

Chapter 10

1. Porter, *Journal*, Vol. 2, pp. 1–5; Feltus, *Journal*, entries from 5 September 1813 to 24 September 1813.

2. Porter, *Journal*, Vol. 2, p. 4.

3. Milton Diamond, 'Sexual Behaviour in Pre Contact Hawai'i: A Sexological Ethnography', *Revista Española del Pacifico* 16 (2004), pp. 37–58.

4. Long, *Nothing Too Daring*, pp. 109–10.

5. Porter, *Journal*, Vol. 2, pp. 5–8; Feltus, *Journal*, entries from 24 to 26 September 1813; Farragut, *The Life of David Glasgow Farragut*, p. 10.

6. Porter, *Journal*, Vol. 2, pp. 9–11.

7. Ibid, pp. 11–14; Feltus, *Journal*, entries from 24 to 26 September 1813.

8. Porter, *Journal*, Vol. 2, pp. 15–17; Feltus, *Journal*, entries from 25 to 26 September 1813; Farragut, *The Life of David Glasgow Farragut*, p. 10.

9. Porter, *Journal*, Vol. 2, pp. 17–18. On Maury see *The Naval War of 1812*, footnotes, p. 769. Also see James Edmonds Saunders, *Early Settlers of Alabama*, New Orleans: L. Graham & Son, 1899, Part 1, pp. 316–18.

10. Porter, *Journal*, Vol. 2, pp. 17–18. On MacDonald see Porter, *Journal*, Vol. 1, p. 11 and Vol. 2, p. 235.

11. Porter, *Journal*, Vol. 2, p. 19.

12. Ibid, pp. 20–1; Feltus, *Journal*, entry 26 September 1813.

13. Porter, *Journal*, Vol. 2, pp. 21–2 and 59–60.

14. Ibid, pp. 23–5.

15. Ibid, p. 26; Feltus, *Journal*, entries for 26 and 27 September 1813.

16. Porter, *Journal*, Vol. 2, pp. 26–7; Feltus, *Journal*, entry for 27 September 1813. On the construction of the Taeeh village see Porter, *Journal*, Vol. 2, pp. 38–40.

17. Porter, *Journal*, Vol. 2, pp. 28–9; Feltus, *Journal*, entry 28 September 1813.

18. Porter, *Journal*, Vol. 2, pp. 32–8; Feltus, *Journal*, entry 29 September 1813; Farragut, *The Life of David Glasgow Farragut*, p. 10.

19. Porter, *Journal*, Vol. 2, pp. 41–5. Porter was right to remain sceptical as the Marquesans were indeed practitioners of ritual cannibalism, a fact attested by Herman Melville, the author of *Moby Dick*, who spent four months living on Nuka Hiva in 1842. By the time of Porter's visit, the islanders had learnt to hide the practice from visitors, but it continued for several generations. The anthropologist A. P. Rice later described the procedure in detail. 'It was considered a great triumph among the Marquesans to eat the body of a dead man', he wrote in a 1910 edition of the *American Antiquarian*. '[They] threw them on the ground and leaped on their chests so that their ribs were broken and pierced their lungs ... Rough poles were thrust up through the natural orifices of their bodies and slowly turned in their intestines. Finally, when the hour had come for them to be prepared for the feast, they were spitted on long poles that entered between their legs and emerged from their mouths.'

20. Porter, *Journal*, Vol. 2, pp. 55–6; Feltus, *Journal*, entry 30 September 1813.

21. Porter, *Journal*, Vol. 2, pp. 65–7; Feltus, *Journal*, entries for November 1813.

22. Porter, *Journal*, Vol. 2, pp. 20 and 50.

23. Farragut, *The Life of David Glasgow Farragut*, p. 10. On Adams and the role of the schoolmaster in the US Navy see McKee, *A Gentlemanly and Honorable Profession*, pp. 194–9.

24. Porter, *Journal*, Vol. 2, p. 63; Feltus, *Journal*, entry for 3 November 1813.

25. Porter, *Journal*, Vol. 2, pp. 74–5. See also Porter to Hillyar, USS *Essex* at Valparaiso, 10 February 1814, ADM 1/1950.

26. Porter, *Journal*, Vol. 2, pp. 76–8.

27. Ibid, pp. 68–72; Feltus, *Journal*, entry for 3 November 1813.

28. Porter, *Journal*, Vol. 2, p. 76; Feltus, *Journal*, entries for 14, 15 and 16 November 1813; Farragut, *The Life of David Glasgow Farragut*, p.10. On the *Albatross* also see William Dane Phelps, *Fore and Aft or Leaves from the Life of an Old Sailor*, Nichols & Hall, 1871, pp. 237–40.

29. Porter, *Journal*, Vol. 2, p. 76; Shillibeer, *A Narrative of the Briton's Voyage*, pp. 71–2. Porter's cruelty was not without precedent. In the summer of 1806, six years before the current hostilities had broken out, the Bostonian had come close to causing an international incident while watering in the harbour of Valletta as commander of USS *Enterprize*. When a drunken British sailor had been 'very insolent' to an American officer, Porter had him taken aboard the *Enterprize* and given twelve lashes. The local Royal Navy commander demanded an explanation and when no suitable reply was forthcoming, the British Governor, Sir Alexander Ball, informed Porter that the *Enterprize* would not be permitted to leave port until the incident had been resolved. Porter refused to back down. Ignoring Ball's threats that the shore forts would fire on him, he upped anchor and 'proceeded to sea without molestation'.

30. Porter, *Journal*, Vol. 2, pp. 78–81.

31. Porter, *Journal*, Vol. 2, p. 81; Feltus, *Journal*, entry for 25 November 1813. On Clapp see J. Neilson Barry, 'What Became of Benjamin Clapp?', *Washington Historical Quarterly*, XXI, 1 (January 1930), pp. 13–17.

32. Porter, *Journal*, Vol. 2, pp. 87–93; Feltus, *Journal*, entries for 27 and 28 November 1813.

33. Porter, *Journal*, Vol. 2, pp. 93–105; Feltus, *Journal*, entries from 29 November to 1 December 1813.

34. Porter, *Journal*, Vol. 2, pp. 105–6; Feltus, *Journal*, entries for 1 to 4 December 1813.

35. Porter, *Journal*, Vol. 2, pp. 106–17; Feltus, *Journal*, entries for December 1813.

36. Porter, *Journal*, Vol. 2, pp. 139–40 and 178. On Coffin see *The Naval War of 1812*, footnotes, pp. 773–4.

37. Porter, *Journal*, Vol. 2, p. 162; Long, *Nothing Too Daring*, pp. 142–3.

38. Porter, *Journal*, Vol. 2, pp. 137–8. On the *Essex*'s cargo of sandalwood see HMS *Cherub*'s Log Book, entry for 10 and 11 February 1814, ADM 53/291.

39. Porter, *Journal*, Vol. 2, pp. 138–9; Farragut, *The Life of David Glasgow Farragut*, pp. 10–11.

40. Porter, *Journal*, Vol. 2, p. 140; Farragut, *The Life of David Glasgow Farragut*, p. 11; Feltus, *Journal*, entry for 13 December 1813.

Chapter 11

1. ADM 52/4237; Gardiner, *Hunting the Essex*, p. 70.

2. ADM 52/4237; Gardiner, *Hunting the Essex*, pp. 71–2. On the *Hunter*, *Hector* and *Boriska* see Strangford to Dixon, Rio de Janeiro, 3 July 1813, reproduced in Graham (ed.), *The Navy and South America*, pp. 101–2; Hillyar to Absacal, HMS *Phoebe* in Callao Bay, 9 December 1813, ADM 1/1948 ; Abascal to Hillyar, Lima, 10 December 1813, ADM 1/1948; Hillyar to Abascal, HMS *Phoebe* in Callao Bay, 10 December 1813, ADM 1/22; Hillyar to Croker, HMS *Phoebe* in Callao Bay, 23 December 1813, ADM 1/22; Vivero to Hillyar, Lima, 17 December 1813, ADM 1/1948; letter written by William Glichrist, Buenos Ayres, 8 May 1813, reproduced in *Niles' Weekly Register*, Vol. 5, 1814, p. 29; Hillyar Coded Journal, Hillyar to Croker, HMS *Phoebe*, 22 October 1814, ADM 1/1950.

3. Gardiner, *Hunting the Essex*, pp. 71–3; Amasa Delano, *A Narrative of Voyages and Travels in the Northern and Southern Hemispheres ...*, Boston: E. G. House, 1817, pp. 486–8.

4. ADM 52/4237; Gardiner, *Hunting the Essex*, pp. 70–1.

5. ADM 52/4237; ADM 53/291; ADM 51/2206; ADM 35/3411; ADM 35/3677; ADM 37/4381; ADM 103/466.

6. ADM 52/4237; ADM 35/3411; ADM 37/4381. On Tucker's beef jerky see Jeffries (ed.), *The Gentleman's Magazine*, Volumes 192–3, July to December 1852, pp. 529–30.

7. Hillyar to Absacal, HMS *Phoebe* in Callao Bay, 9 December 1813, ADM 1/1948; Abascal to Hillyar, Lima, 10 December 1813, ADM 1/1948.

8. ADM 52/4237; ADM 53/291; Gardiner, *Hunting the Essex*, pp. 79–80.

9. ADM 52/4237; ADM 53/291; Vivero to Hillyar, Lima, 17 December 1813, ADM 1/1948.

10. Collier, *Ideas and Politics of Chilean Independence*, pp. 98–100. On the prisoners taken from *La Perla* see ADM 52/4237, entry for 11 January 1814; and *El Monitor Araucano*, Tomo II, no.19, Valparaiso, 11 February 1814.

11. ADM 52/4237; Gardiner, *Hunting the Essex*, pp. 73–4.

12. Gardiner, *Hunting the Essex*, pp. 74–83; Samuel Haigh, *Sketches of Buenos Ayres, Chile and Peru*, London: Effingham Wilson, 1831, pp. 404–6: Delano, *A Narrative of Voyages*, pp. 490–3.

13. ADM 52/4237; ADM 35/3411; Gardiner, *Hunting the Essex*, p. 83. On the *Indispensable* see Elliot Snow, *Adventures at Sea in the Great Age of Sail, Five First Hand Narratives*, Dover Publications, 2011, p. 73.

14. ADM 52/4237; Gardiner, *Hunting the Essex*, p. 92; Hillyar to Croker, Lima, 8 January 1814, ADM 1/1948; Brady Sketches, ADM 344/2303. On Staines see ADM 36/16809 and ADM 37/4380.

15. ADM 52/4237; ADM 35/3411; ADM 35/3677; ADM 103/466; Hillyar to Croker, HMS *Phoebe* at Sea, 24 January 1814, ADM 1/1950; Gardiner, *Hunting the Essex*, pp. 94–6 and 99–100; Hillyar to Croker, 13 November 1814, HMS *Phoebe* at Plymouth Sound, ADM 1/1950. On Crompton see *Boletín de la Academia Chilena de la Historia* no.115, Santiago: 2006, pp. 218–19, and Patricia H. Marks, *Deconstructing Legitimacy: Viceroys, Merchants and the Military in Late Colonial Peru*, Penn State Press, 2007, p. 276, On Royal Navy captains carrying specie see Lewis, *A Social History of the Navy*, pp. 333–40.

16. ADM 52/4237; Gardiner, *Hunting the Essex*, pp. 100–1. On Ingram see Thornton to Thornton, Late United States Frigate *Essex*, Valparaiso Bay, 12 April 1814, reproduced in Gardiner, *Hunting the Essex*, pp. 130–5; Thornton, *Some Things We Have Remembered*, p. 37; Ingram Will, PROB 11/1567.

Chapter 12

1. Porter, *Journal*, Vol. 2, pp. 140–1; Farragut, *The Life of David Glasgow Farragut*, p. 11.

2. Porter, *Journal*, Vol. 2, pp. 141–2; Farragut, *The Life of David Glasgow Farragut*, p. 11.

3. Porter, *Journal*, Vol. 2, pp. 142 and 161; *The Naval War of 1812*, p. 708; Log of the *Comet*, LUB 38/10.

4. Porter, *Journal*, Vol. 2, p. 143. On the *Good Friends* see Hillyar to Croker, HMS *Phoebe*, 30 March 1814, ADM 1/1950; Thornton to Thornton (op. cit.), pp. 130–2. On the *Emily* and George O'Brien see Hillyar to Croker, HMS *Phoebe*, 28 February 1814; and website of Museo Marítimo Nacional http://www.museonaval.cl/es/biografias-de-personajes/251-obrien-jorge.html.

5. Porter, *Journal*, Vol. 2, pp. 143–6; Rippy, *Joel R. Poinsett*, pp. 49–50.

6. Porter, *Journal*, Vol. 2, p. 144.

7. ADM 52/4237; HMS *Cherub* Log, ADM 51/2206.

8. Hillyar to Croker, HMS *Phoebe* at Sea, 24 January 1814, ADM 1/1949.

9. ADM 52/4237; ADM 51/2206; Gardiner, *Hunting the Essex*, p. 101. On Hedges see ADM 37/4380; and *The London Gazette*, 12 November 1811, Issue 16540, p. 2185. On Belcher see HMS *Cherub* Pay Roll, ADM 35/3411.

10. ADM 52/4237; ADM 51/2206; Gardiner, *Hunting the Essex*, pp. 101–2. Farragut mentions Hillyar's jacket: Farragut, *The Life of David Glasgow Farragut*, p. 12.

11. Porter, *Journal*, Vol. 2, p. 144; Farragut, *The Life of David Glasgow Farragut*, p. 12.

12. ADM 52/4237; ADM 51/2206; Gardiner, *Hunting the Essex*, p. 102; Thornton to Thornton, 12 April 1814, Late United States Frigate *Essex* at Valparaiso; and Sampson to Mother, 2 April 1814, HMS *Phoebe*, Valparaiso Harbour, both reproduced in Gardiner, *Hunting the Essex*, pp. 130 and 136; Hillyar to Croker, HMS *Phoebe*, Valparaiso, 28 February 1814, ADM 1/1950.

13. Farragut, *The Life of David Glasgow Farragut*, p. 12.
14. Porter, *Journal*, Vol. 2, pp. 144–5; ADM 52/4237; Farragut, *The Life of David Glasgow Farragut*, p. 12; ADM 51/2206; Gardiner, *Hunting the Essex*, p. 102; Thornton to Thornton, reproduced in Gardiner, *Hunting the Essex*, pp. 130–1.
15. Porter, *Journal*, Vol. 2, pp. 145–6.
16. Porter, *Journal*, Vol. 2, pp. 144–6; ADM 52/4237; Farragut, *The Life of David Glasgow Farragut*, pp. 12 and 14; Thornton to Thornton, Gardiner, *Hunting the Essex*, p. 131.
17. ADM 52/4237; ADM 51/2206; Porter, *Journal*, Vol. 2, p. 146.
18. ADM 52/4237; HMS *Phoebe* Pay Roll, ADM 35/3677; HMS *Phoebe* Muster Roll, ADM 37/4381; Porter, *Journal*, Vol. 2, pp. 147–8; Thornton to Thornton, in Gardiner, *Hunting the Essex*, p. 131; Ingram Will PROB 11/1567.
19. ADM 52/4237; ADM 53/291; Gardiner, *Hunting the Essex*, p. 102; Thornton to Thornton, Gardiner, *Hunting the Essex*, p. 132; Hillyar to Croker, 28 February 1814, ADM 1/1950.
20. ADM 52/4237; Hillyar to Croker, 10 February 1814, HMS *Phoebe* at Valparaiso, ADM 1/1949; Porter, *Journal*, Vol. 2, p. 173; letter of Samuel Burr Johnson, Valparaiso, 27 April 1814, reproduced in *Diarios, Memorias y Relatos Testemoniales*, http://www.historia. uchile.cl/CDA/fh_issue2/0,1392,ISID%253D405%2526JNID%253D12,00.html
21. Collier, *Ideas and Politics*, pp. 109–15 and 201–6.
22. Porter, *Journal*, Vol. 2, pp. 147–8
23. ADM 53/291; HMS *Cherub* Muster Roll, ADM 31/3411; Porter, *Journal*, Vol. 2, pp. 148–50.
24. Thornton to Thornton, Gardiner, *Hunting the Essex*, pp. 131–2; Porter, *Journal*, Vol. 2, pp. 148; Benjamin Vicuña Mackenna, *Obras Completas*, Vol. 3, *Historia de Valparaiso*, Santiago: Universidad de Chile, 1936, p. 17.
25. ADM 52/4237; ADM 53/291; Porter, *Journal*, Vol. 2, p. 149; Hillyar to Croker, 10 February 1814, *Phoebe*, Valparaiso, ADM 1/1949. On Belcher see HMS *Cherub* Pay Roll, ADM 35/3411.
26. ADM 52/4237; ADM 53/291; Porter, *Journal*, Vol. 2, pp. 147–8.
27. Gardiner, *Hunting the Essex*, p. 104; Porter, *Journal*, Vol. 2, p. 150. On the British merchants in Valparaiso see Benjamín Vicuña Mackenna, *Valparaíso y los Ingleses en Tres Siglos: Conferencia Leída en Inglés por Don Benjamín Vicuña Mackenna ante la Young Men's Christian Association de Valparaíso, el Año de 1884*, Santiago: Imprenta Cervantes, 1910, pp. 32–5; Moisés Hasson Camhi, *Viaje y Migracion de los Blest en los Albores del la Independencia* (available online); E. B. Ince (ed.), *The Law Journal Reports*, Vol. 33, 1864, p. 276; Eduardo Cavieres Figueroa, *Comercio Chileno y Commerciantes Ingleses, 1820-1880*, chapter 3, (Universidad Católica de Valparaíso, 1988); David J. Woods, *The Bombardment of Paradise: March 31 1866: Why the Spanish Attacked Valparaiso and the British and American Fleet Merely Watched*, WTA Publishing, 2011, p. 24.
28. Thornton to Thornton, Gardiner, *Hunting the Essex*, p. 135; Porter, *Journal*, Vol. 2, p. 146; Farragut, *Life of David Glasgow Farragut*, p. 12. On the old acquaintances amongst the rival crews compare the muster rolls of the *Phoebe* and *Cherub* with the roll

of prisoners taken by US ships and Porter's lists of casualties and captured men: ADM 35/3677; ADM 31/3411; ADM 103/466; Porter, *Journal*, Vol. 2, pp. 233–41.

29. ADM 52/4237; ADM 53/291; *The Naval War of 1812*, p. 769; Porter, *Journal*, Vol. 2, p. 152; Hillyar to Croker, *Phoebe*, off Valparaiso, ADM 1/22.

30. ADM 52/4237; ADM 37/4381; Porter, *Journal*, Vol. 1, p. 2.

31. ADM 52/4237; ADM 53/291; Gardiner, *Hunting the Essex*, pp. 102–3.

32. ADM 52/4237; ADM 53/291.

33. ADM 52/4237; ADM 53/291; Porter, *Journal*, Vol. 2, p. 152; Crompton to Hillyar, Thursday [23 February 1814] Morning at 10 O'Clock, National Maritime Museum Archives, AGC 23/7.

34. ADM 52/4237; ADM 53/291.

35. ADM 52/4237; ADM 53/291; Crompton to Hillyar, Thursday [23 February 1814], AGC 23/7; Porter, *Journal*, Vol. 2, pp. 152–3.

36. ADM 52/4237; Porter, *Journal*, Vol. 2, pp. 150–4; Hillyar to Croker, HMS *Phoebe* at Sea, 26 June 1814, ADM 1/1950; Gardiner, *Hunting the Essex*, p. 103; British Merchants Resident in Valparaiso to Hillyar, 25 February 1814, reproduced in *The Naval War of 1812*, pp. 718–19.

37. ADM 52/4237; ADM 53/291; Gardiner, *Hunting the Essex*, pp. 103–4; Hillyar to Croker, HMS *Phoebe* at Sea, 26 June 1814, ADM 1/1950; Porter, *Journal*, Vol. 2, p. 154; Farragut, *The Life of David Glasgow Farragut*, p. 12.

38. ADM 52/4237; ADM 53/291.

39. A *Cabildo Abierto* was a general meeting of the elite residents (administrators, clergy, merchants and military) of a Spanish colonial town to discuss a specific political or military matter. They were only called under extraordinary circumstances.

40. Letter of Samuel Burr Johnson, Valparaiso, 27 April 1814, reproduced in *Diarios, Memorias y Relatos Testemoniales*; Collier, *Ideas and Politics*, pp. 99–100.

41. *Niles' Weekly Register*, 20 August 1814; reproduced in *The Naval War of 1812*, p. 721.

42. Gardiner, *Hunting the Essex*, pp. 138–40.

43. ADM 52/4237; Andrew Blest to Hillyar, 15 March 1814, Valparaiso, AGC 23/7; Farragut, *The Life of David Glasgow Farragut*, p. 12; Hillyar to Croker, HMS *Phoebe* at Sea, 26 June 1814, ADM 1/1950.

44. ADM 52/4237; Gardiner, *Hunting the Essex*, p. 138; Porter, *Journal*, Vol. 2, pp. 154–6.

45. ADM 52/4237; ADM 53/291; Crompton to Hillyar, Santiago, 19 March 1814, AGC 23/7.

46. ADM 52/4237; ADM 53/291; Ingram Will, PROB 11/1567.

47. ADM 52/4237; ADM 53/291; Crompton to Hillyar, Santiago, 23 March 1814, AGC 23/7. On Tucker see ADM 51/2675; ADM 103/466; ADM 35/3677.

48. ADM 52/4237; ADM 53/291; Porter, *Journal*, Vol. 2, pp. 163–4; Rippy, *Joel R Poinsett*, p. 54. On Johnson see *The Naval War of 1812*, p. 740, footnote 22.

Chapter 13

1 Porter, *Journal*, Vol. 2, p. 164; Memorial of Mrs. John R. Shaw to the Naval Affairs Committee, 5 February 1839, reproduced in *The Naval War of 1812*, p. 727.

2. The Log Book of the USS *Essex*, reproduced in *The Naval War of 1812*, p. 725; ADM 52/4237; ADM 53/291.
3. ADM 52/4237; ADM 53/291.
4. The following British sources were used in the description of the battle: the log books of HMS *Phoebe*, ADM 52/4237; and HMS *Cherub*, ADM 53/291 (both provide details of damage repaired in the days after the battle); Gardiner, *Hunting the Essex*, pp. 105–7; Hillyar to Croker, HMS *Phoebe* in Valparaiso Bay, 30 March 1814, ADM 1/1950; Thornton to Thornton, reproduced in Gardiner, *Hunting the Essex*, pp. 132–5; Charles Sampson letter, reproduced in Gardiner, *Hunting the Essex*, pp. 136–7; Hillyar to Croker, 6 December 1814, ADM 1/1950 (mentions the role of Mr. Nickenson during the battle); Hillyar to Croker, 5 December 1814, ADM 1/1950 (mentions the role of Master Miller during the battle); Hillyar Memorial in *Colburn's United Service Magazine*, Part 3, 1843, pp. 279–80; *Report of the Proceedings of the Naval and Military Bible Society*, London: 1837. The following US sources were used: Porter, *Journal*, Vol. 2, pp. 163–71 and 234–41; Farragut, *The Life of David Glasgow Farragut*, pp. 12–15; *Niles' Weekly Register*, 20 August 1814, p.420 of Vol. VI of 1814; Saunders, *The Early Settlers of Alabama*, Part 1, pp. 316–18; *Niles' Weekly Register*, Vol. 10, 1816, p. 319; Log Book of the USS *Essex*, reproduced in *The Naval War of 1812*, pp. 725–7; Boatswain's, Carpenter's and Gunner's reports of damage to USS *Essex*, reproduced in *The Naval War of 1812*, pp. 741–4. Also see Vicente Pérez Rosales, *Recuerdos del Pasado (1814–1860)*, Vitanet: Biblioteca Virtual, 2003, pp. 18–9; Benjamin Vicuña Mackenna, *De Valparaíso a Santiago*, Librería del Mercurio, 1877, pp. 24–30.

Chapter 14

1. ADM 52/4237; ADM 53/291; Farragut, *The Life of David Glasgow Farragut*, p. 15; Porter, *Journal*, Vol. 2, p. 171.
2. Farragut, *The Life of David Glasgow Farragut*, p. 16; ADM 52/4237; ADM 53/291; Gardiner, *Hunting the Essex*, p. 107.
3. ADM 52/4237; ADM 53/291; Gardiner, *Hunting the Essex*, pp. 107 and 129; Hillyar to Croker, HMS *Phoebe* Valparaiso Bay, 30 March 1814, ADM 1/1950; Thornton to Thornton (op. cit.), reproduced in Gardiner, *Hunting the Essex*, p. 135.
4. Hillyar to Croker, HMS *Phoebe* Valparaiso Bay, 30 March 1814, ADM 1/1950; Farragut, *The Life of David Glasgow Farragut*, p. 16; Porter, *Journal*, Vol. 2, p. 174.
5. Porter, *Journal*, Vol. 2, p. 169; Gardiner, *Hunting the Essex*, p. 105; Hillyar to Croker, HMS *Phoebe* Valparaiso Bay, 30 March 1814, ADM 1/1950; Thornton to Thornton (op. cit.), reproduced in Gardiner, *Hunting the Essex*, p. 135.
6. Farragut, *The Life of David Glasgow Farragut*, p. 14.
7. ADM 52/4237; ADM 53/291.
8. Boatswain's, Carpenter's and Gunner's reports of damage to USS *Essex*, reproduced in *The Naval War of 1812*, pp. 741–4.
9. ADM 52/4237; ADM 53/291; Porter, *Journal*, Vol. 2, pp. 174–5 and 233–7; Hillyar to Croker, HMS *Phoebe* Valparaiso Bay, 5 April 1814, ADM 1/1950.
10. ADM 35/3677; Porter, *Journal*, Vol. 2, p. 172.

11. Hillyar to Croker, HMS *Phoebe* Valparaiso Bay, 5 April 1814, ADM 1/1950; ADM 52/4237; ADM 53/291; ADM 35/3677.

12. ADM 52/4237; ADM 53/291; Hillyar to Croker, 12 April 1814, HMS *Phoebe* Valparaiso Bay, ADM 1/1950; Hillyar to Croker, 13 April 1814, HMS *Phoebe* Valparaiso Bay, ADM 1/1950; Porter, *Journal*, Vol. 2, p. 171. On HMS *Tagus* see Robert Gardiner, *Frigates of the Napoleonic Wars*, London: Chatham Publishing, 2006, p. 35.

13. Thornton to Thornton, in Gardiner, *Hunting the Essex*, p. 135; Shillibeer, *A Narrative of the Briton's Voyage*, p. 108; Gardiner, *Hunting the Essex*, pp. 108–12.

14. Hillyar wrote a series of letters to Croker detailing his travels in the interior of Chile. See Hillyar to Croker, Santiago, 11 May 1814 and following, ADM 1/1950. Also see Collier, *Ideas and Politics*, pp. 100, 113, 116–18, 120; *El Monitor Araucano*, Tomo II, No. 44. 17 May 1814; Shillibeer, *A Narrative of the Briton's Voyage*, p. 108; Gardiner, *Hunting the Essex*, pp. 170–1; and Edward R. Norman, *Christianity in the Southern Hemisphere: The Churches in Latin America and South Africa*, Oxford: Clarendon Press, 1981, p. 75.

15. ADM 52/4237; ADM 53/291; Gardiner, *Hunting the Essex*, p. 107; Porter, *Journal*, Vol. 2, p. 171; Farragut, *The Life of David Glasgow Farragut*, p. 16. On Cole and Whitney see *Niles' Weekly Register*, Vol. 10, 1816, p. 319.

16. Hillyar to Croker, Santiago, 11 May 1814, ADM 1/1950; *El Monitor Araucano*, Tomo II, No. 44. 17 May 1814; Shillibeer, *A Narrative of the Briton's Voyage*, p. 108.

17. ADM 52/4237; Gardiner, *Hunting the Essex*, p. 113; Hillyar to Croker, Valparaiso, no date (circa May to June 1814), ADM 1/1950.

18. ADM 52/4237; Gardiner, *Hunting the Essex*, pp. 114–15; ADM 37/4381; Hillyar to Croker, Valparaiso, no date (circa May to June 1814), ADM 1/1950; ADM 35/3677.

19. ADM 52/4237; Gardiner, *Hunting the Essex*, pp. 115–18.

20. Porter, *Journal*, Vol. 2, pp. 175–7; Farragut, *The Life of David Glasgow Farragut*, pp. 16–17.

21. ADM 52/4237; Gardiner, *Hunting the Essex*, pp. 115–26; *Colburn's United Service Magazine*, Part 3, 1843, p. 281; Log of HMS *Essex*, ADM 52/4481; Dixon to Croker, Rio de Janeiro, 31 August 1814, ADM 1/1950.

Epilogue

1. Porter, *Journal*, Vol. 2, p. 177; Long, *Nothing Too Daring*, pp. 165–6.

2. *The Naval War of 1812*, pp. 760–72; entries for Kingsbury and Field in War of 1812 Pension Files, US Navy.

3. Long, *Nothing Too Daring*, pp. 165–6.

4. Ibid, pp. 166–71.

5. ADM 52/4237; Hillyar to Croker, 6 December 1814, ADM 1/1950; Hillyar to Croker, 5 December 1814, ADM 1/1950.

6. Hillyar to Croker, HMS *Phoebe*, Plymouth, 13 November 1814, ADM 1/1950; Hillyar to Croker, HMS *Phoebe*, Plymouth, 6 December 1814, ADM 1/1950.

7. Hillyar to Croker, 6 December 1814, ADM 1/1950; Hillyar to Croker, 5 December 1814, ADM 1/1950. On Miller's career see General Service Medals spreadsheet at http://www.google.cl/url?sa=t&rct=j&q=&esrc=s&source=web&cd=1&ved=0

CCEQFjAA&url=http%3A%2F%2Fbritishmedals.us%2Ffiles%2FNGSalpha13. xlsx&ei=_WRsVbTxD4icgwTwgoKoCg&usg=AFQjCNEQE4TvePHWQS40qlOU_ PxSFiomUg&bvm=bv.94455598,d.cGU

8. *Bury and Norwich Post*, 27 December 1815; Dudson, *English Admiralty Reports*, pp. 397–402.

9. Barent Gardenier (ed.), *The Examiner: Containing Political Essays on the Most Important ...*, Vol. 3, 1814, p. 470; Gardiner, *Frigates of the Napoleonic Wars*, pp. 33–40.

10. On Morgan see http://www.dnw.co.uk/auction-archive/catalogue-archive/lot. php?department=Medals&lot_id=98047.

11. Toll, *Six Frigates*, pp. 418–52; Lambert, *The Challenge*, pp. 380–402; Budiansky, *Perilous Fight*, pp. 353–68.

12. *The Sussex Advertiser*, 30 January 1815; *The Morning Post*, London, 15 February 1815; *Hampshire Chronicle*, 15 May 1815; *The London Gazette*, 21 January 1815.

13. Charles Sampson to Mother, 8 August 1815, Sampson Family Papers, 1999/9, Royal Navy Museum Archives. For more on Napoleon's surrender see David Cordingly, *Billy Ruffian: The Bellerophon and the Downfall of Napoleon*, London: Bloomsbury, 2004, pp. 228–53.

14. ADM 52/4237; *Royal Cornwall Gazette*, 26 August 1815. On decommissioning see Lavery, *Nelson's Navy*, p. 322; and Cordingly, *Billy Ruffian*, p. 279.

15. John Gamble, *The Memorial of Lieutenant Colonel J. M. Gamble*, New York: Geo. F. Hopkins, 1828) Porter, *Journal*, Vol. 2, pp. 178–226; McDonald, *Journal*; Shillibeer, *A Narrative of the Briton's Voyage*.

16. Porter, *Journal*, Vol. 2, pp. 245–52; Stephen W. H. Duffy, *Captain Blakeley and the Wasp: The Cruise of 1814*, Annapolis: Naval Institute Press, 2001, pp. 265–73.

17. *The Literary Panorama and National Register*, 1815, pp. 802–3; Stackpole, *Whales & Destiny*, pp. 187–95.

18. *Niles' Weekly Register*, Vol. 10, 1816, p. 319; entry for Cole in War of 1812 Pension Files, US Navy.

19. *The London Gazette*, 9 September 1815.

20. *Bury and Norwich Post*, 27 December 1815; Colonial Secretary Index, Reel 6005, 4/3469, p. 116 and Reel 6027, 4/1717.1, pp. 31–2, available at http://colsec.records.nsw.gov.au/ indexes/colsec/s/F54c_sto-sy-13.htm

21. Lambert, *The Challenge*, pp. 402–57.

22. Long, *Nothing Too Daring*, pp. 160–84.

23. Ibid, p. 161; Lambert, *The Challenge*, pp. 443–4; William James, *A Full and Correct Account of the Chief Naval Occurrences of the Late War Between Great Britain and the United States*, London: T. Egerton, 1817, pp. 305–20, *The Quarterly Review*, Vol. XIII, July 1815, art. 4.

24. Long, *Nothing Too Daring*, pp. 175–320.

25. *Colburn's United Service Magazine*, 1843, Part III, pp. 271–85; Blake, *Evangelicals in the Royal Navy*, pp. 185–6 and 240.

26. Bancroft, Carvill and Wiley (eds.), *The American Monthly Magazine*, Vol. 2, Boston: 1836, pp. 71–8.

27. Charles Lee Lewis, *David Glasgow Farragut: Admiral in the Making*, Annapolis: Naval Institute Press, 2014; Charles Lee Lewis, *David Glasgow Farragut: Our First Admiral*, Annapolis: Naval Institute Press, 2014.
28. John William Marsh and Waite Hockin Stirling, *The Story of Commander Allen Gardiner R.N* ..., Oxford: J. Nisbet, 1867.
29. Thornton, *Some Things We Have Remembered*; William O'Byrne, *A Naval Biographical Dictionary*, London: Murray, 1849, p. 1178.
30. War of 1812 Pension Files, US Navy, entries for Kingsbury and Hughes; Kenneth Douglas-Morris, *Naval General Service Medal Roll, 1793-1840*, Andrews UK Limited, 2012. On Crooney see The National Archives Trafalgar Ancestors search engine.

Bibliography

Primary Sources

National Archives, Kew, London

ADM 1/21, Letters from Commander-in-Chief, Brazil, 1813.

ADM 1/22, Letters from Commander-in-Chief, Brazil, 1814–1815.

ADM 1/1945, *Letters of Captains, Surnames H, 1812.*

ADM 1/1946, *Letters of Captains, Surnames H, 1812.*

ADM 1/1947, *Letters of Captains, Surnames H, 1813.*

ADM 1/1948, *Letters of Captains, Surnames H, 1813.*

ADM 1/1949, *Letters of Captains, Surnames H, 1814.*

ADM 1/1950, *Letters of Captains, Surnames H, 1814.*

ADM 1/1951, *Letters of Captains, Surnames H, 1815.*

ADM 1/1952, *Letters of Captains, Surnames H, 1815.*

ADM 27/18, *Navy Board and Admiralty, Registers of allotments of pay to wives of seamen.*

ADM 52/4236, *Master's Log, HMS Phoebe, 29 October 1812 – 6 September 1813.*

ADM 35/3677, *Master's Log, HMS Phoebe, 7 September 1813 – 28 August 1815.*

ADM 36/16809, *Muster Roll, HMS Phoebe, 1 September 1805 – 20 April 1806.*

ADM 37/4380, *Muster Roll, HMS Phoebe, 1 November 1812 – 31 October 1813.*

ADM 37/4381, *Muster Roll, HMS Phoebe, 1 November 1813 – 31 October 1814.*

ADM 37/5397, *Muster Roll, HMS Phoebe, 1 November 1814 – 31 August 1815.*

ADM 35/3677, *Pay Book, HMS Phoebe, 1 April 1812 – 31 December 1814.*

ADM 35/3678, *Pay Book, HMS Phoebe, 1 January 1815 – 28 August 1815.*

ADM 53/291, *Ship's Log, HMS Cherub, 1 September 1813 – 30 August 1815.*

ADM 37/454, *Muster Roll, HMS Cherub, 1 May 1812 – 30 June 1814.*

ADM 35/3411, *Pay Book, HMS Cherub, 1 May 1812 – 31 August 1815.*

ADM 52/4292, *Master's Log, HMS Raccoon, 7 February 1813 – 9 August 1814.*

ADM 37/4753, *Muster Roll, HMS Raccoon, 1 March 1812 – 31 December 1813.*

ADM 37/4754, *Muster Roll, HMS Raccoon, 1 January 1814 – 31 August 1815.*

ADM 35/3804, *Pay Book, HMS Raccoon, 1 March 1812 – 23 August 1815.*

ADM 101/116/1, *Christopher O'Brien's Medical Report.*

ADM 103/466, *List of British Prisoners of War captured by United States during War of 1812.*

ADM 344/2696, *Philip Brady sketches.*

Trafalgar Ancestors Online: http://www.nationalarchives.gov.uk/trafalgarancestors/default.asp

PROB 11/1567, *Ingram Will.*

Other Archives

Hillyar Papers, National Maritime Museum Archives, AGC 23/7.
Jago Letters, Cornwall Council Archives, X807, documents 2 to 4.
Journal of William W. Feltus, 1812-1814, Historical Society of Pennsylvania, call#Am.0675.
Log of the Ocean East Indiaman, British Library, L/MAR/B/222R.
Sampson Family Papers, Royal Navy Museum Archives, 1999/9.
Transcript of the Voyage of the Comet, National Maritime Museum, Greenwich, LUB 38/10.

Newspapers and Magazines

Bury and Norwich Post, 27 December 1815.
Courier, London, 12 February 1812.
Gazeta do Rio, Rio de Janeiro, 10 and 14 July 1813.
Hampshire Chronicle, 15 May 1815.
London Gazette, various issues between 1811 and 1815.
Lloyd's List, London, 18 June 1813.
Monitor Araucano, Valparaiso, 29 June 1813, and 11 February, 1 March and 17 May 1814.
Morning Post, London, 2 May 1814 and 15 February 1815.
Naval Chronicle, no. 29, 1813.
Niles' Weekly Register, Baltimore, various issues between 1813 and 1816.
Sussex Advertiser, 30 January 1815.
The Times, London, 20 March 1813.

Published Sources

An Alphabetical List of the Pursers, Gunners, Boatswains and Carpenters of His Majesty's Fleet, with the Dates of their First Warrants, London: S. Brooke, 1813.
The European Magazine and London Review, Volume 63, Philological Society of London, 1813.
Dodson, John, *English Admiralty Reports: Reports of cases argued and determined in the High Court of the admiralty ... 1811-1822*, New York: Little, Brown, 1853.
Dudley, W., and Crawford, M. (eds), *The Naval War of 1812: A Documentary History*, 4 volumes, Washington DC: Naval Historical Centre, 1985–2012.
Farragut, Loyal, *The Life of David Glasgow Farragut, First Admiral of the United States Navy, Embodying his Journal and Letters*, Memphis: General Books LLC, 2012.
Gamble, J. M., *The Memorial of Lieut. Colonel J. M. Gamble, of the United States' Marine Corps, to Congress, 1828*, New York: George F. Hopkins, 1828.
Gardener, Barent, (ed.), *The Examiner: Containing Political Essays on the Most Important ...*, Volume 3, 1814.

Gardiner, Allen, and Rieske, John (eds), *Hunting the Essex: A Journal of the Voyage of HMS Phoebe 1813-1814 by Midshipman Allen Gardiner*, Barnsley: Seaforth Publishing, 2013.

Graham, Gerald S. (ed.), *The Navy and South America, 1807-1823, Correspondence of the Commanders-in-Chief on the South American Station*, London: Navy Records Society, 1962.

James, William, *A Full and Correct Account of the Chief Naval Occurrences of the Late War Between Great Britain and the United States*, London: T. Egerton, 1817.

——, *The Naval History of Great Britain: From the Declaration of War by France, in February 1793, to the Succession of George UV, in January 1820*, Volume 6, London: Harding, Lepard, and Co, 1826.

McDonald, John, *Autobiographical Notes*, reproduced in L. R. Mason, *Les Bourgeois de la Compagnie du Nord-Ouest, Recits de Voyages, Lettres et Rapports Inedits Relatifs au Nord-Ouest Canadien*, Quebec: de L'Imprimierie Generale, 1890.

McDonald, John, *Journal*, reproduced in Alexander Henry and David Thompson, *New Light on the Early History of the Greater Northwest*, Cambridge: Cambridge University Press, 2015.

Porter, David, *Journal of a Cruise Made to the Pacific Ocean, by Captain David Porter in the United States Frigate Essex, in the Years 1812, 1813, and 1814*, 2 volumes, New York: 1822.

——, *Constantinople and its Environs in a Series of Letters, Exhibiting the Actual State of the Manners, Customs, and Habits of the Turks*, New York: Harper & Brothers, 1835.

Ray, William, *Horrors of Slavery, or the American Tars in Tripoli*, Troy, 1808.

Russel, John, (ed.), *The History of the War, Between the United States and Great Britain, Which Commenced in June, 1812, and Closed in Feb. 1815, Containing the Correspondence which passed between the two Governments, immediately preceeding, and since hostilities commenced; the Declaration of War, and the Official Reports of Land and Naval Engagements*, Hartford: William S. Marsh, 1815.

Shillibeer, J., *A Narrative of the Briton's Voyage to Pitcairn's Island, Including an Interesting Sketch of the Present State of the Brazils and of Spanish South America*, London: Law and Whittaker, 1817.

Snow, Elliot, *Adventures at Sea in the Great Age of Sail, Five First Hand Narratives*, Courier Corporation, 2011.

Various, *The Literary Panorama and National Register, 1815*, London: C. Taylor, 1815.

Secondary Sources

Atkins, Roy and Lesley, *Jack Tar: The Extraordinary Lives of Ordinary Seamen in Nelson's Navy*, London: Abacus, 2008.

Alexander, Caroline, *The Bounty: the True Story of the Mutiny on the Bounty*, New York: Harper Perennial, 2004.

Bancroft, M., Wiley, J., and Carvill, G., C. & H. (eds.), *The American Monthly Magazine*, Volume II, New York: New York Public Library, 1836.

Barry, J. Neilson, 'What Became of Benjamin Clapp?', *Washington Historical Quarterly*, XXI, 1 (January 1930).

Bennett, Thomas H., and Chase, Washington, *A Voyage from the United States to South America Performed During the Years 1821, 1822 and 1823 . . . in a Nantucket Whaleship*, The Herald Press, 1823.

Blake, Richard, *Evangelicals in the Royal Navy, 1775-1815: Blue Lights & Psalm Singers*, Woodbridge: Boydell Press, 2008.

Bowie, Effie Gwynn, *Across the Years in Prince George's County*, Clearfield Company, 2010.

Budiansky, Stephen, *Perilous Fight: America's Intrepid War with Britain on the High Seas, 1812-1815*, New York: Vintage Books, 2011.

Chamberlain, Paul, *Hell Upon Water: Prisoners of War in Britain, 1793-1815*, Staplehurst: Spellmount, 2008.

Chandler, Charles Lyon, *Inter-American Acquaintances*, Sewanee, TN.: 1917.

Chasteen, John Charles, *Americanos: Latin America's Struggle for Independence*, Oxford: Oxford University Press, 2009.

Clayton, Jane M., *Ships Employed in the South Sea Whale Fishery from Britain: 1775-1815: An Alphabetical List of Ships*, 2014.

Colburn, Henry (ed.), *Colburn's United Service Magazine and Naval and Military Journal*, 1843, Part III, and 1862, Part 3.

Collier, Simon, *Ideas and Politics of Chilean Independence 1808-1833*, Cambridge: Cambridge University Press, 1967.

Cordingly, David, *Billy Ruffian: The Bellerophon and the Downfall of Napoleon*, London: Bloomsbury, 2004.

Darlington, George E., *Recollections of the Old Borough of Chester from 1834 to 1850*, Delaware County Historical Society, 1917.

Daughan, George C., *The Shining Sea: David Porter and the Epic Voyage of the U.S.S. Essex during the War of 1812*, New York: Basic Books, 2013.

Delano, Amasa, *A Narrative of Voyages and Travels in the Northern and Southern Hemispheres. . .*, Boston: E. G. House, 1817.

Diamond, Milton, 'Sexual Behaviour in Pre Contact Hawai'i: A Sexological Ethnography', *Revista Española del Pacifico*, 2004, 16.

Dolin, Eric J., *When America First Met China: An Exotic History of Tea, Drugs and Money in the Age of Sail*, New York: Liveright, 2012.

Douglas-Morris, Kenneth, *The Naval General Service Medal Roll, 1793-1840*, Andrews UK Ltd., 2012.

Duffy, Stephen W. H., *Captain Blakeley and the Wasp: The Cruise of 1814*, Annapolis: Naval Institute Press, 2001.

Federal Writers Project, *Whaling Masters*, Wildside Press LLC, 2009.

Figueroa, Eduardo Cavieres, *Comercio Chileno y Commerciantes Ingleses, 1820-1880*, Universidad Católica de Valparaíso, 1988.

Fletcher, John, *The Wars of Spanish American Independence*, Oxford: Osprey, 2013.

Gardiner, Robert, *Frigates of the Napoleonic Wars*, London: Chatham Publishing, 2006.

Ireland, Bernard, *Naval Warfare in the Age of Sail*, London: Harper Collins, 2000.

Haigh, Samuel, *Sketches of Buenos Ayres, Chile, and Peru*, London: Effingham Wilson, 1831.

Hall, Basil (ed.), *The Letters of Private Wheeler, 1809-1828*, Gloucestershire: Windrush Press, 1999.

Hasson Camhi, Moisés, *Viaje y Migración de los Blest en los Albores de la Independencia*, available online at http://www.irlandeses.org/wp-content/uploads/2012/10/6-Viaje-y-Migraci%C3%B3n-de-los-Blest-en-los-Albores-de-la-Independencia.pdf.

Hay, Robert, *Landsman Hay*, Barnsley: Seaforth Publishing, 2010.

Ince, E. B. (ed.), *The Law Journal Reports*, Volume 33, 1864.

Irvine, Washington, *The Analectic Magazine*, Volume 6, 1815.

Jeffries, F. (ed.), *The Gentleman's Magazine*, Volumes 192–3, July to December 1852.

Johnston, Henry P. (ed.), *The Record of Connecticut Men in the Military and Naval Service of the War of the Revolution 1775-1783*, Salem: Higginson Book Company, 1995.

Lambert, Andrew, *The Challenge: Britain Against America in the Naval War of 1812*, London: Faber & Faber, 2012.

Lambert, Frank, *The Barbary Wars: American Independence in the Atlantic World*, New York: Hill & Wang, 2007.

Lavery, Brian, *Nelson's Navy: The Ships, Men, and Organisation 1793-1815*, London: Conway Maritime Press, 2012.

Lewis, Charles Lee, *David Glasgow Farragut: Admiral in the Making*, Annapolis: Naval Institute Press, 2014.

———, *David Glasgow Farragut: Our First Admiral*, Annapolis: Naval Institute Press, 2014.

Lewis, Michael, *A Social History of the Navy 1793-1815*, London: George Allen & Unwin, 1960.

Linder, Bruce, *Tidewater's Navy: An Illustrated History*, Annapolis: Naval Institute Press, 2005.

Long, David, *Nothing Too Daring*, Annapolis: United States Naval Institute, 1970.

Lloyd, Keith H., 'Voyage of the Isaac Todd', *Oregon Historical Quarterly*, Winter 2008.

Mapes, James Jay, *The Working Farmer, Devoted to Agriculture*, Volume 3, New York: Longett, 1852.

Marks, Patricia H., *Deconstructing Legitimacy: Viceroys, Merchants, and the Military in Late Colonial Peru*, Penn State Press, 2007.

Marsh, John, *A Memoir of Allen F. Gardiner, Commander R.N.*, London: James Nisbett & Co., 1857.

———, and Stirling, Waite Hocking, *The Story of Commander Allen Gardiner R.N...*, London: James Nisbett & Co., 1867.

McGrath, Tim, *Give Me a Fast Ship: The Revolution at Sea*, New American Library, 2014.

McKee, Christopher, *A Gentlemanly and Honorable Profession: The Creation of the U.S. Naval Officer Corps, 1794-1815*, Annapolis: Naval Institute Press, 1991.

Miers, John, *Travels in Chile and La Plata*, Volume 1, Oxford, 1826.

Moore, Charles W., *The Freemasons' Monthly Magazine*, Volume XIII, Boston: Hugh H. Tuttle, 1854.

Norman, Edward R., *Christianity in the Southern Hemisphere: The Churches in Latin America and South Africa*, Oxford: Clarendon Press, 1981.

Orrego de Uribe, Rosario (ed.), *Revista de Valparaiso, Periódico Quincenal*, Numero 1, 1873 (Tornero y Letelier, Valparaiso, 1873).

O'Sullivan, Donald, *The USS Essex in Ireland: A Dún Laoghaire Connection with a Forgotten War*, http://dlharbour.ie/owp-content/uploads/2013/04/The-Convict-Hulk-Essex.pdf.

Paine, Ralph Delaware, *The Ships and Sailors of Old Salem, Massachusetts*, Maryland: Heritage Books Inc., 2007.

Parker, Matthew, *The Sugar Barons*, New York: Walker, 2011.

Payne, John, *Universal Geography, Formed into a New and Entire System, Describing Asia, Africa, Europe, and America...*, Dublin: Z Jackson, 1794.

Phelps, William Dane, *Fore and Aft, or Leaves from the Life of an Old Sailor*, Nichols & Hall, 1871.

Philbrick, Nathaniel, *In the Heart of the Sea,: the Epic True Story that Inspired Moby Dick*, Harper Perennial, 2005.

Pope, Dudley, *The Black Ship*, Barnsley: Pen & Sword Military Classics, 2003.

Purdy, John, *Memoir, Descriptive and Explanatory, to Accompany the Charts of the Northern Atlantic Ocean*, London: R. H. Laurie, 1853.

Reynolds, Jeremiah N., *Mocha Dick: Or, The White Whale of the Pacific*, Michigan, 1932.

Rippy, James Fred, *Joel R. Poinsett: Versatile American*, Literary Licensing, 2012.

Robinson, William, *Jack Nastyface: Memoirs of an English Seaman*, London: Chatham, 1973.

Rodger, N. A. M., *The Wooden World: Anatomy of the Georgian Navy*, London: Fontana, 1998.

———, *A Naval History of Britain*, 2 volumes London: Penguin, 2004 & 2006.

Rosales, Vicente Pérez, *Recuerdos del Pasado, (1814-1860)* (Vitanet, Biblioteca Virtual, 2003).

Saunders, James Edmonds, *Early Settlers of Alabama*, Part 1, New Orleans: L. Graham & Son, 1899.

Schama, Simon, *Rough Crossings*, London: BBC Books, 2005.

Stackpole, Edouard A., *Whales & Destiny: The Rivalry between America, France, and Britain for Control of the Southern Whales Fishery, 1785-1825*, The University of Massachusetts Press, 1972.

Takakjian, Portia, *Anatomy of the Ship: The 32-Gun Frigate Essex*, London: Conway Marine Press, 1990.

Toll, Ian W., *Six Frigates*, London: Penguin, 2007.

Thompson, George Malcolm, *Sir Francis Drake*, Suffolk: Chaucer Press, 1972.

Thornton, Percy Melville, *Some Things we have remembered: Samuel Thornton, admiral, 1797-1859*, London: Longmans, Green & Co., 1912.

Vancouver, George, *A Voyage of Discovery to the North Pacific Ocean and Round the World in the Years 1790-95*, London: Robinson, 1798.

Various, *Boletín de la Academia Chilena de la Historia*, no.115, Santiago: 2006.

Various, *Report of the Proceedings of the Naval and Military Bible Society*, 1837, London: 1837.

Various, *The Literary Panorama and National Register*, New Series, Volume the Second, London: C. Taylor, 1817.

Various, *The Old Dartmouth Historical Sketches, Numbers 1 to 15*, Cornell University, 1903.

Vicuña Mackenna, Benjamin, *De Valparaíso a Santiago*, Librería del Mercurio, 1877.

————, *Obras Completas*, Volume 3, *Historia de Valparaiso*, Santiago: Universidad de Chile, 1936.

————, *Valparaíso y los Ingleses en Tres Siglos: Conferencia Leída en Inglés por Don Benjamín Vicuña Mackenna ante la Young Men's Christian Association de Valparaíso, el Año de 1884*, Santiago: Imprenta Cervantes, 1910.

Wilson, Ben, *Empire of the Deep: The Rise and Fall of the British Navy*, London: Weidenfield & Nicholson, 2013.

Winfield, Rif, *British Warships in the Age of Sail, 1793-1817: Design, Construction, Careers and Fates*, Barnsley: Seaforth Publishing, 2008.

Woods, David J., *The Bombardment of Paradise: March 31 1866: Why the Spanish Attacked Valparaiso and the British and American Fleet Merely Watched*, WTA Publishing, 2011.

Websites

Biography of Jorge O'Brien: http://www.museonaval.cl/es/biografias-de-personajes/251-obrien-jorge.html

Chilean Genealogy Website: http://www.genealog.cl/Chile/S/SantaMaria/

Colonial Secretary Index: http://colsec.records.nsw.gov.au/indexes/colsec/s/F54c_stosy-13.htm

Dictionary of Canadian Biography Online: http://www.biographi.ca/en/index.php

Diarios, Memorias y Relatos Testemoniales: http://www.historia.uchile.cl/CDA/fh_issue2/0,1392,ISID%253D405%2526JNID%253D12,00.html

General Service Medals Spreadsheet: http://www.google.cl/url?sa=t&rct=j&q=&esrc=s&source=web&cd=1&ved=0CCEQFjAA&url=http%3A%2F%2Fbritishmedals.us%2Ffiles%2FNGSalpha13.xlsx&ei=_WRsVbTxD4icgwTwgoKoCg&usg=AFQjCNEQE4TvePHWQS40qlOU_PxSFiomUg&bvm=bv.94455598,d.cGU

Letter of Midshipman Robert Gordon to his mother: http://www.invaluable.com/catalog/viewLot.cfm?afRedir=true&lotRef=221ac52304&scp=c&ri=308

Owemoigne Baptisms: http://www.opcdorset.org/OwermoigneFiles/OwermoignBaps1752-1812.htm

Owermoigne Wills: http://www.opcdorset.org/OwermoigneFiles/OwermoigneWills.htm

National Maritime Digital Library: http://nmdl.org/aowv/whvoyage.
  cfm?VesselNumber=677
US Genealogy Website: http://www.angelfire.com/ks/hagenswain/oswain8.html
William Morgan's General Service Medal: http://www.dnw.co.uk/
War of 1812 Pension Files, U.S. Navy, online: http://www.fold3.com/image/314284970/

Index